ITALIAN INTERVENTION

IN THE

SPANISH CIVIL WAR

Italian Intervention
IN THE
Spanish Civil War

JOHN F. COVERDALE

Princeton University Press
Princeton, New Jersey

Publication of this book has been aided by a grant from
The Andrew W. Mellon Foundation
This book has been composed in Linotype Caledonia

Printed in the United States of America
by Princeton University Press
Princeton, New Jersey

For my parents

TABLE OF CONTENTS

LIST OF TABLES   xi

LIST OF MAPS   xii

PREFACE   xiii

ACKNOWLEDGMENTS   xix

ABBREVIATIONS   xxi

PART I

CHAPTER 1   THE BACKGROUND OF INTERVEN-
             TION: ITALY IN 1936   3
             Mussolini Sends Planes to Franco (3).
             Fascism and Foreign Policy (6). Political
             and Economic Situation of Italy (19).
             Italian Foreign Relations (24).

CHAPTER 2   THE BACKGROUND OF INTERVEN-
             TION: ITALO-SPANISH RELATIONS,
             1922–1936   31
             Primo de Rivera's Dictatorship (31). Early
             Hostility to the Spanish Republic (37).
             Guariglia's Contacts with Anti-Republican
             Conspirators, 1932–1933 (43). The
             March 1934 Agreement with Spanish
             Monarchists (50). Rome Loses Interest in
             Spain (54). Conclusions (65).

CHAPTER 3   THE DECISION TO SUPPORT
             FRANCO: JULY 1936   66
             To Aid or Not To Aid (66). Motives for
             Italian Intervention (74).

CHAPTER 4   THE INTERNATIONALIZATION OF
             THE CONFLICT: AUGUST-NOVEMBER
             1936   85
             Arms Shipments to Spain During Early

August and the Origins of Nonintervention
(85). Growing Aid from Russia, Italy,
and Germany (98). The Birth of the
Axis (110). Military and Naval Aid in
November (113). Italy and Nationalist
Internal Politics (117). Italo-German
Diplomatic Recognition of Franco (123).

CHAPTER 5   "CONTE ROSSI" IN MAJORCA   127
Introduction (127). Military Defense of
Majorca (130). Meddling in Political and
Economic Affairs (138). International
Repercussions (147).

PART II

CHAPTER 6   AN ITALIAN ARMY IN SPAIN:
DECEMBER 1936–MARCH 1937   153
Treaty Between Italy and Nationalist Spain
(153). Mussolini's Plan for Sending
Combat Troops and Hitler's Reservations
(156). Italian Shipments in December
and Early January (165). Mussolini's
Meeting with Göring and Further Shipments
(171). Recruitment of the CTV (181).
Cantalupo and Farinacci (186). The
"Gentlemen's Agreement" (194).

CHAPTER 7   ITALIAN TROOPS IN ACTION:
MÁLAGA AND GUADALAJARA   205
Málaga (205). Genesis and Planning of
the Guadalajara Offensive (212). Initial
Advance (225). Stalemate (230).
Republican Counterattack (242). Signifi-
cance of the Battle (248). Causes of
the Italian Defeat (251).

PART III

CHAPTER 8   INTERNATIONAL TENSION: MARCH–
SEPTEMBER 1937   263
Italian Reaction to Guadalajara (263).

Italy's Commitment Reconfirmed (271). The Northern Campaign (275). Negotiations for a Basque Surrender (284). Formation of the Spanish State Party; Italo-Spanish Economic Relations (294). International Tension (300). "Piracy in the Mediterranean" and the Nyon Conference (306).

CHAPTER 9 TO THE BITTER END: OCTOBER 1937–APRIL 1939   317
Reinforcement of Italian Units in Spain (317). Italian Relations with Spain and Germany (323). Naming of the National Council of the Falange (329). Teruel (332). Franco's First Government; the Spanish Labor Charter; Italo-Spanish Economic Relations (339). The Aragon Campaign and the Easter Agreement (347). Valencia and the Ebro (354). Italo-British Relations (358). Plans for Troop Withdrawal and the Munich Crisis (362). The Occupation of Catalonia and the End of the War (371).

CHAPTER 10 EPILOGUE AND CONCLUSIONS   384
Epilogue (384). Italian Foreign Policy and the Spanish Civil War (388). Italy's Contribution to Franco's Military Victory (391). Effects on the Political Configuration of Nationalist Spain (399). The Spanish Civil War and Italy's Participation in World War II (404).

APPENDIX A. Text of the Secret Italo-Spanish Agreement of November 28, 1936 (413)
APPENDIX B. Officers of the CTV at the Beginning of the Battle of Guadalajara (415)

ix

TABLE OF CONTENTS

APPENDIX   C. Italian Troop Shipments to Spain from
            November 25, 1936–March 15, 1939
            (417)
APPENDIX   D. Italians Killed in Spain by Region and
            Province of Origin (418)

A NOTE ON SOURCES   421

INDEX   439

LIST OF TABLES

1. Italian Foreign Trade 1927–1939   23
2. Italian and German War Material Sent to Spain
   through August 28, 1936   103
3. Italian and German War Material Sent to Spain
   through December 1, 1936   115
4. Italian Troop Departures for Spain through
   December 31, 1936   170
5. Italian Troop Departures for Spain through February
   18, 1937   175
6. Italian War Material Sent to Spain through February
   18, 1937   177
7. Italian War Material Sent to Spain July 1936–
   March 1939   393
8. Italian Forces Sent to Spain July 1936–March 1939   396

xi

LIST OF MAPS

1. Division of Spain: July–October 1936   67
2. Balearic Islands   131
3. Battle of Málaga   208
4. Division of Spain: Feb. 15, 1937   214
5. Battle of Guadalajara: March 8–17, 1937   226
6. Battle of Guadalajara: March 17–23, 1937   244
7. Northern Front: April–October 1937   278
8. Division of Spain: October 1937   318
9. Aragon and Levante Offensives: March–July 1938   348
10. Division of Spain: Fall 1938   373
11. Battle of Catalonia: December 1938–February 1939   377

PREFACE

LIKE the Vietnamese war for my generation of Americans, the Spanish Civil War was a passionate question that left few unmoved. Men of all political persuasions throughout Europe took sides for the Republic or for the Nationalists, with an ardor that arose from their belief that the future of the continent was at stake in Spain. An enormous outpouring of literature, both during the Civil War and after, stands as a monument to the depth of the passions it aroused. Even to this day, the Spanish Civil War continues in some degree to be a live issue that many scholars find it impossible to treat with the emotion-free detachment with which they write about other more recent but less significant topics.

Although thirty-five years have passed since the end of the war, our documentation still leaves much to be desired, particularly as regards developments within Spain itself. The availability of German, American, and British diplomatic documents gives us a much fuller and more accurate picture of the international aspects of the conflict despite the inaccessibility of Soviet and French documents. This book is the first study to be based on a relatively wide range of Italian documents. It may well be many years before scholars are allowed completely free and uninhibited access to the archives, but I am confident that the material I have been able to consult provides a firm base for a detailed examination of Italian intervention in Spain. No doubt my personal political preferences as a moderate and my belief in the polyfactorial nature of most historical causality have influenced my analysis, but I have attempted to write *sine ira et studio*. I hope that I have done justice to the men whose actions I analyze and to the complexity of the issues involved.

xiii

Despite their country's relative isolation, in the mid-nineteen-thirties there were Spaniards to be found wearing all the trappings of each of the three great ideological systems that were struggling for control of Western Europe: communism, fascism, and liberal democracy. When war broke out, both sides immediately turned for help to the foreign governments that seemed most likely to sympathize with their cause. Before the war was two weeks old, the press had reported that France was aiding the Republic and Italy and Germany the rebels. Thus the Civil War took on, in the minds of many, the character of an international ideological conflict being fought out on Spanish soil.

I am acutely aware of the fact that exaggerated stress on foreign involvement in the Spanish Civil War propagated a false image which lives on today. The fact that it was a *civil* war, with roots deep in the social, religious, political, economic, and ideological conflicts of nineteenth- and twentieth-century Spain, is often lost to view when attention is focused on the anti-fascist aspects of the struggle or on the involvement of foreign powers. I do not wish to contribute to that misconception of the most important event in Spain's recent history, even though my study is concerned primarily with Italian intervention in the war.

The issues that were being fought out were colored by European ideological conflicts, but they had affected the everyday lives of millions of Spaniards and had divided the country for years.[1] At the base of the crisis lay the archaic and unjust structure of Spanish agriculture, with its vast latifundia and landless laborers in the south and its economically inefficient minifundia and impoverished peasantry in the northwest.[2] Numerous other problems and

[1] The best general treatments in English of the issues and events of the war are found in Jackson, *The Spanish Republic and the Civil War*, and Thomas, *The Spanish Civil War*. For those who wish to trace the issues further back in Spanish history, the best guide is Carr, *Spain, 1808–1939*.

[2] Malefakis, *Agrarian Reform and Peasant Revolt in Spain*.

conflicts also contributed to the crisis. The rivalry between the powerful anarcho-syndicalist *Confederación Nacional del Trabajo* and the socialist *Unión General de Trabajadores* deeply divided the working class and further embittered labor relations.[3] Violently anticlerical attempts not merely to eliminate undue ecclesiastical interference in politics but to eradicate the church from public life in Spain provoked strong reactions among Catholics.[4] Desires for regional autonomy in the relatively prosperous Basque and Catalan provinces clashed with a rigid Castillian centralism which considered any significant regional autonomy an attack on the unity of the country forged in the sixteenth century.[5] Monarchists opposed Republicans and were divided among themselves on the form a monarchy should take and on who should wear the crown.[6] Civilian reformers attempted to reduce the army's weight in the country's political life, while army officers brooded constantly over the unfair treatment given the army in general and themselves in particular.[7] All these native Spanish divisions were exacerbated by the general European crisis of the nineteen-thirties. The exaltation of violence and the loss of faith in peaceful, democratic methods which characterized the entire European world in the interwar period were reflected in Spain in a climate of violence and intolerance which greatly increased the already existing strains on the social fabric.

In the text I have attempted to give enough information about domestic issues for the reader to understand my subject, and to show how Italian intervention affected the nature and outcome of the conflict. I hope that this analysis will contribute to a more accurate understanding of the

[3] Brenan, *The Spanish Labyrinth;* and Payne, *The Spanish Revolution.*
[4] Sánchez, *Reform and Reaction: The Politico-Religious Background of the Spanish Civil War.*
[5] Payne, "Catalan and Basque Nationalism."
[6] Robinson, *The Origins of Franco's Spain.*
[7] Payne, *Politics and the Military in Modern Spain.*

war and of the importance and limits of Italy's role in it. I do not believe that any useful purpose would be served by lengthening this book with the addition of an examination of the domestic issues involved, which would require an unacceptable degree of condensation and simplification. I prefer simply to warn the readers that my own focus on Italian participation should not mislead them into thinking that the Civil War was primarily an international conflict and to refer those who are interested in the Spanish aspects of the struggle to the growing literature on the subject.

I have divided this book into three parts, which correspond to three distinct phases in the history of Italian involvement in Spain, each with its peculiar characteristics. During the first period, which ends with Italian recognition of Franco in November 1936, the level of intervention was slight. Italy provided arms and small numbers of men who were to act as instructors or use complex equipment in battle, but did not commit any large bodies of combat troops. In keeping with her modest level of support, Rome was scrupulously careful during this period to avoid interference in the internal politics of the Nationalist zone.

The second phase, which extends from November 1936 to March 1937, witnessed not only a vast increase in the scale of Italian aid but a fundamental transformation of its character. Instructors gave way to combat troops, who were formed into separate Italian units and constituted in fact, if not in name, an Italian expeditionary army in Spain. Paralleling this growing military presence was an increased interest in the politics of the Nationalist zone, as Mussolini attempted to influence in various ways the conduct of the military operations and the political structure of Franco's Spain. By February 1937 Italian shipments of troops had been completed, and there is no evidence that at the time Mussolini contemplated any further strengthening of his military presence. It is possible, however, that he would have increased his efforts to influence

xvi

Franco's political and military decisions, had not the Italian defeat at Guadalajara in March 1937 made the prospects for success in such ventures very poor.

Guadalajara marks the beginning of the final and longest phase of Italian involvement in Spain. During this two-year period, a sizable Italian fighting force was maintained in Spain, and arms and supplies continued to flow to Franco from Italian ports, although not at the elevated rates that characterized the second period. The quickening of political life in the Nationalist zone offered new opportunities to exert a certain amount of influence, but the scale of Italian efforts in that direction was very modest. International tension over Spain, and particularly over Italian intervention there, rose to a high during the second and third quarters of 1937, but subsided after the Nyon conference in September 1937. For the next year and a half, Spain constituted an important but generally secondary issue which interacted with other events rather than serving as a primary focus of attention and negotiation.

ACKNOWLEDGMENTS

THIS study originated as a *tesis de licenciatura* under the direction of Professor Vicente Cacho Viú at the University of Navarre and was continued as a Ph.D. dissertation under the direction of Professor Stanley G. Payne at the University of Wisconsin. At various stages many others read and commented on the manuscript: Professors Robert Koehl of the University of Wisconsin, Edward Malefakis of the University of Michigan, Juan Linz of Yale University, Felix Gilbert of the Institute for Advanced Study, Richard Challener, Arno J. Mayer, S. Frederick Starr, and Stanley Stein of Princeton University and Captain Richard Williams and Mr. Paul Atkinson, also of Princeton University. To all of them, my thanks.

This book would not have been possible without the patience and assistance of the staff of the institutions where the research was done: Archivio centrale dello Stato, Archivio storico del ministero degli affari esteri, Archivio del servicio histórico militar, Public Records Office, the New York Public Library, the libraries of the University of Navarre, the University of Wisconsin, the University of Chicago, the Foreign Office, the Royal Institute of International Affairs, and of Princeton, Columbia, Harvard, and Northwestern Universities, the Biblioteca nazionale, the Biblioteca della camera dei deuptati, the Biblioteca di storia moderna e contemporanea, and the Biblioteca della Banca d'Italia.

I wish to acknowledge the financial assistance of the Foreign Area Fellowship Program of the University of Wisconsin, the American Philosophical Society, the History Department, the Shelby Cullom Davis Center for Historical Studies, and the Council for Research in the Humanities and Social Sciences of Princeton University.

ACKNOWLEDGMENTS

Parts of Chapters 6 and 7 were published in the *Journal of Contemporary History*, 9:1 (1974): 53–75, and have been reprinted with permission. Appendix A has been reproduced with permission of The Hamlyn Group, and Appendix B has been reproduced with permission of U. Mursia, Editore.

I am grateful to Mrs. Barbara Clement who typed the final draft of this manuscript, Mr. Jeff Green who was my research assistant during the final stages of its preparation, Mrs. Margaret Case, my editor at Princeton University Press, and Mr. Robert L. Williams of the Yale Map Laboratory who drew the maps.

Many people in Italy helped me with their advice. I wish particularly to express my appreciation to Professors Alberto Aquarone, Giampiero Carroci, Renzo De Felice, Alberto Monticone, and Giorgio Rochat.

A final word of thanks to Dott. Paolo Arrulani, the director of the Residenza Universitaria Internazionale in Rome where I stayed during two research trips to Italy. His cheerful good humor and that of the students with whom I lived there did much to help me through the difficulties that face any historian attempting to do archival research on contemporary Italian topics.

ABBREVIATIONS

ACS	Archivio centrale dello stato (Rome)
B	Busta
C	Carpeta
CP	British Cabinet Papers
DDF	*Documents diplomatiques français*
DDI	*Documenti diplomatici italiani*
F	Fascicolo
FO	British Foreign Office Papers (now in the Public Records Office, London)
FRUS	*Foreign Relations of the United States*
GD	German Documents [*Documents on German Foreign Policy 1918–1945*]
L	Legajo
MAE, Gabinetto	Ministero degli affari esteri. Archivio storico. Gabinetto del ministro: Spagna (Rome)
MAE, Politica	Ministero degli affari esteri. Archivio storico. Direzione generale degli affari politici: Spagna (Rome)
MAE, Ufficio Spagna	Ministero degli affari esteri. Archivio storico. Ufficio Spagna (Rome)
NA T 586	National Archives. Microfilm publication T 586 *Personal Papers of Benito Mussolini Together with Some Official Records of the Italian Foreign Office and Ministry of Culture 1922–1944.*
SHM CGG	Servicio histórico militar. Archivo de la Guerra de Liberación. Documentación nacional. Cuartel general del generalísimo (Madrid).
SHM CTV	Servicio histórico militar. Archivo de la Guerra de Liberación. Documentación nacional. Corpo truppe volontarie (Madrid).

PART I

ONE

THE BACKGROUND OF INTERVENTION: ITALY IN 1936

MUSSOLINI SENDS PLANES TO FRANCO

ON the morning of July 29, 1936, twelve days after the military revolt that touched off the Spanish Civil War, a group of twelve Savoia-Marchetti S 81 bombers of the Italian air force assembled at Elmas airport in Sardinia and were hastily repainted to cover over their military markings and numbers.[1] Their crews were made up of members of the air force who had volunteered for a special assignment outside the country. In the evening the group was visited by the Italian air force chief of staff, General Giuseppe Valle, who briefed them on the mission they were to carry out. The planes were to fly the next day to Spanish Morocco, where the rebels were anxiously awaiting their arrival. Once there, the crews would don the uniform of the Spanish Foreign Legion and place themselves at the orders of General Franco.

At dawn the next morning the twelve planes took off for Morocco, preceded by Valle himself in a long-range sea plane. The general planned to wait for them over the Moroccan coast, circle until they landed, and then return to Italy. Once in the air, the planes encountered unexpectedly strong headwinds that sharply reduced their ground speed. The calculated arrival time went past, and fuel

---

[1] The following account is based on Bonomi, *Viva la muerte*, pp. 1–20; Bolín, *Spain. The Vital Years*, pp. 170–72; and an interview with General Valle in Rome on June 17, 1970. In cases of conflict between Bonomi's account published in 1941 and Valle's testimony, the latter has been preferred.

3

began to run low with no sign of the Moroccan coast. Nine of the twelve S 81s eventually managed to land in Spanish Morocco, with only a few gallons of fuel left in their tanks. The others were not so fortunate: one went down at sea off the coast of French Morocco; the other two crash-landed in French territory, a short way from the border. A Spanish reconnaissance aircraft spotted the downed fliers and dropped Spanish Foreign Legion uniforms together with instructions to cross over into the Spanish zone, but the instructions arrived too late, and the Italian fliers were arrested by French authorities.

Preparations for the flight had been hurried and careless. Few precautions had been taken to prevent identification of the planes in case of a forced landing. Under the fresh paint, Italian military markings could still be made out. Some of the planes' papers revealed the number of the squadrons to which they had previously belonged, and one crew member's documents clearly established that during the month of July he had been on active duty with the Italian air force. The next day newspapers around the world published on the front page the news that the Italian government was providing aid to the Spanish rebels.[2]

Why had Fascist Italy decided to provide military sup-

---

[2] According to General Valle, all the members of the flight crews were regular air force personnel, recruited for the mission in the days immediately preceding their flight to Spain. They were issued false papers to cover their true identity. During the Civil War, pro-Republican propagandists repeatedly affirmed that the pilots' papers showed they were recruited for duty in Spain on July 15. This was adduced as definitive proof of Italian complicity in the preparation of the uprising. An examination of all reliable sources fails to produce any evidence that the pilots' papers in fact indicated they were recruited before the war broke out. This is not surprising since, as we shall see, Rome had no advance warning about the revolt.

The first telegraphic report from Rabat to the French foreign ministry made no mention of the dates on the Italian fliers' papers (DDF, 2, 3, p. 46). Nor was any mention of recruitment prior to the outbreak of the Civil War made in the report shown by the

4

port to a group of rebellious officers who were attempting to overthrow the Spanish Popular Front government elected six months earlier? To answer that question, in this chapter we will examine the Fascist regime that governed Italy in 1936 and the domestic and foreign situation that formed the context of its decision. In the next chapter we will analyze the relations between Italy and Spain since the beginning of the Fascist regime in 1922.

French to American Ambassador Strauss on July 31 (FRUS, 1936, 2, p. 451).

On August 4, the French embassy in London told the British that: a) one crew member still belonged to the Italian air force in July; b) two pilots in the second plane had been recruited only two weeks before; c) two planes formed part of a group of five which belonged to military formations. The second point of the communication stressed how recently the fliers had been enrolled, not how long before the outbreak of the war ("deux pilotes recruités *il y a quinze jours seulement*") (FO W 7665/62/41).

Two days later the French undersecretary of state for foreign affairs, Vienot, told the American *chargé* that there were "certain indications, which the French government was trying to substantiate, that some of these airmen had been enrolled for their duty as early as July 15" (FRUS, 1936, 2, p. 468).

Reporting on the sentencing of the Italian pilots, the *Times* correspondent noted that "some of the prisoners said that they were recruited for their mission three days before the Spanish rising began" [*Times* (London), August 12, 1936]. An official report on these declarations was made by the French embassy in London to the British foreign office on August 17 (FO W 8822/62/41).

The July 15 date was evidently based on declarations made by the captured fliers, and not on anything written in their flying orders or other official papers. There is no need, therefore, to resort to Thomas's explanation that it was a misprint or was the date on which they returned from leave (Thomas, *The Spanish Civil War*, p. 296n).

The Italian airmen testified falsely that they had been recruited by the company to fly the planes to Morocco and then return to Italy. They may have felt that by indicating that the order for the planes had been placed before the outbreak of the rebellion they were lessening their own and their country's responsibility, without realizing that by doing so they made it appear that Italy had helped prepare the revolt.

5

FASCISM AND FOREIGN POLICY

WHEN the march on Rome brought Mussolini to power in 1922, the Fascist party was a diffuse and disparate conglomerate of forces which drew its strength from widely varying groups. Small shopkeepers and angry young soldiers found themselves side by side with landowners, industrialists, and former socialists won over to the doctrines of nationalism. The original coalition contained a considerable percentage of lower middle-class radicals who hoped that a triumphant Fascism would carry out a program of social and economic reform without destroying national unity on the rocks of class conflict.

Mussolini was dependent for his success in national politics, however, on the collaboration of business interests. By the time of the Pact of Palazzo Vidoni in 1925, he had committed himself to controlling labor while leaving business a considerable margin of autonomy in return for continuing support. The party was soon subjected to increasing bureaucratization and rapidly lost its original radical character. An ongoing process of depolitization gradually reduced it to a merely decorative role, without real political power or influence.[3] The establishment of the dictatorship in 1925–1926 was "not so much the party's triumph as Mussolini's; and Mussolini not so much head of the party as head of the government."[4]

Despite its gradiloquent declarations, Fascism never achieved a truly totalitarian regime, and a number of autonomous power centers survived in Italy throughout the Fascist period. The monarchy retained a considerable degree of independent political authority, as was demonstrated at Fascism's demise in 1943. The army, though offer-

---

[3] Carocci, *Storia del fascismo*, pp. 35–36; Aquarone, *L'organizzazione dello Stato totalitario*, pp. 109, 181–82; De Felice, *Il fascismo*, p. XIX.

[4] Aquarone, *L'organizzazione dello Stato totalitario*, p. 47.

ing little resistance to Mussolini's plans, remained faithful to the king rather than to Fascism or the Duce, and the party's militia found itself reduced by the early thirties to an appendage of the army. The church also preserved a considerable degree of independence, especially in the field of education, where the party's efforts to displace it were largely frustrated. Business leaders, as we said, relied on Fascism to discipline their labor force; but in return for their support they continued to enjoy considerable autonomy in the direction of their businesses.[5]

Foreign affairs was perhaps the area in which the regime came closest to achieving its proclaimed goals of totalitarian control. None of the major power centers exercised much influence in this area. Italian industrialists were generally more concerned about economic and social policy than about diplomacy. They were content to allow the government to make its own choices in this field and had little or no influence on any of the major decisions of the thirties.[6] By 1936, top military leaders had renounced all pretensions to influencing Mussolini on questions of foreign affairs, and showed no inclination to oppose him even when his decisions conflicted with what their military training led them to believe were the country's best interests.[7] Until the regime faced the crisis of defeat in war, the king was unable to mobilize his potential political power. The Duce regularly ignored his opinions, particularly in the case of the alliance with Germany, which the king thoroughly disliked. Similarly, the church's protests against Nazi excesses left Mussolini unmoved and in no way deflected his foreign policy from its course. Career foreign service personnel were little more effective. Like their German counterparts,

[5] Sarti, *Fascism and the Industrial Leadership in Italy, 1919–1940,* p. 5 and *passim;* Aquarone, *L'organizzazione dello Stato totalitario,* pp. 252–53, 291–92.

[6] Sarti, *Fascism and the Industrial Leadership in Italy, 1919–1940,* pp. 5 and 125.

[7] Rochat, "Mussolini e le forze armate."

a number of Italian diplomats have attempted in their memoirs to portray the ministry of foreign affairs as exercising a moderating influence on Mussolini and even as working to prevent the realization of his more ill-advised schemes. In fact, however, the influence of the career diplomats was both slight and timid.[8]

Even before Mussolini came to power in 1922, postwar Italy was inclined toward an aggressive and expansionist foreign policy. A widespread sense of injustice and dissatisfaction with the terms of the peace settlement prompted a desire to right the real and imagined wrongs done Italy at the peace table. The country's rapidly growing population and limited natural resources, together with a heavy industrial sector which had been overexpanded during the war, lent urgency to the appeals of those who called for a policy that would win both colonial territories and a larger share in the world's commerce. Finally, many nationalists were determined to show the world that their country was truly a great power, and to claim the influence and prestige they felt was her due.

Under Fascism, these impulses became the basis of an expansionist foreign policy, which espoused the twin doctrines of revisionism and imperialism. Mussolini demanded a larger role for Italy as an imperial power, and called repeatedly for a revision of the peace settlement to give her the voice in world affairs and the territorial advantages she had been unjustly denied. From the very beginning, he couched these claims largely in the context of a Mediterranean policy and of Italy's right to a preponderant role in the *mare nostrum*. Of course, Fascist foreign policy changed over time. Were we attempting to summarize its history, it would be necessary to point out the characteristics of its successive periods. For our present purposes, however, it is sufficient to say that although Fascist expansionism had to be adapted to the concrete situation of

[8] Rumi, "Tendenze e caratteri degli studi sulla politica estera fascista (1945–1966)," p. 159.

8

the changing European diplomatic scene and occasionally almost disappeared from view, hidden under a cover of European collaboration and friendship, it was never far from the surface and is characteristic of Mussolini's entire foreign policy.[9]

In itself, Mediterranean expansionism did not constitute a novelty in Italian foreign policy. It was an element Fascists not only shared with other contemporary political groups but inherited from pre-World War I Italian policy. Giolitti's endeavors in Tripoli and during the Balkan wars clearly reflected the same basic orientation.[10] But if in terms of *aims* and *objectives*, Fascist Italy followed closely in the footsteps of its predecessors, its *motives* and *methods* were radically different. Rome's foreign policy before Fascism was firmly rooted in the Western European diplomatic tradition. It held in high esteem negotiations and the conservation of a delicate European balance, which alone would permit Italy to play a decisive role despite her position as the weakest of the great powers. Italy's leaders also professed, at least in words, their belief in the rights of nationalities and in an international family of nations with common goals and a common stake in civil progress.[11] For all of these values, Fascism substituted the cult of

[9] The continuity of the themes of revisionism and imperialism in Fascist foreign policy has been stressed by Renouvin, Mack Smith, Rumi, Santorelli, *et al.* For a brief review of the literature, see Petersen, "La politica estera del fascismo come problema storiografico," pp. 670–72. This continuity is denied by historians such as Hughes and Salvatorelli, who follow Salvemini in presenting Mussolini as an impulsive policy maker who neither established long-term goals nor laid rational plans for their achievement, but merely used foreign affairs to create stunning effects for internal consumption. This position fails to distinguish between goals and execution in Mussolini's policy. It is undeniable that there was a high degree of improvisation in the execution of Fascist foreign policy, especially from time of the Ethiopian invasion, but this does not rule out the existence of long-range goals.

[10] Santarelli, *Storia del movimento e del regime fascista*, I, 342–43.

[11] Rumi, *Alle origini della politica estera fascista* (1918–23), p. 247.

9

force and an aggressiveness limited only by the constraints imposed by superior power. In his first foreign policy speech as prime minister, Mussolini declared, "We cannot afford the luxury of a policy of foolish altruism or of complete dedication to the plans of others. *Do ut des.*"[12] "I confess," he said in February 1923, "that I do not believe in perpetual peace. . . . In the cemeteries peace is perpetual; but among peoples, despite all the preaching and the respectable ideals, there are facts called race, called development, called grandeur and decadence of peoples, that lead to contrasts. And these contrasts are frequently resolved by recourse to arms."[13]

These declarations did not long remain mere abstract statements of principle. Fascism soon showed its aggressive character in deeds. In August 1923, General Tellini, the head of an interallied commission to determine the boundaries between Greece and Albania, was assassinated by Greek citizens on Greek territory. Mussolini immediately took advantage of the situation to humiliate Greece, and to foster Italy's prestige in the Mediterranean with a policy of force. When Greece rejected the most extreme demands of his ultimatum, the Duce ordered the bombardment and occupation of the island of Corfu, during which about 100 civilians lost their lives. He also threatened to withdraw from the League of Nations if Italy did not receive satisfaction. Only after Greece had paid an indemnity and presented its official excuses did he withdraw the occupation force.[14]

Militarism was an essential part of Fascist ideology. One of the few revolutionary changes Mussolini really did want to accomplish was the transformation of the Italian people into a race of warriors. "We must keep them disciplined and in uniform from morning till night," he said. "Beat

[12] Quoted *ibid,* p. 234.
[13] Quoted *ibid,* pp. 234–35.
[14] Santarelli, *Storia del movimento e del regime fascista,* I, 345–47.

them and beat them and beat them."[15] "There is only one way to create a warlike people; to have ever greater masses who have waged war and ever greater masses who want to go to war."[16] This bellicose posture was partially counterbalanced by the Duce's very real fear of war, but in large measure it set the tone of his foreign policy. In the concrete case of Spain, it added to the other motives for intervention which we will discuss later a desire to use the war as a training ground to prepare the Italians for greater exploits. It was not a question of an organized and rationally planned program for training officers and men but a vague romantic conviction that participation in war in any form was a school of heroic virtue. In November 1937, Mussolini said to his son-in-law: "When Spain is finished, I will think of something else. The character of the Italian people must be moulded by fighting."[17]

The brutally aggressive aspects of Fascist expansion grew out of the basic characteristics of the regime. Classical conservative and authoritarian governments had always tried to depoliticize the masses. Fascism, on the contrary, was a mobilizational regime, which attempted to enlist the active sympathy and support of broad strata of the population. Its propaganda and its institutions were designed to foster a sense of participation in a revolutionary movement which would transform the entire society, while preserving and fomenting national unity. From its inception, the Fascist project for renewing society depended in large part on economic, commercial, and territorial expansion. It attempted to transfer to the international arena the internal tensions which might otherwise have found expression in interclass struggle. In the absence of any coherent attempt to transform the society—an alternative not open to it in view of its close dependence on the former ruling

[15] Quoted in Kirkpatrick, *Mussolini. A Study in Power*, p. 446.
[16] Quoted in Bottai, *Vent'anni e un giorno*, p. 113.
[17] Ciano, *Diary*, November 13, 1937.

groups—it offered Italians the new myth of the rights of "young proletarian" nations in struggle with the "old plutocracies" which they were called upon to despoil.[18]

It is in this light that we can best understand the importance of prestige factors in Mussolini's foreign policy. The Duce's monstrous egotism and overwhelming psychological need for praise and adulation certainly influenced to some degree his policy making. It would be mistaken, however, to stress them to the point of forgetting the functional value of prestige in explaining, for instance, his anachronistic insistence on formal empire and his disdainful rejection of Franco-British proposals for Italian economic and commercial penetration of Ethiopia. In the Spanish Civil War, the regime's need for prestige was especially apparent in its insistence that Italian troops form a separate corps under Italian commanders and in its repeated demands that Franco publicly recognize Italian contributions to his success.

Despite its rhetorical proclamations of revolutionary intent, the Fascist regime was essentially counterrevolutionary in both its domestic and foreign policy. If, as Nolte has maintained, anticommunism was its very essence,[19] we should expect to find anticommunism playing a leading role in Fascist foreign policy. At first glance this might seem to be contradicted by the fact that Mussolini maintained good relations with the USSR during the twenties and early thirties, but his friendship with the Soviet Union can easily be explained in terms of the geographic and political realities of the situation without denying the importance of anticommunism in his foreign policy. The Soviet Union was far enough from Italy and isolated enough politically so that the Duce could afford to ignore its internal regime.

Countries like Spain and France, however, were an en-

---

[18] Rumi, *Alle origini della politica estera fascista* (*1918–23*), p. VIII; De Felice, *Il fascismo*, pp. XIV–XV.

[19] Nolte, *The Three Faces of Fascism*, p. 40.

tirely different matter, given their geographic and political proximity to Italy. In such areas the success of communism—or of any other leftist ideology—was not only distasteful to Italian Fascists; they rightly perceived it as a more or less proximate threat to the internal tranquility, if not the stability, of the Fascist regime in Italy itself. To use a metaphor popular among Fascist leaders, there was a constant danger of "contagion" of revolutionary ideas among the masses, which would weaken support for the regime and perhaps cause serious internal problems. From 1931 on, Italian policy toward Spain exhibited a strongly counterrevolutionary thrust, which was described at the time as "anticommunism," but in fact extended to any leftist regime. This counterrevolutionary mentality explains a large part of Mussolini's antipathy toward the Spanish Republic.

Franco's regime was in many important ways quite different from Italian Fascism, but they were soon identified in the minds of their foes and of many of their supports. This represented an added reason for wanting the Nationalists to defeat the Republic. Mussolini would have been dismayed to see a leftist regime triumph in Spain over, say, a conservative parliamentary one, but he was far more concerned at the prospect that a regime widely considered to be similar to his own might go down in defeat. As Mayer has observed, "the defeat of any kindred movement, or of one that is perceived as such by ideological friends and foes alike, threaten[ed] to undermine the prestige of the counterrevolutionary project in all quarters."[20]

The Spanish Civil War soon came to involve the prestige of Fascism itself as well as of one of Italy's protegés. Virtually from the first day of the war, the conflict was considered throughout the world not as a merely Spanish affair but as the first round in the struggle against Fascism. Few events in the twentieth century have so galvanized public

---

[20] Mayer, The *Dynamics of Counterrevolution*, pp. 99–100.

opinion and contributed so significantly to forming the political conscience of a generation. Even the greater events of 1938–1945 in some sense only confirmed choices which many had made on the basis of the Spanish experience. This is familiar ground to any student of the thirties, and this book makes no attempt to add to the already ample literature on the subject.[21] It is important to bear in mind, however, that the pressure of international public opinion made it inevitable that Mussolini should see the prestige of his own regime at stake in Spain. This explains in part the durability of his commitment to Franco's cause despite many disappointments and reverses.

The fact that an aggressive expansionism so closely correlates with the domestic political needs of the regime and Mussolini's frequent shifts of direction in international affairs have led some commentators to assert that under Fascism foreign policy was entirely subordinate to the needs and demands of internal policy. This thesis has a distinguished pedigree, beginning with Gaetano Salvemini and passing through men such as Salvatorelli and Hughes.[22] It is succinctly put in extreme form by Di Nolfo, who describes Mussolini's as "not a true foreign policy, but rather an internal policy carried out through international polemics. . . . Palazzo Chigi was not so much a foreign ministry as a branch of the ministry of propaganda."[23]

This seems to me a serious misreading of the evidence. There is no doubt that Mussolini used foreign policy with an eye to domestic reactions. His decision to invade Ethiopia may well have been largely a response to the critical

[21] For an introduction to this question, see Watkins, *Britain Divided. The Effects of the Spanish Civil War on British Political Opinion;* Pike, *Conjecture, Propaganda and Deceit and the Spanish Civil War;* Weintraub, *The Last Great Cause. The Intellectuals and the Spanish Civil War;* Guttman, *The Wound in the Heart. America and the Spanish Civil War.*

[22] Carocci, "Salvemini e la politica estera del fascismo"; Petersen, "La politica estera fascista come problema storiografico," pp. 670–72.

[23] Di Nolfo, *Mussolini e la politica estera italiana,* pp. 159 and 45.

problems facing the regime at home,[24] and some of his other concrete decisions may have been taken primarily for internal reasons. Nonetheless, foreign policy goals as such occupy a central role in the Fascist project from the very beginning, even prior to the March on Rome, and cannot be dismissed as merely derivative or instrumental.[25] In fact, Carocci is closer to the truth when he argues that, on balance, "internal politics were subordinated to foreign policy."[26] Mussolini's stubborn insistence on pegging the exchange rate at 90 lire to the British pound in 1927 was a typical example of his subordination of domestic considerations to foreign policy ones. The measure was economically damaging and was opposed by most of the business community,[27] but foreign prestige considerations weighed more heavily in Mussolini's mind.[28] During the thirties, Fascist demographic policy and attempts to bring back émigrées were clearly formulated as a function of a foreign policy of power and prestige, despite their negative influences on an economy already suffering from unemployment and depression.[29] Both during the Republic and during the Civil War, Mussolini's policy toward Spain was determined principally by traditional foreign policy considerations and only secondarily by internal political factors.

I began my research with the conviction, which many of my readers will probably share, that internal public opinion must have been an important factor in shaping Italian policy toward Spain. The results of examining hundreds of files in the Archivio Centrale dello Stato in

[24] Baer, *The Coming of the Italian Ethiopian War*, pp. 31–35; Rochat, *Militari e politici nella preparazione della campagna d'Etiopia*, p. 105.

[25] This is the major thesis of Rumi, *Alle origini della politica estera fascista* (*1918–23*).

[26] Carocci, *Storia del fascismo*, p. 35.

[27] Melograni, *Gli industriali e Mussolini*, pp. 174–75.

[28] Sarti, *Fascism and the Industrial Leadership in Italy, 1919–1940*, p. 137.

[29] Carocci, *Storia del fascismo*, p. 35.

an attempt to find evidence of its influence were disappointingly meager. I am convinced, as I stated above, that Fascist aversion to a Republican victory and determination to see Franco through to final victory were partly prompted by the relationship Fascists perceived between the fate of Spain and their own regime's internal prestige. The decision to seek military vindication after the humiliation of Guadalajara and to recall Ambassador Cantalupo are, however, the only cases in which I can show that internal public reaction to events in Spain led to concrete policy choices.

It is clear that neither Fascist Italy nor any other state is a monolithic unit in which there is an absolute uniformity of opinion and interests. Studies of Italian intervention in Spain in terms of "organizational process" and of "bureaucratic politics"[30] would be useful and informative, and could tell us a great deal about the structure and functioning of the Fascist regime. But the records kept by most Italian government agencies during the Fascist era were spotty and incomplete, and many of them were lost or destroyed during the final months of the regime's life and during the confusion that followed Italy's withdrawal from the war. Consequently, in-depth studies of this type could be carried out only with great difficulty, even if all the materials which have survived were open to scholars and adequately catalogued.

I have attempted to note along the way the most important influences of individuals and agencies on Mussolini's decisions, without pretending to exhaust the subject. My findings confirm once again that policy on Spain was essentially made by one man. It was not the output of a team working together, nor did any individual or group—with the possible exception of Ciano—exercise such decisive influence that the main lines of the story could not be

<hr />

[30] For an interesting discussion of these approaches to the study of foreign policy, see Allison, "Conceptual Models and the Cuban Missile Crisis," pp. 689–718.

correctly identified without referring to them. It seems justified, therefore, to consider Italy's intervention in Spain primarily in terms of the pursuit of goals and objectives set by Mussolini.

The man with whom ultimate decision-making power rested was shrewd and far from unintelligent, but he rarely stopped for any length of time to survey situations and ponder alternatives. Feelings and emotions played a large part in his psychological makeup, and the cold realism on which he prided himself was more a lack of moral scruples than an ability to appraise situations accurately. He was far more given to the striking phrases that make good newspaper copy than to carefully weighed and balanced estimates of a situation. As the years went on, these aspects of his personality came to be more and more dominant. Success in Ethiopia heightened his natural impulsiveness, making him more sure of himself in foreign affairs and more willing to act on intuition or impulse, without careful planning.[31] At the end of the thirties he was described in the following terms by his undersecretary of state for foreign affairs:

He is convinced now that the world must be taken by assault. He says it; he proclaims it in his speeches, causing alarm among the nations, governmental reactions, diatribes in foreign parliaments, and reactions whose potential danger he realizes but against which he fails to prepare any plan. No, he doesn't do this which would certainly be the logical and necessary consequence of his daring thought. He doesn't do it because a concrete plan implies calculating with precision the risks and benefits. It means studying all the possibilities and probabilities, the effects and the consequences. It requires methodical preparation, directing every resource

[31] Chabod, *History of Italian Fascism*, p. 79. The importance of Mussolini's arbitrary decision making is highlighted in Baer, *The Coming of the Italian-Ethiopian War*, p. 165.

and every available energy to the desired goal, in the exact measure determined by the means at hand and their deficiencies. He lacks the patience which mediocre men have to go deeply into problems and the spirit of continuous application of men who lack imagination. Anything that is not spontaneous intuition fails to attract and seduce him. In this way he creates around himself a dangerous atmosphere of messianic expectation, a disconcerting glibness which he enjoys as a sign of blind faith in him. He is indignant if any of the people who should be his closest collaborators raises objective considerations. He thinks that they should be the first to trust in his intuition, in his conviction that he alone can provide for every contingency.[32]

Mussolini rarely set forth in systematic fashion exactly what aims he was pursuing, nor did he calculate explicitly the possible costs. Even less frequently did he prepare or ask his subordinates to prepare detailed written analyses of the general situation, or even of specific problems. Important decisions were often taken after oral discussions of which no minutes were kept. Fascist policy-making methods contrast sharply in this respect with contemporary British practice. The British foreign office was forever studying alternative policies and weighing their costs and benefits. Palazzo Chigi seems never to have been asked for such studies and rarely took the initiative itself.[33] This is not to say that Mussolini did not pursue, over extended periods, certain goals, such as colonial expansion and affirmation of Italy's status as a great power in the Mediter-

[32] Bastianini, *Uomini, cose, fatti. Memorie di un ambasciatore*, p. 42; quoted in Aquarone, *L'organizzazione dello Stato totalitario*, pp. 303–304.

[33] As a result of these practices, the historian attempting to assess the motives of Fascist foreign policy is often forced to fall back on conjecture and on the hints contained in Ciano's diaries and in other memoir sources, even though the archives of the Italian foreign ministry and of Mussolini's personal secretariat have been well preserved.

ranean. But he did not habitually plan carefully how those goals were to be achieved nor weigh the costs against the possible benefits.

POLITICAL AND ECONOMIC SITUATION OF ITALY

What was the internal political and economic situation of Italy in 1936 when Mussolini received Franco's request for assistance? Apart from the comments we have just made about the general nature of the Fascist regime, little need be said about the political situation. During the early summer of 1936, Fascism was at or near the apex of its popularity in Italy. The Ethiopian war had been skillfully used to unite the nation. The League of Nation's ill-fated and ineffectual sanctions had rallied many who might have had some doubt about the economic and moral justification of the campaign and gave many Italians the exhilarating sense of having successfully met the challenge of some of the most powerful nations on earth. Even some opponents of the regime, such as the Republican Mario Bergamo, supported the Ethiopian undertaking and attacked the League of Nations for its hypocrisy and conservative injustice.[34] The idea that Ethiopia would provide a fertile outlet for many of Italy's landless agricultural workers helped to make imperialism a popular cause. The response to the campaign for donating wedding rings and other gold jewelry to support the war, though not entirely spontaneous, indicated that a high degree of enthusiasm had been aroused. The reports of the party's political informants, which had reflected in 1934 and 1935 a certain degree of unrest and discontent, particularly in the major industrial centers of the north, had become far more optimistic and only rarely mentioned any manifestations of disaffection from the regime.[35] As the British ambassador

[34] Salvatorelli and Mira, *Storia d'Italia nel periodo fascista*, p. 877.
[35] Based on a reading of the reports for 1934–1936 of a number of representative provinces (ACS, Partito Nazionale Fascista, Situazione Politica delle Provincie).

in Rome noted at the end of 1936, the Duce was "more popular than he has ever been before."[36]

By 1936 the worst of the depression was also past for Italy, although the economic situation was nowhere near as favorable as the political one. Nominal gross national product, which had stood at 132.9 in 1929 (1913 = 100), had fallen to 125.7 in 1930, recovered to 131.0 in 1934 and then risen sharply to 145.3 by 1936.[37] Much of the growth was due to increasing government payrolls. From 8.6 billion lire in 1934, they grew to 12.0 billion in 1935 and 15.5 billion in 1936, by which time they accounted for 13 percent of the gross internal product, whereas in the decade 1921–1930 they had amounted to only 5.9 percent.[38]

The conditions of the working class continued to be very difficult, since unemployment was widespread. The available statistics are incomplete and inaccurate, but the problem was clearly a serious one. Despite an expanding population, the index number of workers employed in industry published by the Fascist Confederation of Industrial Employers declined from 100 in 1929 to 79.2 in 1934, at which time at least 1 million men were totally unemployed.[39] In that year the regime shortened the normal work week from 48 to 40 hours in an effort to give employment to more men. Apparently this measure and the increase in expenditures occasioned by the Ethiopian war helped to alleviate unemployment, since the index number of workers employed in industry rose to 82.9 in 1935 and 94.0 in 1936.[40]

The reduction in the work week, together with a slight decline in hourly wages in 1935, led to a sharp drop in

[36] Drummond, Annual Report 1936, FO R 3171/3171/22. Catalano describes the Ethiopian conquest as leading to an "almost universal popular unity" (*L'economia italiana di guerra, 1935–1943*, p. 25).

[37] Maddison, *Economic Growth in the West,* p. 202; and La Francesca, *La politica economica del fascismo,* pp. 63–66.

[38] Italy. Istituto centrale di statistica, *Sommario di statistiche storiche dell'Italia 1861–1965,* table 110.

[39] *Yearbook of Labor Statistics,* 1941, table VIII.

[40] *Ibid.,* table V.

real wages per month for workers employed in industry. The index stood at 108 in 1934 and 96 in 1935. During the following year, money wages increased more slowly than prices, so that the index of real monthly wages declined to 94. It would continue to drop over the next two years, reaching a level of 86.6 in 1938.[41] The economic crisis was felt even more sharply in the countryside than in the city. Few statistics are available, but the International Labour Office's calculation that hourly wages of agricultural day laborers fell by more than 25 percent between 1929 and 1936 indicates the gravity of the problem.[42]

The effects of the depression may be observed in the deterioration of the diet of the average Italian. In 1936 per capita daily consumption was only 89 percent of what it had been during the decade 1921–1930 in terms of calories, and 92 percent of what it had been in terms of grams of protein. Already poor consumption levels deteriorated for virtually all items from wheat, olive oil, and tomatoes to beef, green vegetables, fresh fruit, and wine. Except for an increase in the use of milk and milk products, virtually the only areas in which advances were registered were less expensive substitutes for traditional elements of the Italian diet.[43] In its annual economic report for 1936, the British embassy in Rome observed that "wages have fallen to a level at which even the employed workman can barely find the necessities of life."[44]

From 1931 on, government expenditures had exceeded receipts and in 1934 receipts had amounted to only 73.9 percent of expenditures. A sharp reduction of expenditures in 1935 brought the budget closer to being in balance, but the costs of the Ethiopian war caused expenditures to more than triple in 1936, to 66.9 billion lire, with only

[41] *Ibid,* table XIII.

[42] *Yearbook of Labor Statistics,* 1938, table XVIII.

[43] Italy. Istituto centrale di statistica, *Sommario di statistiche storiche dell'Italia 1861–1965,* tables 105 and 106.

[44] FO R 3171/3171/22.

a slight increase in receipts, leaving a deficit of 40.4 billion.[45] In an effort to improve the financial situation, the government began to resort to a series of extraordinary expedients, including forced loans and special taxes on capital as well as the spectacular if ineffective collection of wedding rings and other items of personal jewelry.[46]

The situation was further complicated by Italy's persistent foreign trade deficit. In an economy as heavily dependent as the Italian one on imports of vital raw materials, foreign trade and balance of payments considerations constrained the whole economy to an unusually high degree. Table 1 shows that in some respects the trade deficit problem was alleviated during the 1930s, since the total volume of trade declined and since the decline in Italian exports was less rapid than that in imports. But the problem continued to be a serious one which could be ignored only at the nation's peril.

In an attempt to deal with the problems caused by the depression, Italian foreign commerce was subjected to numerous forms of government control, which led to the substitution of bilateral for multilateral trading. Together with sanctions and the depressed state of world trade, they brought about not only a drop in the value of commerce but a sharp shift in its direction, as can be appreciated in table 1. The growth of Germany's share in Italy's foreign trade and the declining share of Great Britain, and even more noticeably of France, point to the general orientation of Italian foreign policy toward an alliance with Germany.

The policy of autarky, introduced in response to League of Nations sanctions, had not yet had time to take full effect in 1936, but was already beginning to cause notable distortions in the economy as production was forcibly increased without regard for costs. Domestically produced

[45] Italy, Istituto centrale di statistica, *Sommario di statistiche storiche dell'Italia 1861–1965*, table 107.
[46] Salvatorelli and Mira, *Storia d'Italia nel periodo fascista*, pp. 868–72.

TABLE 1

Italian Foreign Trade 1927–1939

Imports

	Total Million Lire	Europe Million Lire	France	Great Britain	Ger- many	Ger- many & Austria
			(as percent of European imports)			
1927	20,375	10,390	17.3	17.6	20.3	25.2
1928	21,920	10,806	19.1	16.6	21.3	26.7
1929	21,303	11,468	17.8	17.8	23.7	27.9
1930	17,347	10,394	14.5	16.1	21.7	25.7
1931	11,643	7,313	11.3	15.0	21.7	25.7
1932	8,268	4,939	9.8	15.0	23.3	27.0
1933	7,432	4,397	9.3	16.5	26.0	29.9
1934	7,675	4,623	9.4	15.3	27.0	31.1
1935	7,790	4,880	9.6	11.6	29.2	34.8
1936	6,039	3,705	3.4	1.4	43.6	53.6
1937	13,943	7,644	6.4	7.3	33.9	42.1
1938	11,273	7,115	3.6	10.2	—	42.4
1939	10,309	6,967	2.2	10.4	—	43.3

Exports

	Total Million Lire	Europe Million Lire	France	Great Britain	Ger- many	Ger- many & Austria
			(as percent of exports to Europe)			
1927	15,519	9,944	12.9	15.4	22.4	27.3
1928	14,444	8,828	15.4	15.9	21.0	25.9
1929	14,767	8,748	14.9	16.7	20.3	25.2
1930	12,119	7,725	16.0	15.4	20.1	25.0
1931	10,210	6,689	16.7	17.9	16.3	21.0
1932	6,812	4,525	11.4	13.3	17.1	21.4
1933	5,991	3,965	11.6	17.4	18.4	21.7
1934	5,224	3,586	9.8	12.0	23.7	26.6
1935	5,238	3,173	11.1	13.5	26.3	31.0
1936	5,542	2,620	7.2	5.9	41.4	48.8
1937	10,444	5,253	8.4	12.2	28.6	34.1
1938	10,497	5,468	6.0	10.7	—	40.3
1939	10,823	6,066	4.0	8.5	—	31.3

SOURCE: Calculated from Italy. Istituto Centrale di Statistica, *Sommario di statistche storiche dell'Italia*, tables 75 & 77.

Italian products had been expensive even before autarky. Coal cost three times as much in Italy as in England, and steel twice as much.[47] The new policy only served to aggravate this condition. Synthetic gasoline and artificial rubber, for example, cost four times as much as imported products.

On balance, the economic situation was difficult and strongly suggested that Italy ought not to become involved in any further foreign ventures which would tax an already overstrained economy; but increasingly after 1935, Mussolini was to subordinate economic considerations to the demands of his foreign policy.[48] Meeting Franco's initial request for aid was no problem since he was able to pay cash, but future arms shipments would cause serious economic difficulties. The scarcity of foreign exchange, with the resulting limitations on imports of raw materials needed to fabricate modern arms and equipment, was a constant concern to the economic ministries, and economic considerations help explain Italy's frequently expressed wish to see the Civil War brought to a quick close.

ITALIAN FOREIGN RELATIONS

In the days that preceded the outbreak of the military revolt in Spain, Mussolini viewed the world with considerable satisfaction and complacency, for his Ethiopian venture had met with success at relatively little cost. Italian East Africa was far from pacified, but that, he felt confident, was only a question of time. The hard realities of economics and geography had not yet worn through the thin plating of dreams and illusions that transformed Ethiopia into a promised land of riches. Italy, so Mussolini declared, had won its colonial empire and was now a satisfied country.

The whole character of the Fascist regime, with its stress on heroic deeds and its constant efforts to mobilize the

[47] Romeo, *Breve storia della grande industria in Italia*, p. 137.
[48] La Francesca, *La politica economica del fascismo*, p. 75.

population for great national undertakings, as well as Mussolini's own restless personality, made it unlikely that Italy would settle down quietly to the relatively dull and glamorless tasks of trying to develop its newly won colonies—tasks for which, it might be added, Italy lacked the necessary financial and technical resources. For the moment the Duce's appetite was satisfied, but sooner or later the regime would feel the need for striking new foreign successes. They would not necessarily take the form of new territorial acquisitions, but some spectacular new affirmation of Fascist Italy's power and prestige would sooner or later be called for.

The most obvious area for such an affirmation in 1936 was the Mediterranean. Largely cut off from the rest of Europe by the Alps, Italy had always been heavily dependent on maritime trade. In 1934 fully 85 percent of her imports arrived by sea. Recognition of her standing as a great power in the Mediterranean had long been one of the Duce's objectives, and had played an important role in his Moroccan policy in the twenties. The conquest of an African empire, linked to Italy through the Mediterranean, had turned his attention more sharply toward winning a special position in that sea.[49]

Italian Nationalists bent on increasing their country's power and prestige had traditionally looked to the Balkans and the Danube basin in addition to the Mediterranean. Mussolini was no exception.[50] In these areas British influence was negligible, but both France and Germany had major interests. After World War I, Paris had carefully built up a clientele among the Central European states. French diplomacy relied heavily upon her special influence in Poland, Yugoslavia, Rumania, and Czechoslovakia. Any

[49] Catalano, *L'Italia dalla dittatura alla democrazia 1919–1948*, p. 232.

[50] Kogan, *The Politics of Italian Foreign Policy*, pp. 29–30; Quaroni, "Le diplomate italien," in Braunias and Stourzh (eds.), *Diplomatie unserer Zeit*, p. 191.

attempt to modify the Balkan or East European situation in Italy's favor would be viewed with alarm in Paris.[51] Germany too was a potential and increasingly important rival, since she also considered the Danube basin an area in which her influence ought to increase, and was actively competing for markets there.[52]

If the Mediterranean and the Balkans represented the two areas in which Italian influence could be expanded, it was Italian relations with the great Western European powers, Germany, Great Britain, and France, which would determine what could be done and how.

In July 1936, the effects of the Ethiopian war were still far from having entirely worked themselves out. It was a moment of transition in European politics, in which Italy's foreign relations might have moved rapidly in any of several directions. Her relations with the Western democracies and with the Soviet Union had been damaged not only by official government policies such as the application of sanctions but by the growth of anti-Fascist sentiment in the press and among gradually increasing sectors of the population. Italy's aggression in Ethiopia, together with Hitler's policy of rearmament and the remilitarization of the Rhineland, lent urgency to the cries of those who saw in Fascism a threat to peace as well as an affront to liberal democratic values.

The ideological similarity between the Nazi regime and Italian Fascism was a constant invitation to closer relations, and since Germany had no major interests in the Mediterranean she might be expected to support Italian claims there as she had done to some extent during the conquest of Ethiopia.[53] The most important obstacle in the way of

[51] "The rival, the only rival when all was said and done, was France." Quaroni, "Le diplomate italien," p. 191.

[52] Weinberg, *The Foreign Policy of Hitler's Germany*, pp. 115–16.

[53] The importance of this factor in bringing Italy and Germany together is discussed in Catalano, *L'Italia dalla dittatura alla democrazia 1919–1948*, p. 232.

better Italo-German relations had been Austria. A German takeover in Austria would not only put Italy in direct contact with a large and potentially aggressive state but would complicate the problem of governing the South Tyrol with its restless German-speaking population. In 1934, when a coup involving the murder of Austrian Prime Minister Dollfuss had made a Nazi takeover seem imminent, Mussolini had even ordered Italian troops on the Brenner pass mobilized, although France and Great Britain had limited themselves to verbal protests.

During the 1934 incident, however, Mussolini became discouraged by French and British passivity. He soon declared that Italy was no longer willing to play the role of sole watchdog of Austrian independence.[54] The League's sanctions against Italy provided Rome the occasion for abandoning Austria to her fate. The weak reaction of London and Paris to his own aggression in Ethiopia confirmed Mussolini's conviction that little positive action could be expected from them, even in defense of their own vital interests, much less to preserve Austrian independence. He was grateful toward Hitler for not applying sanctions and for having averted further Franco-British pressures on Italy by his remilitarization of the Rhineland, even though he was enough of a realist to be aware that the Führer had simply followed his own interest.

On June 6 he advised Austrian Premier Schuschnigg to negotiate an agreement with Hitler, and four days later he dismissed the strongly pro-Austrian Fulvio Suvich and made his son-in-law, Galeazzo Ciano, foreign minister.[55] In July the Austrian government signed a treaty with Germany binding itself to behave in a way that was suitable to "a German nation." Most European observers correctly interpreted this as the death knell of Austrian independence. Mussolini's "sacrifice of Austrian independence on

[54] Baumont, *La faillite de la paix: 1919–1938*, II, 513–15.
[55] Weinberg, *The Foreign Policy of Hitler's Germany*, p. 264; Wiskeman, *The Rome-Berlin Axis*, p. 83.

the altar of German friendship"[56] soon lead to a significant improvement in Italo-German relations,[57] although rivalry for the leadership of the international Fascist camp continued to divide the two countries.

The Ethiopian war had severely strained Italo-British relations, but it is not true that friendship between Rome and London was "beyond repair."[58] Friendship with England had traditionally been a cardinal point of Italian policy, and Mussolini still had a healthy regard for British naval power. There was much to be said for attempting to collaborate with Great Britain in the Mediterranean, and there was no reason to believe that London would refuse Italian friendship. One year earlier, Great Britain had given the world clear proof of her ability to overlook ideological differences by signing the London Naval Pact, and she was clearly desirous of improving her relations with Nazi-controlled Germany, even, if need be, at the expense of her relations with France.[59]

In June and July 1936 London made a bid to improve its relations with Rome. League sanctions were withdrawn. British ships which had been moved to the Mediterranean during the height of the Ethiopian crisis returned to their normal bases, and British guarantees to Greece, Yugoslavia, and Turkey against Italian aggression were ended.[60] Great Britain was not willing, however, to accept Italy's demands for immediate recognition of her empire and explusion of

[56] Salvatorelli, *Il Fascismo nella politica internazionale*, p. 151. Salvatorelli, writing immediately after the end of the Second World War, assumed that Mussolini was informed of the imminence of the Spanish Civil War, and conjectured that he might have been motivated by this knowledge to acquiesce in the first step of German absorption of Austria (*ibid.*, p. 152). As we will see in chapter 2, Mussolini had in fact no advance warning of the outbreak of the Spanish Civil War.

[57] Chabod, *L'Italia contemporanea*, pp. 95–96.

[58] Puzzo, *The Spanish Civil War*, p. 19.

[59] Toscano, *Pagine di storia diplomatica contemporanea*, II, 111; Baumont, *La faillite de la paix: 1919–1938*, II, 528–29.

[60] Duroselle, *Histoire diplomatique de 1919 à nos jours*, p. 210.

Ethiopia from the League of Nations. Since Mussolini was adamant on these points, British overtures of friendship bore no fruit,[61] but no one could have said without the benefit of hindsight that they would remain sterile in the future. At least through the end of 1936 Italy was undecided as to whether to throw in her lot with London or Berlin and was hopeful that she might be able to avoid making a choice at all.[62]

France had joined Great Britain in her overtures of friendship in early summer and had suffered the same rebuff. Relations with France were complicated by ideological hostility after Leon Blum's Popular Front government came to power in June 1936.[63] Aside from ideological considerations, resentment of French attempts to block the growth of Italian influence in Central Europe and the Danube basin was a cause of friction, although prior to the coming to power of the Popular Front it had not proven decisive. The ever-growing volume of criticism of Fascism and the Duce that appeared in the French press after June 1936 annoyed Mussolini, who was also upset by the fact that France provided a haven and a base for the Italian anti-Fascists who had fled their own country.[64] When war broke out in Spain, Italo-French relations were in a transitional phase of increasing estrangement and hostility from

[61] The best discussion of the abortive attempt to achieve a rapprochement in spring and early summer of 1936 is found in Weinberg, *The Foreign Policy of Hitler's Germany*, pp. 264–70.

[62] "Throughout 1936 Fascist foreign policy continued to oscillate between England and Germany" (Santarelli, *Storia del movimento e del regime fascista*, II, 225).

[63] Prior to Blum's government, Italo-French relations had been correct if not cordial (Laurens, *France and the Italo-Ethiopian Crisis*, p. 380). Although France had supported economic sanctions, she had exercised a moderating influence on Great Britain. In recognition of this fact, a group of Fascists had even staged a show of sympathy in front of the French embassy in Rome (Soleri, *Memorie*, p. 218).

[64] For one concrete example of Mussolini's irritation at French hospitality to anti-Fascists, see Rossi, *Trentatré vicende mussoliniane*, p. 386.

which they would not recover, largely because of the effects of the Civil War itself.

Since the Civil War came at a time when Italian foreign relations were in a state of flux and redefinition it will be important to examine closely its influence on them. Particular care will have to be taken to discern exactly how and to what degree it contributed to the eventual alignment of Italy with Germany against the Allies, for most authors simply assert that it was a major factor without attempting to analyze the mechanisms through which it worked. Before we can turn our attention to the Civil War and its effects, however, we must go back to the beginnings of the Fascist regime and examine Italo-Spanish relations during the decade and a half prior to the outbreak of the war.

TWO

THE BACKGROUND OF INTERVENTION: ITALO-SPANISH RELATIONS 1922–1936

Primo de Rivera's Dictatorship

After the last of Napoleon's troops withdrew from the peninsula, Spain lived on the margin of Europe for over a century. She participated to a degree in the cultural life of the continent, and incorporated into her political institutions some of the typical features of nineteenth-century liberalism, but exercised very little influence on the course of events outside her borders. Shorn of most of her colonies during the first third of the nineteenth century, she had ceased to be a power that really mattered in Europe. Although she attempted to exercise an active foreign policy in the early years of the twentieth century, especially in Morocco, she counted for little in Europe's political calculations. Even the First World War passed her by, not only because Spaniards were deeply divided over whether to intervene or not and over which side to support but also because the Allies did not feel it was worth their trouble to press her to enter the conflict.

Like most other European countries, Italy maintained correct but not particularly close relations with Spain during the first two decades of the twentieth century.[1] They had no common borders, and their economies were too similar to encourage any large-scale commerce. On the political level, neither country showed much interest in closer contacts with the other.

Mussolini's rise to power did not immediately change this aspect of Italian foreign policy. During the nineteen-

[1] Giannini, 'I rapporti italo-spagnoli (1860–1955)," pp. 21–24.

31

twenties, his plans for increasing Italian influence, prestige, and power were chiefly concerned with central and eastern Europe and the eastern Mediterranean.[2] Spain lay outside the sphere of his interest. During his first year in office, Madrid made a number of overtures for closer relations, but Mussolini showed no interest in following up on them.[3]

[2] There is no recent scholarly study of the whole of Mussolini's diplomacy. Di Nolfo's *Mussolini e la politica estera italiana* (*1919–1933*) is helpful though by no means definitive. Cassels's *Mussolini's Early Diplomacy* is a thorough study of the first four years of Fascist diplomacy, based on the *Documenti diplomatici italiani*. Carocci's *La politica estera dell'Italia* (*1925–1928*) uses many unpublished documents from the ministry archives to give a detailed picture of a crucial time period. Salvemini's classic *Mussolini diplomatico, 1922–1932* is still useful, although it is based almost entirely on journalistic sources and the author has a tendency to allow his anti-Fascist passion to lead him to deny Mussolini any ability or success. It is available in English in the final edition revised by the author, under the title *Prelude to World War II*. Augusto della Torre's edition of this work in Salvemini's *Opera omnia*, with the title *Preludio alla seconda guerra mondiale*, includes Salvemini's notes for further chapters, including one on the Spanish Civil War. Macartney and Cremona's survey of *Italy's Foreign and Colonial Policy, 1914–1937*, though published in 1938, can still be used for factual data. Santarelli's *Storia del movimento e del regime fascista* is occasionally marred by a dogmatically Marxist approach, but presents an intelligent and interesting view of some aspects of Fascist foreign policy and its relations to domestic events.

[3] King Alfonso XIII had invited the Duce to visit Madrid and had openly suggested to the Italian ambassador the possibility of Italo-Spanish political and military collaboration against France. In February 1923, he had said: "Together we amount to something. If we join our navies, our air force, and our influence, we can help each other greatly. . . . But we need *deeds, deeds, deeds*. And we need to reach a clear understanding about what our common interests are and about who oppose them. Italy can do us great services in the Mediterranean" (Paulucci de Calbali, letter to Mussolini, February 11, 1923, MAE, Politica, b. 1588). Similar overtures had been made by some of the outstanding political leaders of constitutional Spain. Count Romanones, for instance, spoke to the ambassador of the need for "closer links between Spain and Italy to force France to modify her posture and make her realize that the other two Medi-

In addition to traditional strategic, political, and economic motives, ideological considerations also influenced Mussolini's policy. This became apparent in September 1923, when a coup d'état brought General Miguel Primo de Rivera to power in Spain. Primo's dictatorship was designed to solve the political crisis that resulted from the Spanish army's inability to repress the revolt of Abd el Krim in Morocco and a threatened parliamentary investigation of Spain's crushing defeat by the rebels at Anual. The new government presented itself to the world clothed in an authoritarian nationalist guise that immediately aroused Mussolini's sympathetic interest. The moment was especially propitious, since the Duce was in an aggressive and assertive mood (as events in Corfu and Fiume demonstrated), and since his relations with France were at a low point.[4]

Less than a week after Primo came to power, Mussolini drafted in his own hand a telegram to the Italian ambassador in Madrid, suggesting that the new situation in Spain should make it possible to "strengthen in all respects the economic and political understandings between the two Mediterranean countries." "The Fascist Government," he added, "would not be adverse to considering the possibility of reaching a political and military agreement with Spain."[5] Primo de Rivera readily fell in with the idea of an Italo-Spanish agreement as part of an overall anti-French strategy. He suggested that England, too, might be induced to join Spain, Italy, and possibly Portugal in opposing French influence in the Mediterranean.[6]

---

terranean countries do not intend to leave in her hand the keys to their common sea" (Telegram 196, September 7, 1923, MAE, Politica, b. 1588). In a private conversation with the ambassador in June 1923, Santiago Alba expressed his belief in "the firm and solid friendship that should unite our two countries against the common enemy for the defense of the Mediterranean" (DDI, 7, 2, p. 74).

[4] Cassels, *Mussolini's Early Diplomacy*, p. 210.

[5] DDI, 7, 2, p. 378.

[6] DDI, 7, 2, p. 476.

This initial burst of enthusiasm had few practical results. Shortly before King Alfonso's highly publicized state visit to Italy in November 1923, a new commercial convention between the two countries was signed; but Spain steadfastly refused to include a most-favored-nation clause. Prospects for a political understanding faded rapidly as Madrid began to realize the importance of collaboration with France in Morocco, and to weigh more soberly the degree of French opposition to an Italo-Spanish pact. Negotiations dragged on for almost three years. When a treaty was finally announced in 1926, observers felt certain it included secret clauses providing for Italian use of naval bases in the Balearic Islands in case of war with France.[7] In actual fact, it was a banal treaty of friendship and arbitration which an Italian diplomat rightly described as having "no political significance."[8]

The one practical question of some importance that affected the two countries was the status of the international city of Tangiers. Mussolini deeply resented having been excluded from the agreement by which Tangiers' status was fixed and he repeatedly pressed Primo de Rivera to support his demands for a revision of the agreement. The Spanish dictator was lavish in his expressions of good will, but did little to further Italian claims. When a new

---

[7] Rumors about the existence of secret clauses were so widespread that when Ambassador Guariglia spoke to the Spanish foreign minister in 1933 about the possibility of renewing the 1926 treaty, Los Rios thought he was referring to the supposed secret treaty and ordered that a thorough search of the foreign ministry archives be made for its text. The search was fruitless, of course, and Guariglia, who was informed by a ministry official about the situation, wrote a letter to the Spanish director of political affairs explaining the mistake (Report 2637/1469, September 14, 1933, MAE, Politica, b. 4). Historians have generally believed the rumors about secret clauses. See for example Van der Esch, *Prelude to War*, p. 26, and Puzzo, *Spain and the Great Powers*, p. 43.

[8] Guariglia, *Ricordi*, p. 52. The text of the treaty is in *Trattati e convenzione*, XXXVI (1926), 474–80.

agreement was finally negotiated and signed in 1928, Rome gained little in the process.[9]

Primo de Rivera's internal policies were almost as disappointing to Italy as his foreign policy. He had come to power as a result of an army coup and lacked any organized base of popular support. He did enjoy a considerable degree of personal popularity, and made some progress toward giving Spain a rational economic policy. But his regime had almost no adherents among the intelligentsia, and had no ideological program other than a vague "regenerationism," in the tradition of the Spanish social critic of the generation of 1898, Joaquin Costa. Primo de Rivera's state party, the *Unión Patriotica*, was never a real force in Spanish political life and enjoyed little support outside the bureaucracy.[10]

From the very beginning Italian representatives in Spain entertained grave doubts about the new dictator's internal policies. They were particularly concerned about his failure to organize a solidly based party. Only a few days after the coup, the ambassador observed: "The promoter of the Spanish military movement affirms that he was inspired by Fascism. Be that as it may, he committed an error in moving too soon, without considering the necessity of having beforehand the elements with which to rebuild what needed to be torn down."[11]

In the course of the following years, appraisals of the situation naturally varied with the circumstances, but in general Italian observers were quick to point out the defects and weaknesses of Primo de Rivera's regime. A report prepared in the Italian foreign ministry in July or August 1929 accurately summarizes Italian opinion:

[9] Carocci, *La politica estera dell'Italia fascicta, 1925–1928*, p. 217.

[10] On Primo de Rivera's dictatorship, see Ratcliff, *Prelude to Franco;* and Payne, *A History of Spain and Portugal*, II, 618–22.

[11] Unnumbered telegram, September 9, 1923, MAE, Politica, b. 1591.

The Fascist Revolution was passion, struggle, and blood. It had within itself three elements, without which it is almost impossible to bring about the miracle of infusing a new way of life into a people: victory in war, a *condottiero*, a myth. De Rivera's noble movement in Spain was undoubtedly something more than a mere ministerial crisis, but it was certainly much less than a revolution. There was no victorious war. The myth was painfully absent, as has been demonstrated by the pitiable attempt to force the birth of a patriotic party which was completely devoid of soul and vitality. The *condottiero* has proven to be little more than an intelligent and energetic gentleman. His followers are neither numerous nor enthusiastic, and he tends to hold them back rather than to encourage them. . . . [His proposed constitution is an] artificial compilation, a mosaic of timid imitations and of uncertain intentions, half-way between Fascist and democratic-electoral principles.[12]

Although Rome was dissatisfied with Primo's accomplishments, the Italians did not encourage him to imitate more closely the Fascist regime, nor did they otherwise interfere in Spain's internal politics. Even when the Spanish dictator took the complimentary, if highly unorthodox, step of asking Mussolini for comments and suggestions on the draft of his proposed new constitution, the Duce was careful to limit himself to generic, noncommital remarks.

By 1929 Primo de Rivera had lost almost all popular support and faced strong opposition in the university and among intellectuals. A bad harvest and problems with the balance of payments were causing hardship, and King Alfonso XIII was growing restive. When it became clear in January 1930 that the army was also reluctant to continue supporting the dictator, Alfonso dismissed Primo and named an aged general head of the new government. For

[12] Undated and unsigned memorandum for Mussolini, probably prepared in the ministry's political affairs section, MAE, Politica, b. 1591.

the next fifteen months there was little or nothing to report in the field of Italo-Spanish relations.

The significance of the rapprochement between Rome and Madrid during Primo de Rivera's dictatorship has been exaggerated by most historians who treat the question.[13] Primo's six years in power did show that ideological affinities could stir Mussolini's interest and serve as a stimulus to closer relations than were otherwise warranted, but more importantly they demonstrated that such considerations were not sufficient grounds for effective collaboration. It is clear that counting a head of government among his admirers gratified Mussolini's pride, but he had no real desire to foster a Fascist regime in Spain at this time. The fact that Italo-Spanish collaboration was already envisioned as an anti-French strategy was a portent of the future, but nothing concrete came of it at the time.

EARLY HOSTILITY TO THE SPANISH REPUBLIC

The proclamation of the Second Spanish Republic on April 31, 1931, reawakened Rome's interest in Spain. The new regime owed its existence less to the strength of its backers than to the weaknesses and apathy of the throne's supporters. The fall of the monarchy was provoked by the failure of its supporters to win the municipal elections in a number of large cities. The transition to the Republic took place with almost no violence or disorder.

From the day of its birth, the Republic had to face Fascist Italy's hostility. Four factors contributed to the animosity: 1) Fascist scorn for the Republic's liberal parliamentary regime; 2) the overt anti-Fascism of many Republican leaders; 3) Italian fears that liberal democracy would soon lead to Communism in Spain; and 4) Rome's apprehension lest Spain be drawn deeper into the French orbit, to Italy's detriment.

[13] For a typical treatment, see Puzzo, *Spain and the Great Powers*, pp. 42–43.

In Fascist eyes Spain was trying to swim against the current. Fascist propaganda never tired of declaring that liberal parliamentary democracy was a thing of the past, a relic of the nineteenth century that was either dead or dying everywhere. The Weimar Republic was already in crisis and could be ruled only by presidential decree. The French Third Republic was beginning to encounter really serious difficulties, while Great Britain and the United States seemed unable to cope with the problems caused by the depression. Even the one Socialist state, the USSR, was turning to totalitarianism. More and more eyes everywhere were looking toward the apparently more efficient solutions offered by the various authoritarian regimes. Despite all this, Spain had had the audacity, one might even say the effrontery, to reject Primo de Rivera's authoritarian government and turn back to a classical parliamentary democracy, with marked Socialist leanings. A little more than a month after the proclamation of the Republic, Mussolini gave vent to his scorn in a biting aphorism on the fall of the monarchy. "The Spanish Republic is not a revolution but a plagiarism. A plagiarism that arrives a good one hundred and fifty years late. To found a parliamentary republic today means using an oil lamp in the era of electric lights."[14]

Spain's new leaders not only obstinately refused to read the antiliberal and antidemocratic signs of the times, they were also openly and actively anti-Fascist. The new Italian ambassador in Madrid, Ercole Durini di Monzo, who had presented his credentials on April 11, had not had much time to familiarize himself with his new post when the Republic was proclaimed; but it did not take an expert eye to see that "among the Ministers [of the Provisional Government] are to be found the most qualified representatives of the Socialist and Republican parties, the most ruth-

[14] ACS, segreteria particolare del Duce, autografi, 1931, b. 6, f. IX, sf. F. I am grateful to Professor Renzo de Felice for having acquainted me with this text.

less and systematic opponents of Primo de Rivera's dictatorship, of the monarchy, and of Fascism."[15] The Spanish left wing press, released from the control of government censors and filled with enthusiasm for the new Republic, launched out on a campaign of bitter attacks on Fascism and the Duce. The civil governor of Madrid lost no time in offering the city's hospitality to an anti-Fascist rally, and the navy minister expressed in a letter to a French paper his hopes that the repercussions of Spain's example would soon make themselves felt "in the European countries that suffer under dictatorships."[16]

The prospect of Spain's becoming a base for anti-Fascist activities further disturbed Rome. Many Republican leaders had been in close contact with Italian anti-Fascist exiles in Paris, a number of whom soon made their appearance in Madrid. Although they were never very numerous, and their activities were of little practical importance, their presence was an irritant in Italo-Spanish relations.[17]

[15] Telegram 75, April 15, 1931, MAE, Politica, b. 1.

[16] Letter published in *La liberté*, Paris, April 16, 1931.

[17] Roselli, Tarchiani, and Bassanesi of *Giustizia e libertà* were in Madrid some time before the end of April 1931 and saw Prieto, Azaña, and Ramón Franco, whose exploits as an aviator had made him more famous than his brother, General Francisco Franco. Of the three Spaniards, Franco was apparently the most enthusiastic, and reportedly favored bombing Palazzo Venezia. In May Roselli and Tarchiani returned to Spain. In an interview with Azaña they laid plans for a leaflet-dropping flight over Italy, but nothing ever came of the plan. Simultaneously, Facchinetti, a Republican separated from *Giustizia e libertà,* apparently laid his own plans for a leaflet-dropping flight, but once again they came to nothing (Garosci, *La vita di Carlo Rosselli,* I, 235–38). At the beginning of May a group of Italian anti-Fascists comprising Buozzi, Taranto, Facchinetti, Treves, and Campolonghi participated in the International Congress of Syndical Federations and saw privately Eduardo Ortega y Gasset (the civil governor of Madrid and brother of the philosopher), Ramón Franco, and Indalecio Prieto (Telegram 106 of May 2, 1931, MAE Politica, b. 2). Sporadic visits of leading Italian exiles continued, and at least a few Italian anti-Fascists took up residence in Spain. (Some police correspondence on the subject is

Fear that the Republic would open the door to Communism heightened the suspicion and hostility aroused in Rome by its ideology and by its harbouring of anti-Fascist exiles. Even before the proclamation of the Republic, the Italian embassy in Madrid had reported that Communists were making great progress in both the army and the unions.[18] The ambassador was convinced of the existence of a "preestablished and generously financed Communist plan, backed by Russian money," in which even some members of the government were said to be involved.[19] The fact that there was no significant Communist danger in Spain at this time is far less important for understanding Italian policy than is the fact that Mussolini believed there was. Among his aphorisms on the fall of the Spanish monarchy is the following observation: "Kerensky does not recall Nicholas; he prepares the way for Lenin. Today it is no longer a question of republic or monarchy, but of Communism or Fascism."[20]

During the second half of 1931, France made a concerted effort to strengthen her ties with Spain, through tours of deputies and speakers, a visit of the French fleet, payments to the press, intergovernmental loans, etc. Ambassador Durini saw in all this a clear threat to Italy's desire to strengthen her own position in the Mediterranean vis-à-vis France.[21] Fears of a military agreement between Spain and France grew after the victory of the French Left and Tardieu's defeat in the 1932 elections. Significantly enough, Italian naval exercises during the late summer of 1932 were based on the assumption that France had occupied the

---

found in ACS, pubblica sicurezza, affari generali e riservati, prima sezione, 1932, b. 70.)

[18] De Peppo's unnumbered report on the political situation in Spain during 1930, December 31, 1930, MAE, Politica, b. 1.

[19] Report 734/414, May 15, 1931, MAE, Politica, b. 2.

[20] ACS, segreteria particolare del Duce, autografi, 1931, b. 6, f. IX, sf. F.

[21] Report 1987/1117, November 30, 1931, MAE, Politica, b. 2.

Balearic Islands and was attempting to prevent the passage of the Italian fleet from Tripolitania to Italy.[22]

Fear of the possibility of a Franco-Spanish military agreement involving both the use of the Balearic Islands and the right of passage of French troops across Spain was a major factor in Mussolini's decision during the summer of 1933 to sound out the Spanish government on the possibility of renewing immediately the 1926 Italo-Spanish treaty of friendship and arbitration, although it was not due to expire for several years. The treaty was itself virtually meaningless, but Rome apparently felt its renewal would be a valuable sign of good will and something of a guarantee against unfriendly action. The Spanish government failed to realize the symbolic importance that Rome attached to the treaty and showed no interest in anticipating the renewal. This disinterest heightened Italian fears of a Franco-Spanish understanding directed against Italy.[23]

Hostility toward the Spanish Republic soon led Fascist Italy to work for its downfall by aiding and encouraging various anti-Republican conspirators. In April 1932, the Italian air minister, Marshall Italo Balbo, received a visit in Rome from a Spanish aviator and monarchist conspirator, Juan Ansaldo, who had been sent to win Italian support for a military coup under the leadership of General Sanjurjo.[24] Balbo, the Fascist organizer of Ferrara and one of the *quadrumviri* of Fascism, had proposed to Mussolini the year before that Italy attempt to gain control of the Spanish possession of Melilla as a way of strengthening her presence in the western Mediterranean.[25] He now enthusiastically embraced the idea of helping to overthrow

---

[22] Guariglia, *Ricordi,* pp. 186 and 189.

[23] Guariglia's Report 2637/1460, September 14, 1933, MAE, Politica, b. 4.

[24] Ansaldo, *¿Para qué?* pp. 31–33; and Guariglia, *Ricordi,* pp. 188–89. Gil Robles mistakenly places this visit in spring 1933 (Gil Robles, *No fue posible la paz,* p. 712).

[25] NA T 586, roll 1295, frames 112744–45.

the Republican government, and assured Ansaldo he would provide arms and ammunition to Spain as soon as an uprising occurred. The material, chiefly machine guns, was in fact prepared and loaded on a ship, but the August 1932 coup was so poorly planned and executed and so rapidly crushed by the government that the aid never reached the rebels.[26]

As the Italian ambassador in Madrid reported, Sanjurjo's rising belonged to the classic Spanish tradition of *pronunciamientos*. The military had acted largely on their own, without bothering to plan for civilian support. Even in the north, where Monarchist and Catholic sentiment was strong, there had been no reaction among the civilian population. "The uprising that broke out at Madrid and Seville on August 10," wrote Ambassador Durini, "was conducted with extreme, inconceivable frivolity. It is a good measure of the lack of intelligence and the incompetence of its organizers: its chief characteristics are lack of organization, lack of fighting spirit, and lack of resolution in action."

In sharp contrast to the rebels, the government acted with speed and decision to crush the revolt. "The Government's action was rapid and energetic," Durini reported. "The armed forces, generally speaking, remained loyal, and the new police organization created by the Republic, the Assault Guards, responded perfectly and enthusiastically to the authorities' orders. The revolt was thus immediately repressed."[27] Mussolini himself was impressed by President Azana's show of energy, and commented that the Spaniard had "used my very own methods,"[28] high praise indeed coming from the Duce.

[26] Ansaldo, *¿Para qué?* p. 35; Guariglia, *Ricordi,* p. 189; Robinson, *The Origins of Franco's Spain,* pp. 102–103. Friedlander attributes the Italian decision to the fear caused by a supposed agreement between France and Spain reached during Herriot's trip to Spain (*The July 1936 Military Rebellion in Spain,* p. 13). Since the trip did not take place until almost six months later, this is obviously incorrect.

[27] Report 1470/743, August 12, 1932, MAE, Politica, b. 3.

[28] Guariglia, *Ricordi,* p. 190.

42

GUARIGLIA'S CONTACTS WITH ANTI-REPUBLICAN CONSPIRATORS, 1932–1933

The failure of the Sanjurjo *coup* and Mussolini's improved opinion of the Republic's chances for survival led to the appointment in late summer 1932 of a new ambassador to Madrid, Raffaele Guariglia. One of Italy's outstanding career diplomats, he had entered the foreign service in 1909 and had been stationed in London, St. Petersburg, Paris, and Brussels. Since 1926 he had been director general of political affairs for Europe, Africa, and the East. The naming of such a high-ranking career diplomat to the Madrid embassy seemed to indicate that Rome was determined to improve its official relations with Spain. On one level this is true, although Guariglia's ambassadorship also represented the high point of Italian anti-Republican activities prior to the outbreak of the Civil War.

Mussolini told Guariglia prior to his departure for Madrid that the disorganization of the opposition forces in Spain and the urgency of preventing the Republic from drawing closer to France made it imperative to cultivate good relations with the Spanish government. He urged the ambassador to stress the essential similarity of Italian and Spanish interests over and above ideological differences.[29]

During the first year of his mission, Guariglia's effort to cultivate better official relations met with very little success. Official Italo-Spanish relations really began to improve only during the fall of 1933, thanks to changes on the international and Spanish domestic scenes. A growing awareness of the more vicious and potentially dangerous character of the Nazi regime helped turn attention away from Fascism. As the wave of enthusiasm that had accompanied the proclamation of the Republic passed, and as center and right forces regained strength in Spanish politics,

[29] Guariglia gives the text of his instructions in *Ricordi*, pp. 193–199. Except for two omissions, he accurately reproduces the original text which is found in MAE, Politica, b. 3.

there was a distinct improvement in the tone of the Spanish press; attacks on Italian Fascism became less frequent and less virulent.[30] Guariglia attributes part of the improvement to what he describes as "our straight forward political conduct which aims to create better Italo-Spanish understanding without excessive concern over internal political struggles, party affairs and ideological questions used for internal politics."[31] This hardly seems an accurate description of the ambassador's conduct, at least if we are to judge by his own reports, which are full of references to contacts with pro-Fascist Spaniards, as will soon be seen.

By November 1933, the center and right parties in Spain had strengthened their positions sufficiently to administer a stunning defeat to their badly divided leftist rivals in Cortes elections. The majority bloc system of voting made the swing in seats far larger than that of the popular vote. The Catholic CEDA party, led by José María Gil Robles—who refused to declare himself in favor of either the Republic or the Monarchy but guaranteed the protection of the church and of private property—gained 110 seats and became the largest group. It was closely followed by the Radical party, whose urban middle-class voters elected about a hundred deputies. Socialist representation

---

[30] "After Hitler's coming to power in Germany, the Republican press has been less hostile toward us, and the Rightist press has continued to be well disposed and frequently enthusiastically so in our regard. . . . In Madrid, the Monarchist *ABC* still maintains its democratic-liberal dogmatic prejudice, but it shows growing interest in fascism and its accomplishments. The same is true of the Catholic *Debate*, which is openly fascistic. The moderate *Ahora* is still skeptical, but certainly not hostile. The popular *Informaciones* and the conservative *Epoca* have accentuated their philo-fascism. The liberal *El Sol*, the democratic *La Voz* and the radical *Luz* have attenuated their anti-fascism. The only examples left of intransigent anti-fascism are *El Socialista* and the two radical-masonic publications, *El Liberal* and *El Heraldo de Madrid*. Even these three, however, have limited their attacks as a result of scarce public response." Report 972/494, March 20, 1934, MAE, Politica, b. 6.

[31] Report 2381/1319, August 19, 1933, MAE, Politica, b. 4.

was halved to sixty seats, and the Left-Republican parties virtually disappeared.

The new government, made up entirely of Radical deputies but supported by the CEDA and the parties of the right, was a distinct improvement over its predecessor from the Italian point of view. The foreign minister, Leandro Pita Romero, was well disposed toward Italy and not adverse to praising Mussolini, at least in private conversations with the Italian ambassador.[32] Official relations, although they were still far from cordial, rapidly became less tense.

In sharp contrast to the gradually improving atmosphere of official relations stood Italy's continuing support of the Republic's declared enemies. The draft of Guariglia's instructions had originally suggested that he maintain "prudent and indirect contacts with the elements of the opposition," especially with Catholics and rightists, as well as with "the small numbers of young men who are the vanguard of the group which in some degree at least takes its inspiration from the example of Fascist Italy."[33] This paragraph was left out in the final copy of the instructions, but Mussolini may not have resisted the temptation to convey orally some directives of this type. In any case, the new ambassador clearly understood what was expected of him. In the twenties Mussolini had declared that Fascism was not an export article, but all that had changed by the time Guariglia left for Madrid. The Duce now claimed that the twentieth century would be the century of Fascism and the movement in favor of a Fascist international was gathering momentum.[34]

[32] Report 2031/1068, June 14, 1934, MAE, Politica, b. 6.
[33] First draft of the instructions in MAE, Politica, b. 3.
[34] "The twentieth century will be the century of Fascism . . . because outside our principles there is no salvation for individuals or peoples" (Mussolini, *Opera omnia*, XXV, 147). The origins and development of the international Fascist movement are treated in Ledeen, *Universal Fascism.*

Among the Spanish groups that were looking to Fascist Italy for their example, two stood out: The *Falange española* and the *Juntas de ofensiva nacional sindicalista* or *JONS*. José Antonio Primo de Rivera, the son of the late dictator, and several associates who called openly for violence founded the Falange with the express purpose of restoring Spain to its former greatness. The JONS were founded by Ramiro Ledesma Ramos, a young philosopher, and Onésimo Redondo, a peasant labor organizer. The two founders of the JONS shared a virulent anti-Marxism and an inclination toward dictatorship. Neither the Falange nor the JONS was very large. When they merged in February 1934 with the name *Falange española y de las JONS*, the new organization still had only about 3,000 members.[35]

Guariglia did not think highly of the strength and cohesion of the various Fascist and pro-Fascist groups. Most Spanish right-wing parties, he felt, were willing to use Italian friendship for their own purposes, but were far from understanding, much less adopting, Fascist principles in their entirety. He accused them of still thinking in terms of a stronger democratic or autocratic government, without grasping the "healthy and solid concept of a modern state based on Fascist principles."[36] Even more annoying to the ambassador than half-hearted and opportunistic acceptance of Fascist ideology was a lack of fighting spirit. JONS, for instance, talked a great deal about its paramilitary groups, and bragged about its assault squads, strongly reminiscent of the early *Fasci di combattimento*,[37] but during the fall 1933 elections, he reported, they were nowhere to be seen.[38]

Despite the many deficiencies of the various philo-Fascist groups, Guariglia attempted to "cultivate, assist and encour-

[35] Payne, *Falange*, pp. 38–48; Jackson, *The Spanish Republic and the Civil War*, pp. 117–18, 129.
[36] Report 528/316, February 24, 1933, MAE, Politica, b. 4.
[37] Report 2436/1341, August 22, 1933, MAE, Politica, b. 4.
[38] Report 3760/2058, December 14, 1933, MAE, Politica, b. 6.

46

age [them] on every possible occasion and in every possible way." As early as February 1933, he began a program of "clearly Fascist propaganda," starting with a small Fascist information center, housed in the already existing *Casa d'Italia*, and supplied with books and pamphlets on Fascism, current Fascist periodicals, and photographic material to distribute to the press.[39] In May 1934, the Fascist international organization, the *Comitato d'azione per la universalità di Roma*, recruited the extravagant Spanish Fascist writer, Ernesto Giménez Caballero, to organize its Spanish branch. The Nobel Prize winning poet Jacinto Benavente was named president of the Spanish branch the following year.[40]

Guariglia encouraged the nascent Fascist groups to convince the other rightist parties that the only solution to their problems was "a close spiritual unity, designed to create a new state, based on the principle of authority, leaving aside questions of the exact type of regime and of religious policy." He also urged them to take a more active and courageous stand on the problems of the day and be willing to run greater risks in order "to demonstrate to the Conservatives and the partisans of order the practical utility of Fascist organization, by working actively on the industrial and farm laborers who belong to Socialist and Communist unions and by courageously offering their services in strikes and other social conflicts."[41]

[39] Report 529/316, February 24, 1933, MAE, Politica, b. 6. Note for the undersecretary, No. 269671, prepared by affari politichi, ufficio 1, and signed by Buti, March 31, 1933, MAE, Politica, b. 5.

[40] Report dated Rome, June 4, 1934, ACS, ministero della cultura popolare, b. 423, Cat. Prop. I/67/3; Report 873 from Madrid to the sottosegretario di stato per la stampa e la propaganda, March 2, 1935, ACS, ministero della cultura popolare, b. 423, Cat. Prop. I/67/3.

[41] Report 1364/787, May 12, 1933, MAE, Politica, b. 5. In another report dated only a few days later, Guariglia describes in somewhat more detail his policy toward Spanish "neo-Fascism." "We must be at its side. We have to help them for the moment to overcome their

Among the various rightist leaders, José Antonio Primo de Rivera particularly impressed Guariglia, who arranged for him to visit Rome during the summer of 1933.[42] A personal encounter with Mussolini made a great impression on the young Spaniard, who found the dictator a far more human and normal person than the crowd-captivating Duce seen in the press and newsreels. Mussolini doubted the future Falangist leader's ideological orthodoxy, but decided he might have a role to play in Spanish politics and was worth cultivating, if for no other reason than to keep him from falling completely into the German orbit.[43]

The growing prestige of National Socialism presented a new challenge to Guariglia. Until recently there had been no competition for the admiration and loyalties of conservative authoritarian nationalists, who naturally turned their eyes toward Rome. Now Berlin was becoming an important rival. During the months following José Antonio's interview with the Duce, the ambassador worked actively to bring the Falange closer to Italian Fascism rather than to German National Socialism.[44] His task was facilitated by Primo de

---

purely Catholic, Monarchist and even reactionary prejudices. We must aid them to avoid taking up the ideology of *Action Française,* and to forget *primoderiverismo.* Military *pronunciamientos* like Sanjuro's must be avoided. Propaganda among the agricultural and laboring masses is essential. In a word, they must leave behind the antiquated mentality of 1848 revolutionaries, and adopt the modern ideal of unanimous collaboration of all classes, united by the single superior principle of the authority of the State" (Report 1420/816, May 16, 1933, MAE, Politica, b. 5).

[42] On this trip, see Nellessen, *Die verbotene Revolution,* p. 72.

[43] Guariglia, *Ricordi,* p. 204. No official record of this visit has been found in the files of Mussolini's personal secretariat nor in those of the foreign ministry. Shortly after the visit José Antonio wrote an article recounting his impressions. He laid special emphasis on the contrast between Mussolini's public image and the warmth, cordiality, and naturalness he encountered in his private conversation. (The original publication has not been located. A copy of the text may be found in MAE, Politica, b. 49.)

[44] Guariglia, *Ricordi,* p. 205.

Rivera's personality, which was more attracted to the relatively benign forms of Italian Fascism than to the Nazis' brutal exaltation of force. The Falangist leader, however, refused to enter entirely into the Italian orbit. Falangism, he insisted, was an authentic Spanish movement, not a copy of Italian Fascism. For this reason he refused to attend the International Fascist Conference held in Montreux in 1934.

Guariglia, who is at pains in his memoirs to stress the attempts made by career diplomats to limit Fascist influence on Italian foreign policy, in fact encouraged the development of Fascism in Spain more actively than any other Italian representative prior to the Civil War. Ironically, his "Fascist" successor, Orazio Pedrazzi, showed far less zeal for the cause. Even during Guariglia's embassy, however, contacts between Fascist representatives and leaders of the Falange and other philo-Fascist groups had few short term practical results. The Italians offered their encouragement and moral support, but were realistic enough to see that their ideological protégés were too weak to play a significant role in practical politics. If the Republic was to be overthrown, it would have to be by the military or by one of the various Monarchist groups that were in touch with them. This is why the most important contacts between Spanish conspirators and Fascist leaders involved not Falangists or members of the JONS but Monarchists of various persuasions.

In the fall or early winter of 1933, Juan Ansaldo returned to Italy, accompanied by the Monarchist leader, Calvo Sotelo. Guariglia probably contributed to making this trip possible. Calvo Sotelo's energy and determination and his success in the November 1933 elections suggested to the ambassador that the Monarchist leader might be the man to "begin to carry out the political and social reeducation of the Spanish people that would lead them . . . to create the real basis of a modern state as in Italy."[45] According

[45] Report 3504/1934, November 24, 1933, MAE, Politica, b. 4.

to Ansaldo's account, he and Calvo Sotelo met with Marshall Balbo and reached a firm agreement, presumably for
Italian support in case of an uprising against the Republic.[46]
During the same trip Calvo Sotelo also talked with Mussolini, but if the Duce gave him any concrete assurances
no record of them has been found.[47]

THE MARCH 1934 AGREEMENT WITH SPANISH MONARCHISTS

In March 1934, another party of four Spaniards made the
trip to Rome to seek assistance in their struggle against
the Republic. Antonio Goicoechea was a leader of *Renovación española*, a Monarchist group founded less than a
year and a half earlier for the express purpose of preparing
an armed assault on the Republic, by propagandizing
officers and former officers and looking for foreign support,
principally in Italy.[48] Antonio Lizarra Iribarren, the
Navarrese leader of the Carlists or Traditionalists was already actively engaged in organizing Carlist troops and
training them in the mountains of Navarre. Rafael Olazabal, another Traditionalist leader, seems to have been
the man responsible for preparing the meeting.[49] General
Emilio Barrera, the former chief of staff of the Spanish army,
had already been in Rome in 1932 soliciting aid for Sanjurjo's unsuccessful coup. Barrera was the only member
of the group who was not from the Basque country.

The four conspirators assured Mussolini on March 31,
1934, that they were determined to overthrow the Republic
and reestablish the monarchy at the earliest possible opportunity. Olozabal added that following the uprising an army

[46] Ansaldo, *¿Para qué?*, p. 58.

[47] Yangües, *La vida y la obra de Calvo Sotelo*, quoted in Gil Robles,
No fue posible la paz, p. 712.

[48] Gutiérrez-Ravé Montero, *Antonio Goicoechea*, pp. 19–20.

[49] The arrangements were apparently made through a Spanish
Jesuit, P. Segarra, who knew both Colonel Longo and the Italian
air attaché (interview with Francisco Javier Lizarza Inda, Madrid,
September 20, 1970).

officer would probably be named regent, so the problem of which candidate should be named king was not an urgent one.[50]

Mussolini quickly agreed that within a month of a successful uprising and the constitution of a new government, Italy would sign a commercial agreement and a treaty of friendship and neutrality with Spain. The text would be worked out in detail at the time, but would include an article obliging both parties to maintain the status quo with respect to all Spanish territories and protectorates in the western Mediterranean. The Duce demanded as a precondition that the Spaniards denounce the supposed secret Franco-Spanish treaty.[51]

A written agreement by which Italy promised to grant diplomatic recognition to the new regime as soon as that proved feasible was drawn up and signed by the four Spaniards and by Balbo. Mussolini verbally promised more concrete and substantial aid. He offered 10,000 rifles, 10,000 hand grenades, 200 machine guns, and 1,500,000 pesetas in cash immediately, and further aid when conditions justified it. After Mussolini left, the Spaniards continued their discussion with Marshall Balbo. The topics were essentially

[50] Italian minutes of meeting, MAE, Gabinetto, Spagna, 1. Lizarza gives a slightly different but substantially similar version of the conversation. Lizarza Iribarren, *Memorias de la conspiración*, pp. 34–35. In both versions it is perfectly clear that Mussolini was fully aware of the fact that he was dealing with a group of antiliberal Monarchists who were divided over the most suitable candidate for the throne. Though the point is almost too obvious to make, it may be worth while to note that it was also perfectly clear that none of the four Spaniards could with any propriety be considered a Fascist.

[51] Copies of the agreement and of the minutes written by Goicoechea, but not of the official Italian minutes, are most easily found in NA T 586, roll 1062, frames 063027–30. A translation may be found in Askew, "Italian Intervention in Spain: The Agreements of March 31, 1934," pp. 182–83. The Spanish version of the agreement, obviously the original text of which the Italian is a poor translation, speaks of "secret treaties," but it seems doubtful that the Italians really thought there was more than one treaty.

those already covered with the Duce, but Balbo laid special stress on the subject of preserving the status quo in the Mediterranean.[52]

The first installment of 500,000 pesatas was paid the next day to Rafael Olazabal, who eventually also received the balance for distribution between the two Monarchist groups.[53] The Italians also offered to instruct small groups of Spaniards in the use of machine guns and hand grenades. The Traditionalists, who had been training secretly in the mountains, were overjoyed, and seized the opportunity. During the following months three different groups of about fifteen men each received special training courses at an Italian military airport, where they were officially treated as Peruvian officers in order to cover their true identity. The only material that was actually delivered to the conspirators was six small radio-telephone sets. Machine guns, rifles, and hand grenades were shipped as far as Tripoli, but did not reach Spain before the outbreak of the Civil War.[54]

For obvious reasons, Balbo insisted that the Spaniards deposit their copy of the signed agreement and of the minutes they had made in a safe-deposit vault of a Rome bank. Goicoechea nevertheless took the original handwritten draft along with him. A police raid turned up this document in May 1937, and Republican propagandists lost

[52] This conversation is recorded only in the official Italian minutes (MAE, Gabinetto, Spagna, 1). Though his memoirs do not stress this point, Lizarza recalled in later years that Mussolini seemed especially concerned during their conversation about the passage of French troops from Africa to the Continent (Interview with Francisco Javier Lizarza Inda, Madrid, September 20, 1970).

[53] Lizarza Iribarren, *Memorias de la conspiración*, p. 39.

[54] Lizarza speaks of several groups of about sixteen or seventeen, and gives some names of individuals involved (*Memorias de la conspiración*, pp. 48–49). Jaime del Burgo, *Conspiración y guerra civil*, pp. 517–21, provides some purely anecdotal material on this episode. An official Italian report gives the number of groups as three (*Promemoria* dated Rome, November 21, 1936, MAE, Gabinetto, Spagna, 1).

no time in publishing it as proof of Mussolini's complicity in the preparation of the Civil War.[55]

The fact that the agreement was made after the 1933 elections, in which the Center-Right parties administered a crushing defeat to the Spanish Left, shows that Mussolini's continuing hostility toward the Republic was based less on ideology than on old-fashioned political and military considerations. The anti-French thrust of the agreement's provisions is evident and provides the key for understanding it. Italian fears of a secret treaty granting France special rights in the Balearic Islands and the right of passage of troops through the Iberian peninsula were baseless, but nonetheless very real. Mussolini felt only slightly greater affinity with the Monarchists than with the Republicans, but the Monarchists could be useful to him, whereas the Republicans could not. He was willing to help them as a way of reducing French influence in Spain and the western Mediterranean, and they were quite ready to accept Fascist assistance in reestablishing the Monarchy. Political realism led Mussolini to support a group of conservative Monarchists instead of one of the nascent Fascist groups, for whom he had more ideological sympathy, but who exercised almost no influence on the course of Spanish politics.

Most heads of government would have preferred not to meet personally with the conspirators and would not have allowed so high ranking an official as Marshall Balbo to sign an agreement with them. In these purely formal aspects, the agreement is characteristic of the Fascist

[55] The text was first published in Madrid papers on May 14, 1937, and was picked up by much of the world press. In the published versions, the number of rifles and hand grenades promised was doubled to 20,000. The pamphlet, *Documentary Evidence: How Mussolini Provoked the Spanish Civil War*, published in London in 1938, contains a facsimile of the handwritten original in which it is possible to see how the figure 10,000 was written over, changing the one to a two. Although the correct figures have been available for a long time, the inflated ones are still frequently quoted, for example in Gil Robles's *No fue posible la paz*, published in 1968.

regime. Substantially, however, it belongs to the long, if not illustrious, lineage of cases of conivance by foreign powers with conspirators who want to overthrow a legitimate government.[56]

ROME LOSES INTEREST IN SPAIN

The March 1934 Agreement marks the high point of Italian interest and activities in Spain prior to the outbreak of the Civil War. After mid-1934 the general framework of Italian foreign policy shifted, and there was a loss of interest in Spain. Most importantly, planning for the conquest of Ethiopia took on a certain note of urgency after the Walwal incident in December, 1934. Involvement in Ethiopia would eventually lead Italy to greater interest in the Mediterranean, thereby increasing Spain's potential weight in her diplomatic calculations, but for the moment Mussolini and his subordinates were too interested in planning their future conquests to pay much attention to the western Mediterranean.[57] In Europe, Laval's replacement of Barthou as French foreign minister opened up new possibilities

[56] The Spanish Liberal historian Salvador de Madariaga, who played a clearly anti-Italian role as Spain's ambassador to the League of Nations, and who worked actively in favor of sanctions against Italy for its aggression against Ethiopia, has written that the 1934 agreement "can only be exploited as a proof of the origin of the Italian help to the Falange by people without sufficient knowledge of Spanish politics. It is signed by four Monarchists, three of whom happen to be Basques, and it merely states that the Duce will provide arms and money to restore the Monarchy in Spain. The very poverty of these documents suggests that, here as with the Communists, what happened was that Hitler and Mussolini, in fact Germany and Italy, had been spreading their nets in Spain to suit their own ends of military and economic espionage very much as every big power does in greater or lesser degree everywhere; . . . but that definite plans for a Fascist rising had not been established at all despite a number of journeys of military and Falange leaders to Germany and Italy." Madariaga, Spain. A Modern History, pp. 484–85.

[57] Catalano, Italia dalla dittatura alla democrazia, p. 232.

of an understanding with France. An improvement in Italo-French relations was bound to lessen Italian interest in Spain's potential value as part of an anti-French policy. Finally, the assasination of Prime Minister Dollfuss during the attempted Nazi coup in Austria in July 1934 brought to the fore the problems posed by the resurgence of Germany, which threatened to absorb Austria and establish herself on Italy's frontier. Italian attention was drawn away from Spain toward these other more vital or more promising areas.

In the fall of 1934 Guariglia was replaced as ambassador by Orazio Pedrazzi. A forty-five year old lawyer and Nationalist journalist, Pedrazzi had formed part of the government of Fiume in 1919–1920 and had been editor of *Il regno*. He was one of the noncareer diplomats introduced into the foreign service by Mussolini in 1927. In view of his background, he might have been expected to be more active than his predecessor in supporting Spanish Fascist groups and in fishing in troubled Spanish waters. This was not, however, the case.

Pedrazzi did share Guariglia's conviction that Italian propaganda efforts in Spain should be intensified, and could do much to eliminate or lessen hostility toward Italy and Fascism. After the 1934 agreement, the Monarchist press became distinctly more friendly toward Italy.[58] Propaganda activities of the Madrid embassy were modest, however, and were hampered by a restricted budget. In June 1935, apart from special funds for subventions, the embassy had only one thousand pesatas ($137.00) a month for propaganda purposes.[59] On this sort of budget, activities obviously had to be limited to sending out occasional bulletins

[58] An unsigned report on the internal Spanish situation dated March 19, 1935, states: "During the last few months, the Monarchist press, under orders from the party leaders, has supported with every means at its disposal Italian policy and activities" (MAE, Politica, b. 8).

[59] Report 2231, to ministry for press and propaganda, June 11, 1935, MAE, Politica, b. 7.

and articles for publication.[60] In January 1936, just before the vital general elections which would bring victory to the Popular Front, a special grant for propaganda activities was obtained, but it amounted to only 30,000 pesatas ($3,500).[61] The contrast between these paltry sums and the 1.5 million pesatas ($205,000) granted to the Monarchist conspirators in 1934 suggests that the Fascist government did not share the ambassador's enthusiasm for propaganda.

After Guariglia's departure, the embassy's contacts with the Falangists and other philo-Fascist groups became less frequent. Pedrazzi's arrival in Spain coincided with the beginning of a period of polarization in Spanish politics. In October 1934 a proletarian revolt in Asturias brought in elite troops from Morocco. The moderate-conservative coalition that governed Spain from 1934 to February 1936 did nothing to alleviate the problems caused by the depression, and even undid many of its predecessor's efforts to solve the agrarian problem. Discontent was rising steadily when a ministerial crisis led to a dissolution of the Cortes and a call for new elections in February 1936.[62] In the

---

[60] Pedrazzi seems to have prided himself on this aspect of his work and sent detailed reports to the ministry for press and propaganda. His report for November 1935 divides the month's activities into thirteen separate chapters. They come down to the following:

Three communiques issued by the embassy;
One interview granted by the ambassador;
Three issues of the embassy's official information bulletin;
Distribution to the press of several articles on the Ethiopian question and of 4 feature articles;
Distribution of photographs sent by the ministry;
Sending of news bulletins to the local press by consulates, and distribution of news stories picked up from Italian radio broadcasts;
Distribution by the embassy of articles through two small agencies (Report 21506, December 17, 1935, MAE, Politica, b. 7).
[61] ACS, ministero della cultura popolare, b. 171, f. 78.
[62] On developments in Spain during this period, see Jackson, *The Spanish Republic and the Civil War*, pp. 121–83.

shifting and confused Spanish political scene Pedrazzi found it difficult to formulate any hard and fast judgments about the future course of events, but one thing seemed relatively clear, and that was that the Fascist groups were too weak and divided to exercise any real influence.[63] From the fall of 1934 on, the embassy's reports to the foreign ministry consistently either ignored the Fascist groups altogether or criticized their weakness, division, and lack of decision.[64] Pedrazzi also let lapse the contacts which Guariglia had established with Monarchist conspirators.

The only Italian diplomat who maintained important contacts with opponents of the Republic after 1934 was not in Madrid at all, but in Paris. Amadeo Landini, the Italian consul and press attaché in Paris, was an extraordinarily active man and a tireless conspirator. He maintained contacts with numerous informants, politicians, conspirators, and journalists in Paris, and subsidized many of them, including Marcel Bucard, the leader of the French Fascist group *Francisme,* with funds from the ministry of press and propaganda.[65]

On June 3, 1935 Mussolini's son-in-law and under-

[63] In September 1934, the chargé reported from San Sebastian, where the embassy habitually resided during the summer: "In the chaos of Spanish politics, which has given signs of even more intense activity during the past few months, it is almost impossible to distinguish between theory and reality, between what is and what should be, between what really exists and what is a purely Platonic desire of the political leaders" (Report 2943/1511, September 20, 1934, MAE, Politica, b. 6).

[64] The following passage might be considered typical: "As for activities of the fascists, I also have my doubts. The moment, as I said, is extremely favorable, but the fascists lack the means, and I sincerely do not believe that they have the forces and the agility to grasp the opportunity" (Report 3316/1717, October 17, 1934, MAE, Politica, b. 6).

[65] There is much information on Landini's activities scattered through the materials of the ministry for press and propaganda (later renamed ministry for popular culture and so referred to in the following notes), especially in NA T 586, rolls 416 and 418.

secretary of state for press and propaganda, Galeazzo Ciano, ordered Landini to begin subsidizing Primo de Rivera with 50,000 lire ($4,000) a month. After December this subsidy was halved, and from January to June 1936, 25,000 lire a month were sent to the embassy. For some reason Primo de Rivera did not claim the payments for the early months of 1936, and after his imprisonment in March, Landini refused to give the funds to any other representative of the Falange. The money was eventually returned to the ministry in November 1936.

The only correspondence which has been preserved on this subject gives no clue as to the purpose for which the subsidy was given nor exactly how the decision to begin it was taken. The Italian embassy in Madrid was apparently not even informed about it. It is part not of an Italian plot to overthrow the Spanish Republic and establish a Fascist regime in its place but of a general policy of propaganda and support of pro-Fascist groups. Its greatest significance is as a sign of a certain interest in Spain on the part of Mussolini's future foreign minister, Ciano.[66]

For the February 1936 elections, the parties of the left, which had suffered from their disunion in 1933, organized a Popular Front to which the voters gave a slender majority. The majority bloc system of voting that had favored the right in 1933 now worked to the benefit of the left, which received a large majority of Cortes deputies. The center parties virtually disappeared altogether. Under the pressure

[66] The first payment for Primo de Rivera was sent to Paris on June 3, 1935 (NA T 586, roll 416, frames 007527 and 007667). Correspondence on the payments for the months from January to June 1936 is found in ACS, ministero della cultura popolare, b. 170, f. 36. That the payments "did not imply any far-reaching agreement" is conceded by Friedlander, *The July 1936 Military Rebellion in Spain*, p. 58. He is apparently familiar with only a part of the material in the microfilms of the ministry for press and propaganda files, and incorrectly dates the beginning of the subsidies between spring and early summer 1936.

of an outburst of violence in the streets, a new all left-Republican government was immediately formed with Manuel Azaña as prime minister, without waiting for the second round of elections.[67] The new ministry proposed to carry out immediately the Popular Front platform on which it had been elected, including an amnesty for the numerous political prisoners who had been jailed in the fall of 1934 after the Asturian revolt, suspension of evictions of tenant farmers in Extremadura and Andalusia, and restoration of a number of Socialist municipal governments suspended since 1934. The left wing of the Popular Front was not satisfied with these relatively mild measures. In Spain's large cities, massive parades were organized calling for proletarian rule. Demonstrators clashed frequently with the police and both the left and right resorted to violence and assasination.

In the province of Badajoz peasants associated with the Socialist unions could not be persuaded to wait for government measures of land reform and quickly occupied some 600,000 acres. Faced with this *fait accompli,* the government decided to legalize the seizures. By July over 1,250,000 acres had been expropriated, many of them without regard for legal forms.

Early in April the victorious leftist parties joined hands to depose President Alcalá-Zamora on a technicality. The right correctly interpreted this as an attempt to remove the last remaining conservative influence from the government of Spain. Since no other acceptable candidate for the presidency could be found, Azaña abandoned his position as prime minister to become president of the Republic in May. His successor as prime minister, Casares Quiroga,

[67] The following paragraphs on the situation is Spain between February and July 1936 are based largely on Broué and Témime, *The Revolution and the Civil War in Spain,* pp. 74–91; Payne, *A History of Spain and Portugal,* II, 640–43; Jackson, *The Spanish Republic and the Civil War,* pp. 193–230; and Malefakis, *Agrarian Reform and Peasant Revolution in Spain,* pp. 364–74.

would soon prove incapable of dealing with an increasingly difficult situation.

Spring brought with it a rash of revolutionary strikes which reflected the growing radicalization of the Socialist party. Early in June in Madrid alone, 40,000 construction workers and 30,000 electricians and elevator repair men went out on strike. Anarchist labor leaders urged their followers to eat in restaurants and pick up groceries without paying.

There are no accurate figures for the number of outbreaks of violence or for the number of people killed and injured between February and July 1936, but it is clear that Spain was undergoing a serious crisis. In these circumstances, it is not surprising that plans soon began to be laid for a military coup to restore order. A number of meetings were held in March, and serious preparations got under way in May. By early July plans had been made for a revolt between July 10 and July 20. The spark that finally touched it off came on July 12, when a number of police officers avenged the previous killing of a leftist officer by murdering a prominent rightist politician, José Calvo Sotelo. The rising was immediately set for 5 P.M. Friday, July 17 in Morocco, to be followed within twenty-four hours by uprisings in all the major garrisons in the peninsula.

What part if any, did Italian Fascists play in fomenting the disorders that racked Spain from February to July 1936 or the military revolt to which they finally led? Available Italian records offer no evidence that Italian agents were engaged in provoking disorders in Spain. In fact the picture that emerges is one of general passivity. Contacts with right-wing groups that lapsed after Guariglia left Spain in 1934 were not reestablished during the crucial months between February and July 1936.

Italian officials in Spain had no faith in the prospects for a rightist reaction after Feburary 1936. In the weeks and months following the elections, they believed that if anything occured in Spain it was likely to be a social revolution. Until the very last moment, neither Pedrazzi nor his staff believed in the possibility of a successful right-ist—much less Fascist—coup or revolt. In late March he dismissed altogether the possibility of a Falangist-sponsored uprising:

> The only organization that had made a serious effort to oppose with force the lamentable social excesses, Falange Española, has been dissolved and its leaders, starting with Primo de Rivera, arrested. In any case, they were nothing more than sporadic manifestations. . . . There was never any overall plan that might have eventually borne fruit. The present government has nothing to fear, at least for the moment, from its rightist opponents, who are for now politically impotent.[68]

He had also informed the ministry that a military coup against the government was not to be expected. "In my opinion," he wrote, "there is no use fooling oneself this time about the possibility of a military coup d'état like the one that ushered in Primo de Rivera's dictatorship, among other things because the commanding generals are now all leftist sympathizers."[69]

Pedrazzi went on to suggest that Azaña might refuse to allow the Socialists to take power and stage a coup himself, with the help of the army. With the benefit of hindsight the idea may seem fantastic, but it was widely discussed in Spain at the time. The Spanish Falangist author Ernesto Giménez Caballero, in an article written for *Critica fascista*, characterized Azaña as "the only man capable of resolving the dramatic situation of Spain,"[70] and other more influential politicians like Miguel Maura hoped that the president might seize power with military backing.

Toward the end of May, rumors of an impending rightist coup by the army became more insistent, and were reported

[68] Report 871/420, March 31, 1936, MAE, Politica, b. 9.
[69] Report 962/427, March 31, 1936, MAE, Politica, b. 9.
[70] "Lettera dalla Spagna: una situazione drammatica," p. 142.

by the consul in Tangiers.[71] Pedrazzi dismissed them, however, saying that the military's plans seemed "destined for the moment to remain in the area of sterile recriminations, without ever leading to anything practical."[72] Chronic disorder verging on anarchy seemed to him the most likely prospect for Spain in the near future.[73]

Contrary to the allegations of some contemporary observers and of certain recent historians,[74] I find no convincing evidence that Fascist *agents provocateurs* were at work creating incidents in Spain. In the light of their pessimistic estimate of the situation, it seems unlikely that Italian Fascists would have deliberately encouraged or provoked violence which in their eyes had no chance of leading to any positive result. Nor is there any need to resort to hypothetical foreign agents to explain the violence that racked Spain; conditions within the country offer more than sufficient explanation.

There are no grounds in the available records for believing that Italian officials were in contact with the Spanish officers who planned and eventually carried out the revolt against the Republic. If any contacts did take place, the embassy in Spain knew nothing about them, and they have left no trace in the files of Mussolini's personal secretariat nor in those of the foreign ministry that I have examined. The Spanish and Italian participants in the events who have written their memoirs have not been reluctant to speak of earlier contacts, but none of them even hints at any

[71] Telegram by courier 5231/R, May 25, 1936, MAE, Politica, b. 9.

[72] Report 1536/665, May 28, 1936, MAE, Politica, b. 9.

[73] Report 1606/695, May 27, 1936, MAE, Politica, b. 9. About this time the newly appointed naval attaché claims to have sent a report to his superiors, warning that a military revolt was imminent, although Pedrazzi told him that the rumors were ill-founded, and advised him against submitting the report (Gabrieli, *Una guerra civile per la libertà*, p. 9).

[74] Bowers, *My Mission to Spain*, p. 226; Puzzo, *Spain and the Great Powers*, p. 41.

during the vital months when the plans for the military revolt were being laid.[75]

The conspirators did, of course, know about earlier contacts and may well have been encouraged by the thought that if they needed support they could count on Italy. On July 13, after the assassination of Calvo Sotelo, they appear to have sent a message to Mussolini announcing the imminent rising. The courier, however, was stopped in Barcelona and had to destroy the letter he was carrying.[76] There is no evidence of any other attempt to inform Rome about the intended coup or to obtain Italian aid.

Beyond the possibility of falling back on Italy for support if that became necessary, the conspirators gave her no place in their plans, neither asking for nor receiving material

[75] It is interesting to note that the editors of the German diplomatic documents reached a parallel conclusion: "The documents examined in the archives of the German Foreign Ministry do not disclose evidence of German assistance to the Spanish rebels prior to the outbreak of hostilities" (GD, D, III, p. 1). In a study of all available materials on German contacts with Spain prior to the outbreak of the Civil War, Viñas finds no evidence of German complicity in the preparation of the military revolt. (*La Alemania nazi y el 18 de julio*, pp. 255–346). Similar conclusions had been reached by two other recent students of the question. (Horton, *Germany and the Spanish Civil War*, p. 26. Beck, *A Study of German Involvement in Spain. 1936–39*, pp. 34–44).

Alvarez del Vayo's allegation that high-ranking German officials promised aid to Sanjurjo in February 1936 is not supported by other sources and is effectively refuted by Viñas. (Alvarez del Vayo, *Freedom's Battle*, p. 50 and Viñas, *La Alemania nazi y el 18 de julio*, pp. 292–99). There were, however, a few contact between the conspirators and some second or third rank German officials about possible arms supply. (Weinberg, *The Foreign Policy of Hitler's Germany*, p. 286.) In the Italian case there is little reason to believe that even such low level contacts took place. Peman does assert that Italian officials agreed to allow the conspirators to use the embassy during a proposed coup, but he cites no evidence for this statement (Peman, *Un soldado en la historia. Vida del capitán general Varela*, p. 141). Such an agreement may have existed, but if it did it was of little real importance in the genesis of the revolt.

[76] Gutiérrez-Ravé Montero, *Antonio Goicoechea*, p. 36.

or moral support during the crucial months of 1936 that preceded their revolt. Authors who describe the Civil War as "instigated by the army leaders, with German and Italian support"[77] or who assert that "from the beginning, the military plotters had counted on the armed aid of Italy,"[78] vastly overstress the importance of foreign elements in the genesis of the Civil War. In view of the total absence of contacts after February 1936 between the officers involved in preparing the uprising and Fascist officials in Madrid or Rome, it is not accurate to speak of Italian "connivance in the revolt of the Spanish generals."[79] As the author from whom the last quotation is drawn admits, the future Spanish rebels never thought seriously about the possibility of having to fight a lengthy civil war. They hoped for immediate success outside the large cities, and expected that within a few days they would have achieved their aims. On these premises, there was no reason to expect that they would need outside aid, nor indeed that there would even be time for it to arrive.[80]

[77] Van der Esch, *Prelude to War*, p. 14.

[78] Jackson, *The Spanish Republic and the Civil War*, p. 247.

[79] Puzzo, *Spain and the Great Powers*, p. 47. Puzzo rests his case uncritically on authors whose testimony is suspect either because of their partisanship or because they had no reliable sources for the information they claimed to possess. His position is shared by many authors. A well-known historian of Italy, for example, argues that "the promptness of Italian assistance to the rebelling General Franco is clear indication that Italy had been a party to the preparation of the revolt" (Albrecht-Carrie, *Italy from Napoleon to Mussolini*, p. 252).

[80] The most detailed account of the preparations of the uprising thus far published is La Cierva, *Historia de la guerra civil española, I, Antecedentes: Monarquía y República, 1898–1936*. The Navarrese Carlist leader, Antonio Lizarza, has noted that General Mola was reluctant to contract any obligations with the Carlists since he felt they would play a very minor role in the uprising, which he was confident would be very quick and decisive: "It is natural that Mola did not want too many ties with the Carlist Communion, with a force which, when all was said and done, was going to have little to do, on the supposition that the Movement would come down to a march on Madrid" (Lizarza Iribarren, *Memorias de la conspiración,*

Conclusions

The record of Mussolini's relations with Spain over the years prior to the outbreak of the Civil War shows that both ideological and traditional foreign policy considerations determined his attitudes and behavior, but when it came to taking concrete action the latter regularly prevailed. Sympathy with the aspirations of the Falange and of other nascent fascist groups as well as dislike for liberals and socialists explain his hostility toward the Republic and his encouragement of opposition groups, but it was principally concern over Italy's position in the western Mediterranean *vis-à-vis* France and a shrewd estimate of the realities of Spanish politics that led him to provide arms and money to army and Monarchist conspirators.

The extent and importance of his interference in the domestic affairs of the Second Republic has been frequently exaggerated both by propagandists during and after the Civil War and by more recent historians. The available evidence simply does not support the contention that "from April 1931 to July 1936, Rome was the center of the anti-Republican activities of Spanish conspirators."[81] At no time did Rome take the initiative in provoking anti-Republican activities nor did she suggest concrete strategies or otherwise attempt to influence plans for the overthrow of the Republic. Her role was limited to promising to recognize the conspirators' regime as soon as it was established and providing relatively modest quantities of material assistance. For the two years immediately proceeding the army revolt of July 1936, even these activities were largely terminated. Rome's subsidies after 1934 were directed to José Antonio Primo de Rivera, who did not play a central role in the uprising, and there is no evidence of any Italian contacts with the actual organizers of the revolt against the Republic prior to its outbreak.

---

p. 90). The reasoning applies *a fortiori* to contacts with foreign states.

[81] Nenni, *La guerre d'Espagne*, p. 35.

THREE

THE DECISION TO SUPPORT FRANCO:
JULY 1936

To Aid or Not to Aid

THE Spanish Civil War began on July 17, 1936, when the garrison in Morocco occupied Melilla and Tetuán and gave the signal for a series of army risings throughout the peninsula on July 18, 19, and 20. The Popular Front government had placed most of the important garrisons under the command of men of known Republican sympathies. The majority of these generals remained loyal, but many were forced to join the revolt or were replaced by younger Nationalist officers.[1] The outcome of the rising varied from place to place, depending on the political orientation and mobilization of the population, the temperament of the commanders and their subordinate officers, and the response of the troops (see map 1).

By July 20 the rebellion had succeeded in North Africa and in the highly conservative northern areas of the peninsula, with the exception of the Basque country, Santander, and Asturias. In the south, the insurgents took control of the cities of Seville, Huelva, Granada, and Cádiz, despite the hostility of much of the population, but could not control the surrounding countryside. In both Barcelona and Madrid popular support for the government proved decisive in thwarting the rising. Thus the revolt failed in the two largest cities in Spain as well as in most of the northeast, center, and south of the country.[2] Although it is commonly

[1] La Cierva, "The Nationalist Army in the Spanish Civil War," in Carr (ed.), *The Republic and the Civil War in Spain*, p. 190.
[2] The best account of the fighting during the first week of the war is found in Thomas, *The Spanish Civil War*, pp. 181–274.

66

Map 1

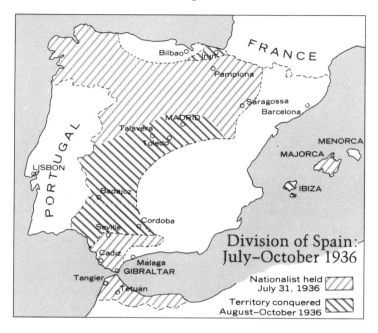

Division of Spain:
July–October 1936

Nationalist held
July 31, 1936

Territory conquered
August–October 1936

asserted that the army went over to the rebels "almost
en masse,"[3] in fact on July 21 the government had fifty
percent of the metropolitan army's men, fifty-five percent
of the civil guards, sixty percent of the caribiñeros, and
seventy percent of the assault guards, together with 250,000
rifles, 400 field guns, and 75 coastal defense guns. More
than half the officers on active duty were in the zone over
which the Republic retained control, and about half of
them supported the government The generals who remained in the service of the Republic outnumbered those
who joined the rebellion by one third. During the last days

[3] Puzzo, *Spain and the Great Powers*, p. 79. Also Madariaga, *Spain:
A Modern History*, p. 487, pp. 601–603; and Alvarez del Vayo, *Freedom's Battle*, p. 233.

of July, there was, then, a rough numerical balance of ground forces, although the rebels controlled in North Africa the most efficient and best trained units of the Army.[4]

Efforts by naval officers to bring their ships over to the rebels failed almost everywhere except in El Ferrol, where Nationalist control of the town made it possible for them to take over ships which could not leave port. In the naval base of Cartagena and at sea, the sailors imprisoned their officers and saved for the Republic the battleship *Jaime I*, three cruisers, and a dozen destroyers. These ships gave the Republic initial control of the sea. In most places the Republic also retained control of the air force. According to one calculation, 173 planes were available to the Republic and 40 to the Nationalists around July 22.[5]

The information reaching Italy about the situation in Spain during the first week of the Civil War was confused and uncertain. Ambassador Pedrazzi and most of his staff had already left Madrid for summer quarters in San Sebastian when the revolt broke out. They were far from the major centers of action and could not verify the innumerable rumors that reached them about the events going on in Spain.

On July 18 Pedrazzi managed to get a telegram through to Rome with news of a rising in Morocco and rumors of disorders in Pamplona and Madrid,[6] but later in the day he found it necessary to resort to diplomatic courier. From July 18 to 21 Palazzo Chigi had to rely on the often contradictory reports of the wire services, which were also the only information available to the Italian press.[7] On

[4] Salas Larrazábal, "The Growth and Role of the Republican Popular Army" in Carr (ed.), *The Republic and the Civil War in Spain*, pp. 161–62; and Salas Larrazábal, *Historia del ejército popular de la República*, vol. I, pp. 181–96 and vol. III, pp. 2422–32.

[5] Gomá, *La guerra en el aire*, pp. 45–46.

[6] Telegram 172, July 18, 1936, MAE, Politica, b. 11.

[7] News from Spain did not make the front page of most Italian papers until July 21. On that date *La tribuna* reported in banner headlines that the rebels had taken Madrid.

July 21 a telegram from the chargé in Madrid, De Ciutiis, was received, but it did very little to clarify the situation. The following day a longer dispatch from Ambassador Pedrazzi, sent by courier on the 18th, finally reached the foreign ministry. Aside from being hopelessly dated, it was of little help. The ambassador was unwilling to venture an opinion about the rebels' probabilities of success. The one certain thing, he reported, was that "whatever the outcome, Spain is entering a period of grave and violent convulsions."[8] Five days after the uprising, Rome still had no trustworthy up-to-date information on what was happening in Spain. What information there was seemed to indicate that things were going poorly for the rebels.[9] Under these circumstances, both King Victor Emanuel and Mussolini were understandably wary about stepping out into the murky waters of the Spainsh situation.

The first concrete requests for aid come from General Franco, commander of the Army of Africa, who arrived in Tetuán from the Canary Islands on July 19. The rebels' original plan had called for at least 17,000 troops to be ferried across the straits from Africa to the peninsula, but the overwhelming naval superiority of the Republic in the waters off Morocco made it impossible to risk the crossing after the first few days, during which fewer than 1,000 men had been able to cross.[10] The alternative was to transport troops by air, but the rebels in Morocco had only three small transports, which could carry fewer than 100 men per day across the straits. They desperately needed aircraft to challenge or offset Republican control of the sea.

[8] Telegram 173, July 18, 1936, MAE, Politica, b. 11.
[9] On July 19 the *Popolo d'Italia* reported that the rebellion would probably be crushed in a few days. Around July 22, Ambassador Pedrazzi expressed his sympathy and condolences for the failure of the rising to its partisans, whom he saw in St. Jean de Luz (interview with the Count of Valdeiglesias, Madrid, September 24, 1970).
[10] Frank, *Seapower, Politics, and the Onset of the Spanish War, 1936*, p. 103.

Franco enjoyed no special authority other than that conferred upon him by his command of the Army of Africa. The titular head of the rising was General Sanjurjo, who was still in Portugal and was to lose his life in a plane crash on his way to Spain on July 20. Its chief organizer was General Emilio Mola, who was five hundred miles away in northern Spain. In European military circles, Franco was known as a bright and ambitious young general, but he had few contacts and his name did not carry great weight in foreign capitals. But there was nothing to be lost by appealing to Rome and Berlin for aid. On July 19 he sent Luis Bolín, a Monarchist journalist who had accompanied him from the Canaries to Morocco, to Rome with a request for twelve bombers and three fighters. Bolín flew to Lisbon to obtain General Sanjurjo's countersignature, and from there to Biarritz in France. From Biarritz he continued by train to Rome, where he arrived on July 21.[11] Before Bolín reached Rome, Franco succeeded in convincing the Italian consul at Tangiers to send a telegram with his request for twelve bombers or even civilian transport planes, but the Duce's replied in one word, scribbled on the bottom of the telegram, which probably reached Rome on July 20: "No."[12]

Despite this first refusal, a Spanish nobleman, the Marqués de Viana, acting in the name of Alfonso XIII, arranged for Bolín to be received by the Italian foreign minister, Count Galeazzo Ciano, on July 22.[13] This was Ciano's first contact with Spanish affairs, in which he was to play a vital role. He was the only son of one of Mussolini's early collaborators, Costanzo Ciano. His father had served with some distinction as a captain in the Italian

[11] Bolín, *Spain: the Vital Years,* p. 167; and Arrarás, *Historia de la cruzada de España,* X, 126.

[12] Ciano told Cantalupo about this incident six months later, before his mission as first ambassador to Burgos (Cantalupo, *Fu la Spagna,* p. 63). Also see Cervera Valderrama, *Memorias de guerra,* p. 68.

[13] Bolín, *Spain: the Vital Years,* p. 168.

navy during World War I, and was made undersecretary of the navy in Mussolini's first government. Subsequently he became minister of communications and president of the Fascist Chamber of Deputies, acquiring a vast fortune over the course of his political career. In 1925 the younger Ciano graduated from the law school of the University of Rome and entered the Italian diplomatic service. After his marriage to Mussolini's daughter Edda five years later, he began to rise rapidly. He was minister to China in 1932, chief of Mussolini's press office in 1933, undersecretary for press and propaganda in 1935, member of the Grand Council of Fascism, and finally, in June 1936, minister of foreign affairs.

Although not entirely lacking in intelligence, Galeazzo Ciano was not well suited for his new post. He was a basically frivolous young socialite, anxious for admiration and attention, with no moral convictions and little or no sense of responsibility. In general he demonstrated far more concern about creating a good impression than about his country's long-term interests, and spent more energy on his intense social life than on the duties of his office. In his brief tenure in office the only serious problem had been obtaining revocation of League sanctions against Italy. The negotiations had been concluded satisfactorily, but this was not the type of success that the vain and ambitious young minister desired. He was looking anxiously for an opportunity to demonstrate his abilities, and the appeal from Franco seemed to be the opportunity he was waiting for.[14]

Ciano's first reaction was to promise Bolín the aid he

[14] Mussolini's biographers Pini and Susmel attribute considerable importance to the young foreign minister's personal interest in the war, and describe him as "anxiously craving to intervene" (Pini and Susmel, *Mussolini: l'uomo e l'opera*, II, 357). This interpretation is supported by the general tone of the earliest entries in Ciano's diary, for instance those for July 27 and 28, 1937. He seems to have sensed in the Spanish conflict the opportunity he was searching for, and enthusiastically supported a policy of intervention, despite his father-in-law's initial caution (Tamaro, *Vent'anni di storia*, III, 200).

requested, but then he began to have second thoughts, perhaps realizing the difficulty of convincing his father-in-law to change his mind. In any case, after questioning Bolín closely about the aims of the rebellion, its leadership, and its popular backing, he instructed him to return the next day for an answer. On July 23 Bolín was unable to see Ciano again personally. Perhaps embarrassed by having to go back on his initial promise of aid, the foreign minister had him received by his secretary, Filippo Anfuso, who told him that his proposals could not be accepted.[15] Another telegram was received at about this time from Tangiers renewing Franco's urgent requests, but Mussolini dispatched it with the simple annotation, "File."[16]

Alfonso XIII, the former king of Spain, also sought and obtained a personal interview with Mussolini, in which he accused France of aiding the rebels. During this interview, the Duce made no specific commitments, but did assure Alfonso that Italy "would not permit the establishment of a Soviet regime in Spain."[17]

The request for aid that finally provoked Italy's intervention in the Civil War came from the chief organizer of the revolt, General Mola. On July 22 he convened a meeting of Monarchist leaders and outlined briefly the military situation. His forces, which were attempting to march on Madrid from the north, had encountered stubborn resistance in the mountain passes of Alto del Leon and Somosierra. They were suffering some 600 casualties a day and ammunition was running short. In the south, little progress could be made, since the failure of the navy to join the uprising made it impossible to bring men and supplies from Africa. Mola admitted the situation was grave, but

[15] Bolín, *Spain: the Vital Years*, p. 168.

[16] Cantalupo, *Fu la Spagna*, p. 63; Tamaro, *Vent'anni di storia*, III, 200. It is possible that a third telegram, whose date cannot be established, was also turned down (D'Aroma, *Vent'anni insieme: Vittorio Emanuele e Mussolini*, p. 242).

[17] Phillips, *Ventures in Diplomacy*, p. 196.

predicted that victory would still be his if France did not intervene to aid the Republic.[18]

Mola wanted the Monarchist leaders, he said, to "go out to the world and find out if the French intend to intervene or not." After one of them suggested that it would also be advisable to warn Berlin and Rome about the danger of French support of the Republic, Mola decided to send Luis Zunzunegui and Pedro Sainz Rodríguez with Antonio Goicoechea to Rome, and the Count of Valdeiglesias to Berlin.[19]

While Mola's envoys were preparing to leave for Rome and Berlin, the French government decided to provide the Spanish Republic with the arms it had requested to quell the revolt. A member of the French government communicated this decision to the German ambassador, who informed his government on July 23. The news was also leaked by the Spanish military attaché to the French right wing press, which began on July 24 a violent campaign against the decision.[20]

The following morning Antonio Goicoechea met with Count Ciano for the first time.[21] The interview began with the Monarchist's account of the situation in Spain and the rebels' urgent need for assistance. He assured the Italian minister that the rebels required only airplanes and perhaps

[18] Goicoechea's minutes of the meeting, in Gutiérrez-Ravé Montero, *Antonio Goicoechea*, pp. 34–35; interview with the Count of Valdeiglesias, Madrid, September 24, 1970.

[19] According to Goicoechea's version of the events, Mola called the meeting with the intention of sending emissaries to Rome to request aid. My narrative follows Valdeiglesias, who maintains that Mola's only purpose in calling the meeting was to ask the Monarchists to use their contacts to find out what French intentions really were. Even at the end of the meeting, according to Valdeiglesias, Mola was opposed to requesting any aid beyond rifle cartridges.

[20] Pike, *Conjecture, Propaganda, and Deceit and the Spanish Civil War*, p. 30; and GD, D, III, 4.

[21] My account of Goicoechea's interview with Ciano is based on Gutiérrez-Ravé Montero, *Antonio Goicoechea*, pp. 35–37; and Arrarás, *Historia de la Cruzada de España*, X, 126.

a few other arms to take the situation in hand. They could capture Madrid quickly and then it would be only a matter of days, or at most weeks, before the entire country would be under their control.

Ciano explained that the Italian government had been reluctant to act because it lacked clear information on what was really going on in Spain. He questioned Goicoechea closely about the leadership and degree of popular support of the movement, and inquired about the willingness of the military leaders to abide by the clauses of the 1934 pact between the Monarchist leaders and Italy. Goicoechea give him ample assurance on all counts. The Italians could be certain, he said, that the leaders of the revolt would honor fully the 1934 agreement, including the clause regarding abrogation of the supposed secret Franco-Spanish treaty.

On the strength of Goichoechea's assurances, and of the information that had been received during the preceeding forty-eight hours about conditions in Spain and about French aid to the Republic, Ciano promised that Italy would send twelve Savoia S 81 bombers to Spanish Morocco by early August.

Besides reaffirmation of the political assurances contained in the 1934 treaty, Ciano demanded that the aircraft be paid for in cash before delivery. The price of the twelve planes amounted to over a million pounds sterling, but Goicoechea had no trouble obtaining this sizable sum from the Spanish financier Juan March. By July 27 or 28 payment had been received and the Italian government began making the final arrangements for the transfer of the planes to Morocco.

MOTIVES FOR ITALIAN INTERVENTION

Mussolini's decision to support the Spanish rebels was determined by traditional strategic and political motives as well as by ideological ones. These motives were intertwined in practice but may be dealt with separately for analytical purposes. There is no need to discuss economic motives at any length here. It has been asserted that a desire for Spanish minerals and markets played an important role in the decision,[22] but this is a misreading of the situation that results from assuming that Rome was moved by the same factors as Berlin. In fact specifically economic considerations, such as foreign trade, control of markets, and access to sources of raw materials played no appreciable part in the Duce's initial decision, and they remained secondary throughout the war. Nor did "ties of race, culture and religion"[23] influence Italian decisions. Mussolini talked occasionally about such things, but did not allow them to affect his foreign policy, as the record of his relations with France clearly shows.

Throughout the years, as we have seen in the previous chapter, Mussolini had thought of Spain largely in terms of Italy's political and military power in the Meditrranean. The acquisition of Abyssinia made it all the more vital to avoid any deterioration of Italy's position on the sea, and to take advantage of any opportunities to improve it. The news that the French Popular Front government had decided to supply arms to the Republic suggested that Spain might be expected to show its gratitude for help in supressing the revolt by drawing closer to France and collaborating more actively with her, to Italy's discomfort. On July 26 Ambassador Pedrazzi called the foreign ministry's attention to an interview with the Spanish Socialist leader Largo Caballero published in *Paris soir*. Largo predicted that after putting down the rebellion Spain would adopt a Socialist government, abandon neutrality, and take its place with other Democratic governments in the struggle against anti-Democratic ones. "This brings out once again," the ambassador commented, "a new international signifi-

[21] Van der Esch, *Prelude to War*, p. 15; Schwartz, *La internacionalización de la guerra civil española*, p. 68.
[23] Van der Esch, *Prelude to War*, p. 14.

cance of an eventual governmental victory over the Spanish National Revolution."[24] On the other hand, should the rebels manage to overthrow the French-backed Republican regime with Italian help, they could be expected at the very least to favor Italian interests and adopt a strongly anti-French line.[25]

The importance of these considerations in Mussolini's decision to provide the first shipment of air planes is clearly indicated by Ciano's insistence in his conversation with Goicoechea on adherence to the terms of the 1934 agreement, which bound Spain to denounce the supposed secret Hispano-French pact. Justifying the decision to aid Franco before the Fascist Grand Council in 1939, the Duce himself insisted on the importance of strategic and political motives, stating that Italian participation in the Civil War responded to "a fundamental historical necessity, Italy's need to obtain free access to the sea."[26]

As a maximum goal, Mussolini may have set his sights on gaining control of the western Mediterranean by establishing Italian naval bases in the Balearic Islands and obtaining the active support and collaboration of a friendly Spain. If the British could be forced out of the straits, Italy's strategic position would be vastly improved. Failing that, the establishment of Italian bases in the Balearics, near Gibraltar, would somewhat weaken Britain's already long and vulnerable lines through Suez and might conceiv-

[24] Unnumbered telegram, July 26, 1936, MAE, Politica, b. 12. See also Siebert, *Italiens Weg in den Zweiten Weltkreig*, p. 50.

[25] Guariglia, *Ricordi*, II, 326; Catalano, *L'economia italiana di guerra*, p. 20. By late July the French government had reversed its position and publically announced its decision to remain neutral and suspend aid to Spain, but officials in Rome did not believe it would abide by this declaration.

[26] NA T 586, roll 405, frames 000039–40. Viñas argues that Hitler's decision to intervene in Spain was also prompted principally by political and military considerations, rather than by economic or ideological ones. (*La Alemania nazi y el 18 de julio*, pp. 436–45).

ably force London to abandon the Mediterranean route.[27] As we have already noted, possession of the Balearic Islands would greatly strengthen Italy's position vis-à-vis France.[28]

It has been frequently asserted that Mussolini was in fact aiming at making the Mediterranean an Italian lake when he decided to support Franco.[29] There is no direct evidence for this, and it seems to me unlikely that he had any very specific or concrete plans.[30] The situation was an open-ended one, and Mussolini was interested in exploiting it for whatever advantages it might offer. While he may have dreamt gradiose dreams for Italian domination of the Mediterranean, he was probably willing to take whatever strategic and political gains he could get in return

[27] Frank, *Seapower, Politics, and the Onset of the Spanish War, 1936*, pp. 209–11.

[28] Blythe's *Spain over Britain*, published in 1937, is the most detailed treatment of the strategic factors involved in the diplomacy of the Spanish Civil War. The author overstresses their importance in the policy making of the great powers, but provides a thorough discussion of the subject. An excellent brief treatment is found in Royal Institute of International Affairs, *Survey of International Affairs, 1937*, II, 127–32. The author draws the conclusion that "in 1936, indeed, Spain was once more the determining factor in a European balance of power" (p. 131).

[29] Cattell writes, "Mussolini coveted Spain as part of his dream to make the Mediterranean an Italian lake, as it had been in the days of ancient Rome. A strong ally in Spain with direct control over bases in the Spanish Balearic Islands would have given Italy an important position in the western Mediterranean and would have made this area untenable for British and French forces" (Cattell, *Soviet Diplomacy and the Spanish Civil War*, pp. 2–3). See also Catalano, *L'economia italiana di guerra*, p. 20.

[30] "It is difficult to say exactly what Mussolini wanted in Spain, for he did not know himself. He had vague plans for an alliance, or at least a close understanding with Spain, which would change the balance of power in the Mediterranean, menace Gibraltar, and create a third front for the French general staff. He had no clear idea, however, of how this alliance was to work" (Donosti, *Mussolini e l'Europa*, pp. 49–50).

for what he thought would be a brief and inexpensive fishing expedition in troubled waters.

Discussion of the ideological motives for Italian intervention in Spain has been clouded by undue insistence on the question of whether or not there was a danger of a Communist take-over in Spain and of whether Mussolini's professed fear of "Communism in the Mediterranean" was real. Italian reports from Spain repeatedly mentioned the threat of a Communist take-over in the country, and the most frequent official explanation of Italian intervention was that it was to prevent Spain from succumbing to Communism. This motive has often been indignantly dismissed as patently false by admirers of the Republic, who point out the small size of the Spanish Communist party in July 1936 and the fact that the first Soviet aid did not reach Spain until long after Italy was already committed to the rebels.[31]

During the early months of the Civil War, when little or no Russian aid was reaching Spain, Mussolini and Ciano were certainly not primarily concerned with avoiding the establishment in Spain of a regime under the direct orders of Moscow, although they occasionally talked about that.[32] It should be remembered, however, that in the Fascist political vocabulary the terms "Bolshevism," "Communism," "Soviet," etc. were often used in a generic sense to in-

---

[31] "The leaders in Berlin and Rome, no matter how Nazi and Fascist, could not seriously think that in July 1936 Spain was a Russian fief or that it was urgently necessary to prevent the Soviet Union's establishing herself in the Mediterranean. They had their Ambassadors in Madrid and in Moscow and elsewhere. They knew, or could know if they wanted to, exactly how things stood" (Valiani, "L'intervento in Spagna," p. 12). "The struggle against 'Bolshevism' . . . was only a facade" (Broué and Témime, *The Revolution and the Civil War in Spain*, p. 346). "Intervention in Spain, disguised before the world as a campaign against Communism would punish them [Spanish liberals] as well as possibly winning the Balearic Islands for Italy" (Mark Smith, *Italy. A Modern History*, p. 457).

[32] Ciano, *Ciano's Diplomatic Papers*, p. 21.

clude any type of leftist revolutionary movement or regime, whether Communist, Socialist or anarchist in its complexion. In this generically counterrevolutionary sense, anti-Communism was indeed an important factor in Mussolini's decision to support the rebels.

From the beginning of the Republic, as we have seen, Mussolini expressed his fears that the Republicans might play the role of Kerensky in ushering in the revolution. In a conversation with the German ambassador on August 6, Ciano confessed his fears:

The general situation was beginning to take on a menacing aspect. The Soviets and the French were unreservedly supporting the Spanish Government, which in reality hardly existed any longer but was entirely in the hands of the Communists. . . . Italy was, like Germany, opposed to the formation of blocs, but the French-Russian behavior was driving Europe directly to a split between Communists and anti-Communists. . . . The French contention that on the one side was the legitimate Government, on the other the insurgents, was not tenable, since actually on the Government side there was no authority but only Red Terror.[33]

The contention that Fascist fears of a revolution in Spain were genuine is supported by the statements of many well-qualified observers in the Italian capital. "Victory for the Spanish Government is regarded here as the equivalent of a victory for Communism," the German embassy in Rome reported.[34] "The Italian government are clearly anxious lest they should be faced with governments in France and Spain

---

[33] GD, D, III, 30. Several weeks later Ciano instructed the Italian embassies in Central and South America to begin a press campaign to alert people to the danger that Communism might spread from Spain to South America (Telegram 3772R/C, August 13, 1936, MAE, Politica, b. 11).

[34] GD, D, III, 40.

in which Communist and anti-Fascist elements may predominate," the British embassy told the foreign office.[35]

Rome's concern over the danger of a revolution in Spain was justified by the situation and by the reports it was receiving. The left-Republican government of José Giral, which took power on July 19, was certainly not itself a revolutionary one. It did not even count any Socialists among its members. By July 25, however, it had to a large degree lost control of the streets and a revolutionary situation was beginning to develop. In Madrid armed bands more or less closely related to the working class parties made it virtually impossible for the government to enforce its will. In Barcelona real power rested with an Anti-Fascist Militia Committee dominated by anarchists, and in several other regions revolutionary committees had also seized power.[36] As the Italian Socialist leader Pietro Nenni was to observe, the situation was soon characterized by "the absence of a centralized authority and direction. Authority, the State, no longer existed."[37]

News of this situation soon began to reach Rome. As early as July 22, the mouthpiece of the Italian foreign ministry, the *Giornale d'Italia*, began to denounce the dangers of Communism in Spain. A telegram from an Italian warship in Barcelona affirmed that local authorities had ad-

[35] FO W 7100/62/41. *L'osservatore romano* warned of the danger of Communism as the *tertium gaudens* in a conflict in which it was not one of the principals in an article entitled "Attenti al terzo" (*L'osservatore romano,* July 29, 1936). The former director of the Italian foreign ministry's special Spanish office, Count Luca Pietromarchi, believed that anti-Communism was an important factor in Mussolini's support of the rebels (interview, Rome, July 7, 1970). According to Horton it is probable that "a hatred and fear of Communism influenced Hitler's decison to aid the rebels" (Horton, *Germany and the Spanish Civil War,* p. 33).

[36] Brenan, *The Spanish Labyrinth,* p. 317; Jackson, *The Spanish Republic and the Civil War,* p. 276; Broué and Témime, *The Revolution and the Civil War in Spain,* pp. 121–48; Payne, *The Spanish Revolution,* pp. 220–24.

[37] Nenni, *La guerre d' Espagne,* p. 32.

mitted to Italian consular agents that armed Communist and anarchist bands controlled the city.[38] In early August, various sources told Ambassador Pedrazzi that both President Azaña and President Companys of the Catalan *Deputaçio* were horrified at the situation and disgusted by the atrocities committed by extremist groups they could not bring under control.[39] The secretary of the Italian embassy, who was still in Madrid, reported by telegraph on August 2 that the city was "completely in the hands of Communist bands, which carry out acts of terrorism."[40]

Observers who were fully sympathetic to the Republic at least partially confirmed the reports of Italian representatives. On July 29 the *Manchester Guardian* argued against sending arms to Spain since "there exist on both sides of the barricade considerable forces which submit to no control. We are therefore free to wonder whether arms dispatched to the Spanish Government would fall into the hands of extremists who, though fighting the insurgents, show no obedience to the central authority.[41] *The New York Times*, in an August 6 article, predicted that a government victory would involve Spain's quickly going Communist.[42]

---

[38] Telegram dated July 24, 1936 in ACS, segreteria particolare del Duce, categgio riservato, 436/R Spagna, sf. 4. The sending of warships did not necessarily imply an intention to intervene in Spain. All the great powers dispatched ships to protect the lives and property of their nationals.

[39] Telegram 200, August 13, 1936, MAE, Politica, b. 11.

[40] Telegram 26, August 2, 1936, MAE, Politica, b. 11.

[41] Quoted in Pike, *Conjecture, Propaganda, and Deceit and the Spanish Civil War*, p 33.

[42] Quoted in Rosachi, *Italian Intervention in Spain. 1934–1939*, p. 26. It has been argued that the danger of a revolution in Spain was subsequent to the military revolt, and it is indeed true that the revolt touched off the revolution its supporters said they wanted to avert. It is also true that German and Italian intervention in favor of the Nationalists in large part prevented the Republic from regaining control of the situation and forced it to throw itself into the arms of the Soviet Union, thereby heightening Russian influence in Spain.

Fascist leaders never tired of speaking of the "Fascist revolution," but in fact the entire regime was fundamentally counterrevolutionary. For the moment it faced no acute crises at home and was, indeed, extremely popular, so there was no need to distract attention from domestic problems with a foreign adventure, as there had been at the time of the Ethiopian crisis. Over the long run, however, prudence dictated avoiding anything that might encourage discontent at home, particularly in view of the continuing difficulties facing the economy.

In this context, the prospect of a successful revolution in Spain was not only distasteful but a cause of concern, since it might encourage revolutionaries in France and all of Western Europe, not excluding Italy herself. This concern is reflected in Mussolini's explanation to his wife that he had decided to help the Spanish Nationalists because "Bolshevism in Spain would mean Bolshevism in France, Bolshevism at Italy's back, and danger of Bolshevization of Europe."[43] According to the French diplomat François-Poncet, who served in both Rome and Berlin, Mussolini "convinced Hitler that the victory of the Spanish Republicans, inflaming the USSR and France by contagion, would give Communism such tremendous impetus as to endanger the totalitarian governments."[44]

Italian aid to the rebels could be viewed, therefore, as a defense of the Fascist regime itself. The idea that aiding the Spanish rebels was a way of safeguarding Fascism is one that recurs regularly throughout the Civil War. In October, 1937, for instance, Ciano was moved to ask himself during a ceremony of presentation of medals to soldiers wounded in Spain whether the loss of so many Italian lives had been justified. "Yes," he responded, "the answer

---

These considerations, however, do not affect the questions of whether or not Rome was genuinely concerned about preventing a revolution in Spain or whether its fears were well grounded.

[43] Rachele Mussolini, *La mia vita con Benito*, p. 137.
[44] François-Poncet, *The Fateful Years*, p. 243.

is yes. At Málaga, at Guadalajara, at Santander, we were fighting in defense of our civilization and our Revolution."[45]

It has traditionally been held that Mussolini was at least as anxious to spread Fascism to Spain as he was to thwart a revolution there.[46] It is significant, however, that Ciano formulated his reply to himself in terms of defending Fascism in Italy, not of spreading it to Spain. The question of the extent to which Italy attempted to foster Fascism in Spain during later periods of the war will be discussed in detail in the following chapters. It is sufficient to say for the moment that there is no evidence to support the contention that short-range plans for converting Spain into a Fascist dictatorship played any significant role in Italian thinking during the early stages of the war.[47]

The majority of those who had risen against the government were conservative authoritarians. Although closer to Fascism than the supporters of the Popular Front, they were not in any strict sense Fascists. Indeed Italian Fascists tended to consider them antiquated and out of touch with modern times. The most important Spanish Fascist group, Falange española, had almost no part in the planning of the uprising, and played no role whatsoever in the contacts with Rome in July 1936. Monarchist conservatives were the only politicians involved in negotiations with Italy, and members of the Spanish nobility made possible their interviews with Ciano and Mussolini. These men could be expected to be somewhat sympathetic toward Fascist Italy, and their success might open the door for future developments, but their own position gave little ground for hopes that Spain would in the immediate future take her place

[45] Ciano, *Diary*, October 29, 1937.

[46] Van der Esch, *Prelude to War*, p. 14.

[47] The Spanish Republican ambassador in France during the Civil War was Luis Araquistain, one of Spain's leading socialist intellectuals. He believed that Mussolini's initial decision to intervene was determined by "a motive of Mediterranean policy and not by his ideological affinities with Spanish Fascism" (Araquistain, "Las grandes potencias y la guerra de España," p. 69).

among the ranks of the Fascist powers. In supporting these men Rome was attempting to head off a successful revolution in Spain, not to establish a Fascist government there.

Mussolini's decision to support the rebels was probably made easier by the knowledge that powerful conservative groups in both France and England were sympathetic toward them. While the entire French rightist press denounced the Spanish Popular Front and the French government's plans to support it, British conservatives were describing the Spanish Republic as "one of the most savage governments, except the Russian, that has ever been seen in Europe."[48] Conservatives would normally have been expected to support a legally constituted government against a revolt and to deplore sending arms to rebels, but in this case political motives prevailed over legal considerations. Their vocal support of the rebels sharply reduced the risk that their governments would react violently to Italian aid should it be discovered. This sharp division of opinion within European countries during the first two weeks of the war presaged the conflicts that were about to arise as the Spanish Civil War rapidly became internationalized.

[48] Watkins, *Britain Divided*, p. 86; and Churchill, *The Gathering Storm*, p. 168. On August 8 Harold Nicolson described the loyalist administration as "a mere Kerensky Government at the mercy of an armed proletariat" (Nicolson, *Diaries—Letters*, p. 220).

FOUR

THE INTERNATIONALIZATION OF THE
CONFLICT: AUGUST–NOVEMBER 1936

ARMS SHIPMENTS TO SPAIN DURING EARLY AUGUST AND THE ORIGINS OF NONINTERVENTION

WHEN the Italian planes reached Franco in Spanish Morocco on July 30, the situation in peninsular Spain was one of temporary deadlock. Mola's forces in the north had reached the passes of the Somosierra and the Sierra de Guadarama, which opened the road to Madrid, but their advance was blocked by militia columns that prevented them from actually attacking the capital. The mountain passes witnessed brief episodes of fierce fighting, but neither side had sufficient trained men or arms to mount a major offensive. In the south the rebels found themselves crippled by their inability to transport the Army of Africa across the straits. Their forces in Andalusia were too weak and dispersed to permit them to begin offensive operations, and they were forced to delay their planned march on Madrid.

The critical factor in this situation was control of the straits. If the rebels could force the straits and bring their highly trained legionaries into the peninsula from Africa, they could proceed with their plans for surrounding and capturing Madrid. If not, the prospects for their success were very slight. Although almost two weeks had passed since the beginning of the revolt, they had succeeded in introducing fewer than 2,000 men into the peninsula; over half of these had been transported by sea during the first two or three days of the war. During the entire following

85

week the few aircraft available to the rebels had succeeded in carrying fewer than 1,000 men across the straits.[1] On July 29, the first of a group of 20 JU–52 transports arrived from Germany in response to Franco's urgent requests for aid. They were immediately put to work ferrying troops to Andalusia. With the aid of Italian and German aircraft, some 6,5000 men would be airlifted into Spain during the month of August.[2]

On August 5, under air cover provided by the Italians, Franco succeeded in forcing the straits with a tiny fleet of ships onto which he had packed 2,500 troops.[3] Even with air support the operation was a daring one, but thanks to the incompetence of the Republican naval crews, who had arrested or killed their commanding officers during the first days of the revolt, the troops disembarked safely on Spanish soil. The crews of the Republican warships made such a poor showing for themselves during August that it is conceivable the straits might have been crossed even without Italo-German air cover. Until the aircraft arrived, however, Franco had shown no inclination to take such a risk and it is highly unlikely that he would have done so.

By enabling the rebels to transport sizeable contingents

[1] Frank, *Seapower, Politics, and the Onset of the Spanish War, 1936,* p. 103; Gomá, *La guerra en el aire,* p. 82; Martínez Bande, *La campaña de Andalucía,* p. 45; Aznar, *Historia militar de la guerra de España,* I, 158.

[2] Frank, *Seapower, Politics, and the Onset of the Spanish War, 1936,* pp. 449–50. Horton puts at 10,000 the number airlifted during August (Horton, *Germany and the Spnish Civil War,* p. 38). Jackson accepts Beumelberg's claim that German planes had carried 15,000 men to Seville by August 5, but this figure seems to me extremely improbable (Jackson, *The Spanish Republic and the Civil War,* p. 248).

[3] The most reliable and detailed account of this operation is Martínez Bande, *La campaña de Andalucía,* pp. 31–46. Bonomi claims that Franco placed him in charge of preparing and executing the entire operation for crossing the straits, but he obviously exaggerates his responsibility and autonomy. Bonomi, *Viva la muerte,* p. 33.

of troops from North Africa to southern Spain during August and September, Italian and German aircraft permitted them to retain the initiative and begin their march to the north. It was soon apparent, however, that a few airplanes would not suffice to guarantee the insurgents' victory. They would clearly need more help if they were to complete the march from Seville to Madrid they began on August 3. The chief of German military intelligence, Admiral Canaris, flew to Italy on August 4 to confer with his Italian counterpart, General Mario Roatta, about the problem. Roatta assured him that Italy intended to provide the needed aid, but no plans were made at this time for ongoing consultation or coordination between Rome and Berlin.[4]

On August 7, Rome dispatched to Franco twenty-seven fighter planes, five tanks, forty machine guns, and twelve antiaircraft guns, together with munitions, bombs, aviation gasoline, and lubricants.[5] As early as the end of the first week of August, then, Italy found herself forced to supply growing quantities of aid to the rebels. The scale was still small, but with the benefit of hindsight, we can see that Rome had set foot on a slippery inclined plane which would soon lead her to massive commitments.

With the aid of Italian and German equipment, Franco's forces gradually fought their way north during the month of August. By August 13, Ciano was convinced that the fall of Madrid was so imminent as to warrant authorizing the Italian embassy personnel in the Spanish capital to leave

---

[4] Frank, *Seapower, Politics, and the Onset of the Spanish War, 1936*, pp. 331–32; Whealey, "Foreign Intervention in the Spanish Civil War," p. 217.

[5] A list of the material sent is contained in an annex to a report on the "Proposals and Requests Brought by Admiral Canaris on August 28 in the Name of the German Government" (MAE, Ufficio Spagna, b. 2). The date of the shipment is given in NA T 586, roll 1062, frame 062961. See also Salas Larrazábal, *Historia del ejército popular de la República,* vol. I, pp. 534–535 and vol. III, pp. 2534–2535.

at their own discretion.[6] On the 14th, the army of Africa took the town of Badajoz in Extremadura and linked up for the first time on Spanish soil with Mola's troops coming down from the north. The capture of Badajoz freed them from the necessity of using Portuguese roads to establish contact. Spirits in the rebel camp were high, and leaders confidently predicted that within a few weeks they would have taken the capital and put an end to the war.[7] During the rest of the month their advance continued steadily if somewhat more slowly than expected. On September 3 the Army of Africa occupied Talavera de la Reina, the last important town before Madrid. Mola's forces in the north occupied Irún, thereby threatening to cut off the Basques from the French border, but did not succeed in dislodging the defenders of the Somosierra and Guadarama, who had been blocking their advance on Madrid for a month.

Events on the international scene moved quickly during August. In the highly charged political atmosphere of Europe in 1936, it was perhaps inevitable that the war in Spain, which had begun as a true civil war between Spaniards over Spanish issues, should soon become internationalized. On the ideological plane, the Spanish conflict quickly took on the aspect of the most important event in the struggle against Fascism. As early as July 28, Carlo Rosselli, in exile in Paris, launched an appeal for support of the Spanish Republic in its struggle against Fascism. Rosselli's slogan "Today in Spain, tomorrow in Italy" stressed the connection between events in Spain and the wider aims of the anti-Fascists. The crash of the Italian bombers in French Morocco only served to confirm this interpretation. Words were soon backed by deeds. During the

[6] Telegram 37, August 13, 1936, MAE, Politica, b. 11.

[7] On August 8, General Mola's son told Ambassador Pedrazzi that his father believed Madrid would fall within ten days. The ambassador found the estimate somewhat optimistic, but reported that the next week might well provide decisive (Telegram 223, August 8, 1936, MAE, Politica, b. 11).

first week of the conflict Nino Nanetti, a member of the central executive committee of the Italian Youth Communist League, arrived in Spain to fight against the rebels. In early August he was joined by the Socialist leader Pietro Nenni. By the end of August a small group of Italian Anarchists had found its way to Spain and had taken up arms on the Aragonese front, where the Giustizia e libertà column entered combat for the first time on August 28 at Mount Pelayo.[8]

Throughout Europe the Socialist, Communist, and democratic press vigorously espoused the cause of the Spanish Republic. Emphases varied according to the political sympathies of each publication, with some stressing the defense of democratic liberties and others empahsizing the elements of class struggle of workers and peasants against oppression. All agreed, however, in categorizing the rebels as Fascists and in denouncing Italian support of the revolt.

The fact that Italy and Germany had decided to provide arms to the rebels not only exacerbated the ideological confrontation but also raised the specter of a possible European war growing out of the Spanish conflict. If France and other nations were to exercise their legal right to sell arms to the Republic to help it put down the revolt, and the Italians and Germans were to persist in supporting the rebels, they might easily find themselves embroiled in a major war. To avoid this possiblility, the French and British developed the policy of nonintervention during the month of August.

The French government had not initially intended to abstain from aiding the Spanish Republic. It had excellent reasons for helping it. The sympathy of most of the supporters of Leon Blum's Popular Front government lay entirely with the Spanish Popular Front, and ideological motives were reinforced by practical political and military considerations. France already had a potentially hostile

[8] Slaughter, *Italian Anti-Fascist Exiles and the Spanish Civil War*, pp. 45–57.

89

Italy and Germany on her borders. The remilitarization of the Rhineland in March 1936 had greatly weakened France's strategic position. A hostile Spain on her southern border would further complicate the situation, making necessary the deployment of forces along the Pyrenees. Even more alarming was the possibility that the use of naval bases in the Balearic Islands by a hostile fleet would make it impossible to move troops from Africa to the metropolis in case of a European conflict.[9] These factors all contributed to the government's July 23 decision to honor the Republic's request for assistance in the form of aircraft.

On the other hand, as soon as the initial decision to aid the Republic became known on July 24, the rightist press led by the *Echo de Paris* began to denounce it scathingly. Many members of Blum's own government, especially the Radicals whose support was essential to its survival, also bitterly opposed aiding the Spanish Republic. There was a grave danger, they argued, that aid to the Republic would lead France into open conflict with Germany and Italy, and it was far from clear that France could count on English support if she became embroiled in a war with Germany over Spain. It soon became apparent that it would be politically impossible for the government to aid the Republic openly, and on July 25 it announced that it had decided for the moment not to sell aircraft to Spain. Air Minister Pierre Cot, however, hurriedly began to arrange for sales of aircraft to third countries for eventual transshipment.[10]

The crash of the Italian bombers in French Morocco on July 30 brought home forcefully to the French the danger of an international conflict. The president of the French Republic, Jeanneney, and powerful Radical cabinet mem-

[9] La Bruyère, "La Espagne et les routes navales de la France en Afrique"; Frank, *Seapower, Politics, and the Onset of the Spanish War, 1936*, p. 197; Van der Esch, *Prelude to War*, pp. 15–16.

[10] Cot, *Triumph of Treason*, pp. 340–55; Warner, "France and Non-Intervention in Spain, July-August, 1936," p. 208.

bers were confirmed in their opposition to open aid of any sort. On July 31, the French Chamber of Deputies instructed the government "to address an urgent appeal to the interested governments for the rapid adoption and rigorous observance of common rules for nonintervention in Spain."[11] On August 1 an appeal in this sense was sent by Foreign Minister Delbos to Italy and Great Britain. It was soon extended to Germany, the Soviet Union, and Portugal, and later to other states.

Up to this point no French aid had actually been sent to the Republic. In view of Italian and German shipments to Franco, the cabinet authorized Cot on August 2 to ship aircraft directly to Spain rather than through third parties, but no official announcement was made and precautions were taken to keep the aid secret. At the same time, another communique was issued calling for a "nonintervention pact." During the next week at least thirty-eight French aircraft reached the Republic. Despite the elaborate efforts made to keep the aid secret, it was denounced in the French Right wing press on August 6 and 7.[12] On August 8 the French government announced that in order to facilitate an agreement it had decided to close its frontiers and prohibit all further shipments of arms to Spain.[13]

[11] Official communique published in *Le temps*, August 3, 1936.

[12] Thomas, *The Spanish Civil War*, p. 305; Pike, *Conjecture, Propaganda, and Deceit*, pp. 44–45.

[13] There is an extensive literature whict attributes the origins of the French nonintervention proposals to pressure from London. Among the more important representatives are: Dreifort, *Yvon Delbos at the Quai d'Orsay;* Thomas, *The Spanish Civil War;* Puzzo, *Spain and the Great Powers;* Van der Esch, *Prelude to War;* Pike, *Conjecture, Propaganda, and Deceit;* Taylor, *The United States and the Spanish Civil War (1936–1939);* Traina, *American Diplomacy and the Spanish Civil War;* Gallagher, "Leon Blum and the Spanish Civil War"; and Kleine-Ahlbrandt, *The Policy of Simmering.* Carlton has recently shown on the basis of the *Documents diplomatiques français* and the foreign office archives, however, that the importance of British influence has been grossly exaggerated. In fact, the policy of nonintervention was proposed by the French largely because of their

Many authors seem to believe that this meant a virtual end to French aid.[14] It did in fact lead to a significant cutback, but sizeable quantities of arms and equipment continued to cross the border into Spain. Between August 9 and October 11, for instance, fifty-six French aircraft reached the Republic.[15] Aid arriving from France contributed significantly to the Republic's ability to resist the rebel advance during late summer and fall. In the meantime, French diplomats strove to win international support for the nonintervention proposal and used the official closing of the French border as an important proof of their country's good will.

Unlike the French government, the British cabinet had decided from the beginning to remain aloof from the conflict. British foreign policy was firmly dedicated to the maintenance of general peace, and pacifist sentiments were strong both within the government and among the public at large. Britain's prime concern was to localize the conflict and prevent it from growing into a European war. Since the end of World War I Britain had in essence followed a policy of balance of power rather than of collective security. She wished to see a strong France, but did not wish French power to be preponderant, lest Germany be driven into the arms of the Soviet Union. Her hopes for peace

concern about the divisive effects that intervention would have in their own country, and because they hoped to avoid a conflict with Italy and Germany. Carlton argues that members of the French Popular Front were partly responsible for spreading the story that they had been subjected to strong British pressure, so as to disarm their leftist critics in France (Carlton, "Eden, Blum and the Origins of Non-Intervention"). Warner notes that British influence was strong but not decisive, and argues that nonintervention was at least partly designed by the French to keep Great Britain from supporting the rebels, since that would have separated London and Paris (Warner, "France and Non-Intervention in Spain," p. 219).

[14] See, for example, Driefort, *Yvon Delbos at the Quai d'Orsay*, p. 49.

[15] Pike, *Conjecture, Propaganda, and Deceit*, p. 48.

were based on combining friendship with France with an understanding with Italy and Germany. This made it essential to prevent the countries who were deeply interested in the victory of one side or the other from becoming so involved in Spain that they could not collaborate with each other on broader European issues. If possible, British statesmen also hoped to prevent the Spanish Civil War from consolidating opposed and conflicting ideological blocs.[16]

These motives for nonintervention, which were derived from Britain's general European policies, were reinforced by a desire to protect British interests in Spain. In addition to having extensive investments there, particularly in mines, London was vitally interested in the security of the Straits of Gibraltar. The chiefs of staff were deeply concerned about the possibility that "a Government inimical to Britain, whether Fascist or Communist, [should] emerge from the present struggle."[17] A victory of the rebels would guarantee the establishment of an authoritarian regime, which would undoubtedly feel sympathy for Italian Fascism and German National Socialism. In the event of a Republic victory, Communists might gain the upper hand. In either case British strategic and economic interests would be threatened. Under the circumstances, the best London could hope for was a stalemate, followed by some sort of negotiated compromise peace which would lead to a coalition government dominated by neither Fascists nor Communists.[18]

[16] *Il corriere della sera* wrote on August 6 that "English policy with respect to the Spanish problem has only one aim, to keep the Powers from turning their attention toward objectives other than those indicated in the communique of the London Conference [on European collaboration and the signing of a new Locarno pact]."

[17] Committee for Imperial Defense Paper 1259–13. A copy is in FO W 9708/62/41.

[18] The Fascist party daily, *Il poplo d'Italia*, assessed the situation quite accurately on August 1: "It is difficult to say which side Great Britain suports. . . . [It seems to be] whichever side is more inclined to live in good relations with England." For a good discussion of British attitudes toward nonintervention, see Puzzo, *Spain and the Great Powers*, pp. 90–103.

93

Great Britain, therefore, accepted the French nonintervention proposal and vigorously supported it. The proposal itself came from France, but it was in effect an Anglo-French initiative, and London was at least as active as Paris in trying to obtain the adherence of other powers. On ideological grounds the Soviet Union would naturally have liked to see the rebels defeated. Early in August Soviet trade unions began organizing a collection of money for Spain. *Pravda* and *Izvestiia* prominently featured speeches by farmers, workers, and academics urging solidarity with the Spanish workers. On August 6 it was publicly announced that $2,400,000 had already been collected to help them in their struggle.[19] The Soviet government, however, was trying at this time to draw closer to Great Britain and France, and consequently abstained from sending Russian military supplies to the Republic. A few Red air force planes may have reached Spain around the first of August, but the evidence is tenuous and this early Soviet aid, if it did exist, was not known and did not affect international affairs.[20]

The Italian ambassador in Moscow reported as early as August 6 that Soviet leaders were greatly distressed by the situation in Spain, which forced them to choose between supporting Spanish Communism, with considerable risk of touching off a general European conflict, or remaining ostensibly neutral in order to preserve the peace, while abandoning their Spanish comrades to what seemed certain defeat. "The Soviet Government," he observed, "has made every effort to commit itself as little as possible. The French proposal for a nonintervention agreement with regard to Spain was received with the greatest relief."[21]

---

[19] Cattell, *Soviet Diplomacy and the Spanish Civil War*, p. 7.

[20] Payne, *The Spanish Revolution*, p. 264.

[21] Report 2475/967, August 6, 1936, MAE, Politica, b. 12. The same note was struck several times again during the month in reports from Moscow. A dispatch dated August 13 concluded that "Soviet leaders have in the final analysis allowed their attitude to be dictated by the demands of peace, which is their principal aim" (Report

On August 23 the Soviet Union formally adhered to the French nonintervention proposal.

Throughout the first three weeks of August, the Italians stalled on accepting the nonintervention proposal, probably because they thought that it would be difficult for them to provide aid to the rebels once an agreement was made, whereas they feared France could easily pass material across the border to the Republic unnoticed.[22] Under pressure from France, Great Britain, and the United States, Rome finally accepted the French proposal on August 21, and three days later the Germans followed suit.[23]

Rome's chief motive for accepting the proposal of a nonintervention pact was to avoid compromising her international position. Ciano had also begun to doubt whether further delay would really serve his purpose. Geographic factors led him to believe that if an agreement were not made soon, French aid to the Republic would reach a scale which Italy and Germany could not match if they hoped to maintain even a semblance of neutrality. It might be easier to conclude an agreement before that happened and while the rebel forces seemed to have the upper hand.

2529/989, August 13, 1936, MAE, Politica b. 12). A week later the ministry was informed that "in fact, the USSR is fearful of international complications and would be extremely pleased if an agreement [on nonintervention] were reached quickly" (Report 2641/1033, August 20, 1936, MAE, Politica, b. 12).

[22] GD, D, III, 40.

[23] Both the British and the French repeatedly requested Italy to accept the nonintervention policy. The French ambassador visited Ciano six times between August 3 and August 17, and the British chargé pressed him for an answer on August 6 and 17 (Ciano, Diplomatic Papers, pp. 25–32). Although the United States was not a party to the negotiations and never signed the agreement, the American ambassador in Rome also urged the Italians to give a favorable reply to the French proposals. The British ambassador in Rome felt American pressure was probably of some importance in the Italian decision to adhere to the Nonintervention agreement (FO W 10293/62/41).

In any case, Italian adhesion to the agreement was from the beginning an empty gesture. The German embassy in Rome noted that the form of Italy's reply was dictated by the desire to reserve freedom of action for all contingencies, and that it was obvious " that it does not intend to abide by the declaration anyway."[24]

By the end of August all the interested European powers except Portugal had accepted the French proposal and it was decided to form a committee of ambassadors in London. The Non-Intervention Committee met for the first time on September 9. By providing an international forum where the problems arising out of the Civil War could be discussed under the moderating influence of a British chairman, the committee helped to dissipate tension and avoid a direct confrontation of the powers, but it was unable to prevent the further internationalization of the conflict. Its activities attracted much attention at the time and were the subject of passionate debate in the European press, but in view of their very limited effectiveness they can be summarized here in a few words.

The first month of activity was taken up entirely with procedural matters, attempts to obtain Portuguese participation, and other minor questions. Italy was at this time devoting her best energies to studying the most effective ways of aiding Franco, and was delighted to see the weeks go by with no substantive debate even begun. Before the first meeting, in fact, the Italian ambassador in London, Dino Grandi, had been instructed to do everything possible "to give the committee's entire activity a purely Platonic character."[25]

Grandi, a Bologna-educated lawyer who served as Mussolini's foreign minister from 1928 to 1932, was a wily and masterful debater, with an excellent sense of timing and unsurpassed dialectical ability. Time and again in the course of the committee's meetings, he successfully de-

[24] GD, D, III, 60.
[25] Ibid., p. 73.

fended his country from the charges brought against it, as often as not managing to direct attention away from Italian violations to those committed by the Soviet Union. His success was due only in part to his astuteness. More important was the fact that neither Great Britain nor France wished to pursue seriously any charges of intervention in Spain, no matter how well founded. They had established the committee in the hope of avoiding direct clashes between the great powers, and preferred to pretend that violations of the agreement did not exist.[26]

The entire month of October was taken up with charges and countercharges against Italy, Germany, and the Soviet Union, but the acrimonious debates produced no concrete results. By early November the committee decided to consider all the accusations unfounded and turn its attention to devising a control system which could check the flow of arms into Spain. During the discussion of the control plan, Grandi strongly insisted on the need for stringent

[26] An unusually frank note by a British foreign office official reveals the true reason why in the entire course of its existence the Non-Intervention Committee never found sufficient evidence to convict Italy, Germany, France, or Russia of violating the agreement which everyone knew they were breaking regularly: "I had thought the Non-Intervention Committee was generally admitted to be largely a piece of humbug," he wrote, "but an extremely useful piece of humbug. Where humbug is the alternative to war, it is impossible to put too high a value upon it" (FO W 16391/9549/41).

Salvemini charges the British with positive complicity in Italy's intervention in favor of Franco: "Mussolini was seconded in the Spanish question not only by Hitler but by the Conservative leaders and the British Government. There was always complete understanding and cordial collaboration" (Salvemini, *Preludio alla seconda guerra mondiale*, appendix F, p. 765). This charge forms part of his larger accusation that "from 1924 to 1940, there is an almost uninterrupted thread of complicity in European politics between British government leaders and Mussolini" (*ibid.*, p. 9). It is more accurate to say that except for the brief period of the Nyon Conference, England did little or nothing to oppose Mussolini's activities in Spain, though she did make half-harted attempts to disuade him from increasing his aid to Franco.

97

regulations to eliminate all possible loopholes and to control all routes to Spain, including not only land and sea but also air. This posed formidable technical problems, and during the month of November the discussions proceeded very slowly.

GROWING AID FROM RUSSIA, ITALY, AND GERMANY

While the diplomats exchanged charges and countercharges in London, the Soviet Union began to intervene more actively in Spain, and Italy and Germany sharply increased the level of their aid to Franco. It was probably between August 20 and August 25 that Stalin decided to support the Spanish government directly. On August 25 the old revolutionary Antonov-Ovseenko arrived in Barcelona as Russian consul general. The following day a high-ranking NKVD officer, Alexander Orlov, was appointed adviser to the Republican government and chief security officer for Russian activities in Spain. Almost simultaneously, Marcel Rosenberg reached Madrid as ambassador, accompanied by an extraordinarily large staff, including military advisors such as Ian Berzin (the former head of Soviet military intelligence), Vladimir Gorev, Y. V. Sumshkevich, P. G. Pavlov, and N. N. Voronov. On September 2, General Walter Krivitsky, chief of Soviet military intelligence in Western Europe, was ordered to mobilize all possible facilities for shipping arms from western Europe to Spain. By November some fifty aircraft purchased by the Comintern in various eastern European countries had reached Spain.[27] Preparations for the shipment of weapons directly from the Soviet Union began on September 14. Soviet intervention in Spain was defensive and aimed at avoiding a Fascist success there rather than at setting up a satellite,[28] but reports of Russian support of the Republic gave rise to

[27] Krivitsky, *I Was Stalin's Agent*, pp. 100–11; Thomas, *The Spanish Civil War*, pp. 335–37; Payne, *The Spanish Revolution*, pp. 267–68.

[28] Ulam, *Expansion and Coexistence*, p. 245; Cattell, *Soviet Diplomacy and the Spanish Civil War*, p. 2.

concern in Rome over Soviet penetration of the western Mediterranean from early September.[29]

The beginning of direct Russian support of the Spanish Republic coincided with the fall of Giral's left-Republican cabinet on September 4 and its replacement by a government of Republicans, Socialists, and Communists. This was the first time that the Communist party joined a western European government, and the Spanish Communist party did so only reluctantly, at the urging of Moscow. The new prime minister, Ernesto Largo Caballero, was a Left Socialist who had become known before the outbreak of the Civil War as "the Spanish Lenin." Ambassador Pedrazzi informed the ministry that the formation of the new government had been "inspired and encouraged by Moscow."[30]

As the fall wore on, Soviet military advisors began to play an increasingly central role in the defense of Madrid. The Republic was desperately short of politically reliable professional officers and was forced to rely heavily on Russian and other foreign military experts, in a way which the Nationalists were not. Meanwhile the Comintern worked feverishly to recruit and organize 10,000 volunteers of various nationalities and various political beliefs into international brigades. During October, Soviet material began to reach Spain in significant quantities. The first major shipment, including forty tanks and thirty fighter planes, arrived at Cartegena during the first week of October.[31] The material was not used in action until the

---

[29] Strangely enough, on September 6 the Italian press was instructed by the ministry of popular culture to stop describing the war in Spain as one between *rebels* and *reds*, and to use the terms *insurgents* or *nationalists* versus *government forces*. Not until November 21, three days after Italy announced her recognition of Franco, were the papers told to employ the terms *nationalists* versus *reds*. At the same time they were instructed to speak of the conflict as an *anti-Communist* or *anti-Bolshevik war* rather than a civil war (ACS, Agenzia Stefani, Directive alla stampa, b. 1).

[30] Telegram 296, September 5, 1936, MAE, Politica, b. 11.

[31] Payne, *The Spanish Revolution*, p. 220.

end of the month, but Franco immediately informed Rome about its arrival.[32] By the month's end, the Soviet Union had supplied the Republic with at least 400 trucks, 50 planes, 100 tanks, and 400 flyers and tank drivers.[33]

Despite growing French and Russian aid to the Republic, Rome was confident that Franco would take Madrid in the near future.[34] What concerned the Italians was the possibility that after the fall of the capital the Republican government would retire to Barcelona and set up a Communist-dominated Republic of Catalonia. In his farewell audience with Mussolini on October 27, the departing French ambassador to Rome received dark hints that Italy would not stand by idly in such a case.[35]

In mid-November the Italian consul general in Barcelona sent the foreign ministry a detailed report on the danger of Catalan independence. Left-Republican Catalans, he said, hoped to be able to win French support for a democratic Catalan republic. Anarchist and Communist groups, he reported, had already reached an agreement with the Russian consul general for the proclamation of a Catalan Soviet Socialist Republic, affiliated to the Third International.[36]

[32] During the first week of October, Franco informed Colonel Faldella that a large Russian shipment had just reached Cartagena. He said he was not advancing any specific requests, but would like Rome to be informed (interview with General Faldella, Milan, October 4, 1970). On the first appearance of Russian equipment in combat, see Fischer, *Men and Politics,* p. 382.

[33] Colodny, *The Struggle for Madrid,* p. 161.

[34] This belief was shared by many who did not support Franco. In mid-September, French Ambassador Herbette was so convinced the northern front and Madrid would soon fall to Franco that he suggested to Pedrazzi that the major powers study the possibility of simultaneously recognizing Franco once he took the capital (Telegram 316, September 14, 1936, MAE, Politica, b. 10).

[35] FRUS, 1936, II, 544–45; and DDF, 2,3, pp. 612–13.

[36] Telegram 665/368, November 11, 1936, transmitted with naval telegrams 149676 and 149677 from the *San Giorgio,* ACS, Marina, Gabinetto, *Rivoluzione in Spagna.*

Soviet arms shipments, the formation of the Largo Caballero government, and fears about a Communist-dominated republic in Catalonia served to increase Italian concern about "red" influences in Spain. The importance which the anti-Communist, and specifically anti-Russian, aspects of the Civil War had acquired in the mind of Italian officials by mid-November may be inferred from an unsigned report to Ciano, probably prepared by his personal secretary Filippo Anfuso:

It is clear that the Spanish Civil War is in itself a purely contingent phenomenon. The Commanders of the Spanish forces in Madrid, Franco told me, are all Russians. The most important elements of Franco's army, on the other hand, are Italians and Germans. The Spanish National Army is held together by the strong metal bands provided by the two great nations with authoritarian regimes. It is, therefore, indispensable that the audacity of the Bolshevic attempt to infiltrate the Mediterranean be definitely crushed, in such a way that it can never return. . . . The Spanish drama, as can be easily seen, is an insignificant episode in comparison with the military struggle between Italo-German and Marxist forces on Spanish territory.[37]

The report exaggerated the extent and importance of both Soviet and Italo-German aid, but was not entirely lacking a foundation in fact.[38] In any case, Italian perceptions are

[37] Unsigned report dated November 18, 1936, ACS, segreteria particolare del Duce, Carteggio riservato. b. 29, f. 14.

[38] George F. Kennan writes: "Within little over two months hundreds of Soviet advisers had arrived in Spain; Soviet tanks and aircraft had been sent, and were in operation; Soviet officers were in effective charge of military operations on the Madrid front. In the face of the weakness and helplessness of the Republican government, Moscow simply took control over whole great areas of the governmental power: particularly military affairs and everything to do with internal security. Within a short time, such key governmental functions as

more important in this context than their degree of correspondence with reality.

Late August witnessed, along with the first major Soviet moves to aid the Republic, a sharp increase in Italian and German support of the Nationalists and the first efforts to coordinate Italo-German policy in Spain. During the forty days since the war had begun, the rebels had used much equipment and ammunition. Until now the aid reaching them from Italy and Germany had not far exceeded the modest levels of support the Republic was receiving from France,[39] but it was becoming clear that more would be needed if the attack on the capital was to be a success.

On August 26 Ciano informed General Roatta that an agreement had been made with Berlin to send an Italian and a German military mission to Franco. The members of the missions were to serve as military advisors to the Nationalist generals, providing them with expert advice on future operations. The chief purpose of the missions, however, was to study the possibilities of providing further support to the Nationalists. Even at this early date, some four months before Italian troops began to arrive in large numbers in Spain, General Roatta was specifically instructed to consider the possibility of sending military personnel, in addition to the aircraft crews which were already engaged in Spain.[40] At the end of August, then, Mussolini was willing to increase substantially Italian commitments in Spain, and provide not only more material in violation

counterintelligence, censorship, and cryptographic communications were largely in Soviet hands. The Soviet government had its own tank and air units, which it operated entirely independently. So far as one can see, this effort of military aid was initially conducted in perfectly good faith, with no other purpose, at the time, than to save Madrid and to assure the victory of the Republic" (Kennan, *Russia and the West*, p. 309).

[39] Frank, *Seapower, Politics, and the Onset of the Spanish War, 1936*, pp. 334–35.

[40] NA T 586, roll 1062, frame 062956.

of the nonintervention agreement, but also soldiers to use it.[41]

Ciano informed Roatta that Admiral Canaris would soon arrive in Rome to work out the details of the mission. At their first meeting on August 28, Canaris gave Roatta an account of the extent of German aid, which proved to be roughly equal to that provided by Italy during the first six weeks of the war, as can be seen in table 2. The

TABLE 2

Italian and German War Material Sent to
Spain through August 28, 1936

	Italy	Germany
Bombers	12	26
Fighters	27	15
Whippet Tanks	5	—
Antiaircraft guns	12	20
Machine guns	40	50
Rifles	—	8,000

SOURCE: "Proposals and Requests Brought by
Admiral Canaris on August 28 in the
Name of the German Government,"
MAE, Ufficio Spagna, b. 2.

two men agreed that their countries would continue to aid the Nationalists in approximately equal measure. The Italian and German soldiers sent to maintain the material would be allowed to take part in war operations whenever necessary, and would be at the orders of the Spanish command for operational purposes. Discipline was to be en-

[41] Ciano later told Hitler that during the struggle for the Balearic Islands, which began in late August, Italy had held in readiness two battalions of Fascist militia. If this is true, it means that during the summer the Italians had already begun to consider the possibility of sending not only technicians but also combat troops to Spain (Ciano, *Ciano's Diplomatic Papers*, p. 58).

trusted to the highest ranking German or Italian officer in the unit or locality. Hitler had originally been opposed to having Germans enter combat in Spain, and had turned down Canaris's proposal in this sense on August 24. He had allowed himself to be convinced only when he learned that Italian pilots had already been authorized to fly combat missions.[42]

Canaris also proposed that both Italy and Germany specifically renounce all territorial compensation for the aid they might provide. Two factors may explain why this proposal was made. Rumors about German designs on Morocco had already begun to circulate, and Hitler may have felt it necessary to assure Mussolini, as he would do through Frank a month later, that Germany had no intention of trying to establish herself in what the Duce was fond of calling "the Roman Sea."[43] The Italians were ill at ease about Hitler's motives for intervening in Spain and anything but pleased at the prospect of increased German influence

[42] Beck, A Study of German Involvement in Spain, 1936–1939, p. 55.

[43] On September 23, the Nazi jurist and minister without portfolio, Hans Frank, visited Rome as Hitler's personal representative to Mussolini. Frank had been instructed to invite both Mussolini and Ciano to Berlin, and to stress Hitler's desire for closer collaboration not only between the two governments but also between the two parties. Frank hastened to explain the German presence in Spain in terms of ideological solidarity. "Germany is giving aid to the Nationalist parties," he asserted," solely because of solidarity in the field of political ideas, but it has neither interests nor aims in the Mediterranean. The Führer is anxious that Italy should know that he regards the Mediterranean as a purely Italian sea. Italy has a right to positions of privilege and control in the Mediterranean."

In response to Hitler's disclaimers of concrete interests in the Mediterranean, Mussolini indicated that Italy had no territorial ambitions in Spain. At the war's end she would expect Spain "to follow a policy which is not contrary to the interests of Italy," but would ask nothing of her "which might modify the geographical situation in the Mediterranean." Italy's support of Franco should be seen, he asserted, as part of her "participation in the anti-Bolshevik struggle" (Ciano, Ciano's Diplomatic Papers, pp. 43–48).

in the Mediterranean.[44] Mussolini was anxious to lessen British influence in the Mediterranean, but he wished to assume for himself any positions they might lose. Nothing would be gained and the situation would be further complicated if a country as potentially powerful as Germany were allowed to gain a foothold there.[45] Hitler was aware of these considerations and anxious to allay such fears and avoid possible German-Italian rivalry in Spain.[46]

The Germans may also have been disturbed by repeated reports of Italian designs on the Balearic Islands and on other Spanish territories. Such Italian ambitions affected no direct German interests, but Hitler may have been concerned to avoid unnecessary international tension that would do nothing to benefit the Reich. Whatever the exact motivation of Canaris' proposal, it is an index of the mistrust that had to be overcome if the two countries were to cooperate in Spain.

[44] The French ambassador in Rome thought this was one of the reasons why Italy accepted the nonintervention proposal (DDF, 2, 3, p. 266).

[45] This concern can be seen even in minor matters of prestige. Early in August, for instance, the Italian consul in Seville reported to the foreign ministry on the enthusiasm generated by a visit of a German warship, and suggested that Italy would do well to send a ship herself. A week later the ministry informed Ambassador Pedrazzi that an Italian ship had been sent to Seville "not only to embark Italians, but also for motives of opportunity and prestige" (Telegram 87778, August 14, 1936, MAE, Politica, b. 11).

Italo-German rivalry also made itself felt in the designation of the members of the military missions to Franco at the end of August. Original planning called for the Italian mission to be headed by Colonel Emilio Faldella, who was outranked by his German counterpart, Colonel Warlimont. Shortly before the group's departure Mussolini ordered General Roatta to accompany the members of the mission, thereby guaranteeing that the ranking officer would be Italian (interview with General Emilio Faldella, Milan, October 4, 1970). After only a few days in Spain, the members of the German mission took their leave of the Italians, preferring to postpone their discussions with Franco to another occasion when the Italians would be absent (Conti, Il processo Roatta. I documenti, p. 204).

[46] Weinberg, The Foreign Policy of Hitler's Germany, p. 292.

Up to this point, the initiative for cooperation had come largely from Germany. Twice in a single month Canaris had traveled to Italy to consult with Italian officials, and the second time he arrived with a series of propositions already prepared. The strategic and political factors that largely motivated Italy's support of the rebels made it difficult for her to rejoice wholeheartedly at the prospect of a German presence in Spain, no matter what its ideological justification, but supporting Franco did create occasions for collaboration between Rome and Berlin. The sessions of the Non-Intervention Committee, and the other occasions on which the international repercussions of the conflict had to be dealt with, were a standing invitation to close ranks and coordinate policy. Whatever their rivalries or distrust, there were obvious advantages to presenting a common front. After Canaris's August visit to Rome, tactics and policy on nonintervention became a matter for routine consultation. Italy soon began to play the leading role in this field, and the German representative on the committee was instructed to second her moves.[47]

Between August 7 and Canaris' trip to Rome, no shipments had been made from Italy. Mussolini probably gave orders for further Italian aid during Canaris's stay in Rome, if not a few days earlier. In late August and early September, six more bombers, twenty-two fighters, and two sea planes were sent to Spain, bringing the total number of Italian aircraft there to sixty-nine, including eighteen bombers, forty-nine fighters, and two seaplanes. On September 3 a cargo ship left, carrying 20,000 hand grenades, 32 machine guns, 5.5 tons of powder, 6,000 bombs weighing from 12 to 250 kilograms, 144,000 2-kilogram bombs, and 660,000 machine gun cartridges, in addition to some of the aircraft just mentioned.[48]

[47] GD, D, III, 78.
[48] "Proposals and Requests Brought by Admiral Canaris on August 28 in the Name of the German Government," MAE, Ufficio Spagna, b. 2. NA T 586, roll 1062, frame 062961. It is not clear if this includes

A few days later, during his discussions with Franco, Roatta agreed to request additional material Franco felt he needed. As a result, ten light tanks, four mobile radio-telegram stations, and thirty-eight 65-mm cannon with munitions were shipped to Spain on September 23.[49] Roatta felt the Spaniards would not be able to handle modern weapons without considerable instruction, so 15 officers, 45 NCOs and 104 troops were sent to serve as instructors and to operate the equipment in combat until the Spaniards learned to do so. This brought the total number of Italians on the Nationalist side at the end of September to about 320, not including the fifty to sixty airmen stationed in Majorca.[50]

Some of the most spectacular Italian activities during the late summer and fall of 1936 took place on Majorca, where a Fascist militia officer, Arconovaldo Bonaccorsi (known in Spain as Conte Rossi), rallied the Nationalist forces in the early days of September. With the aid of a few Italian aircraft purchased by the Majorcan insurgents in August, he helped to repulse the Republican landing and establish Nationalist hegemony on the island. Majorcan Falangists under his leadership soon reconquered the island of Ibiza and threatened the third island of the Balearic group, Minorca. Strong Italian air forces were based on Majorca, and Rossi gained an extraordinary degree of in-

---

the two fighters and three S 81 bombers sent to Majorca in late August.

[49] NA T 586, roll 1062, frames 062963–64. According to General Faldella, the cannon were requested neither by Franco nor by the Italian mission. One day while he was visiting Mola in Valladolid, Faldella observed a group of Republican planes flying unmolested over the city. In reply to his question, Mola told him he had no antiaircraft guns. Faldella accordingly radioed Rome to request 20-mm antiaircraft guns. The message was incorrectly decoded, and some weeks later he was informed that the 65-mm cannon with their crews were already on their way (interview with Faldella, Milan, October 4, 1970).

[50] NA T 586, roll 1062, frames 062963–64.

fluence over the entire life of the island. The details of this episode, which caused great concern in France and Britain, will be discussed in the following chapter.

By this time the Nationalists had taken San Sebastián and completely isolated the Basques from France. The capture of Ronda on September 16 had given them control of all of Andalusia, and in the Tagus Valley the troops had been reorganized for the final drive against Madrid. On September 23, Varela temporarily turned aside from the capital to march on Toledo and relieve the garrison there, which had been besieged in the Alcázar since the beginning of the war and was in imminent danger of falling to the Republic. It took less than a week to occupy Toledo, but not until October 6 would the Nationalist forces be ready once again to resume their drive toward Madrid. In the meantime, on September 29, the battle of Cape Espartel had given them definitive naval control of the straits. Within a few days they transported another 8,000 men from Africa into Spain. In almost two full months the air lift had brought only between 14,000 and 23,000 men into the peninsula, so the new influx represented a very significant increase.[51]

During the month of October the scale of Italian aid for the Nationalists increased further. Italian shipyards fitted the cruiser *Canaris*, the largest ship in the Nationalist fleet, with the guns it was lacking when the Civil War broke out.[52] A large amount of communications equipment for Franco's ground units, as well as some eighteen more fighter and reconnaissance aircraft, also reached Spain during the month,[53] bringing to almost ninety the total number of Italian aircraft sent to Spain by the end of October. Since Germany had sent a hundred planes by October 20,[54]

---

[51] Frank, *Seapower, Politics, and the Onset of the Spanish War, 1936*, pp. 492–94; Gomá, *La guerra en el aire*, p. 92; La Cierva, "The Nationalist Army in the Spanish Civil War," p. 204.

[52] NA T 586, roll 1062, frame 062965.

[53] *Ibid.*, frames 062964–65.

[54] *Ibid.*, frame 062966.

the Nationalists must have received close to two hundred aircraft by the month's end.

For the sake of comparison, we can note that by October 14, ninety-four French war planes had reached Spain. Thirty Russian planes were received by the Republicans early in the month, and at least another twenty arrived before October 31, so by November 1 a minimum of 145 aircraft had reached the Republican zone.[55] Even if none of the original Spanish air force planes which had remained in Republican hands at the beginning of the war are taken into account, the Nationalist air force did not outnumber the Republican by a ratio of more than four to three on November 1. If we accept Salas Larrazábal's estimate that as many as 140 Russian aircraft were in Spain by October 31, the Republican planes outnumbered the Nationalists by nine to eight.[56] Russian I–15 "chatos" were superior in speed and manuverability to the German He 51 and only slightly inferior to the Italian Cr 32. The I–16 monoplanes, known in Spain as "Ratas," were far more modern aircraft, superior in every way to the I–15 and to all other fighter aircraft in service at the time anywhere in the world. In their first engagement over Madrid on November 13, they routed the German Heinkel 51 fighters.

The tanks and artillery pieces sent from Italy at the end of September first appeared on the battlefield on October 21, when Italian ground troops entered combat for the first time on the Spanish mainland, participating in the drive on Madrid.[57] They were grouped into a company

[55] Payne, The Spanish Revolution, pp. 220 and 265; Colodny, The Struggle for Madrid, p. 161.

[56] Salas Larrazábal, "The Growth and Role of the Republican Popular Army," p. 168. Historia del ejército popular de la República, vol. I, pp. 534–35 and vol. III, pp. 2534–35.

[57] The New York Times of October 23, 1936 carried the news under the headlines "Italian Tanks Cut Madrid Defenses. Whippets Rip Barbed Wire and Smash Trenches at Navas del Marques." The correspondent, Frank L. Kluckhorn, reported that there were at least forty tanks involved in the attack, but in fact the total number of Italian tanks in Spain at the time was fifteen.

of fifteen armored cars, eight 65-mm batteries, three anti-tank sections, and a radio-telegraph unit.[58] During the following weeks the Italians were constantly engaged on the Madrid front. By November 17 their casualties amounted to three dead, seventeen wounded and one missing.[59] The Italian tanks weighed only 3.5 tons and were armed only with machine guns. Like the ones being sent from Germany, they were really only armored cars, useful for supporting infantry troops and for attacking machine-gun emplacements, but unable to fight against the medium tanks armed with cannon being sent from the Soviet Union.

THE BIRTH OF THE AXIS

Just as the first Italians were entering the front lines, Mussolini's foreign minister visited Germany. During his meeting with Foreign Minister von Neurath, the two men discussed in detail the course of events in Spain during the preceeding months and the prospects for the immediate future. Ciano concurred in Neurath's diagnosis that Franco's forces, which were advancing very slowly on Madrid, were passing through a "critical phase of inactivity." Mussolini had already decided, he informed him, to "make a decisive military effort to bring about the collapse of the Madrid Government." More planes would be sent and two submarines would be provided to cut the flow of Russian supplies.[60]

When Ciano met Hitler at the Führer's villa in Berchtesgaden on October 24, he aroused Hitler's anger against the British by showing him a copy of a dossier containing thirty-two documents prepared by Anthony Eden for British cabinet members. In the highly secret documents obtained by the Italian secret service, the British foreign

[58] Faldella, *Venti mesi di guerra in Spagna*, p. 122.
[59] A list of the actions in which Italian ground troops took part between October 23 and November 22, together with figures on casualties, is found in MAE, Ufficio Spagna, b. 1.
[60] Ciano, *Ciano's Diplomatic Papers*, pp. 52–55.

minister described Germany as governed by a band of adventurers and recommended speeding up British rearmament while studying the possibility of reaching a *modus vivendi* with Germany.[61] The Führer immediately proposed that Germany and Italy "go over to the attack" against the democracies. A bare and undisguised Italo-German understanding might well arouse suspicion in the smaller European countries, and their fear of Pan-Germanism and of Italian imperialism could drive them into the arms of the democracies, he admitted. Their suspicions could be overcome, however, by presenting the Italo-German front as essentially anti-Communist. The smaller countries "will be brought to group themselves with us if they see in Italo-German unity the barrier against the Bolshevik menace at home and abroad."[62]

It is not clear whether Hitler had previously decided to send the Condor Legion to Spain or whether the decision was taken at this time, as a result of the meeting with Ciano.[63] In any case, it was quickly agreed that both Italy and Germany would increase their aid to Franco in order to counter the growing influx of Soviet material and guarantee his success in the upcoming attack on Madrid.

It can hardly be denied that the Berchtesgaden conversations between Hitler and Ciano represent a step along the path that eventually brought Italy into World War II on

---

[61] Italian diplomatic espionage was extraordinarily active. Colonel Emmanuele testified at Roatta's trial that in the course of one year the Military Intelligence Service (SIM) had taken 16,000 documents from embassies in Rome. Emmanuele himself claimed to have taken seventy code books (Conti, *Il processo Roatta. I documenti*, p. 269).

[62] Ciano, *Ciano's Diplomatic Papers*, pp. 56–60. There is a danger of reading too much into these comments. Hitler clearly suggested using anti-Communism as a cover for an Italo-German front directed not only against the Soviet Union but also against Britain and France. The use of the anti-Communist theme does not, however, authorize us to discount automatically all Italian and German manifestations of anti-Communism as pretexts covering other aims that could not be confessed.

[63] Weinberg, *The Foreign Policy of Hitler's Germany*, p. 294.

Germany's side. Only a few days later, Mussolini was to refer for the first time to the "Rome-Berlin Axis." Care should be taken, however, to avoid overstressing the importance or solidity of the links forged between Germany and Italy by their joint support of Franco. In the speech in which he christened the Axis, Mussolini was careful to stress that it was not intended to be a closed group hostile to the rest of the world, but rather an "axis" around which to build a structure of European collaboration. At the end of the speech he devoted a long passage to discussing Italo-British relations, and called for a "clear, rapid and complete understanding [with England] on the basis of the recognition of our reciprocal interests."[64]

At this time Mussolini was, in fact, probing to see what the real situation was and what price Germany and Great Britain were willing to pay for Rome's friendship. In this respect he was still following the traditional Italian diplomatic system, dictated in large measure by Italy's position as the weakest of the great powers.[65] Ciano's attempt at Berchtesgaden to rouse Hitler's wrath against the British was followed almost immediately by the opening of negotiations between Rome and London. The signing of a "Gentlemen's Agreement" between them on January 1, 1937 was hailed at the time as a return to the policy of friendship between the two countries that had been destroyed by the repercussions of the Ethiopian war.

The fact that the "Gentlemen's Agreement" eventually led nowhere, and that Italy finally entered the war at Germany's side, does not demonstrate that in 1936 she was more firmly committed to one line of policy than to the other. Fascist Italy was attracted to Nazi Germany by ideological considerations, by German willingness to support her claims to great-power status in the Mediterranean, and by the fact that as Germany's ally she could hope for

[64] The text of Mussolini's November 1 speech in Milan is found in his *Opera omnia*, XXVIII, 67–71.

[65] Kogan, *The Politics of Italian Foreign Policy*, p. 31.

tempting rewards in the colonial field from a successful war against England and France.[66] On the other hand, were Germany to defeat France and Great Britain she would dominate the continent, and Italy would find herself reduced to the level of a German satellite. A balance of power within Europe was essential to Italy if she hoped to be able to exercise any influence.[67] In the fall of 1936 Mussolini had as yet made no definite commitments. Italy still had not cast her lot definitely with Germany against England and was trying to follow a policy of friendship with both.[68]

MILITARY AND NAVAL AID IN NOVEMBER

The month following the Berchtesgaden meeting witnessed substantial increases in Italian aid to Franco, in accordance with the decision Mussolini had taken just prior to Ciano's departure for Germany. In November, Rome sent to Spain thirty more fighters and reconnaissance planes, twenty light tanks, fifty-three trucks, and fifty mortars, together with other miscellaneous equipment. This was the first month in which large quantities of munitions for small arms and automatic weapons were sent from Italy.[69]

At the beginning of November, Berlin began assembling in Spain the 5,000 to 6,000-man Condor Legion. This represented a major increase in German commitments to Spain, and was intended to permit Franco to proceed quickly

[66] Macartney and Cremona, *Italy's Foreign and Colonial Policy*, p. 330.

[67] Mack Smith, *Italy. A Modern History*, p. 456; Salvatorelli and Mira, *Storia d'Italia nel periodo fascista*, pp. 946–47.

[68] It is interesting that the British ambassador in Rome, Sir Eric Drummond, believed at the end of 1936 that "even the events of the Spanish Civil War did not lessen Signor Mussolini's strong wish to reach an understanding with the United Kingdom" (Introduction to Annual Report for 1936, FO R 3171/3171/22).

[69] "List of Material Sent to Spain by November 30 or in Shipment by Our Government or That of the Reich," MAE, Ufficio Spagna, b. 2.

to final victory. It included four bomber squadrons with a total of forty-eight JU–52s; four fighter squadrons, comprising forty-eight He–51s; a reconnaissance squadron; a sea plane squadron; four 20-mm batteries; four 88-mm batteries; and four tank companies with forty-eight Krupp Mark I tanks.[70] Table 3 summarizes the aid sent by Rome and Berlin through December 1, 1936. It shows that, contrary to what some authors have maintained,[71] German supplies were clearly much more important than Italian ones at this stage of the war, even from a merely quantitative point of view.

Both the Italians and the Germans tended to keep their aircraft under their own control, but the Italians did so to an even greater extent than the Germans, giving Franco's air force only a small fraction of the available planes. In mid-November the Nationalist air force commanded by General Kindelán could count on twelve bombers, three fighters, and nine reconnaissance planes from Germany, but only six Italian reconnaissance planes.[72] In contrast to the Germans, the Italians also tended to use their own troops to operate the artillery pieces and the tanks they provided. They did not, however, insist on the same degree of nominal independence that the Germans had required as a condition for sending the Condor Legion.

Naval liaison between the Nationalists and their Italian allies had been guaranteed from early October by an "Italian Naval Mission in Spain," headed by Captain Giovanni Ferretti. The naval aspects of the conflict had first been brought up by Admiral Canaris in August, when he

[70] Beumelberg, *Kampf um Spanien,* p. 56; Colodny, *The Struggle for Madrid,* pp. 166–67; "List of Material Sent to Spain by November 30 or in Shipment by Our Government or That of the Reich," MAE, Ufficio Spagna, b. 2; Beck, *A Study of German Involvement in Spain, 1936–1939,* p. 74.

[71] Whealey, "Foreign Intervention in the Spanish Civil War," p. 218; Wiskeman, *The Rome-Berlin Axis,* p. 91.

[72] Roatta's report MMI 502, November 16/17, 1936, MAE, Ufficio Spagna, b. 2.

TABLE 3

Italian and German War Material Sent to Spain through
December 1, 1936

Type	Italy	Germany
Bombers	18	74+
Fighters	69	63+
Observation planes	25	12+
Sea planes	6	—
Unspecified types	—	13
Total Aircraft	118	162+
Whippet tanks	35	60
Antitank guns	12	52
Artillery pieces	42	114
Mortars	50	—
Machine guns	102	300
Ammunition for small arms and automatic weapons (rounds)	16.5 million	37 million
Hand grenades	70,000	40,000

SOURCES: "List of Material sent to Spain by November 30," MAE,
Ufficio Spagna, b. 2; "Data Concerning Material of the
Royal Airforce Sent to Spain. Situation as of December 1,
1936," MAE, Ufficio Spagna, b. 1; Beumelberg, *Kampf um
Spanien*, p. 56; Colodny, *The Struggle for Madrid*, pp.
166–67; Beck, *A Study of German Involvement in Spain,
1936–1939*, p. 74.

proposed that Italy and Germany demand complete freedom of commercial traffic for all Spanish ports, and that
their warships provide protection for merchantmen carrying
arms to Franco. It was also imperative, he said, to
strengthen Franco's tiny navy. Geographic factors made
it easier for Italy to undertake the task, and Canaris suggested that the Italian navy study the possibility of supplying PT boats, manned by Italian crews.[73] Sometime early

[73] Admiral Ferretti's final report on his mission to Spain. Admiral
Ferretti has kindly allowed me to consult his draft of the report.

in the fall, several PT boats seem to have been provided.[74] The Italian navy supported the Nationalists in various other ways as well. Merchantmen carrying supplies to Spain were regularly escorted by Italian warships to defend them from being stopped by Republican vessels, and Italian naval forces provided the Nationalists with detailed information about the movements of ships thought to be carrying arms to the Republican zone. From October 27 to November 7, for instance, two Italian destroyers patroled the straits of Sicily to control the passage of Soviet or other ships carrying troops or arms to Spain. Torpedo boats were deployed for the same purpose in the Straits of Messina.[75]

On November 9, Rome temporarily placed two submarines at the Nationalists' disposition in an effort to reduce the growing flow of supplies reaching the Republic by sea. Berlin had also planned to send submarines to the Mediterranean for the purpose of sinking Republican battleships and cruisers operating there, but when she heard that Italian submarines were already on their way she temporarily desisted.[76] On November 17, at a meeting in Rome, the Italian and German navies agreed to relieve each other in patrolling Spain's Mediterranean coasts. The Italians would take the first tour, which would last until November 30. On that date the Germans would take over until December 11. Both sides agreed that it would be better not to inform the Spanish nationalists that submarines had been deployed.[77]

[74] Cervera Valderrama, *Memorias de guerra*, p. 35. There is no evidence to support this contention in the Italian sources I have consulted, and Cervera Valderrama's chronology may be mistaken.

[75] Telegrams 20810 and 31547, October 27, 1936; and 42199, November 7, 1936, ACS, Marina, Gabinetto, Rivoluzione in Spagna.

[76] Whealey, *German-Spanish Relations January-August 1939*, p. 24.

[77] Translation of an agreement signed by Pini, Giamberardino, Lange, and Heye, Rome, November 17, 1936, German Naval Records T 426 B, PG 80773. This document was supplied to me by Professor Willard C. Frank.

The Italian liaison officer in Spain, Captain Ferretti, was not satisfied that two submarines could effectively reduce the flow of supplies to the Republic. He urged that, in addition, Italy provide another two or possibly four submarines, and at least four destroyers, all with crews. The obvious impossibility of providing large surface ships without being detected led Rome to refuse the request for destroyers, but through February 1937 Italian submarines were constantly active in the Nationalists' service. Their first successful mission took place just after the close of the period dealt with in this chapter, when the *Toricelli* severely damaged the Spanish cruiser *Cervantes* anchored off Cartagena harbor.[78]

ITALY AND NATIONALIST INTERNAL POLITICS

The growing Italian political and military commitment in Spain during the summer and fall of 1936 was not paralleled by an equally active effort to increase Italian political and economic influence in the country. Ciano and Mussolini showed little interest in the domestic politics of the Nationalist zone, and allowed Italy's military personnel in Spain to take precedence over her diplomatic representatives.

In describing to Roatta in August 1936 the functions of the newly formed Italian and German military missions to Franco, Ciano said they were "to guarantee the respective interests of their countries in the political, economic and military field."[79] Implicit in these instructions was the

[78] Admiral Ferretti argued that once Italy had granted diplomatic recognition to the Nationalists, she would be free to provide them ships. The foreign ministry quickly pointed out, however, that this would still involve violating the nonintervention agreement. The information in this paragraph is based on Ferretti's report, on research notes taken in the archives of the Spanish navy by Professor Willard C. Frank of Old Dominion University, and on "Memorandum on Naval Vessels to be Furnished to Spain in View of the Considerations Contained in Report 375 of November 8," MAE, Ufficio Spagna, b. 2.

[79] NA T 586, roll 1062, frame 062956.

predominance of the military in the representation of Italian interests that was to characterize her relations with Spain throughout the Civil War. Though he was a military advisor, Roatta was specifically instructed by the foreign minister to take an interest in the political and economic aspects of the conflict, in addition to his strictly military duties. The military invasion of the civil sphere would have its counterpart in the foreign minister's future asumption of the overall command of Italian military operations in Spain. During the whole course of the war, however, on-the-spot representation of Italian interests was entrusted largely to the military commanders.

Roatta, who commanded the Italian forces in Spain until April 1937, showed little inclination to meddle in the politics of the Nationalist zone, and authorities in Rome did not urge him to do so. Virtually the only area in which the foreign ministry showed some active interest was in securing Italy's future position in Spanish markets, and even in this field its efforts were very modest. On November 10 a clearing agreement designed to facilitate the resumption of trade relations with the territories occupied by the Nationalist army was signed, but little more was done. The Germans were far more energetic and successful than the Italians in creating markets for themselves in Spain and in exploiting Spain's potential as a source of raw materials. Warlimont was chosen to head the German mission to Spain, because as chief of the economic division of the *Waffenannt* in Berlin he was known for his economic as well as military expertise.[80]

The most important Italian decision with regard to the internal politics of the Nationalist zone was that of backing General Franco rather than any of the other military or political leaders. It is quite probable that this policy was never expressly formulated, so it is impossible to fix an exact data on which it was adopted. It is clear, however,

[80] Horton, *Germany and the Spanish Civil War*, pp. 63–64.

that no later than the end of August, Rome was in fact supporting Franco in preference to other leaders. At that time there was still considerable division among the generals. The rebel forces were still split into two bodies—Mola in the north and Franco in the south—with little contact between them. Other lesser figures enjoyed a high degree of autonomy in the areas under their control. Even after the Army of the North and the Army of the South were joined at the end of August, three weeks went by before a single commander-in-chief was selected at a meeting of generals near Salamanca on September 21. The appointment was not made public until September 29, when Franco was named commander-in-chief and "Chief of the Government of the Spanish State."[81]

Support for General Franco as the leader of Nationalist Spain had not formed part of Mussolini's original plans. Franco's first petitions of aid had met with an Italian refusal, and the Duce changed his opinion only after the Monarchist delegation sent by General Mola reached Rome. The first shipment of Italian material had been directed to the forces under Franco's command, and during the following months he continued to receive the bulk of Italian assistance, but this was due at first to the greater ease of transport to the zone controlled by Franco rather than to a political decision to back the Galician general.[82]

Admiral Canaris was an old friend of Franco's. When he visited Rome at the end of August to hammer out the details of Italo-German collaboration in Spain, he went out of his way to insist that aid be provided "only to Gen-

[81] Payne *Politics and the Military in Modern Spain,* pp. 369–72.

[82] On August 6, Italian Undersecretary of State Bastianini told the German ambassador that "the situation of the troops in the north was obviously difficult because of lack of war material—which was all the more regrettable since General Mola was the most competent of the commanders. While the troops in the south were better supplied, the transportation of material to the troops in the north was difficult" (GD, D, III, 30).

119

eral Franco, because he holds the supreme command of the operations and is, therefore, the competent authority to decide on the distribution of the material that reaches the Nationalist troops."[83] It was not in fact true that Franco held the supreme command at this time, but the Italians gladly fell in with the proposal, perhaps because they had already decided to support him before Canaris reached Rome.

On October 1, 1936, Franco was named head of state and installed in Burgos, which remained the official seat of Nationalist government until the end of the war. The Caudillo was not an easy man to deal with, but although on occasions Mussolini threatened to discontinue his aid altogether, he never seriously entertained the idea of supporting any other Nationalist leader in opposition to him.[84] The fact that both Italy and Germany chose to deal exclusively with him and that, apart from a few insignificant German flirtations with the Falange, neither country gave any encouragement to his potential rivals greatly helped Franco achieve and maintain his preeminent position in Nationalist Spain.

Berlin showed more interest than Rome in exploiting the situation to increase her political influence. Ambassador Pedrazzi was seriously concerned about growing German influence, and felt that Italy should adopt a more active line in order to guarantee her own interests. Early in September he warned Ciano:

All information from the territory controlled by Burgos concurs in pointing out the growing popularity of Germany. The Germans take great pains to publicize their aid, and to extend their influence through the press.

[83] "Proposals and Requests Brought by Admiral Canaris on August 28 in the Name of the German Government," MAE, Ufficio Spagna, b. 2.

[84] This impression, which I have derived from many different sources, was confirmed by my interview with Ambassador Pietromarchi in Rome on July 7, 1970.

The responsible military leaders realize that Italian aid has been generous and effective, but the political leaders, who are more influenced by public opinion and by the press, tend to consider Italy's attitude vacillating. This can mean great damage for the future development of the relations between our two countries.[85]

Ciano, however, refused to authorize the opening of even a small office of the Italian news agency, Stefani, in the Nationalist-controlled territory. The ministry for press and propaganda was interested in the idea, but Ciano vetoed it: "It does not seem opportune at the present time," he decided in September, "to carry out new undertakings in the field of the press or other types of propaganda in the zone occupied by the Spanish Nationalists."[86]

By the end of October, Italian propaganda was so inferior to Germany's that Ambassador Pedrazzi had given up trying to compete. By that time the German press agency, DNB, had transferred its offices to Burgos. "It entirely dominates the situation at the moment," he reported, "and constitutes almost the only source of foreign news in the entire territory occupied by the Nationalist troops."[87]

On several occasions Pedrazzi tried unsuccessfully to persuade Ciano to pursue a more active political policy. His most detailed and revealing report on the political situation in the Nationalist zone is from mid-October. Behind the facade of the "National front," he reported, there was deep and bitter division. He found the Spaniards so given to factionalism and ideological jealousy that it was essential to establish a military government with the strength to unify the country. Normal political life could not be allowed to resume immediately, in his opinion, if Spain were to be kept from falling back into ferocious political strife.[88]

[85] Report 2223/987, September 8, 1936, MAE, Politica, b. 23.
[86] Telegram by hand 4288/R September 19, 1936, MAE, Politica, b. 23.
[87] Report 2308/1038, October 23, 1936, MAE, Politica, b. 23.
[88] Report 2297/1079, October 18, 1936, MAE, Politica, b. 11.

When normal conditions did eventually return, he predicted, the old parties would exercise no real influence. The various Monarchist groups, the Liberals, and Gil Robles's CEDA had all lost their power and would have no say in the political future. The dominant force in the new Nationalist Spain would be the Falange:

Its dynamic force, its freshness, and its mysticism which appeals to the impressionable temperament of Iberians guarantee that it will set the tone in tomorrow's Spain. Furthermore, after the victory and the political purge which will follow it, many people from the other band who can accept only the politically most advanced party of the victorious conglomerate will take refuge in its ranks.[89]

Pedrazzi's pleas for a more active Italian political presence fell on deaf ears. Until early December, Ciano would not even sanction an increase in Italian propaganda activities in Spain. Except for Bonaccorsi's backing of the Falangists on Majorca, there is no evidence that either official Italian representatives or the various envoys sent by Ciano and Mussolini and by the Fascist party made any effort to favor the development of one political group or another at this time. Nor did Italian representatives try to sway General Franco's sympathies toward any particular group.

This abstentionism, which clearly represents a conscious policy decision, is at first sight puzzling. The documents offer no explicit statement of motives, but a careful reading of reports on the political situation in Spain offers some clue as to the possible explanation. A long unsigned report to Ciano, dated November 18, 1936, probably summarizes the opinion of his private secretary, Filippo Anfuso, who was the foreign ministry official chiefly responsible for Spanish affairs until the formation of the special Spanish office in early December, 1936. His view of the situation

[89] *Ibid.*

is centered much more on Franco than on the Falange. He dismisses the Falange as "a huge party that was proved by fire before it had time to adopt a real program." "If Italy wants to free Spain from falling, after this cruel conflict, into a rigid feudal and clerical state that would eventually lead to the letting of more blood, she must catechize the Generalissimo properly, and induce him to take care of and temper the Falange." Franco is, in effect, "the only Fascist in Spain. Nazism has no hold on him because he is a *Gallego*, a rational man who wants to see things for himself and understand them."[90]

Aside from his recommendations about catechizing Franco and inducing him to pay sufficient attention to the Falange, Anfuso himself draws no conclusions about Italy's best line of action, but the Caudillo's preeminence would clearly make it advisable to work quietly to win him over, avoiding all direct interference in Spanish affairs. Overt political action or propaganda could alienate the man who seemed likely to be the ultimate arbiter of the situation, whereas a policy of generous military assistance while remaining in the background was well calculated to win his sympathy. This seems to me the most likely explanation for Rome's deliberate refusal to take advantage at this time of the opportunities to influence the domestic politics of the Nationalist zone.

Italo-German Diplomatic Recognition of Franco

Throughout the fall, Franco's armies, strengthened with German and Italian supplies, had been drawing ever closer to Madrid. By November 1 some 25,000 Nationalist troops had begun to enter its southern and western suburbs. In the capital pessimism reigned. On November 6 the Republican government, which had been reorganized two days

[90] Unsigned "Note for His Excellency the Minister," ACS, Segreteria particolare del Duce, Carteggio riservato, b. 29, f. 14.

earlier to include four anarchist ministers, fled to Valencia. On November 7 Nationalist troops under the command of General Varela moved to the attack. Russian tanks had fought for the Republic for the first time on October 29, and on November 8 the first contingents of the international brigades joined the Republican defenders in a desperate defense of the city. Fighting soon became extremely bitter, but much to the surprise of all observers, Madrid's defenses held. The determination of the militia and of the civilian population were essential; but the exertions of the international brigades and of Soviet military advisors, together with the arrival of Soviet tanks and aircraft, which were far superior in quality to their Italian and German opponents, had provided the vital margin that permitted the Republicans to hold the city and bring Franco's offensive to a standstill.

This posed a serious problem to the Italian and German foreign ministries. During Ciano's visit to Hitler, it had been agreed that their two countries would recognize Franco once he took Madrid. At the end of October Ciano suggested naming immediately a "Delegate to the National Government of Burgos" and withdrawing the diplomatic representatives currently accredited to the Republic, thereby granting *de facto* recognition to Burgos even before the fall of Madrid. The Germans refused to accept the suggestion and imposed a more cautious line, among other things because they felt that Franco "might possibly be confirmed in his delaying tactics" by premature recognition.[91]

The matter was allowed to rest there until the afternoon of November 15, when the German embassy in Rome received a telephone call with the news that Berlin no longer "considered it right to wait until the fall of Madrid to recognize the Franco Government."[92] The Italians had been

[91] Telegram 4765/420, October 29, 1936, MAE, Politica, b. 13; GD, D, III, 113.
[92] *Ibid.*, p. 119.

ready for some time, and less than twenty-four hours later they agreed to name a chargé in Burgos.[93]

The step was taken quickly, but it was a serious one. Mussolini had long supported Franco covertly, but now he was openly and irrevocably staking his prestige on the Caudillo's final victory.[94] In a little over one hundred days, Italy had gone from providing a dozen aircraft with falsified papers, through furnishing large amounts of equipment and small numbers of troops, to granting official diplomatic recognition to a regime whose military forces had been brought to a standstill outside of Madrid. The process had been a gradual one, with few sharp breaks in continuity. As Mussolini was to say later, it was mostly a question of having said "A" and finding that it was now necessary to say "B." The result of this gradual process was a complete transformation of the nature of Italy's involvement in Spain. By recognizing Franco as the head of the sole legitimate government in Spain even before the taking of Madrid, Italy and Germany declared to the entire world their determination to see to it that he was not defeated. The decision represented a major political commitment. As the American ambassador in Berlin commented the following day: "Having recognized Franco as a conqueror when this is yet to be proved, Mussolini and Hitler must see to it that

---

[93] The entire question was apparently treated orally. There is no record whatever pertaining to this phase of the process in the Italian foreign ministry's file on the recognition of Burgos.

[94] Germany and Italy were the first two European countries to recognize Franco, although Guatemala and El Salvador had done so on November 8, 1936 (Padelford, *International Law and Diplomacy in the Spanish Civil Strife*, p. 6).

Once Italy had committed herself by recognizing the Salamanca regime as the legitimate government of Spain, she began to press other governments to follow her example. On November 19 Ciano telegraphed the embassies in sixteen countries, urging them "to exercise every possible influence" in favor of recognition of Franco (Telegram 5078, MAE, Politica, b. 13). Count Magistrati, the Italian ambassador in Berlin, was also instructed to request the German government to second Italy's initiative.

he is successful or be associated with a failure. This a dictator can ill afford to do."[95]

[95] FRUS, 1936, II, 561. The unofficial spokesman of the Italian foreign office, Gayda, wrote in an outspoken editorial published in the *Giornale d'Italia* on November 21, 1936: "Italy does not intend to allow a new center of Red revolution to be implanted in the Mediterranean, on Spanish territory . . . . The anti-Communist defense of Italy and Germany in Europe, and of Japan in Asia will not be merely passive. It will not take the offensive, but will react strongly to any aggressive moves on the part of the Soviets and of their Communist committees." The widely-read review *Nuova antologia* was even more explicit: "Italy and Germany have taken a position on a problem of fundamental importance for the future of Europe. They have not hesitated to choose between a Spain regenerated by the National forces and a Spain which would be the beachhead of Bolshevism in the Western Mediterranean. . . . In practice it means above all that they are ready to block any attempt to create a Communist political base on Spanish territory" (December 1, 1936).

FIVE

"CONTE ROSSI" IN MAJORCA

INTRODUCTION

THE Balearic Islands, situated off Spain's Mediterranean coast between Barcelona and Valencia, were geographically removed from the main theaters of action on the peninsula, and followed a course of their own. From mid-August an extravagant Italian Fascist named Arconovaldo Bonaccorsi played a leading role in events there; he soon became known as "Conte Rossi." His activities, which we will examine in detail in this chapter, illustrate a number of interesting aspects of Italian policy in Spain.

Mussolini's interest in the Balearic Islands confirmed the importance of Mediterranean politics in the Italian intervention in Spain. Some authors have argued that he wanted to win positions in Majorca and Minorca principally to threaten British control of Gibraltar,[1] but the islands' chief importance is due to the fact they lie directly across the main routes between France's North African colonies and her Mediterranean ports. In case of a major European conflict, the French general staff planned to move at least a million colonial soldiers over those routes into metropolitan France. If the Italian navy could use ports in Majorca and Minorca to attack that traffic, its position in the Mediterranean would be considerably strengthened and France's correspondingly weakened. This was undeniably a conscious element in Italian policy. In November 1937, for instance, Mussolini told Ribbentrop: "If we use the base in Majorca, that in Pantelleria and others already in exis-

---

[1] Gigli, *La seconda guerra mondiale*, p. 11.

tence and equipped, not one negro will be able to cross from Africa to France by the Mediterranean route."[2]

Events in Majorca also highlight Mussolini's inclination to use unorthodox expedients in the hope of achieving results cheaply. Only an adventurer would have thought of sending a single individual to try to save an island with a population of 300,000 that was being invaded by a force of almost ten thousand men. Furthermore, Bonaccorsi was the sort of agent who could be disauthorized at any time. If his ventures proved successful, Mussolini would be more than willing to reap the fruits. If they failed, it could always be claimed that he was a free agent, an eccentric acting on his own without the approval or knowledge of the government. The entire Spanish venture was originally begun in this spirit, with the dispatch of a dozen disguised aircraft, but Italian intervention on the peninsula rapidly lost its buccaneering quality as the exigencies of the situation forced Rome to supply aid on an increasingly greater scale.

On the peninsula, as we saw in the previous chapter, Mussolini supported Franco without attempting to favor any particular group within his camp. During the early months of the war the Italians were scrupulously careful not to become involved in the struggle between the various Nationalist factions and not even to seem to play any political role themselves within the Nationalist zone. We have suggested that this may have been due both to their perception that Franco was likely to be the real power in Spain, and to their fear of alienating him by meddling in questions that he considered purely domestic. This interpretation is confirmed by the quite different policy that they followed in Majorca.

Rome allowed Bonaccorsi to play an extremely active role in Majorcan politics and to support vigorously the growth and development of the Falange. We shall even see Bonaccorsi and the senior Italian naval officer in the

[2] Ciano, *Ciano's Diplomatic Papers*, pp. 144–45.

island plot a coup against its governor without being rebuked by Rome for stepping out of bounds.

One possible explanation of this radically different policy would be that Italy's strategic interest in the Balearic Islands led Fascist leaders to throw caution to the winds. Majorca was certainly a point of particular interest for the Italians, and they could have thought that if the Nationalists were eventually defeated, they might be able to retain a privileged position there. It seems unlikely, however, that this strategy weighed so heavily in their thinking as to justify spoiling the overall effect of their support of Franco in order to guarantee a special position on the island.[3]

A more probable explanation for their more active intervention was that Majorca was so far removed from the rest of Nationalist-controlled territories that Italian officials believed Franco would pay little attention to events there. Furthermore, if Franco did become upset about Bonaccorsi's activities, it would always be possible to disown him and deplore his excesses. If this was the real rationale behind intervention in the politics of Majorca, it confirms that Italian abstention from political involvement on the peninsula was due not to a lack of interest or desire, but to fear of alienating Franco. It also suggests that Mussolini's loyalty to Franco was based largely on pragmatic considerations, since he seems to have had no qualms about acting behind his back when it appeared he would not be found out.

Finally, it is interesting to note how under these circumstances the Italians did everything in their power to favor the development of the Falange. Part of this may be attrib-

[3] The French ambassador, Herbette, reported on October 5, 1936: "The rumor that Italy is trying to establish herself in the Balearic Islands is absurd. Italy is well aware of the fact that the future Spanish regime will be extremely nationalistic and that anyone who would dare to request any dismemberment of its national sovereignty would be asking for trouble of the worst sort" (DDF, 2, 3, p. 315).

uted to Bonaccorsi's personal attitudes, but it is significant that Ciano specifically urged him to dedicate his attention to organizing the Falange. This seems to indicate that Italy's failure to support it actively in the rest of Spain should be attributed not to a reluctance to see it develop, but to fear of being unduly compromised in a complex and shifting situation in which Franco seemed to hold the only real power.

MILITARY DEFENSE OF MAJORCA

The July rising met with easy initial success in Majorca, the largest of the Balearic Islands. In the second largest island, Minorca, General Bosch proclaimed a state of war, but pro-Republican troops and NCOs prevented him from gaining control of the situation. Within a few days Minorca was securely in Republican hands. In Ibiza and the other smaller islands of the archipelago, the rising met with success (see map 2).

On Majorca the rebels were uneasy. Control of the local population presented some problems, but the real danger was the ever-present threat of invasion from the mainland. The entire Mediterranean coast of Spain, aside from a small section in the province of Cadiz in the far south, was in Republican hands. Almost the whole fleet had remained loyal to the government, and the insignificant Nationalist naval forces could not be expected to come to the island's aid. From July 20, Palma de Majorca was subjected to bombing raids, which did little damage but which presaged an attack and gave heart to the local opponents of the rising.[4]

Just as Franco's request had occasioned the first Italian intervention in the Civil War, in the case of Majorca it was local requests for assistance that provoked Italian aid. On August 2 Captain Juan Thomas and Senor Martín Pou

[4] Aznar, *Historia militar de la guerra de España*, I, 264.

Map 2

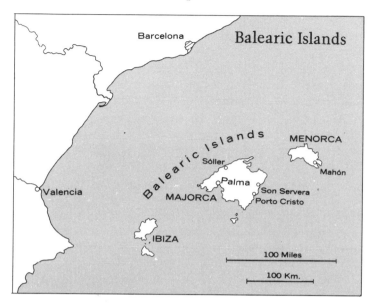

Rodelló left Majorca on a German ship that took them to Italy. Captain Thomas met with little success in his first efforts to obtain aid, and was temporarily jailed by the Italian police after attempting to buy arms from the manufacturers. However, after he made contact with Pedro Sainz Rodríguez, the young monarchist leader who had accompanied Goicoechea on his mission from Mola to Mussolini, his prospects improved considerably.[5] By August 11 Thomas, who belonged to the Falange, could report to the Majorcan Falangist leader, the Marqués de Zayas, that negotiations for the purchase of air planes were proceeding rapidly.[6]

[5] Martínez Bande, *La invasión de Aragón y el desembarco en Mallorca*, p. 269.

[6] Telegram 35872 in ACS, Marina, Gabinetto, Rivoluzione in Spagna. From the beginning of the Civil War until mid-November

They had been seconded by Admiral Magaz, Primo de Rivera's former ambassador to the Vatican, who was acting as the rebels' unofficial representative in Rome, and by the naval attaché of the Spanish embassy, Captain Rafael Estrada.[7]

With the proper contacts, there was little difficulty in obtaining Italian promises of aid. Once Mussolini had decided to intervene in the Spanish conflict, it was only logical to accede to the Majorcan plea. Geographic factors made it particularly easy to ship material to the island, and its strategic position made the prospect of increasing Italian influence there an especially attractive one. The Italians did not, however, offer their assistance free of charge. They demanded three million lire, to be deposited with the Italian consul in Majorca, Abraham Facchi, before delivery of the aircraft.[8] The Majorcan insurgests had no difficulty in obtaining the funds. The wealthy financier Juan March, who had paid for the planes sent to Morocco, was a native of the island and had already indicated his willingness to meet the expenses of its defense.[9] His two sons had also offered to finance the purchase of aircraft, and the funds of the local branch of the Bank of Spain had been put at the insurgents' disposal by order of the military governor of the island.[10]

1936, the minister of the navy kept a special collection of all incoming and outgoing telegrams that referred to Spain. Since the navy served as communications link with Majorca, this collection also includes telegrams sent from or directed to the foreign ministry. In the rest of this chapter, telegrams contained in this collection will simply be cited by number, and any telegram for which no other source is mentioned is found in this collection. Unless otherwise indicated, the date of the telegram is understood to be the date given in the text.

[7] Cervera Valderrama, *Memorias de guerra*, p. 26.
[8] Telegram 35872, August 11, 1936.
[9] Arrarás (ed.), *Historia de la cruzada de España*, XVI, 282.
[10] Martínez Bande, *La invasión de Aragón*, pp. 151 and 269.

On August 13, Zayas telegraphed Rome that the money had already been deposited with the Italian consul, and two days later was informed that three seaplanes equipped for bombing would fly to the island on August 17. They were to be followed on August 19 by a freighter carrying 6 fighter planes and 3 antiaircraft batteries.

By this time, the need for assistance was becoming critical. On August 7 the expected Republican offensive had begun to take shape. An expeditionary force of Catalans and Valencians sailed to the small island of Formentera and occupied it on August 8. On August 9 the Republicans quickly overcame the small garrison of Ibiza with the help of local forces. Four transports, escorted by the battleship *Jaime Primero*, the Cruiser *Libertad*, and two destroyers, appeared off the west coast of Majorca on August 13. After some indecision about where to land, the commander of the expedition, air force Captain Alberto Bayo disembarked at Porto Cristo with 2,000 to 3,000 men at dawn on August 16. A counterattack by the defenders and Bayo's indecision kept the invaders from advancing far from their original beachhead.[11] The next day the Nationalists retook Porto Cristo, but lost ground to the north of the town. During the following days fighting was light and only minor changes in positions took place.[12]

The promised Italian seaplanes did not reach Palma until August 19.[13] The three planes attacked and dispersed units of the Republican fleet lying off Porto Cristo, and bombed the zone where Bayo's forces were concentrated.[14] Their bombs were soon exhausted, however, and without fighter protection they were extremely vulnerable to attack. After a Republican raid succeeded in damaging one of them, the

[11] Ibid., p. 141; Aznar, *Historia militar de la guerra de España*, I, 264–65.
[12] Martínez Bande, *La invasión de Aragón*, pp. 151–55.
[13] Telegram 22398.
[14] Aznar, *Historia militar de la guerra de España*, I, 265.

local authorities agreed it was useless for the two undamaged aircraft to run further risks when they had no bombs, and they returned to Elmas in Sardinia on August 26.[15]

In the week that had gone by since the first landing at Porto Cristo, Bayo's forces had not made any significant advance, although their number had increased considerably, reaching between 8,000 and 9,000 men.[16] The local insurgent commander believed that their numbers and armament, combined with support from the air and from the guns of the Republican navy, would soon prove irresistible. The Falangist leader Zayas still hoped, on the contrary, that with the proper leadership the island might be saved for the insurrection. On August 23 he requested Sainz Rodríguez to ask the Italian government to send a military advisor to direct the defense of Majorca. The following day, Captain Margottini, the commander of the Italian destroyer *Fiume*, at anchor in the bay of Palma, telegraphed his superiors in the navy ministry: "I confirm the opinion that the situation, although subject to collapse at any moment, can still be easily dominated by the prompt and energetic intervention of an advisor and of the aviation. The major problem is the lack of courage of the leaders."[17]

In reply to this petition Mussolini turned his attention not to a regular army officer, but to one of the early members of his Fascist squads, who had risen to the rank of consul in the Fascist militia, Arconovaldo Bonaccorsi. His extravagant name was well suited to the man. A robust Bologna-born lawyer with a great shock of reddish hair, a close trimmed beard, and fiery eyes, Bonaccorsi's energy and fanaticism recommended him for the job of rekindling the enthusiasm of the Majorcan insurgents.

The style of Bonaccorsi's own account of his assignment, dictated to an Italian journalist some twenty years later, gives a revealing picture of the man:

[15] Telegram 10115.
[16] Martínez Bande, *La invasión de Aragón*, p. 141.
[17] Telegram 84272.

Mussolini gave me orders to leave for the Balearic islands and put myself at the orders of General Goded, the Commander of the Military Garrison of Palma de Majorca. His textual words were: "Tomorrow you will leave for Palma. I am sure you will give a good account of yourself. Count Ciano will give you detailed dispositions. I am counting on you. The task Italy is assigning you is a difficult one, but I am certain you will overcome every obstacle. The work you are undertaking is of capital importance for the triumph of Latin and Christian civilization, menaced by the international rabble at Moscow's orders that wants to bolshevize the peoples of the Mediterranean basin."

This was my viaticum, slowly administered with terse precision. I listened with intense emotion and apprehension, because I knew nothing and had been told nothing about the reasons for the interview.[18]

Bonaccorsi reached Palma on August 26 in a seaplane that immediately returned to Italy. He soon encountered the Italian Consul Facchi, and in his company visited the military governor of the island, Colonel Díaz de Freijo. According to Bonaccorsi, the colonel was affable but disheartened and convinced that the situation was irremediably lost. He told him that negotiations with Bayo were already in course and that the island's forces would soon surrender to the Republican invaders.[19]

Mussolini had chosen his man well for a difficult assignment. Together with Zayas, Bonaccorsi began to assemble a Falangist militia to defend the city. Church bells were rung to call the people together, and a manifesto was published exhorting the Majorcans to mobilize. Bonaccorsi, dressed in a black Fascist uniform with high black boots

[18] Quoted in Santamaria, *Operazione Spagna*, p. 21. In fact General Goded had left Majorca for Barcelona on July 19, and had been taken prisoner in an unsuccessful attempt to raise the Catalan capital for the rebellion.

[19] *Ibid.*, p. 22.

and a large white cross at the neck, bedecked himself with pistols, hand grenades, daggers, and ammunition belts. He exercised a great fascination on the Majorcans, and fifty young men were soon grouped into "The Dragoons of Death," at the orders of 'Conte Rossi.'[20] Several audacious *coups de main* against Republican positions near Porto Cristo and Son Servera did much to raise the spirits of the Majorcan insurgents during the last week of August, although they did not modify the military situation.

On August 27 a ship carrying two CR 32 fighters, together with a dozen 20-mm antiaircraft guns, munitions, bombs, and gasoline reached Palma. The fighters went into action two days later and rapidly gained absolute air superiority.[21] On August 31, they were joined by three S 81 trimotor bombers, which attacked Bayo's forces. By early September the Italian air force had sent fifty men to Majorca.[22]

The troops at the insurgents' orders in Majorca still numbered only about 2,500 at the end of the month, when a meeting of military leaders was held.[23] Largely due to the pressure brought to bear by Bonaccorsi and Margottini, who threatened to withdraw Italian support if their demands were not met, the commander of the operational forces on Majorca was deposed.[24] In his place the military governor, Colonel Díaz de Freijo, named Colonel García Ruiz, who till then had been civil governor of the island.[25]

[20] Arrarás (ed.), *Historia de la cruzada de España*, XVI, 297.

[21] Malaparte, *Viva la muerte*, p. 10; Arrarás (ed.), *Historia de la cruzada de España*, XVI, 297; Santamaria, *Operazione Spagna*, p. 23. Martínez Bande speaks of three fighters in *La invasión de Aragón*, p. 162.

[22] NA T 586, roll 1062, frame 062963.

[23] Martínez Bande, *La invasión de Aragón*, p. 164; Santamaria, *Operazione Spagna*, p. 24.

[24] Martínez Bande, *La invasión de Aragón*, p. 164. According to Bernanos, he was not only deposed but imprisoned (Bernanos, *Les grands cimetières sous la lune*, p. 125).

[25] Martínez Bande, *La invasión de Aragón*, p. 165.

The Italian foreign ministry was not long in being informed about strange occurrences on Majorca. Bonaccorsi had raised the Italian and Spanish flags over a fort in Palma and was rapidly becoming the dominant figure, much to the discomfort of the British, who were informed by their vice consul that the population would probably offer Italy some sort of protectorate over the island.[26] On September 1, Ciano instructed the commander of the *Fiume* to order Bonaccorsi to confine his activities to organizing the Falange.[27] Captain Margottini telegraphed back that at the moment it was vitally important for Bonaccorsi to be present at the front and was granted permission to delay transmitting the orders.[28]

The commander of the Italian air force, General Valle, was seriously considering at this time sending a flight of Italian bombers to attack the warships *Jaime Primero* and *Libertad*, which were supporting Bayo's ground forces.[29] Bonaccorsi was enthusiastic about the idea, and stressed in a telegram to the foreign ministry the moral effect that the sinking of a large Spanish warship by Italian-based planes would have on all Spain. The idea was not flatly rejected by the foreign ministry, as one might have expected, but before a final decision was taken circumstances changed, making the attack unnecessary and impractical.

In fact on September 3, much to the surprise of the island's defenders, Captain Bayo began to evacuate his beachhead. By 10 A.M. the next day, the last Republican troops had left the island. Bonaccorsi's enthusiasm and the few aircraft sent from Italy had provided the margin the island's Nationalist defenders needed to check Bayo's advance, but the Republic's abandonment of the effort to

[26] Santamaria, *Operazione Spagna*, pp. 22–23; FO W 10452/9549/41.
[27] Telegram 21324.
[28] Telegram 20021.
[29] Telegram 53342.

conquer Majorca was not due to any overwhelming military superiority of the defenders, nor had the offensive "floundered against Italian air power." In fact three bombers and two fighters constituted the entire Italian air force on the island at this time. It is even more preposterous to speak of Italian "occupation" of the island in early September,[30] when there were probably fewer than 100 and certainly fewer than 250 Italians there.

Bayo's hasty and unexpected withdrawal was not due to the pressure exerted by the Nationalists nor to the strength of Italian forces on the island, but to orders received from Madrid. The attack on Majorca had never aroused much enthusiasm in the capital and Bayo's failure to advance had convinced Republican authorities that it was futile to continue supporting him with units of the fleet that were badly needed in the Straits to interrupt Nationalist traffic with Morocco. The withdrawal was due to the fact that Bayo was ordered on September 3 to evacuate the beachhead within 12 hours or be abandoned by the fleet.[31]

MEDDLING IN POLITICAL AND ECONOMIC AFFAIRS

Bayo's withdrawal made it impossible for Margottini to delay further transmitting Ciano's orders for Bonaccorsi to confine his activities to organizing the Falange on the island. Bonaccorsi, however, was completely undaunted; his Majorcan career had only begun. After the dark days of August, in which it had seemed that defeat was imminent, the Majorcan Nationalists were wild with enthusiasm over their victory. On September 6, Bonaccorsi organized a parade of Falangist troops and organizations. During the preceding days the number of Falange members had grown enormously, and the parade was an impressive suc-

---

[30] Puzzo, *Spain and the Great Powers*, p. 126.
[31] Martínez Bande, *La invasión de Aragón*, pp. 167–71.

cess. Bonaccorsi himself rode on horseback at the head of his troops down the streets of Palma, greeted by cheers of "Long live the hero!" Most of the population was in the streets to do homage to Conte Rossi, who willingly accepted the role of liberator of the island.[32]

Bonaccorsi threw himself passionately into developing the Falange and repressing all resistance to its rule. His flamboyant figure was to be seen everywhere as his sports car shot down the dusty roads of Majorca, followed by several truckloads of his followers. Prior to the rising, the island had lived on the margin of Spanish politics, and even the gravest and most violent crises had barely disturbed the sleepy rhythm of its daily life. The quick success of the rebels in July had given no opportunity for outbursts of popular violence. All in all, the island was very little politicized. Victory over the invaders, nonetheless, signaled the beginning of a period of Falangist terror and violence in which Bonaccorsi played a leading role. It was directed not only against members of the working class, but against everyone who had given the slightest sign of disaffection from the insurgents' cause.

Among the residents of Majorca in the summer of 1936 was the French monarchist novelist George Bernanos, who was staying with his family in the home of the Falangist leader Marqués de Zayas. His 1938 book, *Les grands cimetières sous la lune*, made Conte Rossi infamous the world over for his leadership of the repression. Bernanos estimated that between September and March 1937 some 3,000 Majorcans lost their lives, the majority without trial.[33] The Italian consul in Palma stated in March 1937 that during August and September the Nationalists had executed 1,750 persons.[34] It will probably never be possible to give an exact number of those who were shot, but statistical precision is in this case of secondary importance. The details of Ber-

[32] Telegram 28570.
[33] Bernanos, *Les grands cimetières sous la lune*, p. 130.
[34] Report 94/31, March 26, 1937, MAE, Politica, b. 16.

nanos's picture may be exaggerated and inaccurate, but there seem to be no grounds for doubting that Bonaccorsi and his Falangist squads committed numerous excesses that were not only morally unjustifiable, but politically unnecessary.[35] There is no evidence that Italian authorities in Rome, who on other occasions showed their concern over the excessive severity of the Nationalist repression, made any attempt to moderate Bonaccorsi's zeal.

The Italian's popular success and swaggering manner could not but alienate some Majorcan supporters of the Nationalist rebellion. The majority found it more prudent to hide their feelings and join the popular acclamation of the hero, but some of the military leaders felt certain enough of themselves to oppose his attempts to turn the island into a Falangist fief. The situation, though outwardly calm, quickly became very tense. On September 6, the day of the Falangist parade, Captain Margottini, after consulting with Bonaccorsi, decided to postpone unloading a shipment of arms from the *Neride* until the political situation cleared up.[36] That same day Margottini had a stormy two-hour interview with the military governor, Colonel Díaz de Freijo. Far exceeding his instructions, Margottini demanded in the name of the Italian government greater freedom of development for the Falange and greater scope for Falangist control of local life.[37]

The colonel refused to yield to Margottini's demands, and his attitude encouraged other Majorcans, who sup-

[35] The Italian consul reported: "In the Balearic Islands, on the Red side and on the Nationalist side, all concept of the value of human life has been lost. In the Nationalists' favor there is the fact that their executions in August and September were a reaction to the massacres begun by the other side [on Ibiza and Minorca] and were dictated by the necessity of preventing the subversive elements from joining up with the Red militia that had disembarked in Porto Cristo" (Report 94/31, March 26, 1937, MAE, Politica, b. 16).

[36] Unnumbered telegram of September 6, 1936, ACS, Marina, Gabinetto, Rivoluzione in Spagna.

[37] Telegram 28570.

ported the insurgents but resented Bonaccorsi's methods and his attempts to concentrate all power in the hands of the Falange. On September 9, Juan March, Jr., the son of the financier, declared to Bonaccorsi that he personally was not a Falangist and had no desire to see the Falange dominate Majorcan life. Italy could claim no debt of gratitude for her assistance, he protested, since his father had paid handsomely for it. Furthermore, he had himself spoken with Italian officials in Rome and they had disclaimed all interest in Spanish internal politics. He accused Bonaccorsi of interfering in purely Spanish questions and of far overstepping the bounds of the instructions he had received from Ciano. The interview broke off abruptly. Bonaccorsi was incensed, and dashed off a telegram to Rome requesting permission to get the local authorities to take steps against March.[38]

The same day he found out that it would be some time before the new military governor, Colonel Benjumea del Rey, who had been named to the post on September 5, could be expected to arrive. His hopes of seeing a speedy change were destroyed, and he decided to apply more pressure to clear the way for further development of the Falange. This time he requested Rome to ask Burgos to order the military governor "to give his whole hearted support to the Falangist movement, along the lines indicated by the Italian advisor." Margottini added his personal recommendation that the suggestion be accepted.[39]

Ciano was annoyed by these reports of sharp disagreements between his envoy and such influential figures as March and the military governor. He did not rebuke Bonaccorsi for the concrete incidents, but did send instructions the same day, calling on him to avoid friction with the Majorcans: "You should avoid any conflict with local personalities, and your action should now be directed toward leading the island back to a climate of order, discipline

[38] Telegram 16922, September 9, 1936.
[39] Martínez Bande, *La invasión de Aragón*, p. 178; Telegram 00095.

141

and a sense of national solidarity."[40] Ciano's orders had some momentary effect, and the following day Margottini could report that the situation with March had been sufficiently cleared up to avoid disagreeable consequences.

Bonaccorsi was already anxious for more action. He proposed invading Minorca, although he knew the military governor was opposed to the idea. Ciano did not wish to further antagonize the British and French, who were already disturbed about events on Majorca, and he vetoed the proposal for the moment.[41] Bonaccorsi's impatience broke out again on September 11. He reported that the Falangist movement was making excellent progress, and that it practically dominated the fields of politics and labor. The military authorities, however, continued to oppose its development. He insisted again that "until the new governor is named, Burgos absolutely must be convinced to instruct the governor of Majorca to grant the Falangist movement official recognition and put a halt to Masonic inspired hostility and damaging uncertainty."[42]

Margottini was not content to stand back and merely second Bonaccorsi's requests to Rome. He, too, intervened actively in Majorcan politics, particularly among the military, where he found willing cooperators in the commander of the Spanish naval forces stationed in Majorca and in Major Marín of the military governor's staff. He reported that his own successes "together with the irresistible advance of the Falangist movement under the dynamic influence of Bonaccorsi makes us more tranquil about the future development of the situation. The Command continues its apparent genuflections that only cover its hidden hostility, but it has no following among the people, nor in the army where Bonaccorsi is actively at work."[43]

This intense propagandizing by the Italians and their

[40] Telegram 90952.
[41] Telegram 31785.
[42] Telegram 57042.
[43] Telegram 77744, September 11, 1936.

Spanish Falangist protégés was naturally resented by other political groupings among the insurgents, and particularly by the army officers, who felt their authority being threatened. Late in the afternoon of Saturday, September 12, Margottini reported that a struggle was shaping up between the new civil governor, Colonel Ossorio, and Colonel García Ruiz, who hoped to recover the position as civil governor he gave up in August when he took command of the troops. The situation was confused, but Margottini felt that everything was working to the advantage of the pro-Fascist elements. Control of the island was, in any case, safely in Falangist hands.

A secret meeting of leading Majorcan Falangists was called for the same evening. In attendance were the Marqués de Zayas; Major Marín, the Falangists' chief backer on the military governor's staff; the military judge, Zarranz; navy Commander Rodríguez; Bonaccorsi; and Margottini. The group concluded that within the week some change had to be made. If by Friday the new military governor had not arrived and Burgos had not ordered Colonel Díaz de Freijo to grant official status to Falangist organizations, they would take the situation into their own hands. During the week, Zayas and Bonaccorsi would intensify their propaganda and prepare for a massive display of force by the Falangists on Friday. Meanwhile, Major Marín would also step up his propaganda efforts among pro-Falangist officers. On Friday, if no orders from Burgos had been received, the Falangists would stage a demonstration and immediately afterwards Judge Zarranz would be declared governor, with Major Marín as his chief of staff. Margottini was optimistic and confident. He informed the navy ministry in detail of the plans and concluded that "whatever develops from the present situation, there is no further need for concern."[44]

After Margottini's initial report his telegrams contain no

[44] Telegram 26931.

further references to the plans for a coup, so the news that Colonel Díaz de Feijo would soon be replaced was probably received almost immediately. In any case, on September 18 Lt. Col. Ruiz García was named commander *ad interim* of the forces on Majorca, while Lt. Col. Rubí was made civil governor. Margottini was favorably impressed with Rubí, whom he described as an energetic and able man, known for his public declarations of admiration for Mussolini and for Fascist Italy.[45] Col. Ruiz García met with less favor in the Italian's eyes, but since his was only a temporary appointment the question was of no great moment.

This episode of the short-lived plans for a coup contrasts sharply with Italian policy in the rest of Spain. Neither Bonaccorsi nor Margottini had explicit orders to pursue such an aggressive policy of Italian penetration in Majorca. Their activities were motivated by their own zeal, enthusiasm, and initiative, rather than by orders from Rome. Bonaccorsi had, as we have seen, been specifically ordered by Ciano to confine himself to organizing the Falange and to avoid friction with other groups. On the other hand, neither man made any effort to keep his superiors ignorant of his activities nor even to inform them only after the fact. Margottini's detailed report on the plans for a Falangist coup, for instance, was telegraphed to his superiors in the navy ministry the very evening of the meeting, with a note from Bonaccorsi requesting that it be transmitted directly to the ministry of foreign affairs.

Neither the foreign ministry nor the navy ministry expressed any disapproval of the plans for a Majorcan coup, nor of Bonaccorsi's and Margottini's participation in the plotting.[46] On one occasion in October, Margottini was re-

[45] Telegram 5149.
[46] The documentation on the Majorcan question that I examined in the archives of the foreign ministry is obviously incomplete, since it does not contain all of the telegrams directed to the foreign ministry of which there is a copy in the navy collection. The navy collection, on the other hand, contains only telegrams, to the exclusion of all

buked for exceeding his orders, but in general it seems clear that his superiors were pleased with his activities. Until Italy recognized the Burgos government on November 21, the under-secretary of the navy kept a special file of all incoming and outgoing telegrams on events in Spain, which he evidently followed with particular interest. The fact that Margottini remained continuously in Palma from August until mid-November or later, despite regular rotation of the ships assigned to that port, indicates that he was deliberately kept on the spot to direct Italian activities there. All this shows, as we noted at the beginning of the chapter, that Italy was taking advantage of the island's isolation and of Bonaccorsi's unofficial status to intervene far more actively in politics than she dared do elsewhere in Spain.

Once the crisis on Majorca was over and plans for a coup were abandoned, Bonaccorsi continued his organizing of the Falange. The military governor overcame his initial doubts and began giving him support. Margottini reported that civil governor, Lt. Colonel Rubí, was "fully and enthusiastically intent on carrying out Fascist type projects."[47] Development of Falangist corporative syndicates proceeded especially rapidly since any Majorcan worker who did not wish to incur suspicion of antiinsurgent sentiments enrolled in them. By the end of September Margottini could report after a tour of the island that "Italy, the Fasci, and the Duce are everywhere considered with mystical enthusiasm as the guide and example of the Spanish movement."[48]

Margottini's nonmilitary interests extended not only to politics but also to economics. In mid-September he began

---

other types of correspondence. It seems probable that if any instruction to desist from plotting had been given there would be at least a trace of it in the telegraphic correspondence, but it is impossible to affirm with absolute certainty that no such orders were sent by courier.

[47] Telegram 60014, September 24, 1936.
[48] Telegram 94853, September 30, 1936.

to bombard his superiors with suggestions about the advisability of securing future Majorcan markets for Italy. His first concern was to establish maritime communications between Italy and Palma. Rome immediately approved the idea, and by the end of the month arrangements were made with an Italian steamship line for a regular route to be established.

By that time, Margottini already had larger plans in mind. He was convinced that Italian companies could win control of a large share of Majorcan shipping and commerce. Rome was interested enough in the proposals to give orders early in October for the *Ente Nazionale Fascista per la Cooperazione* to take charge of all Italian commerce with the Balearic Islands. This success only increased Margottini's enthusiasm. On October 11, he proposed that Italy attempt to obtain a formal monopoly of all Majorcan commerce, whatever its point of origin or ultimate destination. This proposal was apparently never taken seriously in Rome.

Italian plans for the economic conquest of Majorca did not meet with any great degree of success. The Tripcovich steamship lines refused to provide the type of service Margottini requested, asserting that they would be unprofitable. The *Ente Nazionale Fascista per la Cooperazione* failed even to establish effective on-the-spot representation in Palma. During the first month of its activities, it did not succeed in putting together any deals whatsoever for the Majorcans. Margottini became so disgusted with its inefficiency that he suggested some other agency be designated for Majorcan trade, and in the meantime refused to allow the *Ente*'s representatives to work from his ship because he did not want to be associated with them.[49] Rome soon dropped altogether the idea of having an agency specially designated to handle Majorcan trade, and simply incorporated it into the new clearing agreement which

[49] Telegram 00854.

was reached for all Nationalist-controlled territories in November.

INTERNATIONAL REPERCUSSIONS

The growing Italian political and military presence on Majorca did not pass unnoticed in other countries. The number of Italians on the island at the end of October was certainly less than 1,200 and nowhere near the 12,000 to 15,000 figure that rumors mentioned and that some historians accept.[50] The Italian presence was sufficient, however, to cause genuine alarm. The strategic position of the islands had created fears of an Italian takeover even before the first Italians arrived there. Foreign Minister Delbos was already firmly convinced in early August that Germany and Italy had made arrangements with the rebels for bases in Spanish Morocco and the Balearic and Canary Islands.[51] On August 5, Admirals Darland and Decoux went to London to consult with the British admiralty about the threat of an Italian occupation of the Balearic group. The British were sceptical about the existence of an immediate danger, for which the French could provide no concrete proof, but they agreed that the situation bore close watching.[52] The following day Admiral Sir William James informed Sir George Mousney of the foreign office about his concern over the stationing of an Italian destroyer at Palma.[53]

Anthony Eden was particularly disturbed by the thought that Italy might attempt to weaken or destroy England's preponderant position in the Mediterranean. On August 19 he told his fellow cabinet members: "We can hardly avoid the supposition that Italy will regard disturbances in Spain not only as a struggle between Fascism and Communism, but also and primarily as a field in which . . . she

[50] Van der Esch, *Prelude to War*, p. 40.
[51] FRUS, 1936, I, 468.
[52] DDF, 2, 3, p. 87.
[53] FO W 7884/62/41.

might find herself at once able to strengthen her own influence and weaken British sea power in the Western Mediterranean."[54]

Toward the middle of August the British foreign office requested the opinion of the chiefs of staff on the dangers of changes in the equilibrium of the western Mediterranean arising from the Civil War. In an August 24th report to the Committee of Imperial Defense, the chiefs of staff concluded that "Italian occupation of any of the Balearic Islands, Canary Islands, and/or Rio de Oro, is highly undesirable from the point of view of British interests, but cannot be regarded as a vital menace."[55] This finding is an important clue to understanding British policy during the following months. It explains what many contemporary observers considered England's inexplicable failure to react to a grave threat to her control of the sea. The foreign office was, indeed, concerned about events in Majorca, but the conviction that no vital British interests were involved lent a less urgent tone to Majorcan affairs and tended to direct attention away from the Balearic Islands to broader issues of Mediterranean policy.

Early in September Eden issued a carefully worded warning to the Italians about British interest in the eventual outcome of events in Spain. In an interview with the British chargé in Rome, Ingram, Ciano had categorically denied any Italian intention of taking advantage of the Spanish Civil War to acquire Spanish territories. Eden seized upon this statement as an opportunity to bring home to Ciano Britain's concern over the question. On September 3, he instructed Ingram: "You should take the early opportunity of informing the Minister for Foreign Affairs verbally that you reported this statement to His Majesty's Government and that you have been instructed to let His Excellency know that His Majesty's Government have received this assurance with satisfaction, as any alteration of the *status*

[54] Cabinet Paper FP (36) 10.
[55] FO W 9708/6/41.

148

quo in the Western Mediterranean must be a matter of the closest concern to His Majesty's Government."[56]

British admonitions may have been responsible for Ciano's decision to instruct Bonaccorsi not to invade Minorca, but they had little other effect. London was well informed about events on Majorca, and by early October had solid evidence of Italian violations of the Non-Intervention Agreement in the Balearic Islands. The foreign office remained convinced, however, that no permanent occupation of the islands was planned and insisted that it was up to the French to bring the question before the Non-Intervention Committee if they so desired. In the absence of British support, the French never raised the question.

The British failed to pursue the Majorcan question with sufficient energy to make any impression on the Italians. On October 13 Eden asked Grandi for assurances about Italian intentions in the Balearics, but he explained that he wanted them in order to be able to assuage the fears of members of Parliament, who were unnecessarily concerned. Encouraged by Eden's apologetic attitude, Grandi categorically denied not only that Italy had any plans for permanent occupation, but even that Fascist militia officers were on Majorca. Eden knew full well that the second statement was false, but failed to press the point.[57]

Again at the end of the month, Sir Robert Vansittart expressed his concern over Bonaccorsi's declarations that Italy would never leave the Balearic Islands and over the continued arrival of men and material. He asked that "Conte Rossi" be requested to moderate his language, and that the men and material be withdrawn or at least not increased. Grandi dismissed Bonaccorsi's declarations as no more important than the anti-Fascist statements of many

[56] FO W 9621/9549/41.
[57] FO W 13608/9549/41. The files of the foreign office show that the British had deciphered the Italian navy code by July 1936. The war office, therefore, had detailed and exact information on developments in Spain and especially in Majorca.

British volunteers on the other side, going so far as to add that the English should be happy Italian volunteers had helped save the Balearic Islands from the hands of Communism.[58]

Perhaps it was the weakness of the British protests and London's supine acceptance of Grandi's impudent lies that encouraged Ciano to belive he could follow an even more active policy in the Balearic Islands. On November 11, when it seemed that Madrid might fall at any moment to the Nationalists, he authorized Bonaccorsi to prepare for the occupation of Minorca, the only island of the group still in Republican hands, and strategically the most important.[59] The invasion did not materialize at this time, but its planning is a clear sign of Italian confidence in British passivity. After early November the repercussions of Italian presence in the Balearic Islands became inseparable from the negotiations for the Anglo-Italian Gentlemen's Agreement, which will be dealt with in chapter 6.

[58] An entire file on Italian relations with Britain and the Balearic Islands is found in MAE, Politica, b. 9.
[59] Telegram 5499.

PART II

SIX

AN ITALIAN ARMY IN SPAIN:
DECEMBER 1936–MARCH 1937

TREATY BETWEEN ITALY AND NATIONALIST SPAIN

By late November it was becoming increasingly clear that if Italy wished to guarantee the success of the cause to which she had just committed herself publicly, she would have to support it on a vastly increased scale. Mussolini was willing to provide the necessary assistance, but he wanted some guarantees for the future. Negotiations for an Italo-Spanish treaty were begun either before or very shortly after diplomatic recognition was extended. By November 28 Filippo Anfuso, Ciano's personal secretary, had succeeded in concluding a secret treaty with the Spanish.

The treaty's importance has been much debated. A distinguished Italian diplomatic historian describes it as "nothing transcendental, a disproportionately small result compared to the military effort made, to the huge expenses incurred, to the risks run and to the damage done to Italy's international diplomatic position."[1] Another Italian historian, on the contrary, maintains that it gave Italy "a full mortgage in the proper sense of the term" on Spain.[2]

The treaty gave Italy a sweeping series of rights. Although it proved to be of little importance in the long run, since Franco successfully avoided fulfilling its stipulations during the Second World War, it was the most important agreement signed between Italy and Spain during the entire course of the Civil War, and it marked the beginning

[1] Toscano, "L'Asse Roma-Berlino," p. 207.
[2] Santarelli, *Storia del movimento e del regime fascista,* II, 264.

of an entirely new period in the history of Italian intervention.

In the first of the treaty's six clauses, Italy pledged "its support and aid for the conservation of the independence and integrity of Spain, including both metropolitan territory and colonies."[3] This clause reflects the concern Nationalist leaders felt about Italy's intentions, particularly in the Balearic Islands. Though ostensibly directed against third parties, it also amounted to an Italian pledge to respect Spain's territorial integrity, and as such had been requested by Franco.[4]

The second and third clauses called for mutual assistance, consultation, and friendship. More specifically the two countries undertook "not to permit the exploitation of their territories, ports and inland seas, for any kind of operation directed against one of the contracting parties, or for the preparation of such operations or for the free passage of the materials or troops of a third Power." They also pledged to consider any previous agreements which were incompatible with this stipulation to be invalid.

These clauses point once again to the markedly anti-French character both of Italy's intervention in Spain, and of her interest in concluding the agreement. The intent of these clauses is exactly the same as that of the 1934 agreement with Spanish monarchists, and reflects Mussolini's anxiety to avoid the shipment of French colonial troops through Spain from North Africa to France. They are obviously designed to secure the revocation of the secret Hispano-French treaty, which the Duce feared had been concluded by the Republic. That this fear should be one of the most important constants in Mussolini's relations with Spain was perhaps inevitable. Given Spain's strategic position and the fact of Italo-French hostility, it was logical that Italy suspect France of trying to guarantee the availability of Spanish transportation facilities in case of war,

[3] The full text of the treaty is reproduced as appendix A.
[4] Cantalupo, *Fu la Spagna*, p. 83.

just as France suspected Italy of establishing bases in the Balearic Islands to cut the vital routes that linked her with her North African possessions.

The fourth clause called for benevolent neutrality in the case of conflict with a third power or in case of the imposition of sanctions. In such cases the two parties also agreed to "guarantee [the other party] the necessary supplies, to put at its disposal all facilities, the use of ports, of airlines, of railways and roads, as well as the maintenance of indirect commercial relations. As the German ambassador, von Hassel, noted, this article entailed "much more than a benevolent neutrality."[5] It gave Italy adequate legal basis for requesting the right to establish bases on Majorca or anywhere else on Spanish territory in the case of a conflict.[6] On the other hand, it did not grant any specific rights. If a conflict arose, the Italians would have to obtain Spanish approval for any bases or facilities they wanted to use, since no provision was made for automatic availability in case of war. The real effectiveness of the agreement would, therefore, depend entirely on the circumstances of the moment when Italy wished to invoke it.

The two final clauses of the agreement reflected Italy's desire to develop her economic relations with Spain, but they were extremely vague and indicated more than anything else how little progress had been made up to this time.[7] Whether anything would come of them would depend almost entirely on future developments.

[5] Note for His Excellency the Minister, prepared by De Peppo after a conversation with von Hassel in Rome on November 28, 1936, MAE, Gabinetto, 1.

[6] D'Amoja, *La politica estera dell'Impero,* p. 63.

[7] Italy was trying to reactivate the commerce of the Balearic Islands but, as we have seen, little had been done, and the market involved was not large enough to offer very attractive prospects for the future. The Tripcovich and Tirrenia Steamship Lines had to be given 100,000 lire per month as subsidies for operating the routes between Italy and Palma and Seville. The air service that was established on the line Rome-Pollenza-Palma-Melillia-Cadiz was of political rather than

With the benefit of hindsight, we can appreciate Franco's skill in avoiding concrete commitments. He promised a great deal, but left unspecified exactly what he would do; any concrete demands that might be made on him would always be subject to negotiation. Rome, however did not yet know him well enough to realize how important this would be. She was pleased with the sweeping character of the concessions she had won and unconcerned about her ability to collect on them.

MUSSOLINI'S PLAN FOR SENDING COMBAT TROOPS AND HITLER'S RESERVATIONS

Once the treaty was signed, Mussolini turned his attention to the military problem of providing Franco the assistance he needed to win the war. The Nationalist attack on Madrid had, for the moment, clearly failed. The stubborn resistance of the city's defenders, the arms and advisors provided by the Soviet Union, and the disciplined forces of the international brigades combined to hold the attackers in the *Casa de Campo,* on the far side of the Manzanares river. The few troops that did cross the river and established a beachhead in the *Ciudad Universitaria* could not be dislodged, but they were unable to advance beyond the School of Medicine. At a meeting on November 23, the Nationalist generals decided to desist from the frontal attack on Madrid.

One major reason for the offensive's failure was lack of men. Four months after the outbreak of the war, mobilization in the Nationalist zone was beginning, but only a fraction of the available manpower had yet been tapped. General Roatta had estimated on November 16 that Franco's combat-worthy troops numbered only about 74,000

economic value. A provisional clearing agreement had been signed on November 23 and some Spanish minerals and olive oil were beginning to flow to Italy, but they did not offset the cost of Italian aid to Franco.

infantry, 5,000 cavalry, and 48,000 militia, excluding forces in the rear areas.[8] The front was very loosely held, but garrisoning a 1,200 mile front in even the loosest of fashions, and maintaining a hold on rear areas where significant parts of the population were hostile to him, required most of Franco's men. In the absence of sufficient reserves, the Nationalists could not create a mass with which to maneuver. It had not been possible to find more than 25,000 men for the attack on the capital.[9] The Italian ambassador in Paris told the American ambassador on November 25 that "it would be impossible for the Italian Government at this time to cease to support Franco even if the Soviet Government should cease to support the Madrid and Barcelona Governments, Franco's effectives being clearly insufficient to enable him to conquer the whole of Spain."[10]

The idea of sending Italian combat troops to strengthen Franco's forces seems to have developed gradually. In a report submitted in early November, General Roatta mentioned the possibility, but still only as an hypothesis that would require certain organizational changes were it to work out in the future. In a letter dated November 20, the correspondent of the *Popolo d'Italia*, Luigi Barzini, whose reports to his editor Mussolini read with interest, suggested that "a division of Black Shirts could take Spain." In his opinion, except for the professionals of the Army of Africa, the Spanish infantry lacked courage. "There is

---

[8] Roatta's report 502, November 16/17, 1936, MAE, Ufficio Spagna, b. 2. On December 10, von Faupel placed the number of men in the Nationalist army at between 180,000 and 200,000, presumably including forces in the rear areas and units in the process of formation (GD, D, III, 148). By early 1937, 270,000 men had been drafted into the Nationalist army (Payne, *Politics and the Military in Modern Spain*, p. 388).

[9] Martínez Bande, *La lucha en torno a Madrid*, p. 30. The Italian correspondent Luigi Barzini placed their number at 10,000 [letter to Barella, November 20, 1936, ACS, segreteria particolare del Duce, carteggio riservato. 241/R (Barzini)].

[10] FRUS, 1936, II, 575.

no comparison with our infantry. There is never any hand to hand combat. The forces being attacked escape first, and if they don't the attacking forces turn back."[11]

Before the end of November, Mussolini began to consider four different options for helping Franco: 1) individual Italians could be allowed to volunteer for service in the Spanish *Tercio extranjero;* 2) mixed brigades could be formed with Spanish troops commanded by Italian officers and NCOs; 3) organized groups of Italians might be sent to fight at Franco's orders as members of the *Tercio extranjero* or other Spanish units; 4) divisional or larger Italian units might be sent to Spain, if international events warranted it.

Allowing individual Italians to volunteer for service in Spanish units presented no particular problem. By late November or early December, Italian officials had given permission for a recruiting office to be established. On November 26 Franco instructed his diplomatic representatives in Rome to begin recruiting immediately, and an office was soon opened in the home of the vice consul in Rome's historic Piazza Navona.[12] Volunteers were lured with offers of a 3,000 lire premium for signing up and forty lire per day pay. Some, not content with volunteering their own services, organized bands to go to Spain in the tradition of the Italian soldiers of fortune.[13] As late as February

---

[11] Barzini, letter to Barella, November 20, 1936, ACS, segreteria particolare del Duce, carteggio riservato, 241/R (Barzini). Gabrieli claims to have convinced Roatta at this time to request that Italian ground units be sent, although he admits he does not know with certainty if the telegram was actually sent. Gabrieli, *Una guerra civile per la libertà,* p. 65.

[12] ACS, pubblica sicurezza, direzione generale degli affari generali e riservati, 1920–1945, 1936, b. 15. Also FO W 19014/9549/41.

[13] On December 21, a certain Raffaele Maestrogiacomo of the little town of Rochetta S. Antonio in the barren southern province of Avellino informed the Spanish embassy that he had a group of 52 people who were willing to enroll with him (ACS, pubblica sicurezza, direzione generale degli affari generali e riservati, 1920–1945, 1936,

1937, there is news of individuals leaving Italy to serve in the Spanish *Tercio extranjero,* but the total number of such volunteers must have been small.

The idea of forming mixed brigades with Spanish troops and Italian officers, artillery men, machine gunners, etc., was first discussed with Franco at the end of November.[14] At the same time preliminary preparations were also being made to dispatch whole Italian units to Spain if necessary. On November 26, Ciano informed German Ambassador von Hassell that "Italy was determined to send to Spain a whole division of Black Shirts, of whom four thousand were already organized into four battalions."[15] The American embassy in Rome believed that as many as ten thousand Black Shirts were being prepared for duty in Spain as well as some four hundred machine gunners and a force of Alpine infantry. It also reported that about two thousand men had sailed for Spain by the end of November.[16] The embassy's information was exaggerated and premature. No concrete plans had yet been made for recruiting ten thousand men, and nowhere near two thousand had already sailed. But the report is indicative of the fact that by late November preparations were already under way on a large enough scale to lend credibility to rumors about plans for very large Italian commitments.

Whatever was going to be done, it obviously needed to be done quickly. On November 27 Ciano requested information on Berlin's view of the situation and plans for the

---

b. 15). On occasion, these undertakings originated in unexpected quarters. In a phone conversation intercepted by the police, Anita Garibaldi told a friend that her younger brother was getting up an expedition to fight *for Franco.* "What is going to happen to our family tradition?" she asked in despair [ACS, segreteria particolare del Duce, carteggio riservato, 463/R (Spagna), Sf. 6].

[14] Undated and unsigned memorandum of the CTV commander, "The Dependence of the Mixed Division Frecce," SHM CGG, L 387, C. 37.

[15] GD, D, III, 139.

[16] FRUS, 1936, II, 582.

future. In his own opinion, he said, "a rapid victory is necessary, time is beginning to work against us."[17] The German foreign minister replied that he was not pessimistic, despite the slowness of Franco's operations, but agreed with Ciano that in general time was working against the Nationalists.[18]

To study future Italian aid to Franco, Mussolini called a meeting for December 6 and requested the Germans to send a representative. The meeting was attended by Mussolini, Ciano, the head of Italian intelligence, and the subsecretaries of the Italian army, navy, and air force. Admiral Canaris represented Germany.[19]

Canaris readily agreed with Mussolini's proposals to strengthen Italian and German air forces in Spain. The Germans would complete the buildup of the bomber strength of the Condor Legion, whereas the Italians would concentrate on developing their fighter units. The Germans had already informed Rome that the distance from their bases would make it difficult for German submarines to share patrol duties in the Mediterranean. Mussolini and Canaris agreed that in the future Italian submarines would take sole responsibility for patroling Spain's Mediterranean coasts and for operations in Spanish harbors, but that German surface vessels would continue their activities, coordinating them with the Italian naval command. Subsequently it was decided that the German surface vessels would limit themselves to the Atlantic, leaving the Mediterranean entirely to the Italians.[20]

[17] Telegram 5167/347 R, November 27, 1936, MAE, Ufficio Spagna, b. 3.
[18] Telegram 561 from Berlin, November 28, 1936, MAE, Ufficio Spagna, b. 3.
[19] This account of the meeting is based on the official Italian minutes, MAE, Ufficio Spagna, b. 2. At this time, Mussolini held the post of minister of all three services, so the subsecretaries were the highest ranking officials after the Duce.
[20] German Naval Attache to Supreme Command of the Navy, B.Nr. 455 g. Kds, Rome, December 15, 1936, German Naval Records T 98 A, PG 33308; draft to be presented to the Commander in Chief,

When the question of sending large numbers of troops to Spain came up, however, Canaris began to raise objections and avoid any commitments. In answer to Mussolini's proposal that Italy and Germany each send a division to Spain, he pointed out the difficulties involved in sending German units. Without flatly rejecting the proposal, he intimated that it would be impossible for Germany to carry this out, since the sixty transports required for a full division with its equipment could hardly make the voyage to Spain without being detected. In discussing the idea of sending Italian and German officers and NCOs to form Spanish troops into mixed brigades, Hitler's envoy stressed the difficulties stemming both from language problems and from the sensitivity of Spaniards who might oppose the arrangement for political reasons. Mussolini came away from the meeting with the conviction that despite the difficulties mentioned by Canaris, the Germans would send men and material for several mixed brigades, but he was badly mistaken.

Canaris's refusal to commit Germany to sending troops to Spain was the result of a fundamental shift in German policy. During the first four months of the war, as we have seen, Germany had supplied considerably more arms and equipment to Franco than had Italy. The secret treaty between Burgos and Rome—which the Italians immediately showed to the Germans—led Berlin to think that Rome's interests in Spain were far more important than her own. As the ambassador in Rome noted:

The interests of Germany and Italy in the Spanish troubles coincide to the extent that both countries are seeking to prevent a victory of Bolshevism in Spain or Catalonia. However, while Germany is not pursuing any immediate diplomatic interests in Spain beyond this, the efforts of Rome undoubtedly extend toward having Spain fall into

dated December 11, 1936, German Naval Records T 98 A, PG 33398. These documents were supplied to me by Professor Willard C. Frank.

line with its Mediterranean policy, or at least toward preventing political cooperation between Spain on the one hand and France and/or England on the other.[21]

The Germans were pleased to see the deepening Italian commitment in Spain, for it threatened no German interests and provided some security that Italy would not allow herself to be drawn away from Germany by the prospect of an understanding with London and Paris:

> Germany has . . . every reason for being gratified if Italy continues to interest herself deeply in the Spanish affair. The role played by the Spanish conflict as regards Italy's relations with France and England could be similar to that of the Abyssinian conflict, bringing out clearly the actual opposing interests of the powers and thus preventing Italy from being drawn into the net of the Western powers and used for their machinations. . . . In my opinion the guiding principle for us arising out of this situation is that we should let Italy take the lead in her Spanish policy, but that we ought simultaneously to accompany this policy with so much active good will as to avoid a development which might be prejudicial to Germany's direct or indirect interests, whether it be in the form of a defeat for Nationalist Spain or in the nature of a direct Anglo-Italian understanding in case of further stagnation in the fighting.[22]

If the Italians wanted a privileged position in Spain, they could not expect Germany to pay the bills. Foreign Minister von Neurath explained the German position:

> The existence of a greater Italian [than German] interest is clearly expressed in the Italian agreement with Franco and will, therefore, also have to be reflected in the amount of aid to be furnished by Italy. I gather . . . that the Italian Government is determined to furnish this aid.

[21] GD, D, III, 157.
[22] Ibid.

A gradual readjustment in the relative strength of German and Italian aid will follow as a matter of course. So far they have been on an equal basis. In the future, provision should be made for reducing German participation as compared with that of the Italians, in accordance with natural interests and local conditions.[23]

Germany was herself rearming and could ill afford to continue sending enormous quantities of arms to Spain. Furthermore, if she were to provide ground troops in addition to the Condor Legion, she might unnecessarily provoke Great Britain and France. She had no desire to abandon Franco altogether, but there were no compelling reasons why she should slow up her own rearmament and create needless international tension by sending him German infantry. If Berlin refused to commit its full resources to helping him, Franco might have to proceed more slowly, but that would not disturb the Germans. In fact, as Hitler pointed out on December 21, it might be to their advantage to see Italy engaged for a long time in Spain.[24] In the light of these considerations, Hitler decided no later than December 2 to let the Italians take the lead in Spain in the future. The flow of German supplies to Spain reached its high point in November 1936, when 26 supply ships

[23] GD, D, III, 142.

[24] In a meeting held on December 21, 1936, Hitler explained his Spanish policy in the following terms: "If the attention of the European powers could further be directed to Spain, this would entail considerable advantages for German policy in Europe. . . . Germany's interests, which alone should be considered, were therefore not so deeply involved in an early conclusion of the Spanish Civil War as to risk a limitation of its own rearmament. On the contrary, German policy would be advanced if the Spanish question continued for a time to occupy Europe's attention and therefore diverted it from Germany" (General Warlimont, who attended the meeting, paraphrasing Hitler; National Archives, Washington, D.C., De Witt C. Poole Mission, interrogation of Warlimont, September 17, 1945). See also the discussion of this point in Weinberg, *The Foreign Policy of Hitler's Germany*, p. 298.

were used to carry men and equipment to the peninsula. In December the number declined to 12. By January, the Germans had sent 4,609 men, 978 vehicles, and 26,000 tons of crated material to Spain.[25] For the next two years Germany continued to provide Franco the large quantities of supplies he needed to wage the war, but refused to send infantry units.

Historians have frequently made much of Hitler's comments about the possible advantages to Germany of prolonging the war and have concluded that Germany in fact deliberately did so.[26] This contention is not supported by the available facts. Throughout the month of December the Condor Legion was continuously strengthened.[27] In January 1937, Berlin sent Franco very large quantities of modern arms and equipment[28] which together with Italian aid, might reasonably have been expected to permit him to crush the Republic. Germany continued to provide substantial aid after Hitler's renewed declarations in the fall of 1937 about the desirability of another three years of fighting in Spain. When Göring proposed dismantling Germany's war effort in Spain to lengthen the conflict, Hitler postponed any decision to an unspecified future date. In fact, the Condor Legion was never dismantled or reduced until the end of the Civil War.[29] Germany's refusal to make an all out effort to end the war quickly cannot be equated with a positive policy of prolonging the conflict, as is often done. It is true that Hitler did not do everything he might have to shorten the war, but that is a far cry from deliberately prolonging it.

[25] Whealey, *German-Spanish Relations January–August 1939*, p. 27; Frank, *Seapower, Politics, and the Onset of the Spanish War, 1936*, pp. 338–39.

[26] Weinberg, *The Foreign Policy of Hitler's Germany*, p. 298. Wiskeman, *The Rome-Berlin Axis*, p. 91.

[27] Horton, *Germany and the Spanish Civil War*, p. 110.

[28] *Infra*, p. 174.

[29] Merkes, *Die Deutsche Politik gegenüber den Spanischen Bürkerkrieg*, pp. 127–28.

ITALIAN SHIPMENTS IN DECEMBER AND EARLY JANUARY

Immediately after the December 6 meeting in Rome, a special office was set up in the Italian foreign ministry, under Ciano's direct authority, to coordinate all Italian aid to Spain. As head of this *Ufficio Spagna*, Ciano chose Count Luca Pietromarchi. The forty-one year old Pietromarchi had entered the diplomatic service in 1923. He belonged to a well-known aristocratic family and fit perfectly the classical type of aristocratic career diplomat. He was not a personal friend of Ciano's and had only returned to Rome recently after seven years spent in the secretariat of the League of Nations. According to his own account, he had made an impression on Ciano by his frank criticism of the young minister's proposals for dealing with the League of Nations, and that is why he was chosen for this important new post.[30]

The new office's functions were very broadly defined: "centralization of all requests from the Military Mission in Spain; coordination of the activities of the three military ministries to expedite reply to the requests; and handling of all affairs related to collaboration with the Spanish Nationalist forces."[31] The office functioned as a situation room and was the exclusive communications link between Italian forces in Spain and all military and civilian authorities in Rome.[32] Special radio facilities were established on Monte Mario to permit communications between the foreign ministry in Palazzo Chigi and the Italian military mission in Spain. The military ministries thus lost all direct contact with events in Spain and much of their decision-making power. The fact that no very serious conflicts arose from this major invasion of the military ministries' sphere of competence reflects their subservience to the regime.

[30] Interview with Count Luca Pietromarchi, Rome, July 7, 1970.
[31] Final report of the Ufficio Spagna, p. 1, MAE, Ufficio Spagna, b. 1.
[32] *Ibid.*, p. 3.

By this time, Mussolini had thoroughly domesticated the armed services and placed at their head men who were unable or unwilling to defend the perogatives and powers of their office against attack, although in most cases they felt no great loyalty to the regime or to the Duce.[33]

The *Ufficio Spagna*, though formally a part of the foreign ministry, was principally concerned with the military aspects of the Spanish problem. It also received all incoming dispatches from Italy's diplomatic and consular agents in Spain, and decided which were to be dealt with by the ministry's political affairs section and which were to be reserved for the minister's personal attention. The political affairs section never even received copies of many of the most important incoming and outgoing telegrams and reports. This bypassing of the ordinary channels of the foreign ministry was not a unique occurrence, characteristic of Spanish affairs alone. It was part of the general pattern of Fascist diplomacy, which tended to concentrate both power and information in the hands of the minister and his personal staff.[34]

On December 7, the Duce placed all Italian forces in Spain under General Roatta's command and instructed him to make contacts with Franco and the German representative, General von Faupel, about the setting up of a joint headquarters staff. On the same day some twenty-three hundred "volunteers" coming from La Spezia and Milan encamped in the province of Salerno. The men were already formed into units and were wearing colonial uniforms, slightly different from those of the troops sent to Italian East Africa. Some of the officers already had Spanish emblems. Soldiers from royal army units who had volunteered for service in an unspecified location outside of the country were being concentrated in Rome, Bologna, Net-

[33] On the relations between Mussolini and his generals, see Rochat, "Mussolini e le forze armate," pp. 3–22.
[34] Gilbert, "Ciano and His Diplomats," p. 519.

tuno, and Civittavecchia. Arrangements for forming these groups had begun before the December 6 meeting. As early as November 23 the police in Massa-Carrara and Grosetto reported that the Fascist militia was beginning to mobilize troops for Spain.[35]

On December 9, Italy formally offered Franco assistance in the formation of mixed brigades to be made up of four or six infantry battalions, one tank company, two groups of artillery, and a company of engineers. The Italian government promised to supply the officers, NCOs, and troops needed to instruct and command the artillery and engineers' companies, and to send complete tank crews, radio-telegraph sections, and one group of artillery for each brigade. In addition, Rome would provide uniforms, arms, and munitions for all the brigades. Franco was asked to specify how many brigades could be organized and what Italian personnel and material would be needed.[36]

No hard and fast decision to send large units of Black Shirts to Spain was made until December 10, although Rome had been discussing the matter for two weeks, and Ciano had told von Hassel at the end of November that everything was ready. On December 10, the head of the *Ufficio Spagna* received a note from Mussolini ordering three thousand volunteers to be sent "to put some backbone into the Spanish National formations."[37] During the preceeding two weeks the militia had enrolled an entire division, principally at Potenza and Reggio Calabria in south central and southwestern Italy. The men were now in training camps in the province of Naples.[38]

On December 11, Pietromarchi and General Russo, the

---

[35] ACS, pubblica sicurezza, direzione generale degli affari generali e riservati, 1920–1945, 1936, b. 15, f. 1.

[36] SHM CGG, L. 387, C. 2.

[37] Final report of the Ufficio Spagna, p. 7, MAE, Ufficio Spagna, b. 1. Interview with Count Luca Pietromarchi, Rome, July 7, 1970.

[38] ACS, pubblica sicurezza, direzione generale degli affari generali e riservati, 1920–1945, 1936, b. 15, f. 1.

167

commander of the Fascist militia, visited the camps to assemble the units, which Mussolini had ordered to have ready for departure within two weeks. The prospects were discouraging. Many of the recruits were unemployed men who were desperate enough to support their families by serving as mercenaries in Spain. Some were habitual drunkards or had long police records. Others were ill or over forty. But time was too short to permit considering alternatives, so orders were given for three thousand men to be ready to leave within a week. Mussolini had said nothing about any further departures, but Pietromarchi requested Russo to begin preparing a second contingent.[39]

On December 14, Colonel Faldella handed Franco a note announcing that three thousand Black Shirts would soon disembark in Cadiz. The troops would arrive already formed into companies commanded by Fascist militia officers. The Italian government requested that the companies be distributed among different regiments of the Spanish Foreign Legion or of the other Nationalist infantry units, but kept under their own company commanders.[40] Franco reacted to the announcement of their arrival with annoyance. "Who requested them?" he asked, stressing that he had not approved their dispatch.[41] He had recently expressed to General von Faupel his interest in receiving well-trained and equipped German and Italian divisions to be used in an attempt to make a breakthrough,[42] but he had no need of three thousand hastily assembled militia under the command of Black Shirt officers. Furthermore, he was offended that Mussolini had given orders for the men to leave for Spain without asking his permission or working out the details with him.

Embarkation date for the first three thousand Black Shirts was set for December 18. Sometime in the course of the

[39] Interview with Count Luca Pietromarchi, Rome, July 7, 1970.
[40] SHM CGG, L. 387, C. 1.
[41] Interview with General Emilio Faldella, Milan, October 4, 1970.
[42] GD, D, III, 147.

intervening week, Mussolini decided to send a considerably larger number of men, and to employ them in purely Italian units, rather than intermixed in the Spanish Foreign Legion or metropolitan infantry.[43] His desire to have them act independently is directly related to his decision to increase their number greatly. As long as only relatively small groups of infantry were contemplated, it would be pointless to demand that they form a separate brigade. Once he had decided to send more than a full division, autonomy began to be a reasonable proposition that offered the possibility of winning recognition and glory for the soldiers of Fascism. Mussolini was being told that "a division or two of an Army like ours would cut through the Spaniards like hot butter, and in a couple of months would finish their stroll with a clean sweep all the way to the coast."[44] It is not surprising, then, that he wanted autonomous Italian units organized so that the glory of their exploits would be reflected directly on Italy, on Fascism, and on their Duce.[45]

The first three thousand Black Shirts sailed for Spain on the old trans-Atlantic *Lombardia* on December 18. They embarked in Gaeta, forty miles north of Naples, where the walls of the ancient port provided protection against curious eyes. At General Roatta's orders, the men went on board in civilian clothes and without their weapons.[46] The *Lombardia's* name had been painted over, and depar-

[43] On December 16, he told German Ambassador von Hassel that the Italians would be employed as "independent columns" (GD, D, III, 156).

[44] Barzini, letter to Barella, December 7, 1936, ACS, segreteria particolare del Duce, carteggio riservato, 241/R (Barzini).

[45] On December 30, 1936, Mussolini ordered the commander of the militia, General Russo, to send soldiers with impressive physiques. The Germans, he said, had made a good impression by so doing [ACS, segreteria particolare del Duce, carteggio riservato, 463/R (Spagna) SF. 6].

[46] On January 25, 1937, Mussolini ordered that later groups be embarked in uniform (NA T 586, roll 1062, frame 062995).

ture was timed so as to permit passing the Straits of Gibraltar in the dead of night with all lights extinguished and in strict radio silence. Few precautions, nonetheless, were taken about arrangements for disembarking the troops unobserved, and their arrival was soon reported in the world press, which generally doubled their number to about six thousand.[47]

During the second half of December, preparations continued at an increasing rate. Three ships sailed from La Spezia between December 23 and 28, carrying some fifteen hundred tank crewmen, artillery men, radio operators, and other specialists. On December 29 the *Lombardia*, whose funnels had been repainted to make identification more difficult, embarked another three thousand men for Cadiz. Two days later the *Sardegna* sailed from Naples with about twelve hundred specialists.[48] Italian troop departures for Spain as of December 31, 1936, including the fifteen hundred men sent by the army prior to December 1, are reflected in table 4.

TABLE 4

Italian Troop Departures for Spain
through December 31, 1936

	Militia	Army	Total
Troops & NCOs	7,591	2,120	9,711
Officers	257	96	353
Total	7,848	2,216	10,064

SOURCE: NA T 586, roll 1062, frame 062980

Final arrangements with Franco for the formation of two mixed brigades had been made on December 17.

[47] *Times* (London), January 5, 1937.
[48] List of ship departures prepared by the Ufficio Spagna for the period from December 23, 1936 to February 17, 1937, MAE, Ufficio Spagna, b. 3; GD, D, III, 170.

Franco would supply the troops and Italy would provide officers, instructors, and specialists. Each brigade was to have six battalions, three 65-mm batteries, two artillery groups with six batteries, a tank company, and an engineers' company. The Italians proposed to send 130 officers, 150 NCOs, and 1,600 troops for each brigade.[49] The personnel was provided by the army, and was largely shipped to Spain between January 1 and January 10. During those ten days another 5,465 men left for Spain. The army provided 290 officers and 3,172 troops, the militia 134 officers and 1,329 troops. This brought the total number of Italian ground forces in Spain to 15,529, of which 60 percent were militia and 40 percent army.[50]

During the month of December, both sides in the Civil War had given most of their attention to rebuilding and reorganizing after the heavy losses incurred in the struggle for Madrid in November. The Nationalists held the initiative, but conducted only probing operations. Early in January they launched a major attack along the Coruña road to the northwest of the capital. Ten days of heavy fighting led to some fifteen hundred casualties on each side, but the battle ended in another stalemate. The Nationalists had advanced some ten kilometers and gained a number of advantageous positions, but had failed once again in their attempt to take Madrid.

Mussolini's Meeting with Göring and Further Shipments

As the battle of the Coruña road was drawing to a close, another important meeting was held in Rome to lay plans for further aid to Franco. Germany was represented by Hermann Göring. It was obvious to all present that by this time the Duce's prestige was so completely involved in Franco's success that he was no longer counting the

[49] SHM CGG, L. 386, C. 2.
[50] NA T 586, roll 1062, frame 062981.

costs of victory: "It is absolutely indispensable," he declared, "that Franco be victorious. Otherwise we would suffer a defeat, and Russia could claim to have won her first victory over Western Europe."[51]

Mussolini was troubled by the fear that Italo-German aid only made Franco more confident of final victory and led him to proceed more slowly, rather than stimulating him to greater efforts. Göring agreed that the aid already provided should have permitted Franco to win the war, if he had used it more efficiently and energetically. The trouble was, in his opinion, that the Spaniards were badly organized. Not only did they fail to plan their strategy effectively, they did not even succeed in distributing the material they received in a rational way. Some areas were badly lacking supplies, while others had more than they could use. The size of Italian commitments in troops as well as in material gave Rome a perfect right, Göring insisted, to urge Franco to proceed more rapidly with the war, and to ask him to accept a joint Italo-German general staff to help plan future operations. The Germans had been insisting on this point for some time. At the end of January, Franco finally did accept the proposal, but little every really came of it.[52]

In any case, Franco would now need additional aid in order to make a successful final offensive possible. Germany would be willing to supply more material, and a certain number of specialists, but Göring said she would not consider supplying a full division or any other organized large units, since the international reaction would be too severe. He pointed out that France would react far more violently to the presence of Germans than to the presence of Italians in Spain, and Germany could not justify the risks involved in provoking the French to such a degree. Mussolini accepted Göring's conclusions without demurring, although

[51] My account of the meeting is based on the official Italian minutes (MAE, Ufficio Spagna, b. 3).
[52] GD, D, III, 124, 137–39, 155–56, 203.

the Italian representative in Berlin had only recently been instructed to urge the Germans to send more troops to Spain.[53]

Mussolini's failure to press Göring for greater German commitments in Spain reflects his hesitation about the growing German presence in the Mediterranean. On the one hand, he would have liked to see Berlin carry a larger part of the burden in Spain. On the other hand, he was anxious to keep German influence there to a minimum. As Ciano told Cantalupo in January 1937, "If we close the door of Spain to the Russians, only to open it to the Germans, we can kiss our Latin and Mediterranean policy goodby."[54]

Italy could not continue sending troops forever, the Duce said, but she could offer 9,000 more. The important thing was to set some clear limit on the amount of aid the two countries were willing to provide and then send it quickly, informing Franco that he should expect nothing further in the future and would have to win the war with his own resources. Whatever was needed could be sent during the next two weeks. The application of international controls would have to be avoided during that period. Then, at the end of the month, Italy and Germany should demand rapid enforcement of the most stringent controls possible to cut off French and Soviet aid.

The impatience and dissatisfaction with Franco's conduct of the war that Mussolini revealed in his interview with Göring, rather than leading to a reduction in Italian assistance, seems to have contributed to its further increase. The Duce was already too deeply committed to draw back, and could not afford to let time take its course, even supposing that it was working in Franco's favor. The most promising plan of action was to send enough men and material to enable Franco to win quickly, perhaps before spring. The nine thousand men mentioned to Göring already had

[53] GD, D, III, 200.
[54] Cantalupo, *Fu la Spagna,* p. 65.

their orders and apparently sailed between January 11 and January 17.[55]

At the meeting it was agreed that Rome and Berlin would draw up a list of what they could provide for what was presumed to be the last big push to put Franco over the top. On January 23 a joint Italo-German note was presented to Franco by the Italian ambassador. It informed him that although all aid would have to cease shortly, the two governments were willing to make a last supreme effort to insure his victory.[56]

The Germans offered no further personnel, but the quantity of material they proposed to ship to Spain was impressive: 60 aircraft, 10 minesweepers, 50,000 rifles, 180 pieces of regimental artillery, 32 77-mm cannon, 12 150-mm cannon, 52 antiaircraft guns, 117 million small-arms cartridges, 450,000 artillery shells, and 65,000 rounds for antiaircraft guns. For the first time the Germans began to provide really modern equipment, including Dornier 17 and Heinkel 111 bombers and a few prototypes of the Messerschmitt 109 fighter. The Me 109s were clearly superior to the Russian *Ratas*, which had swept the He 51s out of the Madrid sky in November, but the first full squadron of Me 109s would not reach Spain until March.[57]

The Italian air force promised to deliver fifteen RO 37 reconnaissance planes, twelve CR 32 fighters, and three S 79 bombers, all with crews and replacement parts. The possibility was held out that another twelve planes might be sent during February. If all shipments had to be finished by January 31, eleven thousand more Black Shirts, formed into six regiments, each with a battery and a mortar platoon, would be sent. They would be commanded by an Italian general. If shipments could continue until February 10, a special army division of another eleven thousand men

[55] FRUS, 1937, I, 230; and DDF, 2, 4, p. 327.

[56] Text in MAE, Gabinetto, b. 1.

[57] Horton, *Germany and the Spanish Civil War*, pp. 131–32; Salas Larrazábal, *La guerra de España desde el aire*, p. 145.

TABLE 5

Italian Troop Departures for Spain through February 18, 1937

Personnel by Arm and Corps	Generals	Colonels	Field Grade Officers	Other Officers	NCOs	Troops	Totals
General Staff (in service or with Diploma of War College)	—	—	33	20	—	—	53
Carabineri	—	1	—	10	35	316	362
Infantry	4	9	41	439	775	9,129	10,397
Artillery	1	2	20	257	282	3,536	4,098
Engineers	1	—	2	32	61	748	844
Medical Corps	—	—	13	97	37	816	963
Commissariat and supply	—	—	6	22	9	130	167
Motorization	—	—	3	49	28	2,571	2,651
Chemical warfare	—	—	—	5	13	264	282
Total army	6	12	118	931	1,240	17,510	19,817
Black shirt militia		8	54	1,100	1,973	25,871	20,006
Totals	6	20	172	2,031	3,213	43,381	48,823

SOURCE: MAE, Ufficio Spagna, b. 2.

would also be sent. In actual fact, the second of these two plans was adopted. Eleven thousand Black Shirts were shipped from Gaeta and Naples between January 23 and January 31, and eleven thousand men of the royal army sailed between February 1 and February 7.

By February 18, the total number of Italian ground forces shipped to Spain had reached almost forty-nine thousand. Approximately 40 percent were members of the royal army, while the other 60 percent came from the Fascist militia. Table 5 gives a detailed analysis of the composition of these forces. By the same date, the Italian air force had sent 277 pilots and 702 other officers and men to Spain, whereas on December 1 there had been only 144 pilots and 205 other officers and men in service there.[58]

The massive Italian troop buildup in Spain between December and February was accompanied by an equally spec-

[58] MAE, Ufficio Spagna, b. 2.

tacular increase in the quantity of Italian material entering Spain. As can be seen in table 6, in two and a half months Rome sent to Spain some 130 aircraft, 2,500 tons of bombs, 500 cannon, 700 mortars, 12,000 machine guns, 50 whippet tanks, and 3,800 motor vehicles. Transporting men and material had required the use of 62 ships, of which 5 carried only troops, 21 carried troops and equipment, and 36 carried only material.

For the sake of comparison, we might note that according to Salas during the first quarter of 1937 the Republic received 184 aircraft from the U.S.S.R and 65 from other countries.[59] According to German observers, from December through February, twenty-four ships passed through the Dardanelles carrying to Republican Spain 18 airplanes, 302 guns, 179 tanks, 135 trucks, 29,500 tons of war material and 10,000 tons of ammunition.[60] In addition the Republic received considerable aid from France, from Russia's Baltic ports, and from Central Europe, but there is no information available on its extent. In any case it seems that at this time Italo-German aid to Franco considerably outweighed aid to the Republic.

By February 16, the Italians in Spain had been organized into four purely Italian divisions that formed the Corps of Voluntary Troops or *Corpo Truppe Volontarie* (CTV) under the Command of General Mario Roatta:

–1st Black Shirt Division, "Dio lo Vuole," commanded by General Edmondo Rossi;

–2nd Black Shirt Division, "Fiamme Nere," commanded by General Amerigo Coppi;

–3rd Black Shirt Division, "Penne Nere," commanded by General Luigi Nuvoloni;

–Littorio Division (army), commanded by General Annibale Bergonzoli.

[59] Salas Larrazábal, *Historia del ejército popular de la República*, III, p. 3422.

[60] Watt, "Soviet Military Aid to the Spanish Republic in the Civil War 1936–1938," p. 541.

TABLE 6

Italian War Material Sent to Spain through February 18, 1937

	Through Nov. 30, 1936	Dec. 1, 1936– Feb. 18, 1937	Total as of Feb. 18, 1937
Bombers	19	21	40
Fighters and assault planes	69	86	155
Other aircraft	30	23	53
Total aircraft	118	130	248
Bombs (metric tons)	1,500	2,471	3,971
Cannon	54	488	542
Mortars	50	706	756
Rifles	—	105,000	105,000
Machine guns	102	1,211	1,313
Submachine guns	—	2,109	2,109
Hand grenades	70,000	2,130,000	2,200,000
Artillery shells	148,000	1,150,000	1,300,000
Ammunition for small arms and automatic weapons (millions of rounds)	16.5	123.5	140.0
Whippet tanks	35	46	81
Trucks, ambulances, automobiles, etc.	53	3,730	3,783

SOURCE: MAE, Ufficio Spagna, b. 2.

The organization of the mixed Italo-Spanish brigades was proving considerably more difficult. Franco had decided that they should be manned by members of the Falangist militia, rather than by troops from regular Nationalist army units. At a meeting between the future Italian commander of the 2nd Mixed Brigade, Colonel Sandro Piazzoni, and Falange leaders from the province of Badajoz, where the brigade was to be formed, it was decided that the Falange would provide some NCOs and officers up to the rank of captain, in addition to troops. The Falangists expected to give the brigades a distinctively Falangist tone, using their own terminology, uniforms, and emblems. On the basis of this understanding, four hundred Falangists were mobilized and dispatched to the brigade as officers and NCOs to begin preparing for the arrival of the troops.

Early in February, Piazzoni changed his mind and informed the Falangists that they would have to be content to serve as simple soldiers and that he was unwilling to have them employ their terminology or uniforms and emblems. This naturally caused great discontent. Tension grew to such a point that on February 8 the provisional national head of the Falange, Manuel Hedilla, ordered that no more Falangists be incorporated into the brigade.[61] Franco's energetic intervention temporarily solved the crisis, forcing the Falangists to give way on most substantive points. New difficulties developed later in the month, when the Falangist militia men began to be incorporated. The Spanish liaison officer with Franco's headquarters reported on February 24 that the Falange was sending its least able elements. The men were lacking in military discipline, and many were physically unfit for duty. Italian doctors had rejected three hundred out of one group of seven hundred.[62] Of forty-six hundred Falangists sent in February and March, about 30 percent were rejected. Early in March, Franco was forced to use a thousand army recruits to complete the unit's strength.[63]

Franco's plans for using Falangists proved even less successful in the case of the 1st Brigade than of the 2nd. The Seville Falange, which was to provide five thousand men, proved totally unable or unwilling to do so. By early

[61] Hedilla, letter to Franco, February 6, 1937, SHM CGG, L. 387, C. 7; note on a telephone call to Franco's headquarters from the military governor of Badajoz, February 8, 1937, SHM CGG, L. 387, C. 7.

[62] Captain Barba, letter to Colonel Barroso, February 24, 1937, SHM CGG, L. 387, C. 6.

[63] Piazzoni, letter to Franco, March 6, 1937, SHM CGG, L. 387, C. 12. Complete data on the composition of the brigade are not avail-

March the brigade had its full complement of officers and most of its equipment, but no troops had arrived. Franco, in disgust, finally gave up the idea of using Falangists and sent 5,000 army recruits.[64] Only the 2nd Mixed Brigade, therefore, was actually made up principally of Falangists.

At sea as well as on land, Italian aid to the Nationalists grew. From mid-November on, two Italian submarines operated off the Spanish coast, using the Spanish Nationalist flag, but manned by Italian crews and based in Italian ports. On November 22, one of them, the *Toricelli*, was submerged off the port of Cartagena when it sighted the Republican cruiser *Jaime Primero* and a few minutes later the destroyer *Miguel de Cervantes*. After waiting for a British warship to enter the port, the commander of the *Toricelli* attacked the *Cervantes*, hitting it with two torpedoes and severely damaging it.[65]

Since it could be demonstrated that Franco had no submarines of his own, it was clear that the *Cervantes* had been torpedoed by either an Italian or a German submarine, and geographic factors pointed to Italy. Subsequent protests did not discourage Rome from leaving the submarines in the Nationalists' service, and even increasing their

---

able, but the following partial figures give some idea of its composition. It seems unlikely that the number of Italians increased significantly after March 1.

Date	Officers	NCOs and Troops
January 18, 1937	72	500 (all Italians)
February 10, 1937	145	2,500
March 1, 1937	161 (103 Italians)	5,600 (1,154 Italians)
March 20, 1937	217	8,000

SOURCE: Piazzoni, *Le "Frecce Nere" nella guerra di Spagna (1937–1939)*, pp. 18 and 27; Invrea, "La verità su Guadalajara," p. 22.

[64] Note on Barroso's report of March 2, 1937, SHM CGG, L. 387, C. 10.

[65] Mission report by the commander of the *Toricelli*, MAE, Ufficio Spagna, b. 3.

number to six in December, but severe restrictions were imposed on their activities. Italian commanders were ordered to avoid launching torpedoes if there was any possibility that Nationalist naval units or airplanes could achieve the objective. In no case was an attack to be carried out against merchantmen unless they were clearly identified Republican or Russian ships, entering port with a cargo. Even then the attack was always to take place within the three mile limit, not on the high seas.[66]

These conditions hampered the Italian subs, since it was virtually impossible to identify with certainty a merchantman flying a false flag, but their presence did not become useless. The Republican fleet had been circumspect since the beginning of the war, and after the torpedoing of the *Cervantes* it became even more timorous, hardly ever venturing out of port, for fear of Italian submarines. This paralysis of the Republican fleet gave the inferior Nationalist surface fleet a free hand to carry out its war on traffic.

Italian naval activity in support of Franco grew steadily. By mid-February 1937, 13 cruisers, 22 destroyers, 2 PT boats, and 7 auxiliary ships had navigated 117,000 miles, engaged mostly in escorting merchantmen and in exploratory and protective missions. On two occasions Italian surface vessels had carried out shore bombardments. A total of 42 Italian submarines had operated off the coasts of Spain, navigating 200 days on the surface and 135 days under water. They had sighted 133 vessels suspected of being Republican warships or merchantmen carrying supplies to the Republic. In the 15 cases in which they had been able to identify positively the ship as being Spanish, they had launched 27 torpedoes, sinking one freighter and damaging another, in addition to crippling the *Cervantes*.[67]

[66] Cervera Valderrama, *Memorias de guerra*, pp. 60–63; unsigned report of the navy ministry on "Italo-German Collaboration in Spain," December 4, 1936, MAE, Ufficio Spagna, b. 3.

[67] Report prepared by the Ufficio Spagna, MAE, Ufficio Spagna, b. 2; and research notes of Professor Willard C. Frank.

Between December 1936 and February 1937, the character of Italy's military intervention in the Spanish Civil War had been completely transformed. From providing instructors and advisors, Rome moved rapidly to establishing an expeditionary army in Spain. The process was carried out piecemeal. Mussolini made decisions on the spur of the moment, and orders were given for their implementation without any serious attempt to coordinate them. Despite the existence of the *Ufficio Spagna*, no overall plans were established and no timetable or order of priorities was set down.

In this entire process, the initiative lay with Rome. The first contingents of troops were already on their way to Spain before Franco was even notified of Italy's intentions. He does not seem to have been consulted frequently about plans for subsequent troop shipments, except as regards the mixed brigades. On at least one occasion during the period we are discussing here, the Caudillo showed his annoyance with Italy's cavalier attitude toward his authority, and this would become a continuing problem, with important implications for Italo-Spanish relations.

RECRUITMENT OF THE CTV

Where did the forty-eight thousand Italians sent to Spain come from? What were their motives, and how did they feel about the Spanish conflict? An important part of the answer is found in the figures already given: fully 43 percent of the Italian troops were members of the regular Italian army. The army "volunteers" were, of course, by no means a homogenous group. Many were authentic volunteers, attracted by the possibilities of experience and promotion and by the better pay that service in Spain offered, or motivated by a desire to fight against Communism, or simply by a desire for adventure. It is impossible to estimate the number of such volunteers, but it seems reasonable to suppose that they constituted a high percentage of the officers and other professional soldiers who eventually found their way to Spain.

To judge from mortality statistics, it seems that the army personnel sent to Spain was recruited in disproportinately large numbers from southern Italy and the islands. Northern and central Italy accounted for almost two thirds of the country's population, but only slightly more than one third of the mortalities. The South and islands, with roughly one third of the population, suffered two thirds of the mortalities. As much as 8.3 percent of the men killed were from Sardinia, which had only 2.4 percent of the population, whereas only 2.8 percent of the men killed came from Piedmont, which had 8.0 percent of the population.[68]

The conditions of service were quite favorable, especially for officers. They could improve their promotion prospects by serving in Spain, and the pay was good. A general received a special indemnity of 3,534 lire upon departure and the same amount after four months in Spain. A colonel received two payments of 1,767 lire, and a lieutenant 1,060 lire at departure and 707 after four months. Supplementary Italian pay for Spanish duty was 192 lire per day for a general, 100 for a lieutenant colonel, 73 for a lieutenant, 27.5 for a sergeant, and 20 for a soldier. A number of benefits granted to veterans of the Abyssinian campaign, such as preferential treatment for employment, were extended to veterans of the Spanish war. Furthermore, the Spanish government granted a monthly supplement of 2,800 pesetas for a general, 1800 for a colonel, 713 for a lieutenant, 542 for a sergeant, and 150 for a soldier. When army units were requested to provide small numbers of troops from the various specialities (tank corps, artillery, machine gunners, etc.) for "duty outside the country" the reply was often enthusiastic. According to reports reaching the French embassy in February, a request to an artillery regi-

[68] See appendix D.

ment stationed in Florence for seven NCOs had been answered by twenty-three volunteers.[69]

The men of the Littorio division constituted a separate case among the regular army personnel sent to Spain. The troops of this division were men who had been drafted later than usual and averaged about twenty-six or twenty-seven years of age. During the month before it was sent to Spain, the division had been employed as extras for one of the more successful Italian films of the period, "Scipione l'Africano." In view of its high average age, it was intended for relatively light guard duty in Africa. The entire division seems to have been simply assigned to duty in Spain, without even a pretext of individual volunteering.[70]

The question of the origin of the Black Shirt volunteers is far more complex and difficult than that of the regular army volunteers. The war in Spain does not seem to have generated a great deal of pro- or anti-Nationalist enthusiasm in Italy during its early months. Police informants did report a certain revival of Marxist propaganda among the working classes, who were stimulated by what little news they could get of the revolution going on in Spain and of the successful defense of Madrid against "Fascist" attacks. But the phenomenon was of limited importance and never reached what could be called widespread support for the Republic or opposition to Mussolini's intervention in favor of Franco.[71]

Before the Fascist party began its official recruiting efforts, some thirty-five hundred to four thousand individ-

[69] Final report of the Ufficio Spagna, pp. 25–27, MAE, Ufficio Spagna, b. 1; DDF, 2, 4, p. 417.

[70] Interview with General Emilio Faldella, Milan, October 4, 1970; Conforti, *Guadalajara*, pp. 185 and 318–19; Lajolo, *Il "Voltagabbana,"* pp. 35–40. The commander of the division, General Bergonzoli, is reported to have told the journalist Sandro Sandri that he had 2,000 or more grey-haired married men in the division (NA T 586, roll 492, frame 048683).

[71] *Infra*, pp. 264–71.

uals volunteered for duty in Spain by contacting the Spanish embassy, or by writing directly to Mussolini, one of the Fascist party leaders, or some other prominent personality. There is no way of telling what percentage of these men eventually joined the Black Shirts in Spain, but an analysis of their characteristics can tell us something about the prevailing climate of opinion in Italy when the party began its recruiting efforts. Half of the group was made up of men over thirty; one fourth was between twenty-five and thirty, and only one quarter were under twenty-five. More than 15 percent were over forty, whereas a meager 6 percent were under twenty. More than 69 percent of the classifiable individuals were manual workers and only 4 percent were students. Almost exactly 25 percent had penal precedents. The group's high average age and low socio-economic status seem to point clearly to economic necessity and social inadaptation as the primary motives for volunteering. Coupled with the low absolute number of men who volunteered before December 1936, this confirms that the early stages of the Spanish Civil War aroused little enthusiasm in Italy for the Nationalist cause.[72]

Judging once again from mortality statistics, it seems that the militia units sent to Spain were more geographically representative of the country than were the army ones. The North again provided a smaller share of the mortalities than its population would have warranted, but the difference was not great and the provinces of Lombardy and Emilia both provided their full share. The South and Center contributed more heavily to the mortalities than to the population, but the islands did not, since Sicily, with 9.3 percent of the population, accounted for only 7.3 percent of the mortalities.[73]

[72] Based on an analysis of data in ACS, pubblica sicurezza, direzione generale degli affari generali e riservati, 1920–1945, 1936, b. 15–17 and 1937, b. 15–17. For further information on this group, see Coverdale, "I primi volontari italiani nell'esercito di Franco," pp. 545–54.

[73] See appendix D.

The first of the three Black Shirt divisions was hastily assembled with troops gathered at random under the auspices of the Fascist Militia (MVSN). The second two were more systematically organized by requiring Black Shirt Legions to provide fully organized battalions. At Bari, around mid-January, the local *fasci* were functioning as recruiting offices. At first, the more fervent local Fascists were called in and requested to place themselves "at the Duce's service" without any further explanation. Until a few days before departure, they were not advised of their destination. When the news finally came, it rapidly cooled the enthusiasm of many, and a good number reported sick in order to avoid departing, for which they were expelled from the party. This first experience taught the local authorities to proceed rapidly and get the men on their way as soon as possible after calling them up.

At Bari recruiting was never a very serious problem since the economic misery of the surrounding countryside was so great that many young men were willing to enlist for the pay.[74] In more prosperous regions, the prospect of better pay was not always attractive enough to bring in a sufficient number of volunteers. At a meeting of the 92nd Legion in Florence on January 20, only one volunteer could be obtained from the three hundred people present. The other fifteen or twenty volunteers the legion was expected to provide had to be drawn by lot.[75] Pressure and deception were frequently used to secure "volunteers." Some men were called up or volunteered to go to Africa as colonists, only to find themselves days or weeks later on their way to Spain. Others were told their true destination, but as-

[74] Final report of the Ufficio Spagna, p. 10, MAE, Ufficio Spagna, b. 1; DDF, 2, 4, p. 327. Reports from the French embassy in Rome are an excellent source of information on the recruiting of Italian volunteers for Spain. Comparisons of French diplomatic reports with secret official Italian reports on sailings show that the French embassy had an extremely good information service in Italy.
[75] DDF, 2, 4, p. 371.

sured they would see no frontline duty. Perhaps more frequent were the cases of men who were subjected to various forms of political and economic pressure by local Fascist authorities. In the atmosphere of Italy in 1937, it was difficult indeed for a man to refuse a preemptory invitation to "place himself at the Duce's orders."

In a few cases, men who were recruited under false pretexts for the Black Shirt Militia were able to obtain redress. Two civilian drivers who refused to don militia uniforms and embark for Spain were jailed but eventually set free because they testified they had been told they would be sent to Africa.[76] The number of those who had the courage and the good fortune to regain their freedom once incorporated into a unit bound for Spain was, however, small indeed.

The majority of the militia men were probably neither deceived nor coerced, but simply sought in enrollment a way to keep their family alive. In April 1937, their average age was between twenty-eight and thirty-two. A group of twenty-three hundred men was reported to have some seventy-three hundred children, or an average of more than three each.[77] The liberal *Manchester Guardian* summarized the situation quite accurately: "Italians have no desire to go and fight for 'National' Spain for sentiment's sake. But thousands have volunteered in a genuine enough sense for the sake of the pay offered them."[78]

CANTALUPO AND FARINACCI

As Italy's military aid to Franco multiplied, her political presence in Nationalist Spain also became more active. The first sign of a new attitude came in early December when Ciano, who had previously refused to authorize more

[76] ACS, pubblica sicurezza, direzione generale degli affari generali e riservati, 1920–1945, 1936, b. 15.
[77] Interview with General Emilio Faldella, Milan, October 4, 1970.
[78] *Manchester Guardian*, February 17, 1937.

active propaganda efforts, requested the ministry for press and propaganda to send to Spain publications on Italian corporativism, the *dopolavoro* organization, labor tribunals, and all other outstanding aspects of the regime. He also requested large quantities of photographs of Mussolini and of the ministers and party leaders for distribution to the Spanish press, as well as newsreels to be shown in Spain.[79] In February 1937, an Italian press and propaganda office was opened in Salamanca with considerable financial resources.[80] The head of the office, Danzi, was a personal friend of Ciano's and reported directly to the foreign minister, escaping altogether the control of the embassy.[81] The office was charged with publication of a daily press bulletin, distribution of photographs and propaganda pamphlets, radio propaganda, and so forth.[82]

The question of appointing a regular ambassador to replace the chargé d'affairs, who had been named when recognition was granted to Franco, was taken up in Rome in early January 1937. Apparently, Mussolini first considered the Cremona Fascist leader Roberto Farinacci, ex-secretary general of the Fascist party and member of the Fascist Grand Council.[83] This would have signaled a radical shift in Italian policy, to one of working actively for a Fascist Spain. There is no way of knowing how seriously Mussolini considered making Farinacci ambassador but the fact that two months later he sent him on a special mission to Spain seems to indicate that he was in fact tempted to abandon the policy of allowing Franco to make his own political decisions in favor of an effort to implant a Fascist regime in Spain.

[79] Telegram by hand 15057, December 10, 1936, MAE, Politica. b. 23.

[80] Interview with Bruno Morini, Rome, May 10, 1970.

[81] Artiere, *Quattro momenti di storia fascista*, p. 205.

[82] Final report of the Ufficio Spagna, pp. 100–101, MAE, Ufficio Spagna, b. 1.

[83] Cantalupo, *Fu la Spagna*, pp. 75–77.

Farinacci's appointment would have been totally unacceptable to France and England, since it would have been interpreted as an unequivocal sign of Italy's desire to increase her political influence in Spain. Farinacci was also known for his overtly anti-British posture. In February 1937, for instance, his Cremona-based newspaper *Regime fascista* was confiscated for printing a bitter attack on England. "We do not forget," the article said, "that thousands and thousands of our legionnaries have fallen in Spain, thanks above all to the arms and munitions sent by the Franco-Russo-English bloc. Torrents of blood divide today two conceptions and two aims."[84] Franco would have been very unhappy with the appointment also because of Farinacci's violent anti-Catholicism. Franco was not particularly religious himself, but he owed many of his adherents precisely to the Republic's sectarian anti-Catholicism and he could not afford to alienate them. For these reasons, Mussolini abandoned any idea of sending Farinacci, and named as his ambassador Roberto Cantalupo. Cantalupo was not a professional diplomat but a journalist. An exmember of the Nationalist party, he had been sent by Mussolini as Italian representative to Cairo in 1930 and as ambassador to Brazil in 1932. He was certainly more identified with the regime than most of the career diplomats, but he was, of course, far less politically significant than Farinacci.

The new ambassador was given his instructions not by the Duce but by Ciano. Despite increased Italian propaganda in Spain, the foreign minister stressed that he did not want Cantalupo to become involved in the infighting between the different factions of the Nationalist band. As for Italy's longer range objectives in Spain, Ciano disclaimed any interest in seeing a Fascist regime established there: "It is sufficient for us that Bolshevism does not take root in Spain. This is the only true scope of our diplomatic presence in Salamanca. The ideological question in Spain

[84] FO R 1704/23/22.

188

is secondary for us. The principal thing is the defense of Western civilization."[85]

At a second interview, Ciano insisted again on the same point, stressing his desire to avoid any unnecessary European tension. He disclaimed any desire of provoking France, much less England, with whom Italy needed to cooperate in East Africa. Italy, he said, did not want to take over the Balearic Islands permanently nor establish a Fascist dictatorship in Spain.[86] Cantalupo specifies that Ciano claimed this policy as his own and asserted that Mussolini "would be overjoyed" with a totalitarian regime in Spain. The Duce, he said, had wanted to send Farinacci "to make Spain Fascist."[87]

[85] Cantalupo, *Fu la Spagna*, p. 62.

[86] *Ibid.*, p. 77.

[87] *Ibid.*, pp. 75–77. No copies of Cantalupo's written instructions have been found in the archives of the Italian foreign ministry, but one of his first dispatches from Spain confirms his allegation that Ciano instructed him to refrain from trying to influence the internal political development of the Nationalist zone: "As soon as I set foot on Spanish territory, I received proof of the great utility and far-sightedness of Your Excellency's instructions not to show any direct interest in internal politics, and much less give the impression of wanting to intervene in them. This directive of the Fascist Government is the only one that reflects at present the real situation of the parties in Spain with respect to General Franco, and it is therefore, the only one that protects our interests" (Report 235/108, February 11, 1937, MAE, Politica, b. 14). This confirmation of one of the central parts of Cantalupo's thesis lends credibility to his other affirmations, which can neither be confirmed nor disproved with the available archival evidence. The material reproduced in the text seems plausible enough to be accepted, for want of other evidence, as a fairly accurate statement of Ciano's policy in January 1937.

Some aspects of Cantalupo's version of his instructions seem, however, extremely implausible, particularly the affirmation that Ciano instructed him to work for a "liberal and Catholic" Spain and to "avoid the eventuality that Franco, once he takes Madrid, found a totalitarian regime there" (Cantalupo, *Fu la Spagna*, p. 75). I have argued that Italy did not aim at implanting a specifically Fascist regime in Spain, but it is difficult to believe that Ciano would have favored the establishment of a "liberal" regime on "a democratic

There can be no question of Ciano's following a policy of his own in opposition to Mussolini,[88] but there does seem to have been a certain tension between the Duce's tendency to support the development of Fascism in Spain and his son-in-law's efforts to keep Italy out of Nationalist politics. Shortly after Cantalupo arrived in Spain, in fact, Mussolini sent Farinacci on a special mission "to take stock of the situation of Nationalist Spain," and to acquaint Franco with his "ideas about the future."[89] Farinacci's trip apparently signifies that despite having renounced the idea of making him ambassador, Mussolini had not abandoned his plans to promote Fascism in Spain.

Farinacci attempted to convince Franco of the necessity of preparing a concrete program for governing Spain after the war was won, and above all of the necessity of creating a "Spanish National Party" which could be "inserted in each and every agency of the state." He urged that other political parties be abolished, and that there be "only one press, the national press." For the moment, the party's program should not be spelled out in detail, he said, but it ought immediately to take a favorable stance toward the working class.[90]

Franco told Farinacci that he did not intend to count on either the Falangists or the Carlists for the reconstruc-

---

and Christian base" (*ibid.*, p. 76). It seems likely that Cantalupo's desire to present himself as the ambassador of Italy rather than of Fascism has led to some distortion of Ciano's instructions. Cantalupo published his Spanish memoirs in 1948, when his political ambitions would have been badly compromised by any confession of having worked for a totalitarian Spain.

[88] As the dean of Italian diplomatic historians has pointed out, "even in the field of foreign affairs final decisions were made only by Mussolini, and his collaborators were limited to acting in those areas where *il Duce's* will had not yet been determined" (Toscano, *The History of Treaties and International Politics*, I, 276).

[89] Mussolini to Franco, March 1, 1937, ACS, segreteria particolare del Duce, carteggio riservato, 463/R (Spagna), Sf. 6.

[90] Farinacci to Nicolas Franco, March 10, 1937, quoted in Fornari, *Mussolini's Gadfly*, pp. 162–63.

tion of Spain, since neither party had first-rate leaders. Nor was he particularly concerned about the monarchical and dynastic question. "First I have to create the nation: then we will decide whether it is a good idea to name a king."[91] If, as Cantalupo maintains, Farinacci had been sent to Spain to propose that a member of the Savoy family might be chosen to occupy the Spanish throne, this declaration must have caused him to abandon the idea.[92]

The mass executions taking place in the Nationalist zone disturbed Farinacci. On that score, he told Mussolini, there was not much to choose between the two sides:

> To tell the truth, Red and Nationalist atrocities are equivalent here. It is a sort of contest to see who can massacre more people, almost a sport. It seems impossible that a day can go by without a certain number of people being sent to the other world. . . . The population is used to it by now and pays no attention: it is only we sentimentalists who create a tragedy over people who don't deserve it.[93]

The issue seemed to him one on which Rome could take a stand, to show that it had intervened in Spain to protect Fascism from Communist attack, not to support senseless vengence. Without consulting or advising the ambassador, he presented on his own initiative a strongly worded protest to Franco.[94]

At Ciano's instructions, Cantalupo himself had raised the subject of executions with Franco, who had expressed

[91] Farinacci to Mussolini, March 5, 1937, NA T 586, roll 438, frames 026380–81.

[92] Cantalupo, *Fu la Spagna*, pp. 153–54. The idea seems a fantastic one, particularly in view of the clamorous failure of Amadeo of Savoy as king of Spain in the nineteenth century. It cannot be entirely discounted, however, since most of the rest of Cantalupo's version of Farinacci's trip seems to be corrorborated by Farinacci's report to Mussolini.

[93] NA T 586, roll 438, frame 026383.

[94] Cantalupo, *Fu la Spagna*, p. 138.

his concern but indicated that he was not in complete control of the situation.[95] Again on March 7, the foreign ministry instructed the ambassador to protest about the severity of the repression in Málaga, in whose capture Italian troops had played an important part. The province had been the scene of particularly sharp social tensions and of considerable violence during the months immediately preceding and following the outbreak of the civil war and passions were running very high. According to Italian estimates some 2,800 official executions took place in Málaga in February alone, and in all some 5,000 people were executed there, with similar numbers losing their lives in Seville, Caceres, and Badajoz.[96] At Cantalupo's suggestion, an official request was made in Mussolini's name that all political trials be put off until the end of the war. The concrete results of this request were the removal of two particularly severe military judges in Málaga and clemency for nineteen Masons who had been condemned to death there.[97]

On May 21, 1937, the consul in Seville, Conti, reported that executions were still being carried out in Málaga at a rate of twenty per day, although the frantic pace of the earlier days had given way to greater calm and greater legal guarantees for the accused. According to the consul's report, ten thousand people were still being held in prison on Málaga, whose population in 1934 was two hundred thousand. The Italian consul in Málaga was still actively engaged in assisting the families of those in jail and of the executed, but the introduction of greater legal formalities in the proceedings had considerably diminished his effectiveness in obtaining clemency for men condemned by the tribunals.[98]

[95] *Ibid.*, pp. 130–34.
[96] MAE, Ufficio Storico-Diplomatico, *Spagna. Situazione Politica, 1937*, p. 8, in NA T 586, roll 1291 (no frame numbers).
[97] NA T 586, roll 492, frames 048712 and 048755.
[98] Report 1806/121, May 21, 1937, MAE, Politica, b. 14.

Farinacci was not impressed with Franco's potential as an aspiring Fascist political leader. He correctly noted that Franco had little interest in political theory and was concerned only with winning the war and maintaining for a long time afterwards a dictatorial government. "The man," he wrote to Mussolini, "is politically thin." He described him as "a rather timid man, whose face is certainly not that of a *condottiere*."[99] In their assessment of Franco, if in little else, Farinacci and Cantalupo seem to have agreed. In describing the presentation of his credentials, Cantalupo wrote: "He stepped out with me on the balcony that offered an incredible spectacle of the immense piazza, but was incapable of saying anything to the people that applauded and waited to be harrangued; he had become cold, glassy and feminine again."[100]

Farinacci did not limit himself to talking to Franco, but made direct contact with the Falangist leader, Manuel Hedilla. He gives no details of the contents of their conversation, except to say that the Falangists had agreed to meet with him and a group of Requeté leaders "to lay the foundations of a new national movement, which Franco ought to strengthen and use."[101] His conversation with Hedilla strengthened Farinacci's conviction that the Falange was the only group in Spain that was oriented toward Rome and regarded Fascism enthusiastically.

The Falangists and Requetés had already been in contact with each other to discuss possibilities of unification. Their conversations had come to an end in late February without any concrete results, but on an amicable note.[102] If the meeting that Farinacci announced to Mussolini ever took place, it had no practical consequences. The fusion of the Falange and the Traditionalists would soon take place,

[99] Farinacci to Mussolini, March 5, 1937, NA T 586, roll 438, frame 026380.
[100] Report 404/197, March 1, 1937, MAE, Politica, b. 29.
[101] NA T 586, roll 438, frame 026384/1.
[102] Thomas, *The Spanish Civil War*, pp. 527–28.

but at Franco's order and with very little consideration for the feelings of the leaders of the two parties, and without regard for his allies' opinions.

Farinacci's attempts to promote Fascism in Spain had few if any practical consequences, and Italy soon returned to a less aggressive line with respect to Nationalist politics. This may have been due to Mussolini's loss of interest in the topic or to a change of opinion, but it may also have been an indirect result of the Italian defeat at Guadalajara. Even if the Duce wished to continue encouraging the growth of Fascism in the Nationalist zone, his possibilities of exercising a real influence were much reduced by the loss of prestige suffered at Guadalajara. Had the outcome of the battle been favorable to the Italians, it is possible that Farinacci's mission would have been the starting point of a new Italian policy. In fact, however, it stands out as an isolated incident.

The "Gentlemen's Agreement"

During the period we have been discussing in this chapter, Spain occupied a central place on the international scene. The arrival of the Condor Legion, the international brigades, and the Italians of the CTV lent an air of urgency to efforts to contain and circumscribe the conflict and prevent it from growing into a European war. On the surface, it seemed that considerable progress was being made. Italy and Great Britain reached a "Gentlemen's Agreement" in which they pledged to respect the status quo in the Mediterranean, and the Non-Intervention Committee managed not only to prohibit the departure of volunteers for Spain but to develop an international control scheme to enforce the prohibition. All of this, however, seems curiously unreal when viewed against the background of massive Italian shipments of men and material to Spain. In fact, the characteristic note of most of the international relations surrounding the Spanish question during this period seems to be precisely their disjunction from reality.

The ostensible aim of both London and Rome was not only to avoid drifting further apart but to reestablish the cordiality that had existed between them prior to the Ethiopian crisis and the outbreak of the Spanish Civil War. On November 1, in the same speech in which he coined the term "Axis" to describe the relations between Rome and Berlin, Mussolini made a bid for talks with London. The response was favorable, although Eden was not convinced that Italy was sincere in her desires for better relations with England. Time and again, Mussolini had affirmed that his final aim was to reestablish a Roman Empire. As long as he held that goal, Eden maintained, Italy could "hardly enter into sincere collaboration with England, the one great obstacle in her path." Tactical motives, he believed, made it advisable, nonetheless, not to rebuff the Italians and so keep them from coming too close to Germany or becoming too much of a nuisance in the Arab world.[103]

The announcement of Italy's recognition of Franco took London by surprise, but had little appreciable influence on Italo-British relations. Eden's concern over Italy's intervention in Spain was limited to preserving the territorial status quo. He wanted to prevent Italy from taking control of any Spanish territory or establishing permanent military or naval bases in Spain or her colonies. If that could be achieved, he would not complain that Italy continued to support Franco. In response to a question in the House of Commons on November 19, Eden declared that other governments were more guilty than Germany and Italy in questions of intervening in Spain. The war office's report that the available evidence did not support his statement did not lessen his desire to improve Britain's relations with Italy.[104] His declarations in the House of Commons had

[103] Eden, *Facing the Dictators*, p. 482.
[104] FO W 16391/9549/41.

been less a statement of objective fact than a sign of his willingness to overlook possible obstacles to an agreement. Actual negotiations opened in early December and were carried out in Rome. The basic agenda for the discussions and their limitations had been outlined by Eden in mid-November. The heart of the agreement would be a mutual recognition of Mediterranean interests and a declaration of the intention to respect them. England would not for the present recognize the Italian conquest of Abyssinia, but wished Rome to accept the territorial status quo in the Mediterranean and to stop anti-British propaganda in the Near East.[105] Italy accepted the agenda and conditions without difficulty, but refused to accede to Britain's desire to have France participate in the agreement.

As Italo-British negotiations were getting under way in Rome, a flurry of other activities related to Spain took place on the European diplomatic scene. On December 2, the Non-Intervention Committee approved the general lines of a plan for the control of Spanish ports, airfields, and borders in order to stop the flow of arms.[106] Until this time, the Non-Intervention Committee had dealt exclusively with the supply of war material to the two sides in the Spanish conflict. The growing influx of fighting men into both camps now made it seem that some steps would have to be taken to prohibit the entrance of volunteers if the danger of a European conflict were to be averted. At the suggestion of Lord Plymouth, the British chairman of the committee, an ad hoc subcommittee was designated to study this new aspect of the problem.

The concern of Paris and London over the arrival in Spain of the German Condor Legion moved them not only to press for progress in the Non-Intervention Committee, but to make proposals outside its cumbersome framework. In a note sent directly to Germany, Italy, Portugal, the USSR, and the United States, they invited them to: "re-

[105] Eden, *Facing the Dictators*, pp. 482–83.
[106] Vedovato, *Il nonintervento in Spagna*, I, 59–61.

nounce all direct or indirect intervention, to work in the NIC for an effective control scheme, and to try to mediate the conflict."[107] The Italian reply to this note, sent on December 14, did not flatly reject the mediation proposal, but pointed out the practical difficulties involved in carrying out any sort of plebiscite in Spain and cynically suggested that "the Spanish people have already sufficiently expressed their consensus in favor of the national Government, which has progressively won the consent of the majority of the population and control of the majority of the national territory."[108]

Even before the Italian reply was received, Eden had attempted another expedient. It took the form of a proposal to Grandi that the Spanish question be discussed by Great Britain, France, and Italy alone, to the exclusion of Germany and Russia. It is understandable that Eden was impatient with the Non-Intervention Committee's endless debates and almost inexhaustible possibilities for delay, but the move was a clumsy one. Unless she were offered a proportionate incentive, Italy could hardly be expected to accept a proposal that would necessarily be interpreted in Berlin as an abandonment of her German partner. Furthermore, in tripartite meetings with France and Great Britain about Spain, Italy could expect to find herself regularly in the minority. Eden's proposal was rejected and Rome notified Berlin of its contents.

Action was also proceeding on another front. From December 10 to 16, the League council met in Geneva to hear an appeal from the Spanish Republican government. Neither England nor France was pleased at the prospect of bitter debates in Geneva at a moment when they were trying to put forward their mediation proposal. Eden and French foreign minister Delbos both refused to attend the meeting. Secretary-General Avernol was eager to avoid em-

[107] Royal Institute of International Affairs, *Survey of International Affairs 1937*, II, 271.
[107] Quoted in Vedovato, *Il nonintervento in Spagna*, I, 60.

broiling the League in the conflicts arising out of the Spanish question.[109] As the Fascist press gleefully pointed out, even the Soviet foreign minister refrained from going to Geneva.[110] Consequently, the League council could only adopt a series of innocuous proposals, expressing its hope for the acceptance of the recent Franco-British proposals, and exhorting the members of the Non-Intervention Committee to work to make its activities more effective.

In both Paris and London, concern over Italian activities in Majorca was increasing. The ever growing Italian air strength stationed on the island, the construction of three new airports, the introduction of Italian as a compulsory language in Majorcan schools, and Bonaccorsi's control of the Falange were all viewed with alarm in both capitals. The French chargé in Rome told Ciano that his government was giving its full attention to developments in the Balearic Islands. "The establishment of any foreign authority over a position which dominates France's lines of communication with North Africa," he warned, "would affect French vital interests and create a situation which no French Government could regard with indifference."[111]

On December 14, Eden presented the cabinet with a memorandum on Italian activities in the Balearic Islands. Its tone was grave, even alarmist. Eden suggested that Italy seemed to be on the verge of establishing a protectorate there and that the conclusion the chiefs of staff had reached in August—that Italian control of Majorca would not threaten vital British interests—might need to be revised in view of the construction of new military airports on the island. In any case, he argued, from the strictly political point of view, leaving aside all military considerations, England could ill afford to let Italy gain effective control of the Balearic Islands, since that

[109] Barros, *Betrayal from Within*, pp. 146–52.
[110] *Nuova Antologia*, December 16, 1936, p. 466.
[111] The French embassy in London communicated the text of his instructions to the foreign office (FO W 18182/9549/41).

would damage the prestige on which the British empire depended for its survival.[112] Neither Eden's fellow cabinet members nor the chiefs of staff shared his alarm, so no action was taken beyond a request to Rome that the Gentlemen's Agreement include a clause in which both countries would proclaim that they did not intend to take control of any Spanish territories.[113]

In the light of all this activity, one might have expected the Spanish question to have occupied a paramount position in the negotiations between Rome and London for a general Mediterranean agreement. In fact, except for the question of the Balearic Islands, Italian intervention in Spain was not much discussed. Far more attention was paid to anti-British propaganda in the Near East than to Italian arms shipments to Spain.[114] As a concession to the British, Bonaccorsi was withdrawn from Majorca shortly before Christ-

[112] "The Abyssinian crisis, discovering as it did the inadequacy of British military preparations and a widespread reluctance in this country to employ a threat of armed resistance to a course on Italy's part which was diametrically opposed to the declared policy of England as of other members of the League of Nations shook British prestige as nothing else had done since the conclusion of the war. . . . I do not like to contemplate how grave would be the risk to our position in the Mediterranean if Italy were permitted with impunity to make another move such as the establishment of Italian control in the Balearic Islands. . . . No man can foresee what disastrous modifications might not take place in the status of an Empire depending for its paramountcy not only upon armed strength but upon opinions, nor what unexampled efforts in arms might not be exacted from us before the position could be reestablished" (FO W 18182/9549/41).

[113] Eden, *Facing the Dictators*, pp. 484–85. On January 19, 1937, the chiefs of staff reaffirmed their position that Italian occupation of the Balearic Islands threatened no major British interests [CP 10(37)].

[114] FO R 7373/226/22. On December 16, 1936, in response to a question, Mussolini told the German ambassador that the British had not brought up the Spanish question during the negotiations in course (GD, D, III, 156). The archives of the British foreign office confirm that this was substantially true.

mas.[115] The arrival of the first contingent of three thousand Italian Black Shirts in Cadiz on December 22, however, was not even reflected in the negotiations.

The text of the Italo-British agreement signed on January 2 contained no specific mention of Spain, but it declared that the parties "disclaim any desire to modify or, so far as they are concerned, to see modified the *status quo* as regards national sovereignty of territories in the Mediterranean area." This was made more explicit in a separate exchange of notes in which Ciano assured Eden that "so far as Italy is concerned, the integrity of the present territories of Spain shall in all circumstances remain intact and unmodified."[116]

British foreign office officials were jubilant over the treaty and particularly over the notes on Spain. The head of the southern division observed on January 1: "We have obtained all our requirements, and what is particularly satisfactory is the acceptance without alteration of our formula regarding Spain." Eden himself was hardly less enthusiastic: "I agree that this is very satisfactory . . . . It is particularly satisfactory that we should have obtained our formula regarding Spain and I am glad that we were firm about this."[117]

At the very moment the treaty was being signed, Rome was preparing fresh contingents of troops for embarcation. No effort was made to hide the fact that Italian troops were pouring into Spain in increasing numbers, although Ciano did try to maintain the fiction that they were volun-

---

[115] British representatives in Rome had repeatedly requested Bonaccorsi's removal, and the foreign office believed that it took place in response to British pressure (FO W 18772/9549/41).

[116] The English text of the agreement is found in Eden, *Facing the Dictators*, pp. 484–86. The Italian text is in *Trattati e convenzioni*, 51, pp. 26–27. Ciano had refused to include a specific reference to Spain in the agreement itself, alleging that to do so would be insulting to Franco. He did not, however, object to the publication of the exchange of notes.

[117] FO R 12/1/22.

teers for whom the government was not responsible.[118] From a strictly juridicial point of view, sending troops to Spain could not be said to be a violation of the terms of the agreement. As the British authors of the *Survey of International Affairs* noted, "The published terms of the declaration of the 2nd January, 1937 . . . left Signor Mussolini free to follow this path, for . . . it made no mention of any undertaking to respect the independence of Spain or refrain from intervention in her internal affairs."[119]

British leaders were, nonetheless, understandably disturbed by the massive shipments of Italian troops and material to Spain during January. The arms and ammunition were being sent in clear violation of the Non-Intervention Agreement, and the shipments of troops were, they felt, contrary to the spirit, if not to the letter, of the Gentlemen's Agreement. The Italians, for their part, regarded London's expressions of shock at their continuing aid to Franco as naive and disingenuous. During December, Italy had clearly expressed her determination to secure Franco's victory.[120] The British had been willing to sign the agreement despite Italian troop shipments in late December and

[118] Ciano, *Ciano's Diplomatic Papers*, p. 78. The German ambassador in France remarked to his superiors: "The principle followed by the Italians of conceding a part [of the truth about their intervention in Spain] and representing this as being an answer to French assistance is undoubtedly more effective [than a flat denial]" (GD, D, III, 191).

[119] Royal Institute of International Affairs, *Survey of International Affairs 1937*, II, 280.

[120] Several times during the final weeks of negotiations, authoritative organs of the Italian press openly hinted that Italy did not intend to stand by idly in the presence of a Communist threat in the Mediterranean. The *Giornale d'Italia* stated in an editorial on December 15: "The Franco-British [mediation] proposals do not seem to take into account that in Spain an irreconcilable war is being fought between order and disorder, between the Nation and the anti-Nation." On the same day, the Fascist party daily *Popolo d'Italia* commented that "for a thousand reasons, and especially because of the inadmissability of the eventual establishment of a Bolshevik state in Catalonia,

had not even insisted on receiving a reply to their note on volunteers before doing so. These factors, combined with Rome's general conviction that London wanted Franco to defeat the Republic, may have led the Italians to suppose that their aid to Franco need not damage their relations with Great Britain. The shipments of arms and men to Spain after the signing of the "Gentlemen's Agreement" does not necessarily imply that Mussolini did not really desire a détente with England. It certainly does mean, however, that he was willing to risk spoiling the effects of the Gentlemen's Agreement if that proved to be the price of insuring a rapid Nationalist victory.

A week after the Gentlemen's Agreement was signed, Italy and Germany finally responded to a Franco-British note of December 26 about the prohibition of volunteers. Like the earlier Portuguese and Russian replies, their notes professed willingness to prohibit the enlistment and departure of volunteers providing others did the same. Eden wanted to take them at their word and offer the services of the royal navy for the necessary control. His fellow cabinet members, however, were unwilling to commit the British navy to policing a ban on volunteers, so London simply welcomed the replies of the other powers and noted the general desire to exclude foreign volunteers from Spain.[121]

During the first two weeks of January, authorities in Rome apparently believed that Italy would soon have to accept some form of effective international control of shipments to Spain. Their plan was to pour large quantities of aid into Spain before controls were initiated, and then press for their stringent application. Mussolini's conversation with Göring on January 13 was based on the premise that Italo-German shipments to Spain would have to be completed by February 1. The note given to Franco on

---

it would be impossible to expect an Italo-German adhesion" to the mediation proposal.

[121] Eden, *Facing the Dictators*, pp. 489–491.

January 23 still contemplated the possibility that all shipments might have to cease by February 1, although it held out the hope that they might possibly be continued until midmonth. It is not at all clear why Mussolini thought an agreement would be reached so quickly. The Non-Intervention Committee had already shown its almost infinite capacity for delay. Even had all parties been animated by the best of intentions, formidable technical problems stood in the way of implementing an effective control scheme in a period of three weeks.

On January 25, Italy declared her willingness to prohibit the recruiting and departure of volunteers, provided that other governments did the same and that an effective control scheme was established. By this time, Rome and Berlin had made plans for completing their own shipments to Spain. It was in their interests to cooperate with the British to prevent further men and material from reaching the Republican zone, so they dropped their previous condition about establishing effective international controls before taking other measures. On February 20, Italy and the other members of the Non-Intervention Committee that had not previously done so put into effect bans on volunteering.[122]

The Non-Intervention Committee seemed to be making rapid progress. By February 16, it had hammered out the outlines of a control system to be put into effect on March 6. New difficulties arose over the presence of international controllers on the Portuguese frontier, and over the Soviet Union's demand to be allowed to participate in naval control on an equal footing with Great Britain, France, and Italy, but these obstacles were soon overcome. On March 8, the plenary meeting of the Non-Intervention Committee agreed on a control scheme to go into effect on March 13.[123]

The rapidity and apparent ease with which work in the

[122] Vedovato, *Il nonintervento in Spagna*, I, 94.

[123] Royal Institute of International Affairs, *Survey of International Affairs 1937*, II, 289–92.

committee was progressing created an international atmosphere of détente and confidence. There were, however, grounds for a less sanguine estimate of the situation. As Italian troop commitments had grown, the Italian press had become increasingly open about the presence of Italian "volunteers" in the ranks of Franco's army, although any official intervention in Spain was still systematically denied. In early March, the Grand Council of Fascism went much further toward officially identifying Italy with Franco's cause by approving an order of the day which expressed solidarity with Nationalist Spain and saluted Franco's armed forces.[124] As Ciano noted when instructing Cantalupo to read the document to Franco, this constituted a "public solemn manifestation of solidarity."[125] Under these circumstances, only the most optimistic observer could have expected the control plan to go into effect without serious difficulties, even had events on the battlefields of Spain not profoundly modified the situation.

[124] *Nuova antologia*, March 16, 1937, p. 211.
[125] Telegram 528/R 175, March 3, 1937, MAE, Politica, b. 14.

SEVEN

ITALIAN TROOPS IN ACTION: MÁLAGA
AND GUADALAJARA

MÁLAGA

As Italian troops poured into Spain in January 1937, Franco's forces held about 60 percent of the country, leaving the Republicans in control of two separate blocks. Their northern sector comprised a 200-mile long strip on the Atlantic coast, including the Basque provinces, Santander, and part of Asturias. The main body of Republican territory included the Mediterranean coast from the French border to Marbella, 50 miles northeast of Gibraltar. Within it, three areas were easily distinguishable. In the north, Catalonia and Aragon formed a truncated inverted right triangle, 175 miles deep at its base at Port Bou on the French border, but tapering down to about 70 miles in depth at Castellón de la Plana, 250 miles to the southwest. The southern sector was a strip of coast twenty-five miles deep running a hundred miles from Marbella to Motril, in the provinces of Málaga and Granada. Between these two lay the largest block of Republican territory, a rough square stretching from Castellón to Motril and reaching inland an average of 250 miles from the coast to its western border, which ran northeast to southwest from the Sierra de Guadarrama to the Sierra de Guadalupe, passing El Escorial and Talavera de la Reina. In the vicinity of Madrid, a dangerous bulge had been created in the Republican front during the Nationalists' fall offensive. Thirty-five miles west of the city, the front turned sharply and ran almost due east to the outskirts of the capital, where it turned south for 25 miles to near Aranjuez before jogging west again along the south bank of the Tajo River. This gave the Nationalists control of an area 50 miles long and 25 miles deep immediately south and southwest of Madrid, between the Tajo River and the city. With the northern border of the Republican territory situated only 40 to 50 miles north of Madrid, the capital was in constant danger of encirclement.

Studying this map, Roatta decided to employ his forces for the first time in an attack on Málaga, the Mediterranean port situated in the narrow strip of territory that ran from Marbella to Motril. Málaga was near the disembarcation point of the Italian troops in Cádiz and was one of the few areas in which relatively favorable weather for an offensive could be expected in midwinter.

Ciano enthusiastically approved the attack on Málaga, which fitted in perfectly with his outline of what he hoped would be the decisive actions of the war. In mid-January the young foreign minister explained to Ambassador Cantalupo that Italian forces under the command of General Roatta would first capture Málaga and then continue up the coast to Valencia, where the Republican government had taken refuge in November, when the fall of Madrid appeared imminent. The troops would then be transported to Guadalajara to participate in an attack on Madrid, forming the northern half of a pincers that would close around the city. After the fall of the capital, Bilbao and Santander would be taken, leaving Catalonia to face alone the combined onslaught of all the Nationalist forces, aided by their Italian allies.[1]

The beginning of the first part of this triumphal march through Spain was delayed by organizational difficulties. The Italian units had been hastily assembled and many of the officers and men lacked training and experience. Their material had also been hurriedly prepared and shipped. During a storm many of the trucks stowed in the holds of the transports had broken loose and had been badly damaged. Crates lacked adequate marking, and con-

[1] Cantalupo, *Fu la Spagna*, p. 64.

fusion reigned supreme on the wharf, where they were unloaded in haphazard fashion. When the moment to leave Cádiz finally arrived, it became clear that many of the men enlisted as drivers had never driven a truck before. During the ninety mile trip from Cádiz to Seville accidents were frequent (see map 3).

By the end of January, most of the difficulties had been overcome and the 1st Black Shirt Division began to occupy its starting positions for the attack on Málaga. The operational plans drawn up by Roatta and distributed on January 30 called for an attack by three columns. The right column, which would attack from Antequera through Almogia to Málaga, would be made up of three battalions and supporting artillery, a tank company, an armored car platoon, an engineers' platoon, and two 105-mm batteries. The central column was to be the strongest, with four completely motorized battalions and their supporting artillery, one tank company, one company of motorized machine gunners, four batteries, and one engineers' company. It took up positions in Loja and was to occupy Colmenar before descending on Málaga. The left column was to begin its attack from Alhama, proceeding from there to Vélez Málaga. It was made up of three battalions with supporting artillery, a 105-mm battery, a 20-mm battery, and an engineers' company. A reserve of three battalions and an armored car platoon was situated at Villanueva de Tapia.

The Italian forces were to attack simultaneously with a Spanish column that would proceed along the coast from Marbella through Fuengirola and Torremolinos toward Málaga. Three other Spanish columns would operate to the west of the Italians' right wing, in the sector between Ronda and Antequera, and a fifth Spanish column would operate between the Italian right and center columns. The main role, however, belonged to the Italians, whose superior firepower and mobility would enable them rapidly to outdistance the slower Spanish forces.[2]

[2] Martínez Bande, *La campaña de Andalucía*, pp. 160–62.

Map 3

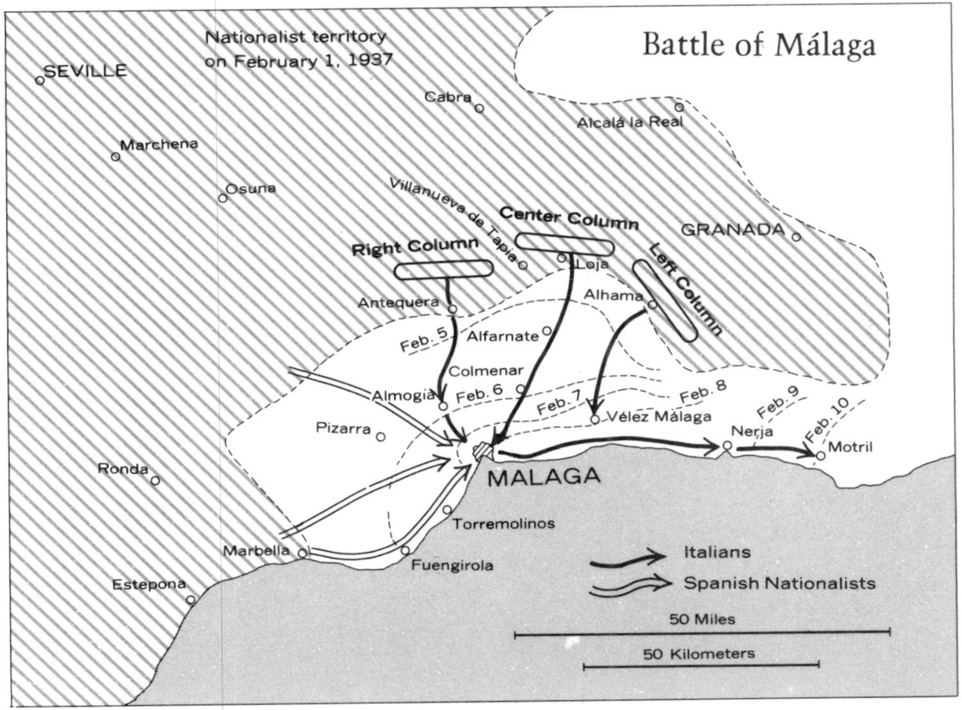

Battle of Málaga

Nationalist territory
on February 1, 1937

SEVILLE

Marchena

Osuna

Cabra

Alcalá la Real

GRANADA

Villanueva de Tapia

Antequera

Ronda

Pizarra

Almogía

Colmenar

Alfarnate

Alhama

Loja

Left Column

Center Column

Right Column

Feb. 5

Feb. 6

Feb. 7

Feb. 8

Feb. 9

Feb. 10

Vélez Málaga

Nerja

Motril

MALAGA

Torremolinos

Fuengirola

Marbella

Estepona

Italians

Spanish Nationalists

50 Miles

50 Kilometers

The attacking ground forces were supported by some fifty aircraft: thirteen bombers, six reconnaissance planes, and thirty fighters, based in Seville and Granada.[3] Naval support was provided by the Nationalist cruisers *Canarias* and *Almirante Cervera*, as well as by four Italian PT boats that were towed to the area by the Italian destroyer *Da Verazzano*.[4]

The assault began at dawn on February 5. Surprise was only partially achieved, but the Italians' rapid advance disoriented the defense. The central column met the stiffest resistance and had to be reinforced on the 5th and 6th with three battalions taken from the reserve. General Roatta was wounded while trying to get the stalled central column going again, but he retained overall command of the Italian forces until the end of the operation. By February 7 all resistance had been overcome. The next day the Italian right and center columns, together with Spanish forces, occupied Málaga, while the Italian left column took Vélez Málaga.[5]

The coastal route from Málaga to the east had deliberately been left free to encourage the Republican forces to flee rather than make a desperate last stand. After the fall of the city, a column was organized to pursue the fleeing militia forces. At midnight of February 8 an infantry battalion, supported by a tank company and a group of 100-mm cannon set off in pursuit, reaching Vélez Málaga on February 9. There the column was reinforced with troops from the forces that had occupied Vélez Málaga. Italian aircraft strafed retreating militia men and civilians, who were pursued by the ground units until February 14, when a halt was called at Motril, some fifty miles up the coast from Málaga. Ciano's fantastic plans for marching

[3] *Ibid.*, p. 161.
[4] Final report of Admiral Ferretti, head of the Italian naval mission in Spain, consulted by the author through the courtesy of Admiral Ferretti.
[5] Martínez Bande, *La campaña de Andalucía*, pp. 164–66.

all the way to Valencia, 375 miles away, were out of the question. It might have been possible to reach Almería, seventy miles up the coast from Motril, but the city could have been held only by advancing the whole Granada front and occupying the passes of the Sierra Nevada, an operation which would have required considerably more manpower than was available.[6] Italian casualties during the operations were relatively heavy, considering the brief duration of the fighting. There were 9 officers and 85 men killed, and 26 officers and 250 men wounded for total losses of 372, including 2 men missing in action.[7]

During the Málaga campaign the Italians employed their recently developed *guerra celere* tactics, a sort of *blitzkrieg* in which motorized columns moved ahead very rapidly, spearheaded by armored cars. After the first day of the attack, little effort was made to protect the flanks of the attacking columns despite the rugged terrain, which would have facilitated a counterattack. Their security was entrusted almost exclusively to the rapidity of their advance, which was expected to disorganize the defenders and prevent them from reacting.[8]

If the tactic was successful, it was largely due to the weakness of Málaga's defenses. There were only about twelve thousand Republican defenders for a 175-mile front, and their armament was deficient. On January 11, 1937, the sector could muster only eight thousand rifles, fifty-

[6] Faldella, *Venti mesi di guerra in Spagna*, pp. 249–50.

[7] Secret official figures contained in a report of the Ufficio Spagna on losses in Spain from October 29, 1936 to September 15, 1937, MAE, Gabinetto, b. 2. The *Almanacco del Regio Esercito, 1939–1940*, p. 480, gave losses as 500. I have generally accepted and given in the text the secret official casualty figures compiled by the Ufficio Spagna for internal use. It is possible, of course, that they may have been mistaken or even deliberately falsified, but I have found no concrete evidence that convinces me that they are not the most accurate sources available. It is worth pointing out that these figures were not intended for publication.

[8] Faldella, *Venti mesi di guerra in Spagna*, p. 248.

seven submachine guns, sixteen cannon, and twenty-two mortars. Ammunition even for the available arms was sorely lacking.[9] Italian submarines operating off Spain's Mediterranean coast had made supplying Málaga difficult and risky, and had discouraged the Republican fleet from venturing from its harbors to contribute to the city's defense.

The state of the Republican forces in the province had changed very little since July. Militia bands without solid military discipline, which had been replaced in the rest of Spain by more organized and disciplined forces, were still the chief defense of Málaga.[10] President Azaña wrote of Málaga: "We had an extraordinary military commander there a short time ago. 'I don't build fortifications,' he said, 'I sow the revolution. If the rebels enter, they will be swallowed up by the revolution.' With that sort of morale they hoped to prepare the defense of a city which is by nature weak and disorderly. The surprising thing is that it wasn't taken sooner."[11]

The Málaga campaign was a minor one, but not without importance. The occupation of the city shorted the front by about 150 miles, and gave the Nationalist control of a Mediterranean port.[12] Some ten thousand prisoners were taken, many of whom were eventually incorporated into the ranks of the Nationalist army. The victory also did much to boost the morale of Franco's forces, who were depressed by their failure to take Madrid; their morale would be sorely tried again during the futile offensive on the Jarama.

[9] Martínez Bande, La campaña de Andalucía, p. 146.

[10] "The Republican forces that defended the Málaga front, a series of battalions and of small militia columns, with a total of about 15,000 men, were in virtually the same precarious state of organization seven months later as at the outbreak of the war." Ibarruri et al., Guerra y revolución en España, II, 237.

[11] Azaña, La velada en Benicarló, pp. 46–47; quoted in Martínez Bande, La campaña de Andalucía, p. 176.

[12] On the effects of the campaign, see Faldella, Venti mesi di guerra in Spagna, pp. 193–94.

Italian authorities were elated, and failed to give sufficient weight to the deficiencies of the defending forces when they drew their lessons from their first action in Spain. As a result, they were badly deceived about the fighting capabilities of the hastily assembled units they had sent to Spain. Predictions that Italian troops would cut through Spanish resistance like hot butter seemed fully confirmed, and the *guerra celere* was judged to be a complete success.

GENESIS AND PLANNING OF THE GUADALAJARA OFFENSIVE

By the end of the Málaga operations, the CTV was fast becoming an expeditionary army of almost fifty thousand men, commanded by 6 generals, 20 colonels, and 172 other field grade officers, including 33 members of the Italian army general staff and graduates of the War College. The division commanders, Edmondo Rossi, Amerigo Coppi, Luigi Nuvoloni, and Annibale Bergonzoli, were older men, formed in the battles of the First World War. Among the staff officers were many of the best graduates of the War College, the 'young lions' who were to lead Mussolini's new Roman legions to victory: Giuseppe Bodini, Aristide Nasi, Bruno Lucini, Giacomo Zanussi, Giorgio Morpurgo, Emilio Molteni, Giuseppe Amico, Massimo Invrea.[13] Mussolini hoped that the CTV would win two or three stunning victories that would put an end to the Civil War, or at least place Franco in a situation of permanent superiority before the nonintervention control scheme came into effect. If their victories were to prove to the world that the new generation of Italians were worthy successors of their Roman ancestors, it was essential that the CTV be used as a single unit under Roatta's orders, in rapid attacks on important objectives.

One of the most promising prospects seemed to be an

[13] The names of the officers of the various units of the CTV are given in appendix B.

attack from Teruel, 150 miles east of Madrid, to Sagunto on the Mediterranean coast just north of Valencia. It would cut the main Republican zone in two, separating Madrid, Valencia, and Alicante from Barcelona and the rest of Catalonia, and would put the Nationalist forces in a favorable position for an assault on Valencia.[14] As a preliminary to this ambitious operation, the CTV planned to use one Black Shirt division and Spanish forces to launch a diversionary attack from Sigüenza toward Guadalajara. In the face of a threat of encirclement of Madrid, the Republican commanders would not dare to move their reserves away from the capital, and the attack on Sagunto could be carried out unmolested (see map 4).

A few days after the fall of Málaga, Roatta returned to Rome to have his wounded arm examined by specialists, leaving his chief of staff, Colonel Emilio Faldella, to make arrangements with Franco for future operations. Faldella reached Salamanca on February 12 and requested an appointment for the following day. During the afternoon Colonel Antonio Barroso, Franco's chief of operations, visited Faldella and discussed with him the offensive which the Nationalist "Reinforced Division of Madrid" had launched to the south and southeast of the capital on February 6. The troops had just succeeded in crossing the Jarama River, and Barroso was jubilant. "Within five days we will reach Alcalá de Henares, cutting all the communications between Madrid and Valencia," he declared.[15]

[14] Faldella, *Venti mesi di guerra in Spagna*, p. 253. The text reflects Faldella's contention that the immediate objective was to be Sagunto, not Valencia itself. As will be seen, however, Franco treated this proposal as one for the taking of Valencia.

[15] Conforti, *Guadalajara*, p. 29. The following account of the genesis of the Guadalajara offensive is based on the material contained in the official report on the battle prepared for Mussolini by the Ufficio Spagna (NA T 586, roll 492, frames 048602–86), hereafter cited as *Report*. The original is found in ACS, segreteria particolare del Duce, carteggio riservato, 186/R Guadalajara. I also make considerable use of Conforti, *Guadalajara: la prima sconfitta del fascismo*. Although

Map 4

Division of Spain:
Feb. 15, 1937

CTV planned offensives

Nationalist territory

When Faldella mentioned that he planned to propose an Italian offensive against Sagunto and Valencia, Barroso immediately replied that it was out of the question. Franco, he said, could never allow the Italians to carry out an independent attack on the seat of the Republican government.

After his conversation with Barroso, Faldella revised the

Conforti's book is marred by inventions and selective use of material to demonstrate a thesis, and he does not cite his sources, it is clear that he has had access to important archival materials not open to other writers. General Faldella has confirmed in a letter to me dated March 25, 1971, that Conforti's account of his conversations with Barroso and Franco prior to March 8, 1937, is substantially correct.

text of the CTV's note to Franco, suggesting that the CTV might be used either for an attack on Sagunto and Valencia, or in large scale offensive from Sigüenza toward Guadalajara.[16] In the second case, the Italians would be the northern half of a pincers whose southern half would be formed by the Spanish forces moving up from the Jarama. The two would meet near Alcalá de Henares, sealing off Madrid. The offensive could begin toward the end of February.[17] On February 13 Faldella and the assistant chief of staff of the CTV, Lt. Col. Giacomo Zanussi, met with Franco, Barroso, and General Moreno. If Faldella had expected to be thanked or congratulated for the Málaga offensive, he was sorely disappointed. Franco said not a word about Málaga, but criticized the CTV's note as "an imposition in the fullest sense of the term."

> When all is said and done, Italian troops have been sent here without asking my authorization. First I was told that companies of volunteers were coming to be included in Spanish battalions. Then I was asked to form Italian battalions and I agreed. Next field grade officers and generals arrived to command them, and finally already-formed units began to arrive. Now you want to force me to allow these troops to fight together under General Roatta's orders, when my plans were quite different. . . . The usefulness of these troops is greatly reduced by the requirement that they always be used together. This is a special kind of war, that has to be fought in a special way. Such a large mass cannot be used all at once, but spread out over several fronts it would be more useful.[18]

[16] Villella is wrong in suggesting that the plan for the offensive was put forward by the Nationalist command (Villella, *Rivoluzione e guerra di Spagna*, p. 219–21).

[17] *Report*, frame 048605.

[18] Conforti, *Guadalajara*, pp. 30–32.

Faldella had strict orders from Rome about using the CTV as a unit in decisive actions designed to contribute to ending the war soon, and he was personally convinced this was the best course.[19] He argued that it was far better not to disperse in different directions a force which could break the existing equilibrium and decide the outcome of the struggle if it were used *en masse,* simultaneously with the rest of the Nationalist army. Franco could hardly disagree on the level of pure military strategy, but he stressed once again that a civil war was a different matter from an international conflict. In a civil war, he preferred slow systematic occupation of territory, with time for the *limpieza* needed to guarantee the political security of the conquered areas. Rapid defeat of his adversaries would leave the country infested with enemies.

Faldella insisted once again:

Your Excellency is undoubtedly right from a certain point of view, but we must consider another vitally important factor: the need to put a rapid end to things. If a violent, rapid attack led to the occupation of Valencia, enemy resistance would crumble everywhere, and Your Excellency could carry out with greater tranquility the political purge that you want to effect in all of central Spain. Furthermore, the action would have many other favorable military and political repercussions.

Franco, however, was adamant and broke off the interview:

I am absolutely opposed to employing the Italian Legionaries against Valencia, because Valencia must be occupied by National troops. . . . I reserve my decision on the employment of the mass of Italian troops, which I would like to use, as I had planned, on different fronts. But I will probably ask you to attack Guadalajara.[20]

[19] Faldella, letter to the author, March 25, 1971.
[20] Conforti, *Guadalajara,* pp. 32–33.

216

Franco's written reply on February 14 grudgingly accepted the Italian proposal for an attack on Guadalajara, but not without stressing again that the Italian plans were far from coinciding with his own desires:

The proposal made by the Italian Military Mission in Spain for the occupation of the central part of Spain coincides in general lines with the decisions of the High Command on future operations. The employment *en masse* of Italian troops was not, however, foreseen. Every effort has, in fact, been made not to give the impression that Italian forces were acting alone and independently. To do otherwise might cause fruitless international tension and could create difficulties and even provoke other interventions.

From the point of view of our internal politics, it is also necessary that decisive actions against politically transcendental objectives not be carried out without the joint action of the Spanish and Italian units. . . .

The action from Siguenza toward Guadalajara whose execution by Italian forces has been proposed, coincides exactly with the general plan described above, and can be carried out within the established limits. The Italian troops can operate in the general direction Siguenza-Guadalajara, establishing their left flank against the Tajuña.[21]

Meanwhile the fighting in the Jarama sector had become extremely bitter, and both sides were incurring heavy losses. By February 16, the Nationalist forces commanded by General Varela had lost all their offensive capabilities, and their attack ground to a halt after one last attempt to advance on February 17.[22] The next day the Republicans began to counterattack, and Varela soon found himself in grave difficulties. His troops were exhausted and fresh re-

[21] *Report,* frames 048603–604.
[22] Martínez Bande, *La lucha en torno a Madrid,* p. 99.

217

serves were nowhere to be had. On February 17 Colonel Barroso requested Faldella to begin as soon as possible the Italian offensive in order to relieve the pressure on Varela.[23] Two days later the proud and battle-scarred commander of the Spanish Foreign Legion, General Millán Astray, again pleaded with the Italian chief of staff to act immediately. Eighteen Italian battalions of the 2nd and 3rd Divisions were being assembled in the Aranda-Almazán area, along the Duero River to the north of Segovia and Sigüenza. It should be possible, he said, to mount at least a small offensive with a few brigades, even though they were not yet fully organized.[24]

The Italians were not willing to sacrifice their men in obscure actions designed to assist the hard-pressed Spanish forces on the Jarama. They considered the CTV an army of shock troops, destined to win resounding victories, not cannon fodder to be consumed in diversionary actions. Faldella, therefore, took refuge in the fact that his units were still being organized and limited himself to promising to do everything possible to speed the beginning of the offensive.[25]

Fortunately for the Nationalists, the Republican forces attacking them in the Jarama had also suffered heavy losses during the previous ten days' fighting and were unable to dislodge them from their bridgehead on the east bank of the Jarama. By February 23 fighting in the sector had died down, due to the exhaustion of both sides. It flared up again briefly at the end of the month, but for all practical purposes the battle was over. In all the Nationalists

---

[23] Faldella, *Venti mesi di guerra in Spagna,* p. 255.

[24] Conforti, *Guadalajara,* pp. 34–36. Faldella stresses that the Spaniards never requested that Italian troops be used in the Jarama sector itself, as Conforti's text seems to imply (letter to the author, March 25, 1971).

[25] Faldella, *Venti mesi di guerra in Spagna,* p. 255; Cantalupo, *Fu la Spagna,* p. 186; Roatta telegram, March 25, 1937, summarizing the battle, NA T 586, roll 492, frame 048777; interview with Count Luca Pietromarchi, Rome, July 7, 1970.

suffered some six thousand losses on the Jarama. Republican losses were probably close to ten thousand.[26]

Roatta was fully aware of the fact that the Nationalist troops on the Jarama had been badly mauled. In a summary of the military situation sent to Rome on March 4, four days before the beginning of the Guadalajara offensive, he reported:

> The adversary, alarmed by the news of our concentration in the Sigüenza area . . . has begun to let up his pressure on the White troops in the Jarama sector and to move International Brigades toward the northeast. The White troops are gradually recovering their breath, but it will certainly be some days before they can carry out a great offensive. All eyes are, therefore, on us.[27]

Despite this fact, Italian planning went ahead steadily, without important modifications. Rome expected the operation to be a major one, culminating in the encirclement of Madrid, as is evident in Mussolini's telegram of March 6 to Roatta: "I have studied the plan that is about to be put into effect and consider it excellent for definitively encircling Madrid and perhaps provoking its surrender."[28]

Franco's attitude toward the impending operations is more difficult to define. After their refusal to allow him to use the CTV at his own discretion, contacts between him and the Italians took place in an atmosphere thick with ambiguity and equivocation. A leading Nationalist

---

[26] Martínez Bande, *La lucha en torno a Madrid*, p. 111. Thomas puts losses on the Jarama at 20,000 Nationalists and 25,000 Republicans (Thomas, *The Spanish Civil War*, p. 492). He adds (p. 493) that the Nationalists lost another 6,000 men in attacks on February 23 and March 1. The second affirmation is obviously based on Cantalupo, *Fu la Spagna*, p. 197. Martínez Bande has correctly pointed out, however, that the 6,000 casualties Cantalupo reports on February 25 and March 1 should actually be referred to the entire offensive (*La lucha en torno a Madrid*, p. 160 n).

[27] *Report*, frames 048607–608.

[28] *Report*, frame 048611.

military historian maintains that after mid-February Franco did not believe that "the projected offensive against Guadalajara would prove decisive, among other things because of its lack of coordination with the Jarama offensive."[29] In his conversation with Roatta on March 1, Franco did stress the difficulties facing the Nationalist forces on the Jarama, but he also assured the Italian commander they would attack simultaneously with the CTV.[30] Roatta's operational order number 12, issued the same day, stated:

The Supreme Command has decided to launch an all-out attack against the Red forces in the Madrid region. It will act against them and against their lines of communications simultaneously from the southeast and the northeast. The action from the southeast will be carried out by the units of the "Reinforced Division of Madrid,"

[29] Martínez Bande, La lucha en torno a Madrid, pp. 117–18. He maintains that the decision to carry it out anyway was based only on the desire to relieve the pressure on the Jarama front and on the vague hope that the Republican defenses might simply collapse. Although he has access to the entire archives of the Nationalist army, Martínez Bande bases this allegation solely on Cantalupo's published account. According to the Italian ambassador, Franco told him at their first meeting, which took place in mid-February, that after the failure of the Jarama offensive the attack on Guadalajara had lost its strategic objective of completing the encirclement of Madrid and would serve merely to lessen the pressure on the Jarama (Cantalupo, Fu la Spagna, p. 109). It is possible that during the dark days around February 20, when his forces were in danger of being thrown back over the Jarama, Franco may have described the actions that he was pressing the Italians to carry out immediately as merely diversionary. It is unlikely that he would have said the whole Guadalajara offensive had lost its strategic objective, since he knew full well that the Duce and Roatta were anxious for spectacular victories and unwilling to use their four divisions to lessen the pressure on Nationalist forces.

[30] Roatta telegram, March 25, 1937, summarizing the battle, NA T 586, roll 492, frame 048778. Salas asserts that the Nationalists on the Jarama were to attack only after the Italians had broken the front in their sector, but he offers no proof for this statement. Salas Larrazábal, Historia del ejército popular de la República, vol. I, p. 864.

which will renew their recently interrupted advance from the Jarama river toward Alcalá de Henares. The attack from the northeast will be carried out by the Voluntary Troops at my orders, who will attack in the direction Sigüenza-Guadalajara. Other Spanish forces will cooperate with us, attacking concentricly from the line Guadarrama-Somosierra-Sigüenza.[31]

Roatta was not alone in believing Franco was still intent on encircling Madrid. General Moscardó, the commander of the Nationalist Soria Division, which was to operate in the Guadarrama-Somosierra sector, issued an order on March 4 that described the objectives of the upcoming operations as being "to cut completely the communications between Madrid and the rebellious zone to the east, closing the circle and forcing the surrender of the city."[32]

The final communications between Roatta and Franco prior to the attack took place in an exchange of letters on March 5. The Italian commander informed Franco that he had set the attack for March 8. In his reply Franco pointed out once more the difficulties facing the Nationalists on the Jarama. In view of their "limited possibilities of penetration, . . . the union of the voluntary troops with those of General Orgaz is a function of the resistance that the latter meet on their front." Nonetheless, Franco accepted "in principle that the union take place southeast of Alcalá, in the region between the Henares and the Tajuña, whose center is Pozuelo del Rey."[33]

Roatta should, perhaps, have read between the lines of Franco's letter the message that he would have to count almost exclusively on his own forces and on those of the 2nd Nationalist Brigade stationed on his right in Somosierra. It is not clear exactly what interpretation he did

---

[31] The entire order is reproduced as an appendix to Martínez Bande, *La lucha en torno a Madrid,* pp. 197–202.

[32] Quoted *ibid.,* p. 203.

[33] Quoted *ibid.,* p. 132 n.

give it. It is unlikely that he would have gone ahead with his plans had he known that during the first days of the offensive the Nationalist forces in the Jarama would fail to move at all.[34] He was not overly concerned, however, at the thought that their attack would be of limited effectiveness. The easy success of his *guerra celere* tactics at Málaga had led him to think his forces could overwhelm the Republican defenders and advance rapidly enough to keep them from massing any significant reserves before he had reached Guadalajara. This, at least, was the underlying assumption of the CTV's plans, prepared by Faldella and only slightly retouched by Roatta after his return from Italy:

> It is my intention to proceed rapidly, by the shortest possible route and in the shortest possible time, to the point at which we can give battle to the main body of the enemy (Guadalajara) or from which, at least, we can manuever against it. This will be achieved by a rapid violent rupture of the enemy defenses across the line Sigüenza-Guadalajara, immediately followed by the advance of a motorized mass on Guadalajara.[35]

For the attack on Guadalajara, Roatta had on paper the most powerful striking force assembled by either side during the first nine months of the Civil War, totalling about thirty-five thousand men. The 1st, 2nd, and 3rd Black Shirt

[34] This point is stressed by Faldella in his letter to the author of March 25, 1971. Canevari, who visited Spain at this time as Farinacci's military advisor, affirms that Franco actually told Roatta his forces could not participate in the action and asked him to call it off until more Spanish units and heavy artillery could be assembled, but that "Roatta, confident of his troops, decided to attack alone anyway" (Canevari, *La guerra italiana*, I, 470). This statement is in conflict with all the evidence cited above and seems to have been dictated by Canervari's personal aminosity toward Roatta, whom he bitterly attacks.

[35] Operational order 12, March 4, 1937; quoted in Martínez Bande, *La lucha en torno a Madrid*, p. 198.

Divisions each had three infantry regiments, plus a 65-mm battery and an engineers and services company for a total of sixty-three hundred men. The Littorio Division was composed of seventy-seven hundred men, formed into two infantry regiments, a machine gun battalion, two 65-mm batteries and an engineers' and services company. The infantry was completed by two independent regiments, the 4th and 5th, with eighteen hundred men each. The corps artillery had two groups of 75-mm guns, four of 100-mm, two of 105-mm, and two of 149-mm, as well as four self-moving batteries, one of 20-mm and the other of 75-mm. Roatta's forces were completed by a tank battalion with eighty-one whippet tanks armed only with machine guns, a company of eight armored cars, a company of motorized machine-gunners, and a corps motor pool.[36] The CTV was extremely well armed by the standards of the Civil War, although it did not enjoy the overwhelming advantage in armament with which many authors credit it.[37]

One of the distinguishing features of the Italian forces in comparison with both their Republican adversaries and Franco's other units was their relatively high degree of motorization. They were not, as many authors contend, however, fully motorized.[38] Trucks and tractors had completely replaced animal traction for transporting material and drawing artillery pieces, but the infantry generally advanced on foot, except when vehicles of the motor pool were temporarily assigned to transporting them, since none of the Black Shirt divisions had sufficient vehicles of its own to carry the troops.[39] Each of the three Black Shirt

[36] *Ibid.*, p. 123.

[37] Thomas, for instance, multiplies by three its number of tanks, which he puts at 250 (*The Spanish Civil War*, p. 495).

[38] Colodny mistakenly asserts that each battalion had seventy trucks in addition to the divisional truck parks (*The Struggle for Madrid*, p. 129). Thomas also gives a figure of seventy trucks per battalion (*The Spanish Civil War*, p. 495).

[39] This point is particularly stressed by Invrea, "La verità su Guadalajara," p. 27. Major Massimo Invrea was the assistant chief

divisions had only about two hundred trucks permanently assigned for carrying its supplies, munitions, and equipment. The Littorio Division was better equipped, with slightly over four hundred trucks. Another fourteen hundred trucks were assigned to the artillery and engineers and to the corps motor pool.

The CTV was to be supported by the Nationalist Soria Division operating on its right flank under the command of General Moscardó, famous for his defense of the Alcázar of Toledo. Moscardó's forces were divided into two brigades. The 1st, commanded by Colonel Infantes, was situated in Somosierra and had a total of about forty-eight hundred men. The 2nd Brigade, commanded by Colonel Marzo, was immediately to the right of the Italians and would collaborate closely with them in the offensive. Its thirteen battalions and three artillery groups had a total of eighty-five hundred men, making it larger than any of the Italian divisions. In preparation for the attack, the recently formed 3rd Brigade was also placed at Marzo's disposition, bringing the total number of men at his orders to well over ten thousand.[40] The forces available for the offensive were, therefore, approximately fifty thousand men, counting the Littorio Division, which was not yet in the sector when the attack began on March 8.

The forces facing the Italians and Spaniards in the Guadalajara-Somosierra sector on March 8 were the ten thousand men of the Republican 12th Division.[41] These troops had carried out a minor offensive against Sigüenza in January with some slight success, but the sector's organization was rudimentary, with the defenders strung out in a single line and no defensive works of any consequence.

---

of staff of the 3rd Black Shirt Division at Guadalajara. The article published in *Secolo XX* was written in 1938 for the war ministry's journal *Rassegna di cultura militare,* but was not published at the time.

[40] Martínez Bande, *La lucha en torno a Madrid,* pp. 124–25.

[41] Lister, *Nuestra guerra,* p. 106.

INITIAL ADVANCE

Roatta's plans called for the 2nd Black Shirt Division to open the attack on March 8, breaking the lightly held Republican front and advancing to the line Almadrones, Hontanares, Alaminos (see map 5). There the 3rd Division, transported in the trucks of the corps motor pool, would execute a passage of lines and continue the offensive along the Saragossa highway toward Torija and Guadalajara. On the morning of the 8th rain was falling and a cold wind swept the plateau, but Roatta was unwilling to delay the attack. At 7:00 A.M. the artillery barrage began, and at 7:30 the 2nd Division was ordered to advance. The troops, who had never seen combat and were discouraged and weakened by the unfavorable weather, showed little tendency to attack.[42] It was around three in the afternoon when the right column reached the outskirts of Almadrones, just to the west of the Saragossa highway. The town was defended by not more than two hundred men and four tanks, but night was falling and the division commander, General Amerigo Coppi, an artillery general who suddenly found himself commanding an infantry division, ordered the attack suspended for the night.[43] When the fighting ceased at the end of the first day the center column had reached Hontanares, but the left and right columns were both stopped short of their objectives, Cogollor-Masegoso and Argecilla.

The first day's operation had witnessed an advance of from four to eight miles despite bad weather, but the lightly held enemy front had not been completely broken and the 3rd Division had not been able to begin its advance down the Saragossa highway toward Torija.[44] In an offen-

[42] "Report of the Royal Carabinieri on the Taking [sic] of Guadalajara," NA T 586, roll 492, frame 048689.

[43] Ibid., frame 048690.

[44] Colodny is mistaken in asserting that the 3rd Division entered combat on the eighth (The Struggle for Madrid, p. 131).

Map 5

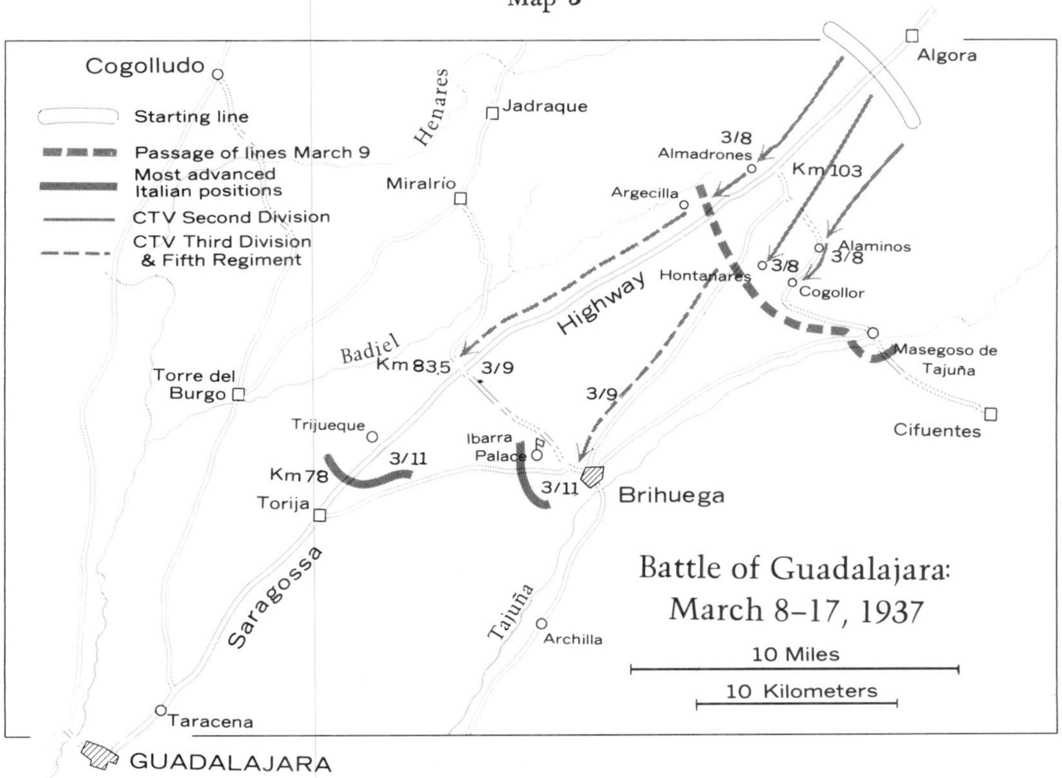

Battle of Guadalajara:
March 8–17, 1937

10 Miles

10 Kilometers

Cogolludo

Starting line

Passage of lines March 9

Most advanced
Italian positions

CTV Second Division

CTV Third Division
& Fifth Regiment

Algora

Km 103

Álaminos

3/8

3/8

Cogollor

3/8

Masegoso de
Tajuña

Cifuentes

3/8

Almadrones

Argecilla

Hontanares

Highway

3/9

Brihuega

3/11

Archilla

Tajuña

Jadraque

Henares

Miralrío

Badiel

Km 83.5

3/9

Ibarra

Palace

3/11

Trijueque

3/11

Km 78

Torija

Saragossa

Torre del
Burgo

Taracena

GUADALAJARA

sive in which rapidity and surprise were to be the chief factors, the delay was important, especially since the Spanish forces in the Jarama sector had failed to attack as agreed. Roatta's information services told him the Republicans were already beginning to rush reinforcements up from Madrid toward Guadalajara. In the evening he formally requested Franco to order an attack in the Jarama sector the following day to fix the Republican reserves around Madrid and prevent their being massed against him.[45]

March 9 was to prove the most successful day of the Guadalajara offensive for the Italians. By 10:00 A.M. Almadrones and Cogollor were taken. The original objectives had still not been fully obtained, but Roatta felt confident enough to order the 3rd Division to execute a passage of lines and begin its advance at 1:30. On paper the operation was a simple one, but the passage of lines proved more difficult than expected. Distances were not properly kept and traffic jams soon developed along the road. It was late in the day when the 3rd Division began to advance along the Saragossa highway toward Trijueque and Torija, and along the road that leads from Almadrones to Brihuega.[46]

Meanwhile the first Republican reserves were being moved into the sector. At midafternoon, small advance units of the XI International Brigade went into action on the Saragossa road, but were unable to stop the advance of the 3rd Division.[47] By 7 P.M. the vanguard of the Italian right column had advanced twelve or thirteen miles, to km. 83 of the Saragossa highway, where it is intersected by the highway that runs from Miralrío southeast to Brihuega. The left column, reinforced by the 5th

---

[45] Conforti, *Guadalajara*, p. 62; *Report*, frame 048615.

[46] Martínez Bande, *La lucha en torno a Madrid*, p. 199; *Report*, frames 048618–19.

[47] Delperrie de Bayac, *Les Brigades Internationales*, p. 249; Martínez Bande, *La lucha en torno a Madrid*, p. 136.

Regiment commanded by Militia Consul Francisci, had advanced down the Almadrones-Brihuega road to about two and a half miles northeast of Brihuega. The position of the Republican forces was extremely critical. Vicente Rojo, who directed the defense of Guadalajara, describes the Republican front as completely broken by evening of the 9th.[48] As night fell, however, the commander of the 3rd Division, General Nuvoloni, called a halt.

The decision could be justified on many grounds. The right column of the 3rd Division was spread out for fifteen miles on the Saragossa highway, and many of the trucks had still not passed a detour at km. 103. The weather was foul, and the men were tired and hungry. It is impossible to say whether the vanguard of the 3rd Division's right column could have succeeded in advancing another five miles to Torija during the night. The XI International Brigade, reinforced with a company of Russian T–26 tanks, was already taking up positions across the Saragossa road and in the woods along the southern edge of the road to Brihuega, but these forces were still not organized and might have been overcome. The risk would have been great, but it could have been justified both in terms of the need to advance rapidly and in terms of the strategic position of Torija. Had the Black Shirts been able to win control of the town during the night, they might well have prevented the Republicans from bringing reserves into the upper part of the plateau. This was all the more important since, despite Roatta's request, Franco's forces in the Jarama had again failed to attack on the 9th, leaving the Republican commanders free to concentrate their forces to the north.[49]

[48] Rojo, *Así fue la defensa de Madrid*, pp. 174–75.

[49] Invrea, "La verità su Guadalajara," p. 25. On March 9 Miaja ordered to the Guadalajara sector "all currently available reserves and any that can be quickly constituted" including all available tanks. Salas Larrazábal, *Historia del ejército popular de la República*, vol. I, p. 869.

The only CTV force that did advance during the night was the 5th Regiment, commanded by Enrico Francisi. Marching the last two and a half miles that separated him from Brihuega before dawn, Francisci burst into the town, taking prisoner the commander of the garrison, 5 officers, and 130 troops, together with two cannon.[50] Francisci's Black Shirts were not, however, the only Italians who were moving in the Guadalajara sector. The Garibaldi Battalion of the XII International Brigade reached Torija during the night and continued to advance toward Brihuega. Early on the morning of March 10 the Garibaldi Battalion took up positions in the woods to the southwest of Brihuega. Simultaneously, other units of the XII International Brigade were entering the Brihuega woods, and El Campesino's 1st Assault Brigade was stationed in Guadalajara in reserve.[51]

Roatta and his staff had no accurate information about the Republican troops movements, but they were unconcerned and exuberant. The Republican front had been broken and its defenders were retreating in disorder. Italian casualties had been relatively light. In the flush of success, it was easy to overlook some of the disquieting defects that had shown up during the first two days' operations.

The light Italian tanks, armed with only machine guns, could not stand and fight against the heavier Russian T–26 tanks equipped with cannon. This made the absence of adequate antitank weapons all the more critical. The infantry had to rely for antitank actions on regular artillery pieces. Until a cannon could be dragged into position and put into action, hours could go by and an entire column could be held up by one or two tanks.

Long lines of trucks loaded with supplies and troops were an inviting target for Republican aviation. During

---

[50] Roatta's telegram of March 10, NA T 586, roll 492, frame 048701.

[51] Longo, *Le brigate internazionali in Spagna*, pp. 227–29; Martínez Bande, *La lucha en torno a Madrid*, p. 138.

the first two days of combat, few serious losses had been incurred, but isolated incidents had shown the vulnerability of columns spread out on the long straight highway that provided a perfect point of reference for Republican planes diving out of the clouds and mist. The combination of bad weather and temporary air fields with dirt runways often prevented Italian planes from getting off the ground to provide air cover against the Republicans, who could take off from the cement runways of the airports around Madrid. The few 20-mm antiaircraft batteries supplied to the advancing columns provided almost no protection against bombing and strafing.

<h2 style="text-align:center">STALEMATE</h2>

Italian headquarters were little concerned about these factors on the evening of March 9 as they planned another spectacular advance for the following day. In fact, however, the CTV's offensive was soon to be brought to a complete halt as the Republicans first held the line and then counterattacked. The next nine days' action was to be concentrated in the small area in which the CTV and the Republican troops were already established by the morning of March 10. The theater is a rough equilateral right triangle whose legs are formed by the Saragossa road from km. 83.5 to Torija (a distance of about six miles), and by the road from Miralrío that runs southeast from km. 83.5 of the Saragossa road to the town of Brihuega; the road running southwest from Brihuega to Torija forms the third side of the triangle. The area is mostly covered with woods, which provide good support for a defensive action on the otherwise featureless plateau. There are few buildings in this sparsely inhabited area. The most important group of buildings is the Ibarra Palace, made up of a villa with a small tower on one side, stables, storage buildings, and several peasant houses, all enclosed by a six-foot wall. It is situated in the woods a few hundred yards off the road that runs from Brihuega to km. 83.5 of the Saragossa highway, about three miles from the town.

Brihuega itself is a town of about three thousand inhabitants, situated in the valley of the Tajuña river. The roads that climb up from the town toward the west twist and turn in rapid ascent before reaching the plateau. To the southeast a bridge over the Tajuña gives access to the area between the Tajuña and Tajo rivers.

On March 10 the attempt to continue the Italian offensive was entrusted to the 3rd Division, which operated in two columns, the left along the highway from Brihuega to Torija, and the right along the Saragossa road. The 2nd Division was gradually being brought up and assembled at Brihuega, but did not participate in the day's action. The advance of the left column was soon halted by the Garibaldi and André Marty battalions of the XII International Brigade. Repeated attempts by the Black Shirts to advance along the road were repulsed. The CTV's light tanks were unable to penetrate into the woods from the road, and artillery support was insufficient to overwhelm or dislodge the defenders.

During the morning Francisci's men, who had remained behind at Brihuega, crossed the bridge over the Tajuña without encountering resistance, and established a bridgehead. They committed the serious error of occupying only a very small area in the Tajuña valley, neglecting the heights on the left bank of the river, although at this time they could have occupied them without difficulty. As night fell, the 3rd Division's left column was still stopped only a short distance from Brihuega, while Francisci's men held a perilously small bridgehead across the Tajuña.[52]

Along the Saragossa highway the 3rd Division's right column also met heavy resistance when it attempted to resume its advance. The 1600 men of the three mixed bat-

[52] Martínez Bande, *La lucha en torno a Madrid*, p. 139.

talions of the XI International Brigade had taken up defensive positions in the woods dominating the highway, and they held up the column during the entire day.[53] The day's fighting took a heavy toll of the Republican defenders, but the Italians also incurred heavy losses and were suffering greatly from the weather, for which they were ill-equipped, and from the defects of their supply system.

By the morning of March 11, the 2nd Division, which had been used for the initial assault on the Republican lines, was drawn up at Brihuega. The forces of the 3rd Division were concentrated along the Saragossa road for another attempt to break through the Republican defenses and take Torija, while the 2nd Division was to attack along the Brihuega-Torija road. In view of the exhaustion of both the 2nd and 3rd Divisions, CTV headquarters ordered no action for the morning, with the attack to begin about noon. The *guerra celere* was already slowing to an *andante ma non troppo* on the fourth day of combat.

The 2nd Division's attempt to advance along the road to Torija was brought to a halt, after a gain of less than three miles, by the tenacious resistance of the defenders established in the woods, although one group of Black Shirts did manage to infiltrate the woods and occupy the Ibarra Palace. Their tactical victory was offset by the loss of a group of thirty-one men and three officers, who were surprised in the dark by men of the Garibaldi battalion and taken prisoner. The 3rd Division, operating along the Saragossa highway, was somewhat more successful. Using flame throwers with devastating effect against the Edgar André Battalion established in the woods along the highway, they managed to take the town of Trijueque and advance about a mile beyond.[54]

---

[53] Roatta's telegram of March 10, NA T 586, roll 492, frame 04872; Faldella, *Venti mesi de guerra in Spagna*, p. 263; Delperrie de Bayac, *Les Brigades Internationales*, p. 250.

[54] Longo, *Le brigate internazionali in Spagna*, p. 280; Conforti, *Guadalajara*, pp. 187–90; Delperrie de Bayac, *Les Brigades Interna-*

This was not the sort of easy success the Black Shirts had been led to expect, and their morale was sinking badly. Mussolini, who was on his way to Libya, could telegraph, "I am certain that the impetus and tenacity of our Legionaries will break the enemy's resistance. Overcoming the International forces will be a victory of great political value as well. . . . Tell the Legionaries that I follow hour by hour their action, which will be crowned with victory."[55] But Roatta, who was closer to the problem, was less sanguine about the morale of his troops. On the evening of the 11th, he decided to call a twenty-four hour halt in the operations in order to allow them to rest, and in the hope that a promised attack in the Jarama sector the following day would relieve some of the pressure on his men.[56] During the first four days of the Guadalajara offensive, the Jarama sector had been almost completely quiet, except for one minor action on March 9. Roatta was furious at the Nationalist failure to launch at least a small offensive that would fix Republican reserves and prevent them from massing against him.

The unexpectedly stiff resistance being met in the Brihuega woods and along the Saragossa highway led the CTV to propose a variation in the original plan of the offensive. The fresh 1st Division would attack in a southerly direction along both banks of the Tajuña River toward the town of Armuña, located twenty miles south of Brihuega on the east bank of the Tajuña. This attack, proposed for the 14th, was to be preceded on the 13th day by a rapid march from Brihuega to Budia, twelve miles southeast of Brihuega and only three miles west of the Tajo River. These

---

tionales, p. 250; Martínez Bande, *La lucha en torno a Madrid,* p. 141 n; Roatta's telegram, March 11, NA T 586, roll 492, frame 048705; Faldella, *Venti mesi di guerra in Spagna,* p. 267.

[55] Telegram sent from Libya, March 11, 1937, NA T 586, roll 492, frame 048754.

[56] Roatta's telegram, March 11, NA T 586, roll 492, frames 048705–706.

two operations would considerably widen the front, expanding it to include the area between the Tajuña and the Tajo rivers. Franco was absolutely opposed to the new plan, which he considered unnecessarily risky. He informed Roatta that he considered the CTV's present position safe, since its flanks were protected by the Badiel and Tajuña rivers, whereas operations to the southeast of the Tajuña would leave the left flank open. Furthermore, the Spanish troops who had advanced as far as Miralrío could not continue their march if the CTV stopped its advance between the Badiel and the Tajuña.[57]

Quite aside from Franco's opposition, events which were taking shape on the other side of the front would soon render impractical the plans for operations between the Tajo and the Tajuña. Through the evening of March 11, the Republicans had fought a purely defensive holding battle, favored by the terrain and by the weather, which badly impeded the CTV's movements and grounded its aviation. The Republicans were also suffering from the inclement weather, but its effects on them were less serious since their aviation, based in airports with hard-surface runways, managed to take to the air, and since their lesser degree of motorization and basically defensive posture made the condition of the roads less critical for them. In a meeting at Torija on the night of March 11 to 12, they decided to attempt a counterattack the next day.[58]

The Republican attack on March 12 was supported by powerful artillery barrages and aerial bombardment. During the previous days, the Republicans had generally enjoyed air superiority, but their attacks had been of limited intensity and effect. Now, for the first time, the right column of the 3rd Black Shirt Division was subject to repeated machine gunning from the air and bombing with fragmen-

---

[57] Faldella, *Venti mesi di guerra in Spagna*, p. 266; Roatta's telegram, March 25, summarizing operations from March 8 to March 24, NA T 586, roll 492, frame 048775; *Report*, frame 048635.

[58] Lister, *Nuestra guerra*, pp. 108–109.

tation bombs. Fighting on the ground was also heavy, and the battle swayed back and forth along the Saragossa road as now one side, now the other attacked and drove its opponents back a mile or two. In one of the attacks, the commanding officer of the CTV's 11th Regiment, Console Alberto Liuzzi, was killed, apparently by a bomb.

It is impossible to reconstruct with any accuracy the exact course of events on the Saragossa road between March 12 and March 14, but the general outlines are fairly clear. After an entire day of combat, at midnight on March 12, the Black Shirts still held approximately the same lines as they had when the day began, but losses had been heavy and their morale was falling rapidly. Panic had taken hold on several occasions during the day and the troops had retreated in disorder. In one precipitous retreat, five artillery pieces which had been emplaced far forward in antitank positions were lost to the Republicans. The officers not only failed to keep up the morale of their units, but committed serious tactical errors that unnecessarily increased their losses and contributed to the troops' insecurity.[59]

Around midnight on the 12th, when fighting finally ceased, Roatta reported to Rome that the situation was "completely reestablished,"[60] but the 3rd Division badly needed to be replaced. The 2nd Division had been less severely mauled during the day, but it had been subject to heavy artillery attacks and Roatta decided to withdraw both divisions. The 1st Division, which he had planned to use for the offensive between the Tajuña and the Tajo, was ordered to take the place of the 2nd Division in the lines along the Brihuega-Torija road, and the Littorio Division moved up to replace the 3rd on the Saragossa road.[61]

[59] Faldella, *Venti mesi di guerra in Spagna*, pp. 267–68; Roatta's telegram, March 13, NA T 586, roll 492, frame 048716; *Report*, frames 048630–37.

[60] *Report*, frame 048632.

[61] *Ibid.*, frames 048629–30.

Putting the Littorio and the 1st Divisions into the line left Roatta without fresh reserves, and deprived him of the possibility of exploiting a breakthrough in the now unlikely event that his troops should manage to rupture the Republican defenses. The Guadalajara offensive as originally planned was now over,[62] but Roatta failed to take up defensive positions, and the two fresh divisions were thrown into the combat under unfavorable circumstances. General Coppi, the commander of the 2nd Division, described the situation in a report written after he was removed from his command and sent back to Italy:

The Legionary troops, and especially those of the 1st Division [at Brihuega] were in a situation similar to that of a person who is arrested after taking a running start but remains balanced on one foot, knowing full well he cannot complete the jump, but refusing to put both feet solidly on the ground or take a step backward if necessary in order to be able to resist any blow.[63]

During the night of March 12–13, the replacement of the 2nd and 3rd Divisions began. By the time it was completed, Trijuque had been abandoned.[64] The Ibarra Palace was lost on March 14 in the only significant fighting that took place between March 14 and 17.

The morale of the two fresh divisions had been lowered by their contact with the withdrawing troops and was further depressed by the loss of the Ibarra Palace. From March 15 to 17, they were not subject to military pressure, but to a massive Republican propaganda offensive that took

[62] Barzini wrote to Barella that on March 11 and 12 he began to tone down his dispatches for *Il popolo d'Italia* because it was clear to him that "the action was destined to gradually die out" [Barzini, letter to Barella, March 23, 1937, ACS, segreteria particolare del Duce, carteggio riservato, 241/R(Barzini)].

[63] Coppi, *La seconda divisione volontari 'Fiamme Nere' alla battaglia di Guadalajara* (typescript), p. 91, MAE, Ufficio Spagna, b. 3.

[64] Faldella, *Venti mesi di guerra in Spagna*, p. 270; Martínez Bande, *La lucha en torno a Madrid*, p. 146.

its toll. Large scale propaganda had begun around March 11, particularly in the Brihuega sector, where the Italians of the Garibaldi battalion faced the Black Shirts. The Italian Communist Luigi Longo based the propaganda on a guarantee for the lives of those Black Shirts who would surrender, and an appeal to their sentiments of national and class solidarity. Propaganda leaflets with a picture of the soldiers captured on the 11th and the text of a declaration they were said to have made were hurriedly printed and dropped in large numbers on the Italian lines:

> Comrades and fellow soldiers! We are 31 soldiers of the 1st machine gun battalion. On March 10 we were sent forward "to take Guadalajara." No one told us that we would have to fight other Italians, brothers of ours. The battle was hard, and we suffered heavy losses. At night we were marching in the woods when we heard voices shouting in Italian: "Drop your arms!" We didn't shoot. How could we shoot at our brothers? But we were afraid nonetheless. We had been told, "If they take you prisoner, they will shoot you." Instead of shooting us, they have treated us like brothers. They gave us food and drink and cigarettes. They have talked to us not as enemies but as brothers, not as prisoners but as comrades. A veil has fallen from our eyes. The stories about "red bandits," "incendiaries," and "assasins" are all lies. The men who oppose us are workers and peasants like ourselves. They have explained to us why they are fighting, and we have seen they are right. They are volunteers who fight to help the Spanish workers and peasants, to prevent the government from falling into the hands of a pack of Generals and Barons who not only make Spanish workers suffer but will go on preparing wars that benefit only the rich, never us.[65]

Huge loudspeakers mounted on trucks boomed out their messages through the woods. Recently captured prisoners

[65] Quoted in Longo, *Le brigate internazionali in Spagna*, pp. 286–87.

talked to their own units, citing names and facts that left no room for doubt as to the real identity of the speaker. Popular Italian songs were played throughout the night, interspersed with propaganda well designed to weaken the spirit of the Black Shirts: "Italians! Soldiers and Black Shirts, return to your homes! Your families are weeping for you. Return to your homes. You have no reason to die." "Italians! Soldiers and Black Shirts, return to your homes! Pass over to the Republican ranks. Come with the *Garibaldini.* You will be received like brothers."[66]

The damaging effects of the Republican propaganda campaign made Roatta all the more desirous of withdrawing his troops from the Guadalajara sector. Without fresh reserves, the possibilities of obtaining any significant success by pressing the attack were very small, and there was little incentive to leave the troops exposed to the inclement weather and the continuing barrage of Republican propaganda. Up to this point, the Italians had failed to achieve any striking success, but at least they had not been humiliated. Roatta was anxious to avoid the possibility of a clamorous defeat. On March 14, he telegraphed Mussolini, "Given our special situation, we can content ourselves temporarily with a partial success, but cannot, without very grave necessity, expose ourselves to the possibility of failure."[67]

The following afternoon, Roatta went to discuss the situation and future courses of action with Franco, but the two men failed to reach any agreement on the fundamental question of whether or not the Guadalajara offensive could still be expected to contribute significantly to the fall of Madrid. The positions were completely reversed from what they had been in February. Franco, who had objected to the plan for an Italian offensive in the Guadalajara sector, now insisted that the "final solution should be sought in the Madrid region, continuing the operations in course."

[66] *Ibid.,* pp. 288–89.
[67] *Report,* frame 048639.

Roatta, on the contrary, now maintained that nothing could be gained by pressing the attack and wanted to withdraw his troops for use elsewhere.[68] For the immediate future, they agreed that the Italians would pause until March 19, and then take advantage of the first opportunity to drive the Republicans out of the Brihuega woods, establishing their front lines beyond the edge of the woods. Franco apparently interpreted this as the first step in a renewed offensive, but Roatta considered it a mere rectification of the lines, prior to replacing the Italian troops with Spaniards.[69]

As soon as he returned to his headquarters, Roatta wrote Franco a long letter that falls into two parts. In the first, he tried to dissuade Franco from carrying out further operations in the Madrid sector, arguing that neither the CTV nor Franco's troops on the Jarama were in any condition to wage a major offensive. These arguments had already been presented unsuccessfully in their conversations during the afternoon, however, and Roatta had scant hope of convincing Franco. In the second part, therefore, the Italian commander turned his attention to possible plans for continuing the offensive in the Guadalajara sector, while withdrawing Italian troops from the line as soon as possible. Franco had already vetoed the Italian plan for an offensive between the Tajuña and the Tajo, and Roatta now discarded the possibility of continuing the attack down the Saragossa road against the mass of the Republican defenders. This left, he suggested, only the possibility of an attack "in the north, with the right wing straddling the Henares River." Though still in the Guadalajara-Somosierra sector, and therefore ostensibly in accordance with Franco's desire to continue the offensive, this was in fact a proposal for an entirely new set of operations that would make it neces-

[68] *Report*, frame 048642.
[69] Roatta's telegram, March 25, summarizing the battle, NA T 586, roll 492, frame 048776; Martínez Bande, *La lucha en torno a Madrid*, p. 149.

sary for the Black Shirts to "be withdrawn from the present sector and transported to the region north of Jadraque-Cogolludo."[70]

While Roatta tried to convince Franco to take the CTV out of the line, the Republican commanders decided to attempt a counterattack against Brihuega. They spent March 15–17 preparing for their offensive, while the CTV let the days slip past without accomplishing anything, paralyzed by the impossibility of reaching an agreement with Franco. Neither Roatta nor Franco seems to have felt the least concern about the possibility of a Republican counterattack. This is all the more surprising in view of the fact that the Italian commander knew full well the morale of his troops was very low.[71] The only apparent explanation

[70] *Report*, frames 048641–44.

[71] On March 16, Roatta issued his order number 3002 on "Moral Preparation" (reproduced as document 100 in the white book presented by the Spanish Republican Government to the council of the League of Nations on May 28, 1937, *Documentos ocupados a las unidades italianas en la accion de Guadalajara*):

"Although the units are composed of troops with a high morale and ready to follow their leaders, they are often lacking in dash and aggressiveness, and allow themselves to be impressed too easily by the vicissitudes of battle. . . . This state of affairs, which is already sufficiently regretable in itself, might become a real danger if, in addition, there was a tendency to overestimate the value of the enemy, especially in the sense of crediting him with an ability to do with ease things which we ourselves cannot even attempt. Obviously, units commanded by officers holding this point of view would be placed at the outset in a state of inferiority to the enemy.

"The commanders must react urgently, energetically, and constantly against such defects and such a mentality. . . . They should endeavor to produce a state of exaltation—that is to say, they should explain carefully to those under their command that our troops in the past few days have gained an important tactical success, rapidly overrunning several lines of enemy trenches in the most unfavorable weather conditions, that they have conquered in one blow an enemy zone thirty-six kilometers in depth, that they have beaten and taken the positions of some of the best Red troops—the Internationals—that they have repulsed several attacks by the latter, that we have stopped

for Roatta's failure to take defensive measures seems to be that he continued to underrate the capabilities of his adversaries, despite the painful lessons of the preceeding week.

On March 18, Roatta was informed that Franco wished to see him and left his headquarters for Salamanca, leaving

---

only to allow our valiant troops the rest they have earned. . . .

"Commanders, by simple and elementary reasoning, should make it clear to their subordinates (and in some cases to themselves) how absurd it is to attribute fantastic powers to the enemy: forces that attack in daytime without cover or artillery preparation or after only a few rounds, detachments that steal upon us by night over unknown ground between the positions occupied by our troops and then advance several kilometers in order to cut off our regiments, etc. . . .

"Reflect and make others reflect. At the very moment when one of you becomes anxious and exclaims: My God! What will the Reds do next? On the other side, the Reds are asking each other in agitation, By Lenin! What are the Whites going to do?

"In clear cases of lack of energy, of authority, and of courage, and when punishment will be exemplary, it should be meted out without pity. . . . There is no room for men who are 'lost.' Picking them up is not a mere logistic operation, as if they were lost material. It is the first step in the process of military justice, which must determine the error or the fault, and in the latter case the penalty. . . .

"Explain that because of the blockade the possibilities of receiving new supplies are limited and nothing should be thrown away. Even a child should be able to understand that. Take steps against this deplorable abuse!

"Every opportunity of instructing the units must be taken advantage of. It is all a question of good will. Anyone can learn the elementary things that need to be known in war: use and care of arms, of radios, etc.

"'Move! Be demanding! Command! Above all, make your men understand that we are not fighting at home, lost in the midst of a huge mass, where one unit's defects can be compensated by the brilliant actions of others. Here on foreign soil we are the representatives of Italy and Fascism, by the side and under the close observation of our allies and under the distant but searching scrutiny of the entire world. By our actions will be judged the moral and technical quality and efficiency of Italy in the year XV. . . .

"We have an enormous responsibility, and we must make ourselves worthy of it, even though we lose our lives. . . ."

his chief of staff, Colonel Faldella, to handle what he expected to be the day's routine business. He went, not to
request Moroccan units to aid in the next stage of the
offensive, as one historian claims,[72] but to press once again
for the withdrawal of his troops from the sector. In Salamanca he soon found that his arguments in favor of shifting
the CTV to another sector had failed to convince the Generalissimo. Franco was not even willing to consider pulling
the Italians out of the line to regroup and mount a new
offensive in another part of the Guadalajara-Somosierra
front. They enjoyed, he said, clear superiority in men and
material, and the Republicans had no significant fortifications in the entire sector. Furthermore, the Italian and
Spanish troops in the Guadalajara sector were now in "an
optimum tactical situation that permits us at any moment
to encircle the enemy on the right wing." Franco offered
Roatta his choice of several plans, all of which called for
at least two Italian divisions to continue their attack on
Torija and Guadalajara. Roatta had just tentatively accepted one of them when he received a telephone call
from his headquarters with the news of a violent attack
against the Italian front.[73]

REPUBLICAN COUNTERATTACK

The first sign of the impending attack had come at 1:30
P.M., when waves of Republican planes began to bomb
the Italian lines, concentrating their attack on Brihuega
and its immediate neighborhood. No sooner had the last
airplanes dropped their bombs and turned south again,
when Russian tanks began to appear around Brihuega,
closely supported by infantry (see map 6). Pittau's 6th
Regiment, which was holding the small bridgehead across
the Tajuña from the town, seems to have been entirely

[72] Colodny, The Struggle for Madrid, p. 142.
[73] Report, frames 048649–52.

caught off guard and reacted very slowly. The error made days earlier in not occupying the high ground beyond the immediate bridgehead now became apparent as the soldiers were subject to intense fire from the heights. According to rumors circulating among the troops of the CTV several weeks after the battle, an officer was heard to cry "Each man for himself!" Whether this was true or not, the Italian military police reported that panic took hold of the men and that the lines were abandoned *en masse*. In their flight back into Brihuega, the Black Shirts failed to destroy the bridge across the Tajuña, and El Campesino's troops poured unobstructed into the town from the east.[71]

Along the road from Torija to Brihuega, the Republican attack was spearheaded by the Garibaldi Battalion, supported by Russian tanks under the command of General Pavlov. Facing them was the 1st Division's 1st Regiment, under the command of Colonel Frezza, who held the left flank of the CTV's line. Immediately behind Frezza's regiment lay the vital intersection between the Torija-Brihuega road and the road which runs northwest from Brihuega to km. 83.5 of the Saragossa road. It was supposed to be defended by other elements of Pittau's 6th Regiment, which were to take up defensive positions across the intersection. In the initial attack Colonel Frezza was killed and his troops decimated by the deadly fire of Pavlov's tanks. Disorganization soon set in, and within an hour the 1st Regiment was disbanded. Pittau's troops did no better in defending the intersection than they had the bridgehead, and it soon fell to Republican tanks.[75]

Colonel Salvi, whose 2nd Regiment was slightly behind the main line in ready reserve, took up improvised positions just west of Brihuega. He incorporated into his unit elements from the now retreating 1st and 6th Regiments and

---

[71] Conforti, *Guadalajara*, p. 305; "Report of the Royal Carabinieri on the Taking [*sic*] of Guadalajara," NA T 586, roll 492, frame 048691.

[75] *Report*, frame 048655; Conforti, *Guadalajara*, p. 295.

Map 6

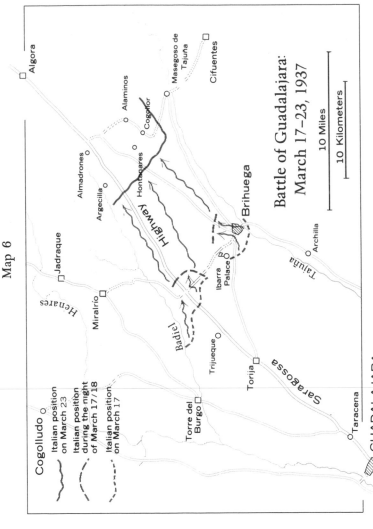

Battle of Guadalajara:
March 17–23, 1937

10 Miles

10 Kilometers

Algora

Masegoso de Tajuña

Cifuentes

Alaminos

Cogolor

Almadrones

Hontoares

Argecilla

Brihuega

Highway

Archilla

Ibarra Palace

Tajuña

Jadraque

Henares

Miralrio

Badiel

Trijueque

Saragossa

Torija

Torre del Burgo

Taracena

GUADALAJARA

Cogolludo

Italian position on March 23

Italian position during the night of March 17/18

Italian position on March 17

did his best to establish defensive positions, but by mid-afternoon Brihuega was in Republican hands and the left wing of the Italian line had been broken. Further to the west, the 1st Division's 3rd Regiment, under the Command of Colonel Mazza, resisted the initial attack of the 70th Brigade.

Bergonzoli's Littorio Division was also attacked along the Saragossa road. Bergonzoli repelled the first attack, and around 5:00 P.M. counterattacked strongly with heavy artillery support, breaking a hole between the XI International Brigade and the 2nd Spanish Brigade. This put the Republicans in a critical situation, since the Littorio menaced the highway from Brihuega to Torija, but Lister managed to repel the counterattack with the aid of two tank companies and two battalions rushed up from the reserve.[76] As evening came on, the Italians were holding the line across the Saragossa highway and down to about km. 5 of the road from Brihuega to Miralrío. The 1st and 6th Regiments, however, had been driven back and the left flank was undefended except for Salvi's 2nd Regiment. At 6:00 P.M. Colonel Salvi received an order to dig in and hold the line, establishing contact with Pittau on the left and Mazza on the right.[77] By this time, however, Pittau's troops had completely abandoned their positions, and Mazza had also begun to retreat under the pressure of renewed Republican attacks. The order was clearly impossible to fulfill.

During most of the afternoon the commander of the 1st Division, General Edmondo Rossi, had let events take place without making any appreciable effort to regroup his troops for a counterattack or to establish a defensive perimeter. At 7:15 he called CTV headquarters to report that his troops were in "irremediable retreat" and that he himself was withdrawing to a position further behind the

[76] General Rodimtsev, "En la dirección de Gaudalajara" in *Bajo la bandera de la España republicana,* pp. 306–308.

[77] Conforti, *Guadalajara,* p. 297.

lines.[78] Rossi's message precipitated events. If the 1st Division was retreating all along the line, the Littorio's left flank was completely exposed and in grave danger of being attacked and encircled. Colonel Faldella informed General Bergonzoli, who decided to order the Littorio Division to retreat, although by this time the Republicans had ceased their attack.

General Rossi must bear a large part of the blame for the Italian defeat on the 18th. The positions of the 1st Division at Brihuega and on the bridgehead across the Tajuña were extremely insecure, if not indefensible. Rossi had inherited them from the 2nd Division when he replaced it on March 13, but in the intervening days had done little or nothing to improve them. Pittau's group had given clear signs of its weaknesses and disorganization, but Rossi failed to remedy the situation. On the 18th he utterly failed to provide the leadership and direction which might have stopped the Republican attack, apparently overestimating the extent of the collapse of his own front. When Rossi informed CTV headquarters that his men were in "irremediable retreat," Pittau's troops had lost the bridgehead and the intersection to the west of Brihuega, and the town was solidly in Republican hands. But Salvi's 2nd Regiment, plus the units he had picked up from Frezza's and Pittau's regiments, was still intact and well armed. Mazza's regiment was retreating, but in a relatively orderly fashion. More importantly, the Republican attack was already coming to a halt. The situation was difficult but did not justify precipitous abandonment of the sector.[79]

[78] *Ibid.*, p. 312.

[79] *Report*, frame 048658. General Biondi-Mora of the Italian army historical office, writing under the pseudonym "General Belforte," accused Rossi of being responsible for the defeat, although without mentioning his name: "The retreat was due to a mistaken judgment, not to the pressure of the enemy, which never managed to break the superb resistance of the Italian volunteers, despite the enemy's numerical superiority, which was overwhelming in some sectors" (Belforte, *La guerra civile in Spagna*, III, 134). Biondi-Mora's accu-

On the evening of March 18 the Republicans broke off all contact with the retreating Italian units. During the entire withdrawal, which lasted well into the next day, no Republican units even molested the Italians.[80]

Despite the quiet reigning on the front on March 19, Roatta was extremely concerned. The previous day's experience had opened his eyes to the effects on his troops of 10 days of bad weather, constant harrassment from the woods and from the air, and an ably directed propaganda campaign. He feared they would prove incapable of resisting another strong attack, and requested Franco to replace them immediately with Spanish troops. Despite the previous day's debacle, Roatta had the cheek to say that his were shock troops, destined for offensive operations, not for holding a line.[81] Franco, who had long experience of commanding the Spanish Foreign Legion, must have been amazed at Roatta's idea of shock troops. In any case, he showed no inclination to move quickly to substitute his troops for the Italians.

Not until March 20 did the Republicans return to the attack. A column attempted to advance on the Saragossa road, spearheaded by eight Russian tanks, but it was repulsed with the loss of two tanks, destroyed by the Italian artillery. On the 21st, another Republican attack was repulsed.[82] The morale of the troops was greatly improved by their success in withstanding attacks of considerable

---

sation echoes Mussolini's, published in an unsigned article in *Il popolo d'Italia* on June 17, 1937; "Up to this point no mistakes had been made by the command, but then an order to retreat was given. Why? The Legionaires had not been beaten ever. The decision is inexplicable. Afterwards, when it had time to consider the situation more carefully, the command admitted to having committed an error, a grave error. The real truth is that the command failed to overcome a moment of moral crisis that affected it, not, let it be clear, the troops who felt, and who were, victorious."

[80] *Report,* frame 048655.
[81] *Report,* frame 048655–56 and 048659.
[82] *Report,* frames 048660 and 048664.

force, but their commanders were becoming more nervous by the hour. At the urging of Roatta's liaison officer at Franco's headquarters, Ambassador Cantalupo requested Franco to withdraw the Italian troops immediately. Franco agreed to begin the substitution on the 23rd.[83] Although the Italians had to repulse one more Republican probing attack on the 22nd, the battle of Guadalajara was now over.

SIGNIFICANCE OF THE BATTLE

Measured in purely objective strategic and tactical terms, Guadalajara was a relatively minor success for the Republicans. A weak and poorly organized line had been broken by the Italian attack, but the CTV's advance had been stopped before it reached any vital objectives. Although the Italians had thrown all four of their divisions into the battle, the Republican units had held their ground and eventually managed to throw them back part of the distance to their initial starting points. They had thus successfully parried another threat to Madrid, as they had done in the fall at the University City and in February on the Jarama; but they had not been able to make any significant gains, nor even recover all of the ground they had lost in the initial stages of the fighting.[84]

Republican losses appear to have been heavier than those they inflicted on the Italians. According to the best estimates about two thousand Republicans were killed at Guadalajara, and about twice that number wounded.[85] According to the secret official casualty figures compiled by the Ufficio

[83] Telegram, March 21, 1937, NA T 586, roll 492, frame 048750; and *Report*, frame 048666.

[84] The Italian forces retained at the end of the battle between six and thirteen miles of the terrain they had gained in the initial advance, but it was of no strategic or tactical significance.

[85] Conforti calculates Republican losses at some 2,200 killed, 4,000 wounded, and 400 prisoners or missing in action (*Guadalajara*, p. 376). Delperrie de Bayac concurs in this estimate, putting total Republican losses at about 6,000 (*Les Brigades Internationales*, p. 258).

Spagna, about four hundred members of the CTV were killed and eighteen hundred wounded, while some five hundred fell prisoner or were missing in action.[86] The Italians had also lost significant quantities of arms and supplies, including at least 25 artillery pieces, 10 mortars, 85 machine guns, 140 submachine guns, 822 rifles, and 67 trucks.[87]

[86] A telegram from the Italian military mission in Spain to the Ufficio Spagna on April 16, 1937, estimated 616 killed, 2,120 wounded, and 585 prisoners or missing (*Report*, frame 048671). Further investigation led to a reduction of these figures to 415 killed, 1,832 wounded, and 496 prisoners (note of Ufficio Spagna on "The Spanish Question from March 1937 to February 1938," MAE, Politica, b. 33). I see no reason to doubt that these figures are approximately accurate, as I explained in note 7 of this chapter, although they are considerably lower than those given not only by Republican propagandists but also by impartial historians and pro-Nationalist sources. One of the lowest estimates is given by Largo García, who lists 1,000 killed, 2,500 wounded, and 800 prisoners ("La batalla de Guadalajara," pp. 28–30). Thomas estimates 2,000 killed, 4,000 wounded, and 300 prisoners (*The Spanish Civil War*, p. 500). The Spanish military historian Aznar gives figures of 1,375 killed, 2,400 wounded, and 300 prisoners for both the Italians and the Spanish Soria Division (*Historia militar de la guerra de España*, II, 116). Martínez Bande places Italian losses at 3,000 killed, 1,500 wounded, and 300 prisoners (*La lucha en torno a Madrid*, p. 174).

[87] This data is taken from a table contained in the second edition of the official report on Guadalajara prepared by the Ufficio Spagna and found in ACS, sergreteria particolare del Duce, carteggio riservato, 186/R Guadalajara. The addition of this table is the only substantive difference between the second edition and the first edition, which is found in NA T 586, roll 492. Republican sources give considerably higher estimates. Lister, for instance, claims the Republicans took 65 cannon, 13 mortars, 500 machine guns, and more than 3,000 rifles (*Nuestra guerra*, p. 111). According to official figures, the Littorio Division lost almost no armament except for that belonging to the machine gun brigade, which was surprised in the Brihuega woods on March 11, when the rest of the division was not yet in line. The heaviest losses of artillery pieces were incurred by the 1st Division, which lost nine 65-mm, five 100-mm, and one 149-mm cannon during its retreat from Brihuega on the 18th. The 3rd Division's losses of 7 cannon, 33 machine guns, 71 submachine guns, 558 rifles, and 59 pistols took place mostly during the fighting on the Saragossa road around Trijueque on the 12th and 13th.

The true importance of Guadalajara is not measured, however, in purely numerical terms. Not unlike the battle of the Bulge, it was far more important from a moral and psychological point of view than from a strategic or tactical one. The Fascist regime traded heavily on the myth of the Duce's infallibility and invincibility. "Mussolini is always right" was a slogan painted on the walls of buildings in every Italian town. Guadalajara provided the material for a countermyth.[88] Fascism had massed its forces against the Republic and had been turned back. The magnificent Republican propaganda machine soon went into action to trumpet to the world the news of the Italian defeat. Republican sympathizers vied with each other to see who could give the highest figures for Italian losses and prisoners and the most injurious stories of Italian cowardice. The battle rapidly grew to epic proportions. Ernest Hemingway, for instance, wrote: "I have been studying the battle for four days, going over the ground with the commanders who directed it, and I can state flatly that Brihuega will take its place in military history with the other decisive battles of the world."[89] The morale of Madrid's defenders and of their supporters throughout the world was greatly raised by this success.

Fascist propaganda was not long in responding. On March 24, Vigilio Gayda published in *Il giornale d'Italia* a long front-page editorial entitled "Facts and Figures and the Rumors about Spain":

The Nationalists believed it necessary to rectify a few advanced lines in order to establish a more solid and unified front. The brief, partial withdrawal was conducted in perfect order, accompanied by continuous vic-

[88] This aspect of Guadalajara was stressed by Randolfo Pacciardi in an interview with the author in Rome on September 12, 1970.

[89] Hemingway, dispatch for the North American Newspaper Alliance dated March 28, 1937. I am indebted to Professor Carlos Baker for copies of Hemingway's dispatches on the battle as originally distributed by NANA.

torious combat, during which the Legionaries took 300 Red prisoners, destroyed 20 tanks (almost all of which were Russian), downed 20 aircraft and inflicted on the enemy 6,000 casualties. At the end, they still held positions far advanced with respect to their starting points, all the way across the line.

This is all there was to the great Red victory, proclaimed by the still furious partisans of sanctions. It was nothing more than an episode which was uncertain in its immediate results and unimportant in the overall course of the Spanish war.

By June 17, when Mussolini published his unsigned article on "Guadalajara" in *Il popolo d'Italia,* he was no longer content to claim that the outcome of the battle was uncertain. Apparently acting on the theory that a strong offense is the best defense, Mussolini declared that Guadalajara was, in fact, an Italian victory:

> Of the 40 kilometers gained in their advance, the Legionaries retained 20 at the end of the battle. The Legionaries were so clearly victorious that the Reds did not dare to follow them. Among other things, they had suffered 5,000 losses. Thus, the war of positions resumed. What then was the 10 day battle of Guadalajara? A victory. An authentic victory which could not be exploited because of subsequent events.

Whatever their propagandists might claim, the Italians knew that at Guadalajara they had suffered a stinging defeat. And no one knew it better than the troops and officers who had been engaged there. Before the CTV could return to action, it would have to be purged and completely reorganized.

Causes of the Italian Defeat

What were the reasons for the Italian defeat? The strength and rapidity of the Republican reaction must evidently be ranked among the most important causes, although it is beyond the scope of this book to examine in detail the political, ideological, and military factors that made that reaction possible. Clearly the fact that the main thrust of the offensive was being made by an Italian corps did much to stimulate the reaction. Spanish xenophobia and the anti-Fascism of the members of the international brigades were a powerful incentive for a maximum effort. As Vicente Rojo has testified, Guadalajara was "the most rapid and orderly concentration of forces ever carried out by the Republic."[90]

Almost all available Republican tanks and airplanes were thrown against the Italians at Guadalajara.[91] By the end of the battle, fifty-two Republican battalions were in line or in reserve in the sector, with a minimum of thirty to thirty-five thousand troops.[92] Between March 8 and March 21, therefore, a minimum of twenty to twenty-five thousand Republican troops were brought into the sector.

The Republican buildup of men and material was made possible in large part by the failure of Franco's troops on the Jarama to mount an offensive that would have busied the Republican units in that sector and prevented the reserves around Madrid from being concentrated to the north of the capital.[93] A significant part of the units rushed to Guadalajara by the Republicans had taken part in the battle of the Jarama, including the XI and XII International Bri-

[90] Rojo, Así fue la defensa de Madrid, p. 176.

[91] The Republicans employed about 90 tanks and 120 airplanes in the Guadalajara sector (Aznar, Historia militar de la guerra de España, II, 102).

[92] Martínez Bande, La lucha en torno a Madrid, pp. 171–72. For further details on the Republican forces employed in the battle see Salas Larrazábal, Historia del ejército popular de la República, vol. I, p. 879.

[93] Roatta identified this as the chief cause of his defeat: "The essential cause of the failure to reach our objective is the lack of support by the Spanish troops on the Jarama who were supposed to represent the other arm of the pincers of which we were the east [sic] arm" (Report, frame 048672).

gade, the LXX Brigade, and El Campesino's Assault Brigade. These units accounted for nineteen of the forty-two Republican battalions present in the Guadalajara sector on March 16, and more importantly were among the protagonists of the battle.[94] Some of them had already been taken out of the Jarama sector before March 8 for a period of rest and reorganization; but had Franco's forces attacked more strongly in the south, some of them, and some of the other units rushed from Madrid to Guadalajara, would certainly have been sent to the Jarama or maintained in ready reserve at Madrid.

The failure of Franco's troops on the Jarama to support the CTV's offensive points up the special difficulties of a combined offensive between one of the parties to a civil war and a foreign army. The well-known problems of wartime alliances are greatly complicated by the special demands of a civil war. Franco badly needed Italian arms and technical assistance, but the presence of an expeditionary army, which he had not requested, did nothing to strengthen his political position. Furthermore, the Italians were anxious for a quick end to the war, which would enable them to devote their undivided attention to the final pacification of Ethiopia and allow them greater freedom of action on the international scene. Franco, on the contrary, had learned over the course of the preceding months that pacification and political consolidation were slow, time-consuming processes. He feared that too rapid a victory would not give him sufficient time for purging the conquered territories and might lead to serious problems in the future.[95] Most importantly, the Italians were anxious for spectacular victories that would redound to their own glory and, therefore, insisted on using their troops as a body in decisive actions. Franco, however, could not help but be displeased at the prospect of an independent

[94] Martínez Bande, *La lucha en torno a Madrid,* pp. 150 and 171.

[95] See the discussion of Franco's interview with Faldella on February 13, *supra,* pp. 215–16.

Italian force winning a major battle, especially one that might provoke the complete collapse of the Republic. If he hoped to govern the country at the war's end, he could ill afford to have the fall of Madrid attributed to a foreign army.[96]

Franco had made it clear to the Italians that he did not approve of their plans for the Guadalajara offensive, but in view of his dependence on Italy as a source of arms and diplomatic support, he could not reject the proposal out of hand. Furthermore, an Italian attack north of Madrid would have the advantage of taking pressure off his own forces south of the city, even if it did not suceed in its major objectives. Under these circumstances, although he accepted the Italian plan and agreed to mount at least a minor offensive on the Jarama, neither he nor his subordinate commanders had any reason for sacrificing their troops to facilitate an Italian victory. This would seem to be the probable explanation of the lack of adequate Spanish support during the offensive. The Nationalists on the Jarama were probably not capable of any major fighting, as Franco had pointed out to Roatta before the battle began. After two weeks of rest and reorganization, however, it seems that a more substantial diversionary attack than the very minor actions carried out on the 9th, 13th, and 14th could have been organized. Had the men attacking Guadalajara been Spanish rather than Italian, the troops on the Jarama would probably have been asked for greater sacrifices.

[96] During the February 13 Faldella-Franco interview, Franco's aide, Colonel Barroso, had insisted that "the prestige of the Generalissimo is the most important factor in this war. It is inadmissible that Valencia, the seat of the Republican government, be occupied by foreign troops" (Conforti, *Guadalajara*, p. 33). The first director of information of Franco's National Press Service has observed that "if Roatta had triumphed at Guadalajara, it would have been difficult for Franco to acquire the prestige and independence he needed to put an end to the political differences that existed in the Nationalist zone." (Garriga, *Guadalajara y sus consecuencias*, p. 208).

After the Italian attack was halted by the Republicans, the conditions of the alliance again influenced the course of events. Roatta was convinced that no further progress could be made in the Guadalajara sector, or at least that the possibility of obtaining a rapid and decisive victory without heavy losses had now disappeared. He was anxious to remove his troops from the line as quickly as possible, but could only do so if he could convince Franco to replace them with Spanish units. Franco justified his refusal on the grounds that the prospects for a successful offensive were still good, but it seems unlikely that he was really convinced this was the case.

A more plausible explanation for his insistence that the Italians continue the offensive is that he was not displeased to see them play a thankless and inglorious role and had no reason to hurry to their relief. No direct evidence on Franco's motives or attitudes is available, but it is clear that Italian arrogance and superior airs had annoyed many Spaniards. As early as August 1936, Queipo de Llano's propaganda chief had noted: "The Germans behave with dignity and avoid showing off. The Italians are quarrelsome and despotic bullies."[97] After the battle of Guadalajara many Nationalists, including members of Franco's staff, toasted the health of the Republicans who had demonstrated that Spaniards, even Red Spaniards, could always get the better of Italians.[98] Franco himself must have found exasperating the importunate pressure of his allies, who had forced him to accept a combined general staff and refused to let him run the war in his own way and at his own pace. Now that the roles were momentarily reversed and the Italians had to request his assistance, he was not anxious to relieve them. This explains why, when the Republican counterattack came on March 18, the Italian troops were still in the line despite Roatta's urgent requests that they be re-

[97] Bahamonde, *Memoirs of a Spanish Nationalist,* p. 128.
[98] Cantalupo, *Fu la Spagna,* p. 207; Jackson, *The Spanish Republic and the Civil War,* p. 352.

placed. It has been suggested recently by an Italian author that Franco designed the Italian defeat at Guadalajara.[99] There is no evidence that he foresaw or desired their actual defeat, but the political considerations we have discussed and the frictions and rivalries existing within the alliance clearly contributed to it.

The causes of the Italian defeat are not confined to factors beyond their control, such as the unexpected strength of the Republican reaction or the failure of the Spanish Nationalists to collaborate in the offensive. The weaknesses and deficiencies of the CTV, in both troops and commanders, also contributed importantly to its defeat. The Italians apparently grossly overestimated the capabilities of their troops, or failed to realize the demands that would be put upon them in operations of the type they had planned. In view of how the men were recruited, it is not surprising that many were not physically fit for combat duty, much less for a *blitzkrieg* attack. In a report to Rome on March 20, 1937, General Roatta complained about "the numerous older married men who are not very aggressive."[100] Most of the twenty-three hundred men Faldella inspected in April 1937 were between twenty-eight and thirty-two. As mentioned earlier, among them they had some seventy-three hundred children, on an average of more than three each.[101] The director of the Italian hospital at Sigüenza reported: "Among the soldiers there are men unsuited to the toils of war. Men rejected for military service, and at times too old. Many of them suffer from hernias, appendicitis, syphilis, gonorrhea, gastric disturbances, etc."[102] These troops had received only the most summary training. Some did not even know how to operate their individual weapons properly, and many of the drivers and other spe-

[99] Conforti, *Guadalajara*, p. 360.
[100] *Report,* frame 048673.
[101] Interview with General Emilio Faldella, Milan, October 4, 1970.
[102] *Report,* frame 048680.

cialized personnel were unfamiliar with the equipment they were expected to employ.[103]

Perhaps even more important than the physical deficiencies and lack of training of the troops was their lack of motivation. Both before and during the battle, Italian propagandists attempted to build their morale. The Republicans were represented as barbarians guilty of innumerable atrocities and the war was depicted as an anti-Communist crusade. Appeals were also made to a sense of personal loyalty to the Duce and to the troops' responsibility as the representatives of Fascism on foreign soil.[104] This propaganda, however, was an evident failure. An Italian journalist observed in a letter:

No one feels this war spiritually, and no one understands its importance. The territory lost, they say, is Spanish and doesn't hurt Italy. They feel they have been sold out: cannon fodder and nothing else. They do not hate the enemy.[105]

While the battle was still in course, Roatta had noted that among the most important defects of his troops was the fact that "they do not hate the enemy."[106] Even Musso-

---

[103] *Ibid.*, frames 048673 and 048680.

[104] The propaganda of the CTV is most easily studied in the copies of its newspaper, *Il Legionario*. Some of Roatta's orders of the day are reproduced in Spain, Ministerio de Ultramar, *Spanish White Book. The Italian Invasion of Spain: Official Documents and Papers Seized from Italian Units in Action at Guadalajara* (Washington, D.C., 1937).

[105] *Report*, frame 048683. Ernest Hemingway observed in a dispatch to the North American Newspaper Alliance dated March 23, 1937: "Generalissimo Franco . . . now finds that he cannot depend on the Italians, not because the Italians are cowardly, but because Italians defending the line of Piave and Mount Grappa against invasion are one thing, and Italians sent to fight in Spain when they expected to go on garrison duty in Ethiopia are another."

[106] *Report*, frame 048674.

lini himself was forced to admit to the Fascist grand council that lack of motivation had been an important factor in the defeat. A "doctrinal war," he observed, is always difficult. When the soldiers do not feel they are defending their own homes, "it is not easy to develop a military spirit."[107] When compared with Roatta's admission that the members of the international brigades fought "with skill and above all with fanaticism and hatred,"[108] these observations constitute a striking confession of the failures of Fascist propaganda and go far toward explaining the CTV's lack of fighting spirit.

An important share of the responsibility for the Italian defeat must be attributed directly to Roatta and his staff. The Italians clearly underestimated their adversary, supposing that once the Republican front was broken a single Italian division could carry the offensive all the way to Guadalajara. This was perhaps understandable in the light of their experience at Málaga, although more careful study would have revealed that Málaga was one of the weakest sectors of the entire Republican zone, and that around Madrid much stiffer resistance could be expected. What is surprising is that after their offensive was brought to a halt on March 10, and even after the heavy fighting along the Saragossa highway on March 13, the Italians still continued to underestimate the enemy and failed to take steps to counter a possible Republican counteroffensive, which caught them entirely by surprise on March 18.

Italian planning for the attack was hasty, incomplete, and based on inadequate information. The area between Sigüenza and Guadalajara is a plateau whose average altitude is about thirty-five hundred feet. Its relatively flat surface is swept by bitter winds, and storms are frequent. Troops operating there in March should be equipped and trained for a winter campaign, but the Italians failed to

[107] Quoted in Giuseppe Bottai, *Vent'anni e un giorno*, p. 110.
[108] *Report*, frame 048673.

take this into account. During the first days of the battle, many of the soldiers had only colonial uniforms, which were totally inadequate for the freezing temperatures they encountered.

The clay surface of the plateau is easily crossed by motor vehicles when dry, but becomes impassable as soon as rain begins to fall. The thick heavy mud that forms rapidly after a storm makes it difficult even for a man afoot to proceed across country, and restricts trucks to hard-surface roads. The rudimentary highway network of the sparsely populated region around Guadalajara was totally inadequate to permit the flow of twenty-four hundred trucks, in addition to artillery pieces, tanks, staff cars, and advancing columns of soldiers. Tie-ups frequently brought traffic to a virtual halt, leaving the front line troops without supplies, and exposing the columns on the road to aerial and artillery attack. These difficulties might easily have been foreseen, but they were not.

Successful execution of a *blitzkrieg* attack such as Roatta planned requires absolute superiority in aviation and armor, and highly trained troops. Due to unusually unfavorable weather conditions, which may have been impossible to foresee, air superiority during most of the battle lay with the Republicans. It should have been clear to Italian planners, however, that their 3-ton whippet tanks, armed only with machine guns, were no match for the 37-mm cannon of the 8.5–ton Russian T–26 tanks, which had given good proof of themselves in the battle for Madrid the previous fall.

Little attention seems to have been paid to a study of the terrain. Battalion commanders were often given no maps at all, and Rotta's order of operations relied on the Michelin 1 to 400,000 highway map, whose lack of detail and of topographical information made it wholly inadequate for planning a battle.[109] As Farinacci's aide remarked, what Roatta and his staff had prepared was not a battle

[109] Martínez Bande, *La lucha en torno a Madrid,* p. 198.

plan but a plan of march.[110] It was apparently their faith in the effects of a rapid breakthrough, followed by a swift advance of a motorized column, that led them to neglect the study of many of the factors which proved vital in the actual course of the battle. It must be added, however, than an effort to speed up the tempo of the preparations in order to satisfy Spanish requests for a prompt attack may also have had a negative influence on Italian planning.[111]

Some European military leaders and theorists, especially in France, attempted to draw conclusions about the effectiveness of *blitzkrieg* tactics and about the merits of tactical air support from the Italian experience at Guadalajara. The special conditions under which this battle was fought would make it difficult to draw any valid generalizations from this case, but in Italy and elsewhere defenders of more traditional tactics were confirmed in their opinions, and proponents of the newer system were embarrassed by what seemed to be a striking failure.

Guadalajara and Málaga were the only two battles of the Civil War in which Franco allowed the Italians to play a central role independently. In all future actions, he would insist on their operating as part of larger units made up primarily of Spanish troops and commanded by Spanish generals. Neither battle was of great military importance, but Guadalajara fixed in the public mind an image of Italian intervention in Spain which has proved indelible. It marks the end of a period of constantly growing Italian commitments in Spain, and ushers in the final, longest period during which Rome found herself forced to pay the price of the commitments she had made.

[110] Canevari, *La guerra italiana*, I, 47.
[111] Faldella, letter to the author, March 25, 1971.

PART III

INTERNATIONAL TENSION: MARCH–
SEPTEMBER 1937

ITALIAN REACTION TO GUADALAJARA

AN "absurd sense of satisfaction" at the Italian defeat reigned at Franco's headquarters at the close of the battle of Guadalajara, according to Cantalupo's report to Rome. Many Nationalists were openly saying it would be wiser not to link Spain too closely to Italy and Germany. In view of this situation, the ambassador suggested that the entire Italian involvement in the civil war ought to be reassessed in the light of its costs and potential risks and benefits.[1]

A number of factors made it highly unlikely that Mussolini would at this point seriously consider withdrawing from Spain or sharply reducing Italy's commitments there. The first was his unwillingness to admit defeat to the world. Guadalajara had occupied the front page of newspapers around the globe, and most had interpreted it as a crushing defeat for Italian Fascism. The prestige of Italy, of the Fascist party, and of Mussolini himself had clearly suffered a devastating blow. The derision being poured on Italian soldiers in the anti-Fascist press throughout Europe threw the Duce into such a towering range that he vowed the Italian commanders in Spain would never return home alive if they did not win a victory to cancel out the memory of Guadalajara.[2] To a much greater degree than Hitler, Mussolini had allowed his personal prestige to become involved in the Spanish venture, and his vanity required

[1] Cantalupo, *Fu la Spagna*, pp. 207–208.
[2] GD, D, III, 259.

263

a military victory to reestablish his reputation as well as that of Fascism.

A second and related reason was the Duce's concern for appearing loyal. Although loyalty was not in fact one of his outstanding character traits, he often gave signs of intense concern over appearing disloyal. In March 1939, for instance, after the German takeover of Bohemia, he commented to his son-in-law: "We cannot change politics, because after all we are not prostitutes."[3] Particularly at a moment when things were not going well for Franco, he was loath to give his critics an opportunity of charging him with having deserted a cause he had taken up.

In terms of the international situation, the moment was not a propitious one for a change of policy. Neither London nor Paris seemed particularly anxious to improve relations with Rome and there was nothing in the diplomatic correspondence from those two capitals to indicate that either of them would be willing to make any substantial concessions in return for a change in Italian policy in Spain.

Finally, the regime needed a military victory in Spain to silence its critics at home. Thus far we have not looked closely at the reaction of the Italian public to the war in Spain. It may be worthwhile to suspend for a few pages our account of the aftermath of Guadalajara in order to examine this question.

From the very beginning of the Civil War, Italian propaganda officials were chiefly concerned with keeping events in Spain from arousing unnecessary excitement or unrest. As soon as news of the army revolt reached Rome, the Italian press was ordered to restrict its coverage to simple news stories, under pain of sequestration. On July 22 more specific instructions were given. Newspapers were directed to devote no more than one and a half columns to Spain, to use no more than two-column headlines, and to refrain absolutely from publishing any commentary or photo-

[3] Ciano, *Diary*, March 20, 1939.

graphs. These early instructions set the tone for those that would be given throughout the war. Only rarely was the press positively instructed to give any particular piece of news other than items about French and Russian violations of the nonintervention agreement. But editors were reminded with monotonous regularity to "play down events in Spain," to limit their headlines to one or two columns, and to avoid using sensational photographs.[4]

After Italy officially recognized Franco, the press consistently described the Civil War as a struggle against Communism. This approach was well chosen to appeal to the regime's adherents. In 1922 Fascism had won the support of many Italians by offering itself as the savior of the country from Communism. The Civil War was presented as the same sort of operation, being repeated not on the national but on the international plane.

Since the unification of Italy, public opinion had been formed by two institutional sources, the government and the church. During the Fascist period, church-related newspapers and magazines were the one legally available source of news not directly controlled by the party. Only on rare occasions did the church openly oppose the regime; but as in any country with press censorship, readers soon became skilled interpreters of significant silences, differences of emphasis, and varieties of approach.

On the question of Spain, the church strongly reinforced what the regime was already saying. This is not to imply that the Catholic press approached the issue in exactly the same way as other Italian publications. Catholic opinion laid major emphasis on the religious aspects of the war. The violent persecution of the church in Republican Spain, where thousands of bishops, priests, and religious were

---

[4] ACS, agenzia Stefani, carte Morgagni, direttive alla stampa. In general, Fascist propaganda officials were more concerned with what was not to be said than with positive efforts to promote certain ideas. Tannenbaum, *The Fascist Experience*, pp. 223–24.

murdered during the course of three years, was a constant topic of the Catholic press and of sermons from the pulpit.[5] In sharp contrast, the secular press devoted very little attention to the subject, mentioning it rarely, and then only in passing. A regular reader of the Fascist party's daily, *Il popolo d'Italia*, for instance, might well have had no idea that a bloody religious persecution was in fact going on in Spain. The anticlerical element in Fascism was too strong to allow the party's propaganda machine to make use of the religious issue, even though it would certainly have moved large sectors of Italian public opinion. This difference in emphasis did not render less effective the basic agreement of both official and Catholic opinion on the anti-Communist character of Franco's movement and on the desirability of supporting it. If anything, the fact that state and church presented diverse arguments in favor of the same course of action probably served to unite behind it a broader spectrum of support than could have been won by any single unified presentation.[6]

From the beginning of the war, Italian anti-Fascist exiles recognized in the Spanish conflict an excellent issue. On August 2 the Paris-based socialist newspaper *Avanti!* published a salute from the Italian Socialist party to its Spanish brothers, expressing its confidence that "the grandeur of their experience will be a lesson and a stimulus to the world proletariat in the difficult but grandiose struggle against the tyranny of fascism and of the capitalist regime." *Giustizia e libertà* developed the same theme: "If until yesterday the European proletariat could only lay claim

---

[5] This generalization is based on a reading of *L'avvenire d'Italia*, *L'osservatore romano*, and *La civiltà cattolica*. It is confirmed by Tannenbaum, *The Fascist Experience*, pp. 198–99.

[6] I am indebted to the late Professor Giampaolo Nitti for an illuminating discussion on this subject and on the general topic of Italian public opinion on the Spanish Civil War. The best treatment is Alberto Aquarone's brilliant essay, "La guerra di Spagna e l'opinione pubblica italiana." I believe, however, that Aquarone undervalues the divergence beween the positions of the Catholic and the official press.

in the postwar period to resistance and glorious defeats, today it can offer the testimony of the practical results of five months of revolution."[7] The Italian Communist party attacked the Fascist government for spending "millions to support the enemies of freedom in Spain" when Italian workers did not have enough to eat.[8] It also attempted to use the Spanish issue to win support from Italian Catholics whom it tried to convince that most Spanish Catholics were supporting the Republic and collaborating with the Communists.[9]

To judge from the reports of Fascist party informers, it seems that the Spanish Civil War, and particularly the idea that events in Spain would trigger changes in Italy, did strike a responsive chord among some of the regime's opponents.[10] The popularity Mussolini had won with the Ethiopian venture and his successful defiance of the League's sanctions had profoundly depressed them, so they welcomed any indication that the struggle against Fascism was not doomed to failure. As early as July 22 a party informant in Milan reported that some sectors of public opinion that had seemed won over to Fascism were following events in Spain with great interest and revealing in their commentaries their sympathy for the Republic.[11] By early August the police were reporting signs of unrest in

[7] *Giustizia e libertà*, January 1, 1937.

[8] *L'unità* XIII, 9 (1936).

[9] Manifesto of the Central Committee of the Italian Communist Party, no date, ACS, ministero del interno, pubblica sicurezza, direzione generale degli affari generali e riservati, 1903–1949, Cat. F 1, b. 7.

[10] These reports are one of the few indices available for judging the state of public opinion, but they are extremely difficult to evaluate. The paid informant was naturally anxious to report something that would justify his salary, and there is no way of controlling the accuracy of any given piece of information. The repetition of roughly similar comments from a number of informers does, however, offer grounds for granting them some credence.

[11] ACS, partitio nazionale fascista, situazione politica delle provincie, Milano.

Padova, Genoa, Milan, Trent, and Verona.[12] A typical report is that of a party informant in Genoa.

> The attention of the masses is always fixed on events in Spain. They are discussed frequently and people say that the red militia will win. Some do not hide their hope that the victory of the red militia will unleash "something" in other nations as well, including Italy. It seems that every evening many workers join their friends who have radios to listen to the programs from Barcelona, Madrid, Bilbao, etc.[13]

Events in Spain came much closer to home when men began to be recruited for duty there. The numbers who went unwillingly were not high enough to cause any serious problems to the regime. They did, however, cause some hostility and discontent. The political repercussions of recruiting would have been much greater had more taken place in the northern industrial centers, where opposition to the regime was always strongest. The fact that disproportionately large numbers were drawn from rural areas in southern Italy helped to limit the amount of discontent that was generated.

The most significant sign of unrest was a demonstration in favor of the Madrid government that took place in the Venetian shipyards. Information reaching the British embassy indicates that some two hundred arrests were made, although only about twenty men were retained in custody.[14] Incidents of this magnitude were extremely rare. Response to the war in Spain, even among the politically conscious individuals in the larger towns, was mostly confined to listening to Radio Barcelona or writing "Long live the Span-

[12] ACS, segreteria particolare del Duce, carteggio riservato, 463/R Spagna, sf. 4; ministero del interno, pubblica sicurezza, direzione generale degli affari generali e riservati, 1920–1945, 1936, 22.

[13] ACS, partito nazionale fascista, situazione politica delle provincie, Genova.

[14] FO R 3171/3171/22.

ish workers!" on the walls of a building.[15] Dormant hopes and ambitions were stirred, but not sufficiently to present any real threat to the regime.[16]

Criticism of Italy's role in Spain was not limited exclusively to opposition groups. Among the regime's supporters there was also a certain amount of dissention. The party's left wing, sections of which had hoped to see realized in Spain the revolutionary programs that were so frequently mentioned in Fascist propaganda, were angered to find that their country was contributing to the establishment of a reactionary regime there. As one young Fascist wrote:

What it all comes down to is that we look to the left while we move decidedly to the right. We talk about a proletarian, antibourgeoise revolution, while we take up the defense of the most retrograde group of generals, latifundia owners, and exploiters that exists in Europe. We are obliged to fight side by side with the enemies of progress, with the gravediggers of democracy, with those who administer the holy oils at the bedside of every revolution.[17]

In this respect the Spanish Civil War marked a decisive turning point in the history of Fascism. Italian support of Franco dashed the last hopes of those in Italy and else-

[15] Radio Barcelona broadcast regularly in Italian on the theme put forward by Carlo Roselli, "Today in Spain, tomorrow in Italy." Within Italy a number of clandestine transmitters also spread the same message (ACS, ministero della cultura popolare, b. 105, f. 20).

[16] In November 1936 the ministry of the interior prepared a twenty-seven-page report for Mussolini on subversive activities during the fourteenth year of the Fascist era (October 1935–October 1936). Considerable stress was laid on the repercussions of the Ethiopian campaign, but hardly any mention of Spain was made except to say that Barcelona was a center of anarchist activity. The ministry appears to have felt no concern at this time over the possible effects of events in Spain on the Italian political situation (ACS, segreteria particolare del Duce, carteggio riservato b. 30, f. 14).

[17] Gambetti, *Gli anni che scottano*, p. 277.

where in Europe who had hailed Fascism as a movement that could combine radical social reform with nationalism. The Spanish experience definitively alienated many of those who had continued to believe in Fascism as a movement of the left, despite all previous evidence to the contrary.

Within the higher ranks of the state there was some disagreement that could not be kept entirely silent, although it was never, of course, reported in the press. At one point, for instance, rumors were circulating in Genoa, Liguria, and Piedmont about General Badoglio's opposition to the use of army troops in Spain. The police called the matter to Mussolini's attention and the Duce ordered the general to give some public sign of his support of official policy.[18]

As news of what had happened at Guadalajara began to trickle into Italy through the numerous holes that Fascist censorship never managed to plug, signs of mounting public discontent began to appear. The police reported a number of arrests for listening to Radio Barcelona, for commenting favorably on the Republic's success, and for writing "subversive" phrases like "Viva la Spagna" on the walls of public buildings.[19] None of the individual incidents was particularly serious and their number was not high enough to indicate widespread popular reaction,[20] but Mussolini, who

[18] ACS, segreteria particolare del Duce, carteggio riservato, b. 63, f 389/R Badoglio.

[19] Incidents are reported in the following telegrams received in the ministry of the interior between March 19 and April 5, 1937: 19053, 19522, 19561, 19592, 20076, 20380, 20425, 20442, 20616, 20619, 20680, 20892, 21057, 21068, 21461, 21544, 21731, 21880, 21933, 22105, 22320, 22322, 22504, 22713, 22795 (ACS, ministero del interno, ufficio cifra, telegrammi in arrivo).

[20] The best summary of the situation is perhaps found in the British embassy's annual report for 1937: "Intervention in Spain was unpopular with the country at large, and regarded with anxiety on account of the serious complications in which it was thought it might involve Italy. In 1937, as in 1935, rising prices and consequent distress occasioned considerable discontent, and business men viewed the future with increasing alarm. But in 1937, as in 1935, these murmurs did

was always very sensitive to criticism, authorized the party secretary, Starace, to take special repressive measures. At least in the province of Genoa there was talk of organizing Fascist squads once again to deal with the subversives.[21] The Duce told the Grand Council of Fascism a few weeks later: "At a certain point I said to Starace, 'Let's see if the wine of Squadrism which we've had in the cellar for so long is still good. Open up a few bottles.' The wine is still excellent. A few heads and a lot of radios were smashed, and everything is back to normal."[22] While the party took its own repressive measures, the police and the courts continued their usual activities. Penalties for dissent could be harsh. Being overheard saying "Let's hope the Reds win," or writing "Viva Lenin" on the walls of a urinal could result in a sentence of from three to five years forced residence in an out-of-the-way village.[23] These various repressive measures were quite effective in silencing criticism, but the pressure of adverse public opinion contributed to the Duce's determination to vindicate Fascism with arms.

ITALY'S COMMITMENT RECONFIRMED

As early as March 24, Mussolini told Franco's personal emissary, Colonel Villegas, that Spain could continue to count on Italian aid.[24] The following day, he sent Ambassador Grandi a telegram announcing his determination not to withdraw Italian units from Spain until Guadalajara had been vindicated. No more troops would be sent, but those already there must win a victory that would cancel

---

not constitute any serious danger to the stability of the regime" (FO R 692/692/22).

[21] ACS, partito nazionale fascista, situazione politica delle provincie, Genova.

[22] Bottai, Vent'anni e un giorno, p. 110.

[23] Examples in ACS, ministero del interno, direzione generale degli affari generali e riservati, 1903–1949, Cat. C 2, b. 6–10.

[24] Cantalupo, Fu la Spagna, p. 210.

out the memory of the defeat. After that, they might be withdrawn, if other countries were willing to do the same, especially since the Spanish Nationalists' attitude toward their allies was far from clear. "I do not want," Mussolini wrote, "to accept at face value Cantalupo's reports that Italians are 'surrounded by the icy indifference of the Spaniards which,' he says, 'will change into open resentment, but the Spaniards certainly show us no great affection."[25]

The previous eight months had taught Mussolini little or nothing about the real pace of events in Spain. Time and again he had been told that victory was just around the corner, only to find a month later that it was still as far off as ever. Nonetheless, he now predicted that the victory that would vindicate Italian honor could be expected in the next ten days to two weeks.

On March 31 Ambassador Cantalupo was recalled to Rome to confer. In fact, his recall was to prove permanent, for during his brief stay in Spain he had succeeded in alienating the party, the military, and members of Ciano's entourage in the foreign ministry. Among his most bitter enemies and critics was Farinacci, who was urging against the ambassador's advice Italian support of the Falange and of a one-party system in Spain. He was annoyed by what he considered Cantalupo's unduly alarmist insistence that Spain was not half Nationalist and half Red, but rather "a Red mass with a thin white crust on top,"[26] and irritated by the ambassador's attempts to maintain an independent position and preserve the prerogatives of his office in the face of the party's encroachments.[27] In a three-page letter

[25] Telegram 649 R/C of March 26, 1937, MAE, gabinetto, b. 1.
[26] Cantalupo, *Fu la Spagna*, pp. 155–56.
[27] According to the head of the Spanish office, Farinacci was offended by Cantalupo's failure to meet him when he arrived in Spain. Cantalupo makes it appear in his memoirs that he was anxious to see the Fascist leader, but that Farinacci refused to see him (interview with Count Luca Pietromarchi, Rome, July 13, 1970). The two versions may be complementary, and in any case certainly indi-

to Mussolini dated April 11, 1937, he attacked Cantalupo for criticizing the Axis, for "condemning our intervention in Spain," and for lack of personal courage. He also accused him of bringing bad luck, pointing out that shortly after the ambassador's arrival the CTV had suffered the reverse of Guadalajara, and reminding Mussolini that in recent times he had received proof of the problems caused by those who bring bad luck.[28]

Outside the ranks of the party, Cantalupo had also made enemies for himself in the army. The Italian consul at San Sebastian at the time, Cavalletti, attributes the ambassador's downfall largely to his arguments with Roatta, whom he accused of incompetence after Guadalajara.[29] Cantalupo himself recounts that the top military leaders in Rome criticized his having intervened with Franco to obtain the replacement of the Italian troops on March 22, even though he had done so at the explicit request of the military authorities on the spot. They interpreted this action, like his insistence that military victory was still far off, as a sign of "defeatism."[30]

Even at the foreign ministry, Cantalupo's reports had aroused considerable antagonism. The head of the Spanish office, Pietromarchi, and other officials viewed his descriptions of the Spanish situation as symptoms of "alarmism" and excessive excitability. Even more jarring in the atmosphere of Palazzo Chigi in the 15th year of the Fascist era was Cantalupo's critical spirit, which called into ques-

cate that there was friction between the two men before Farinacci's mission had fairly begun.

[28] Farinacci, letter to Mussolini, April 11, 1937, NA T 586, roll 462, frames 033867–69. When the issue of Cantalupo's return to Spain was still undecided, some lower-ranking party hierarchs sent an emissary to Spain to inform Franco's brother that he was opposed to continued Italian participation in the war. Cantalupo, *Fu la Spagna*, pp. 268–69.

[29] Interview with Francesco Cavaletti, Rome, August 2, 1970.

[30] Cantalupo, *Fu la Spagna*, p. 202.

tion the basic framework of Italian policy in Spain.[31] The career diplomats knew only too well that "Mussolini is always right" was a propaganda slogan for the masses, but over the years they had grown accustomed to acting as if they were convinced it were true, since neither the Duce nor his young son-in-law was favorably disposed toward frank criticism.

When Cantalupo reached Rome, Ciano intimated that if he wished to return to Salamanca he would have to accept the government's policy of continued support for Franco.[32] The ambassador refused to change his stance. In a memo to Mussolini he criticized Franco's political leadership as "feeble." He questioned whether Fascist Italy, with its claims of being revolutionary in character, should be supporting the reactionary military regime that would result from a Franco victory. On the military level, he argued that the failure of the Jarama and Guadalajara offensives and the influx of French and Russian supplies had reversed the relatively promising situation of two months earlier. The outcome of the war was now uncertain, and it was probable that Republican superiority would increase in the future unless Italy and Germany were willing to increase their aid radically. In the absence of an internal revolution in one of the two parts of Spain or of international mediation of the conflict, he predicted that the war could well develop into a stalemate that might last for years. Under these circumstances, he suggested, Italy would be well advised to consider reducing her commitments in Spain and carrying on "international diplomatic activities designed to search for a political solution which would pacify Spain with full Italian participation, while making a Communist regime impossible there."[33]

Catalupo's pleas for a complete policy review fell on deaf ears and served only to guarantee that he would not

[31] Interview with Count Luca Pietromarchi, Rome, July 13, 1970.
[32] Cantalupo, *Fu la Spagna*, p. 247.
[33] *Ibid.*, pp. 249–57; quoted material is found on p. 257.

return to Spain. Mussolini was unwilling to withdraw his support of Franco, and from this point on his commitment to aiding him may be considered definitive. On several occasions over the next two years Mussolini would grumble and threaten to stop helping Franco if the war was not pursued more vigorously, but the threats were idle. More than any victory could have done, Guadalajara had bound Italy to the Spanish cart.

THE NORTHERN CAMPAIGN

If the Italians were to remain in Spain and recoup their lost prestige, the CTV would clearly need to be reorganized. To announce publicly an immediate change of commanders, however, would be to admit defeat, and that Mussolini was unwilling to do. On March 26, he confirmed Roatta in his command of the CTV, while informing him that General Mario Berti would soon arrive to help with the reorganization of the Italian units. A few weeks later, when public interest in Italian doings in Spain had lessened and it had become apparent how thoroughly the CTV needed to be reorganized, Roatta was replaced by General Ettore Bastico, who had commanded the 3rd Army Corps in Ethiopia.

Bastico's observations when he reached Salamanca on April 16 confirmed his worst suspicions: "Discipline is still in its beginning, training is very deficient, and administration chaotic."[34] During the month of April, far-reaching changes were made in the commanders and in the structure of the CTV. In addition to Bastico and Berti, Generals Frusci, Manca, Favagrossa, Mozzoni, Alegretti, and Terruzzi were sent to Spain. Colonel Faldella was replaced as chief of staff by Colonel Gastone Gambarra, and General Berti was named assistant commander. Some thirty-seven

[34] Bastico, letter to Pariani, April 16, 1937, reproduced in Canevari, *La guerra italiana*, I, 487.

275

hundred men were pulled out of the CTV and sent back to Italy.[35] The Littorio Division was left substantially unchanged, except that losses were filled in. The 1st and 3rd Black Shirt Divisions were dissolved, and their better elements used to reinforce the 2nd Division, under the command of General Mario Frusci, and the March 23rd Group (later transformed into a division) under the command of Consul General Francisci. The two mixed Italo-Spanish brigades, which had not yet seen any substantial action, were left untouched. During the period March 1 to May 31, 1937, almost no troops were sent to Spain. Of the 363 men added to the CTV during the period, 180 were officers and 99 NCOs.[36] By mid-May, 1937, there was a total of 2,536 Italian army and militia officers in Spain, including 13 generals.[37]

The entire spring and summer following the battle of Guadalajara was a quiet period in terms of Italian shipments of troops and material. Official Italian records show that no troops left for Spain in March and April, and only twelve hundred men left from May through August. Not until September would the need to maintain the strength of the Italian units in Spain make it necessary to send large numbers of new troops.[38]

During the late winter and spring the Soviet Union was particularly active in aiding the Republic. According to German reports from Istambul, in the four months from February through May, 113 aircraft, 430 guns, 375 tanks, 37,250 tons of material, and 6,525 tons of ammunition passed through the straits on their way from Russia to

[35] Note of the Ufficio Spagna on the Spanish Question from March 1937 to February 1938, MAE, Politica, b. 33.

[36] Ufficio Spagna, Final Report, Annex 5, MAE, Ufficio Spagna, b. 1.

[37] Report from the Ministry of War to the Ufficio Spagna, May 20, 1937, MAE, Ufficio Spagna, b. 3.

[38] Ufficio Spagna, Final Report, Annex 5, MAE, Ufficio Spagna, b. 1.

Spain.[39] The Italian press also carried frequent stories about large shipments of Russian and French aid, which it claimed was being passed across the Pyrenees. Mussolini believed that these shipments had given the Republicans air superiority, so in April he decided to send another 72 fighter planes to Spain.[40] Twenty-four planes were sent immediately. It is not possible to determine precisely when the remaining 48 were shipped to Spain, but by May 1937, Nationalist air strength was certainly at least equal to that of the Republic, if indeed it had ever really been inferior.[41] By September 22, 1937, the Italian air force had sent a total of 418 aircraft to Spain, of which 42 were handed over to the Spanish Nationalists and 376 retained under direct Italian control.

The failure of the Guadalajara offensive had finally convinced Franco that further attacks on Madrid would be fruitless. He now turned his attention to the northern front, which had been relatively quiet since the early days of the war (see map 7). Victory in the north would free troops for other sectors and would give him control of the coal, iron, and steel of the Basque country, as well as of important manufacturing facilities. The central objective on the northern front was clearly Bilbao, but before the heavily fortified city could be attacked, the Nationalists needed to penetrate far enough into Vizcaya to establish themselves in striking position. Mola began preliminary operations on March 31 with the air support of Italian fighters, bombers, and reconnaissance planes, but his progress was painfully slow.[42]

---

[39] Watt, "Soviet Military Aid to the Spanish Republic in the Civil War 1936–1938," pp. 540–41. Salas describes the spring of 1937 as the most active single period of Russian supply shipments. Salas Larrazábal, "The Growth and Role of the Republican Popular Army," p. 180.

[40] GD D, III, 266.

[41] Salas Larrazábal, *La guerra de España desde el aire*, p. 196.

[42] Belforte, *La guerra civile in Spagna*, III, 146.

Map 7

Northern Front: April–October 1937

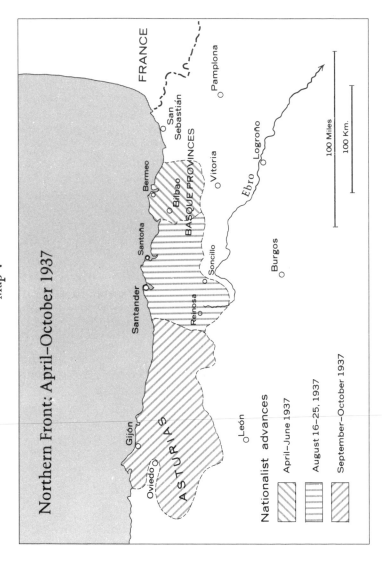

FRANCE

Pamplona

San
Sebastián

BASQUE PROVINCES

Bermeo

Bilbao

Vitoria

Logroño

Ebro

Santoña

Santander

Soncillo

Reinosa

Burgos

Gijón

Oviedo

ASTURIAS

León

Nationalist advances

April–June 1937

August 16–25, 1937

September–October 1937

100 Miles

100 Km.

All of April and May and over half of June would go by before the Nationalists finally took Bilbao.

By the end of April, Italian commanders in Spain were becoming extremely impatient with the progress of the Nationalist campaign, and pessimistic about its eventual outcome, to the point of asserting that without a radical change in tactics Bilbao would not be taken nor the war won.[43] This attitude was shared in Rome, where as early as April 23 the American ambassador reported he had received a definite impression that "the Italian government is becoming increasingly anxious to liquidate its participation in the Spanish conflict."[44] On May 3, Mussolini told von Neurath that if Franco had made no progress by the end of the month, he would offer him the alternatives of "either a rapid advance or the withdrawal of Italian troops."[45]

Although the Italians were anxious for a quick victory, this desire was clearly subordinated in practice to their need for a spectacular success to avenge Guadalajara. By late April or early May, their forces had been completely reorganized and were ready to be committed again. General Mola was anxious to use them in his operations against Bilbao, but refused to give them a central role before they had been tried in minor actions. Bastico, on the other hand, was unwilling to allow his forces to be employed in secondary or diversionary attacks. The CTV, he insisted, must be employed to break the front.[46]

A deadlock was reached over this point. Despite Franco's repeated requests for active Italian collaboration, Bastico refused to undertake the minor actions offered him, so the main body of his forces was held in reserve during the

[43] GD, D, III, 274–75.
[44] FRUS, 1937, I, 287.
[45] Ciano, *Ciano's Diplomatic Papers*, p. 115.
[46] Bastico, letter to Ciano, May 31, 1937, quoted in Canevari, *La guerra italiana*, I, 490–94.

entire Bilbao offensive.[47] The Italian aviation flew some twenty-eight hundred hours and dropped 140,000 kilograms of bombs in support of the attacking Nationalists,[48] but the only Italian infantry that participated in the operations were the "Agrupación legionaria," composed of the March 23 Group and the Italian-led Black Arrows Brigade, commanded by General Roatta, to whom Mussolini had promised a promotion if he successfully led a division in battle.[49]

On April 30, a battalion of Black Arrows occupied the Basque fishing port of Bermeo, but a Republican counterattack succeeded in cutting the road and surrounding the town, which was not relieved until May 3. For several days the fighting was heavy and the Italians suffered almost three hundred losses.[50] The incident was of negligible military importance, but gave rise to violent press polemics which in some sense justify Steer's description of it as "a second Guadalajara" and make it the only aspect of Italian infantry participation in the Bilbao offensive that merits attention.[51] For all practical purposes, the Italian infantry was entirely absent from the offensive up to the capture of Bilbao on June 19.

During the second phase of the northern campaign, after the fall of Bilbao, Bastico was more successful in convincing the Nationalist commanders to grant his troops an important role. Plans were made for an offensive from Reinosa to Soncillo, designed to cut off the Republican troops south of the Cantabric Mountains, prior to launching an attack against the city of Santander fifty miles to the northwest of Bilbao. For this operation, Bastico obtained the use of

[47] Franco to Pedro Garcia Conde, September 23, 1937, enclosure, SHM CGG, L. 387, C. 38.

[48] Belforte, *La guerra civile in Spagna*, III, 158. The Condor Legion also provided aerial support for the Nationalists, including the bombing of Guernica.

[49] Faldella, *Venti mesi di guerra in Spagna*, p. 312.

[50] Piazzoni, *Le "Frecce Nere" nella guerra di Spagna* (1937–1939), p. 202.

[51] Steer, *The Tree of Guernika*, p. 268.

Franco's Fourth Navarrese Division to complement his own forces. Early in July, the CTV began taking up positions for the offensive.[52] Only July 6, however, the Republicans launched an attack against the town of Brunete, to the west of Madrid, which threatened to cut off the besiegers of the capital. Franco immediately ordered the Italian air forces to the Madrid front to assist his hard pressed troops. By July 13, the Brunete offensive had been brought to a halt, although bloody fighting continued in the sector until the end of the month. Italy's planes contributed significantly to blunting the edge of the Republican offensive. Her bombers dropped 106,000 kilograms of bombs, while her fighters put in twenty-seven hundred hours of combat missions, downing a number of Republican aircraft.[53]

The arrival of large numbers of Italian planes during the spring had already given the Nationalists numerical superiority in the air. The extent of its losses at Brunete placed the Republic at a marked disadvantage in the air war, from which it was never to recover.[54] By the end of the Brunete offensive, the balance was clearly inclining in favor of the Nationalists in terms of artillery and infantry reserves as well. According to Faldella, Franco had almost 50 percent more artillery pieces and fifty thousand more men in reserve, although the total number of men under arms on the two sides was approximately equal.[55]

Not until August 14 did the long-planned second phase of the northern offensive finally begin. The main body of the CTV occupied the middle of the Nationalist line, with

[52] Belforte, *La guerra civile in Spagna*, III, 181.
[53] Belforte claims 105 Republican planes shot down, but the real figure is probably lower. Belforte, *La guerra civile in Spagna*, III, 172.
[54] Kindelán, "La aviación en nuestra guerra," *Guerra de liberación*, p. 369.
[55] The nationalists had 1,252 artillery pieces to the Republicans' 800; and 100,000 men in reserve to the Republicans' 50,000. The total number of men under arms was 432,000 and 425,000, respectively (Faldella, *Venti mesi di guerra in Spagna*, p. 357).

Navarrese brigades operating on both flanks. The extreme right of the Nationalist line was held by the newly organized Arrows Division under the command of General Roatta.[56] The first part of the offensive consisted in encircling the Republicans south of the line Reinosa-Soncillo, between the Ebro River and the Cantabric Divide. In this phase, the CTV operated against the Escudo Pass from the east, while the Navarrese attacked Reinosa from the west. With overwhelming air and artillery support, the Navarrese and the CTV reached their first objectives in three days, cutting off some ten thousand Republican troops. Franco telegraphed Mussolini his congratulations on the Italian success in occupying the critical Escudo Pass, defended by rugged terrain and solid fortifications.

After two days of reorganization and mopping-up operations, the attack on Santander itself began. Developments were closely followed in Rome. Ciano took boyish glee in playing the general at a distance, telegraphing instructions to the Italian commanders to cut the city's water supply in order to hasten its surrender.

On August 25 and 26, with all escape routes to the west virtually cut off by the Navarrese brigades, the Basque forces surrendered to the CTV at Santoña.[57] Almost simultaneously, the Republican units from Santander and Asturias also decided that further resistance was useless. On August 26 the last defenders of the city lay down their arms and the Nationalists entered Santander unopposed, led by the CTV.

The Italian press had already begun to treat the Santander offensive as a great Italian victory. With the fall of the city, all the stops were pulled. Full page headlines announced: "A Great Victory for Franco. Santander Con-

[56] The division was formed in mid-July by joining the Blue and Black Arrow Mixed Brigades, SHM CGG, L. 387, C. 26. During the Santander offensive, Roatta actually had only the Black Arrow Brigade at his orders, since the Blue Arrows were in Extremadura (Faldella, *Venti mesi di guerra in Spagna*, p. 408).

[57] For details of the surrender, see *infra*, pp. 291–92.

quered. Italian Volunteers at the Head of the Forces of Liberation."[58] Victory parades and demonstrations were organized throughout Italy.[59] Front page editorials claimed Santander as a Fascist triumph:

Franco's victory, which crowns the irresistible march of the Nationalist and Legionary troops on the Santander front is an essentially Fascist and Italian victory. The strategic and tactical conception of the offensive were Fascist and Italian, as was the overwhelming character of the advance. Two divisions of Italian volunteers participated in the formidable action in fraternal and comradely collaboration with Franco's National forces. . . . In addition, impressive units of Italian volunteers were included in the mixed brigades.[60]

On August 28, the entire Italian press published Mussolini's telegram to Franco celebrating the victory. Unusually detailed information was given to the press about the composition of Italian units in Spain.[61]

Franco at first collaborated closely with Italian propaganda efforts, incorporating into his official daily war bulletins information on Italian units prepared by the head of the Italian delegation to his headquarters, Colonel Gelich. Soon, however, the blatant exaggerations of the Fascist press, which gave all the credit for the success of the operations to the CTV, began to irritate the Spaniards. General Bastico was forced to take measures to moderate the tone of press dispatches from Spain.[62] In addition

[58] *Corriere della sera*, August 26, 1937.

[59] See telegrams to the ministry of the interior from the provincial prefects in ACS, presidenza del consiglio dei ministri, gabinetto, 1937–1939, 15, 2, 47.

[60] *Corriere della sera*, August 27, 1937.

[61] The *Avvenire d'Italia* published on August 28, 1937, the names of eleven Italian generals who had participated in the campaign, of whom three belonged to the Fascist militia, one to the air force, and seven to the royal army.

[62] Gelich, letter to Commando Truppe Voluntarie, September 25, 1937, MAE, Politica, b. 20.

to annoying her Spanish protegées, Rome's press campaign gave Republican propagandists an opportunity to exaggerate the size and importance of the Italian contribution to Franco's forces, so as to be able to request more aid from their own French and Russian supporters. Republican sources even began to report the presence of Italian units in Asturias, where in fact no Italians had set foot.

After the capture of Santander, fighting throughout Spain became sporadic and desultory for more than a month. The Nationalists in the north made only slight progress in their advance on Gijón and the rest of Asturias during the month of September. At the beginning of October, however, the morale of the Republican defenders, whose ammunition was almost exhausted, suddenly collapsed. By October 21, the Nationalists had taken Gijón, thus liquidating the entire northern front.[63]

The fall of Gijón marks the end of a cycle. For fifteen months the war had been fought in two separate theaters. Until Guadalajara, most of the action had centered around the Nationalists' attempts to take Madrid and the Republicans' stubborn defense of the capital. The last six months had seen most of the attention shifted to the northern theater, except when the attack at Brunete momentarily drew it away. Now Franco was free to concentrate all his forces for a new attack on the capital, without the distraction of a second front, and considerably strengthened by the occupation of one of Spain's richest industrial areas. The CTV, having obtained the propaganda victory Mussolini so desperately wanted, was withdrawn from the front lines. It would see very little action before spring 1938.

NEGOTIATIONS FOR A BASQUE SURRENDER

The elimination of the northern front had taken more than half a year. Rome, which was increasingly anxious to liqui-

[63] Thomas, *The Spanish Civil War*, pp. 609–11.

date its commitment in Spain, had hoped that it could be done much more quickly if the Basques could be induced to surrender by the offer of a reasonable settlement and of an Italian guarantee that Franco would respect the terms once they had laid down their arms. This hope explains why Italy had reversed its policy of not interfering directly in the internal politics of the Nationalist zone, and attempted to negotiate a Basque surrender.

Since the beginning of the war, the Basque provinces, together with Santander and Asturias, had been cut off from the main body of Republican territory and could be supplied with arms only with difficulty. Politically, the Basque position within the Republican coalition was an anomalous one. The region had long been one of the most devoutly Catholic areas of Spain and, outside the industrial city of Bilbao, most of its inhabitants were socially conservative small farmers. On both political and religious grounds, therefore, the Basques had little in common with other Republican groups. Their support of the Republic was primarily a result of their regional nationalism. The Basques sought only to defend and preserve their regional autonomy. Republican leaders, who were fully aware of the Basque's Catholicism and bourgeois leadership, were unwilling to expend any significant proportion of their resources in the north when they were urgently needed in the critical central and southern theaters.

The Italians had no particular sympathy for the Basques or their cause and no special desire to help them, but they thought they perceived in the anamolous situation an opportunity to hasten the end of the war. If the Basques could be convinced to surrender, their withdrawal might provoke the collapse of the northern front, and would certainly somewhat shorten the fighting.

As early as the second week of March 1937, the recently appointed Italian consul in San Sebastian, the Marchese di Cavaletti, reported that only fear of a blood bath at the hands of Franco's troops was keeping the Basques in the line, and that if they had adequate guarantees against reprisals, they might be willing to abandon the struggle.[64] On March 21 Cardinal Gomá contacted Cavaletti to suggest that Italy offer her good offices in arranging a negotiated peace.[65] Cantalupo was interested in this possibility and, after sounding out Franco on his attitude, he querried his government about its willingness to guarantee a Basque surrender.[66] The proposal did not evoke any great enthusiasm in Rome, but around April 12 the foreign ministry did authorize offering the Basques an Italian guarantee.[67]

A month later, Cavaletti contacted for the first time the man who would carry out most of the negotiations for the Basques, Fr. Alberto Onaindía. Onaindía, a strongly nationalistic Basque canon, was a close personal friend of the president of the Basque government, José Antonio Aguirre, and of other prominent members of the Basque Nationalist party. After his first interview with Cavaletti, Onaindía discussed the Italian diplomat's proposals with Doroteo Ciaurriz, the president of the Junta Suprema of the Basque Nationalist party. Ciaurriz was enthusiastic about the possibility of a surrender, since by this time Mola's forces had advanced a considerable distance into the Basque country and the siege ring around Bilbao was being inexorably closed. He urged Onaindía to fly immedi-

[64] Telegram 334, March 8, 1937, MAE, Politica, b. 20.

[65] Granados, *El Cardenal Gomá*, p. 156.

[66] Cantalupo, *Fu la Spagna*, pp. 224–27; interview with Francesco Cavaletti, Rome, August 3, 1970.

[67] No copy of Cavaletti's dispatch nor of the ministry's response has been found in the archives of the ministry of foreign affairs. The tenor of the response may be inferred from Cavaletti's report 974, May 12, 1937, MAE, Politica, b. 20. There are very considerable lacunae on the Basque question in the files of the Italian foreign ministry that I was able to consult. They are probably due to vagaries of the filing system rather than to suppression of the documents. Fortunately, the unpublished memoirs of one of the chief Spanish actors, Fr. Alberto Onaindía, which will be quoted frequently in the following pages, permit a reasonably accurate and reliable reconstruction of Italian policy.

ately to Bilbao to consult with Aguirre.[68] Aguirre also showed some interest in the Italian offer, but was cautious and noncommital. The reply he authorized Onaindía to make was vaguely worded and offered no prospects of immediate action.[69] The contrast between Ciaurriz's enthusiasm and Aguirre's guarded caution reveals not only the president's greater reserve but also his fundamental distrust of the Italians. Aguirre does not appear ever to have taken the Italian proposals seriously. He saw in them a way of gaining time, rather than a possible solution to the Basque problem.

During the following month, Cavaletti maintained close contacts with Onaindía, to whom he suggested the advantages of surrendering Bilbao to the Italians rather than to Franco's troops, hinting that his government might not be disinclined to establish some sort of protectorate over the Basque country for a number of years after its surrender.[70] Onaindía kept Aguirre informed about these contacts, but the Basque president showed no interest in pursuing them, so no progress was made.

On June 11 the Nationalists relaunched their offensive against the Basque capital, soon penetrating the "iron ring" of fortifications that had been expected to defend Bilbao against attack. In view of the critical situation, the president of the Basque Nationalist party, Juan Ajuriaguerra, asked Onaindía to inform Cavaletti that the Basque troops would keep order in the city until the last moment and that they hoped the Italians would intervene to protect the lives of civilians. On the morning of June 19, Nationalist troops entered Bilbao unopposed. Basque leaders fulfilled their promises, handing over to the Nationalists political prisoners who might otherwise have been executed by Communist

[68] Report 974, May 12, 1937, MAE, Politica, b. 20.

[69] Onaindía memoirs, p. 9. I am grateful to Professor Stanley G. Payne of the University of Wisconsin for making the typescript of these unpublished memoirs available to me.

[70] Ibid., p. 25.

or anarchist groups, and preventing the destruction of buildings within the city. To avoid reprisals and disorders, Franco allowed only small bodies of troops to enter Bilbao. All Basque leaders had withdrawn with the retreating troops the day before, and few arrests of civilians were made. Franco's moderation was partially due to Mussolini's intercession. Sometime before the fall of the city, the Duce had suggested to Franco that the Basques might still be won over to the Nationalist cause,[71] and as soon as Bilbao was taken, he telegraphed to Franco, again urging moderation.[72]

The capture of Bilbao did not signify the liquidation of the northern front, since Santander and parts of Asturias remained in Republican hands. Cavaletti was still determined to negotiate. On June 21, he visited Onaindía to suggest that it would be worth the Basques' while to consider the possibility of surrender to Italian units rather than to Franco. Italy, he said, would be willing to study the possibility of evacuating the Basque population from Santander and allowing Basque leaders to flee the country.

On June 25, a delegation led by the president of the Basque Nationalist party, Juan Ajuriaguerra, met at midnight in the port of the little town of Algorta with Colonel De Carlo of the CTV. De Carlo, who used the pseudonym Da Cunto, assured the Basques that if they were willing to surrender to the Italians, the lives of the civilian population, of the Basque soldiers and wounded, and of Spanish army officers fighting on the Basque side would be guaranteed. An arrangement would also be made to take care of the political leaders.[73] De Carlo stressed, however, the importance of swift action. A new offensive against Santander might begin any day and it was imperative that an agreement be reached before it did.

At the end of June, Ajuriaguerra, acting in agreement

[71] Interview with Francesco Cavaletti, Rome, August 3, 1970.
[72] Ciano, Diary, January 25, 1939.
[73] Onaindía memoirs, pp. 36–48.

288

with President Aguirre, instructed Onaindía to go to Rome to explain the nature of the Basque question and their reasons for participating in the war. In characteristic fashion, he expressed his hope that the Duce would support the Basques' aspirations, but made no mention of any concessions they would be willing to make to the Italians. Throughout these contacts the Basques repeatedly made appeals to the good will and benevolence of the Italians, while offering nothing in return. If Rome was interested in a possible special settlement with the Basques, it was certainly not because of abstract humanitarianism nor of particular sympathy for Basque aspirations. Rome's interest arose primarily from a desire to see the war brought to a speedy conclusion. If they wanted to obtain Italian support, the Basques would have to offer something concrete in return.

On July 6 Onaindía reached Rome and was immediately taken to Ciano. The foreign minister showed clearly that he was concerned about obtaining a quick surrender rather than about Basque liberties or whether or not the Basques should be considered Spaniards. Nonetheless, Onaindía's appeal for a humanitarian intervention on Mussolini's part interested Ciano insofar as it could be tied to a rapid Basque surrender. That same day Mussolini sent a personal telegram to Franco, urging him to avoid reprisals against the civilian population and to leave Basque prisoners under Italian control without forcing them to fight in the Nationalist ranks. He argued that a Basque surrender would lead to the immediate collapse of the whole northern front, and would have beneficial results on the international political scene and on Catholic opinion throughout the world.

Franco agreed on July 8 to accept Mussolini's suggestions, although he expressed his doubts that the Basque troops would obey orders to surrender and that their surrender, even if it did come about, would actually lead to the collapse of the northern front.[74] In the light of Fran-

[74] *Ibid.*, pp. 57–58 and 62.

co's response, Onaindía considered his mission in Rome successfully completed. Further negotiations would be necessary, but they would have to be carried out on the spot.

After Onaindía's return to St. Jean de Luz, talks were initiated to establish the timing and modality of the surrender. Since the Italians believed that the political and diplomatic questions had already been solved and that what was lacking was a technical military agreement, Cavaletti was replaced in the negotiations by Colonel De Carlo, Major Beer, and General Roatta. For almost a month no substantial progress was made. The relative success obtained by the Republicans in the battle of Brunete and the consequent postponement of the second phase of the offensive in the north encouraged Aguirre and other Basque leaders, who still hoped to avoid surrender.

To speed up the negotiations, the CTV proposed late in July a meeting between President Aguirre and General Roatta or the Italian ambassador in Paris, Cerrutti. Aguirre, however, refused to even consider meeting with them. Meanwhile, on several occasions the Basques violated the terms of the agreement under which the Italians allowed ships to visit Santander to evacuate civilians. These factors, and the general slowness of the negotiations, eventually convinced the CTV that the Basques were merely playing for time. As preparations were stepped up in early August for recommencing the Nationalist offensive, the Italian military withdrew from the negotiations, putting them back in Cavaletti's hands on August 10.[75]

The second phase of the Nationalists' northern offensive, which was to lead to the capture of Santander, began on August 14. Among the Republicans, and especially among the Basques, who had little interest in carrying on the struggle now that their homes had already fallen to Franco, morale was low. On August 20 a Basque delegation led

[75] Report 1961, August 10, 1937, MAE, Politica, b. 20. Onaindía memoris, pp. 69–98.

by Juan Ajuriaguerra agreed to surrender to the CTV, in return for an Italian promise to guarantee the lives of the Basque combatants and to allow Basque leaders and officials to leave the country. The Italians also pledged that they would consider the Basques who surrendered free of all obligation to take part in the Civil War, and would guarantee that the civilian population not be persecuted for having adhered to the Basque government.[76]

On August 21 the CTV set a deadline of midnight August 24 for the surrender, notifying the Basque representatives in St. Jean de Luz that the conditions fixed on the previous day would not be respected if the surrender had not taken place by that time.[77] The following day the bulk of the Basque forces began withdrawing toward the fishing port of Santoña, twenty miles east of Santander, where their surrender was to take place. While the Basque forces withdrew to the east, Navarrese brigades reached and occupied the road from Santander to Asturias, cutting off any possibility of escape for the now encircled defenders of the city.

On August 24 the Basques retreated without firing, but did not surrender.[78] The next day a few Basque battalions

[76] Bowers, *My Mission to Spain*, pp. 349–50; Onaindía memoirs, pp. 106–107.

[77] Bastico, letter to Ciano, September 9, 1937, MAE, Politica, b. 20.

[78] Late on the evening of August 24 several Basque staff officers presented themselves at the front lines of the Black Arrows Brigade to establish the timing and modality of a surrender. The seven-point agreement they signed on the 24th provided that "the surrender is unconditional, as specified by His Excellency the Generalissimo, respecting the lives of all except those who have committed crimes." (The original handwritten text of the surrender is found in SHM CGG, L. 388, C. 64 bis.) On August 25, however, the CTV command informed the Basque representatives in St. Jean de Luz that whether or not the previously agreed to conditions would be respected depended on the way the surrender was carried out and the number of men who surrendered (Onaindía memoirs, p. 118). It seems, therefore, that the agreement signed during the night of the 24th repre-

surrendered to the Black Arrows. On August 26 Basque emissaries arrived to settle the conditions for the surrender of the remaining battalions. At Bastico's orders they were given a note stating that any surrender would be unconditional, but holding out the hope of lenient treatment from the Italians. The following day the CTV occupied Santoña, where eleven Basque battalions surrendered.

When the Italians occupied Santoña, some one thousand Basque civilians were in the town, including a large number of exleaders or officials of the Basque government. Many of these people clearly belonged to the category whose expatriation had been provided for in the original agreement. Some two hundred had already embarked on English ships, but could not leave the port, whose exit was blocked by Spanish Nationalist ships. On August 27 the Nationalist supreme command ordered the Black Arrows Brigade to disembark them forcibly and to search the ships. The Italians refused to fulfill the order, but advised the Basques to leave the British ships, trusting the goodwill of the Italians.[79] This they did.

The men who surrendered were taken prisoner and, like other civilian and military prisoners, were held under guard in Santoña by purely Italian units. At the end of August, however, General Franco issued a formal order to Bastico for the immediate surrender of all Basque prisoners to the Spanish authorities.[80] In view of the assurances received from Franco's aide, Colonel Antonio Barroso, that the Basques would be given lenient treatment, that none but criminals would be executed, and that the Nationalists

---

sented a purely local battlefield episode that did not modify the previously established situation. Martínez Bande is mistaken in considering it proof that the surrender of the Basques took place under the same conditions as those of other units (Martínez Bande, *El final del frente norte*, pp. 97–98).

[79] Bastico, letter to Ciano, September 9, 1937, MAE, Politica, b. 20.

[80] SHM CGG, L. 387, C. 27.

would consult the CTV about the entire question, General Bastico ordered on September 4 that they be handed over.[81]

No sooner were the prisoners in Nationalist hands than summary trials began. Bastico attempted to secure favorable treatment for the Basques, partly out of fear that Basque exiles might publish accounts of the surrender that would damage Italy in the eyes of the world opinion. On September 8 he sent General Roatta to Salamanca to plead that no one be executed, that Basque leaders be allowed to flee the country, and that the troops be set free. Roatta argued both that a moral obligation existed toward the troops who had surrendered in good faith, and that there was a danger of an anti-Italian propaganda campaign. Franco was totally unmoved by these considerations. Roatta then advanced the suggestion that Basque leaders might be allowed to leave the country on foreign ships—thus freeing the Italians from all responsibility—and then taken prisoner again on the high seas by Nationalist warships. Understandably, Franco did not pursue this bizarre idea.[82]

As a concession to the Italians, Franco did agree to allow an Italian officer to sit on the commission for the classification of the prisoners. Early in November, when the initial screening was completed, 11,000 individuals had been set free, 5,400 assigned to labor battalions for having volunteered for service in the Basque army, and 5,600 were still in prison. By that time, 510 death sentences had been pronounced and 57 executed.[83]

During the following year approximately another 145 capital sentences were pronounced and 85 carried out,

[81] Bastico, letter to Ciano, September 9, 1937, MAE, Politica, b. 20.

[82] Roatta, letter to Bastico, September 8, 1937, MAE, Politica, b. 20.

[83] Gambarra's report 335 to Colonel Gelich in Burgos, November 7, 1937, MAE, Politica, b. 20. Among the men executed were three who had left the ships in Santoña harbor—all three of whom, Gambarra hastened to add, were accused of homicide and other criminal offenses.

bringing the total number of capital sentences to 655 and of executions to 145. Of the remaining 510 Basques condemned to death but not executed by August 1938, 55 had been exchanged for prisoners held by the Republicans and 230 had already had their sentences changed to life imprisonment or were sure to do so, leaving about 225 still liable to the death penalty.[84] Italian authorities were convinced that the presence of an Italian officer on the classification commission and the appeals made by him and by the embassy had greatly reduced the number of capital sentences and executions. Ambassador Viola affirmed that the majority of those condemned to death were in fact guilty of serious nonpolitical offenses.[85]

The initiative in all the negotiations with the Basques had rested with the Italians. They informed Franco about the major steps and obtained his approval, but it is obvious that it was grudgingly given. If Franco had been free to decide, he would have preferred to avoid Italian interference in this question, which involved the delicate issue of Basque regional nationalism. The Italians had pressed ahead with their plans despite Franco's lack of enthusiasm primarily because they believed that by so doing they could shorten the war.

FORMATION OF THE SPANISH STATE PARTY;
ITALO-SPANISH ECONOMIC RELATIONS

In contrast to their active role in initiating and pursuing negotiations with the Basques, the Italians were passive observers of the formation and development of Franco's

[84] This is the best calculation that can be made from the somewhat confused and contradictory information given in the Italian embassy's Report 3853/1194, August 10, 1938, MAE, Politica, b. 20, and in Gambarra's report of November 7, 1937. The figure of 655 death sentences has been calculated by adding the other categories. In report 3853/1194, however, the total number of death sentences is given as 455.

[85] Report 3853/1194, August 10, 1938, MAE, Politica, b. 20.

official state party, the *Falange Española Tradicionalista y de las JONS*. During the early months of the war, the two most important political groups in the Nationalist zone had been the Falange and the Traditionalists. In early 1937 they began negotiating with each other in desultory fashion about possible unification, but little or no progress was made. It was clear that Franco was determined to bring them together and to reduce the influence of the left wing of the Falange, but few clues were given as to when or how it would be done.

Franco carried out the unification without consulting his foreign supporters and with very little concern for the feelings and opinions of the leaders of the two parties. He simply took advantage of a violent struggle between two factions of the Falange to assert his own control and to join the Traditionalist Communion to it on April 19, 1937.[86] The preamble of the decree of unification specifically cited the example of other totalitarian countries,[87] and it is clear that the Fascist and Nazi parties represented the models for the new creation.[88]

News of the unification was given prominently in the Italian press, which only rarely gave any news at all about political events in Nationalist Spain. The *Corriere della sera* described it as an historic event, which joined all the healthy political forces of the nation and gave them a totalitarian physiognomy, while eliminating dangerous dissidence. In a front-page editorial, it called the unification an important sign that the youthful forces of renovation in Spain were capable of sacrificing some of their private and personal interests in favor of the common cause. More realistically, the editorialist pointed out that the decree "confirms that Franco's authority imposes itself against all autonomistic and dissident tendencies."[89]

[86] Payne, *Falange*, pp. 164–66.
[87] Clark, *The Evolution of the Franco Regime*, appendix I, p. 43.
[88] Reyes Heroles, *Tendencias actuales del estado*, p. 328.
[89] *Corriere della sera*, April 21, 1937.

Mussolini was encouraged by the unification, which seemed to him an important step in the right direction. Rome, however, had been a passive observer of the scene. It played no role in the unification process and made no efforts to influence the preparation of the new party's statutes. The ministry of popular culture apparently even forbade any explicit comparisons between Franco's new party and the *Partito Nazionale Fascista*. Neither the *Corriere della sera* nor any of the other major Italian papers even used the word Fascist or Fascism in referring to the new party.

Unification was a largely negative and preventive measure, designed to guarantee Franco's continued hegemony and to prevent damaging in-fighting among his supporters rather than to create a new power base. It demonstrated that no one in the Nationalist zone could even remotely challenge his position, but it led to no sudden changes. Months went by without the new organization's doing anything significant. Not until August did Franco even publish its statutes.[90]

The publication of the statutes of the *Falange Española Tradicionalista y de las JONS* coincided with the arrival of a new Italian ambassador, Guido Viola. To replace Cantalupo, Mussolini had chosen a fifty-four year old aristocrat who had spent much of his career in various positions in the foreign ministry in Rome, most recently as head of the ceremonial office. Viola was calm and serious, but not very strong willed. The Duce clearly wanted a representative who would not cause problems, and in Viola he had found the man he wanted. The new ambassador reported that the statutes Franco had just published clearly had a "more Fascist than Nazi character."[91] Mussolini was very pleased with this news and instructed him to "express to Franco my lively pleasure with his recent measures. One party, one militia, one syndicate. On these three pillars

[90] The text of the statutes is found in Clark, *The Evolution of the Franco Regime,* appendix I, pp. 67–71.
[91] Report 2360/977, August 8, 1937, MAE, Politica, b. 14.

tomorrow's great Spain will be securely built."[92] Rome was satisfied with the results, but had done nothing to shape them. She had been a passive observer of the scene, just as she had been months earlier when the party was formed.

The lack of initiative that characterized most of Rome's activities with respect to the internal politics of Nationalist Spain also extended to the economic sphere. Italy's economic relations with Franco were centered around the twin problems of reducing the immediate strain on the Italian treasury and guaranteeing that over the long run she would be paid for her aid. They did not extend to trying to win a lasting place in Spanish markets, nor to taking control of Spanish mineral resources.

The failure of the Guadalajara offensive and the slow progress of Mola's operations in the north made it seem probable during the spring of 1937 that the end of the Spanish Civil War was still far off. Italy could expect to have to make significant new contributions if Franco were to go on to victory. The minister of foreign commerce, Felice Guarnieri, was alarmed at the prospect of further large shipments to Spain because of their effects on the Italian economy. Especially critical, in his opinion, was the strain on Italy's foreign exchange position, since many of the raw materials needed to manufacture war material had to be imported.

The commercial agreement signed in November 1936

[92] Telegram 1386 R/536, MAE, Politica, b. 14. The Italian ministry of foreign affairs was not deceived about the scope and effectiveness of Franco's fusion of the parties. In its secret-print report on the political situation in Spain for the year 1937, it noted that despite the initial enthusiasm with which the decree was greeted in Spain, it had remained dead letter. The *Falange tradicionalista* was "an artificial creation, with no echo in the opinion of the people who remained what they had been: Falangists, Requetés or Alphosine monarchists." Only Franco's energetic discipline kept the latent conflicts beneath the surface. (NA T 586, roll 1287, no frame number, Quaderno 59, p. 7.)

and the clearing agreement of December 21, 1936, were entirely insufficient to meet the demands of the new situation, and were replaced by two new agreements in April and August 1937. The April agreement was negotiated by Vincenzo Fagiuoli, president of the state-owned *Società Anonima Fertilizanti Italia* (SAFNI). At Fagiuoli's urging, the Spaniards agreed to pay 150 million lire per year beginning in January 1938 on debts that were estimated at 1.5 to 2 billion lire. Under the terms of the November 1936 agreement, they would have had to pay only 30 to 40 million annually on a debt that size, so the new agreement represented a considerable step forward for the Italians. Fagiuoli also received a promise that before December 31, 1937, the Spaniards would pay 75 million lire against their outstanding debts in iron ore, unwashed wool, hides, and free currencies.[93] The Italians, like the Germans, had their eye on the high-grade iron ores from Spain's Riff mines, but Fagiuoli tried in vain to obtain some definite commitment of future production. He had to be content with a vague assurance that after January 1, 1938, the Spaniards would no longer be bound by their existing international agreements controlling the mines and would make no further commitments without consulting the Italians.

In late June 1937, Franco requested almost 200 million lire in new arms shipments. In response to this request, Ciano's personal secretary, Filippo Anfuso, was sent to Spain to discuss the entire question of arms shipments and payment. Anfuso succeeded in radically scaling down Franco's requests, but the new material Italy promised to provide was still valued at 85 million lire. Anfuso agreed that 75 percent of this amount be added to the Franco-Fagiuoli account established in April, but insisted that the remaining 25 percent be paid in free currencies and iron ore.[94] In the light of Nicolás Franco's avowal that the Salamanca government had a total of only a hundred thou-

[93] The text of the agreement is found in MAE, Politica, b. 32.
[94] Telegram 540, July 7, 1937, MAE, Ufficio Spagna, b. 3.

sand pounds sterling in foreign exchange, the prospect of receiving any sizeable payments in free currencies seemed very slight.[95] Anfuso returned to the question of Riff ores, suggesting this time that the Spanish government might cede some of the company stock to Italy, but the suggestion was rebuffed.[96]

Economic issues were raised again in early August, when Nicolás Franco visited Rome. During his stay in the Italian capital, yet another Italo-Spanish agreement was signed, the Ciano-Franco agreement of August 11, 1937. To reduce the strain on the Italian treasury, a consortium of banks, headed by the Banca d'Italia, was induced to agree to loan the Salamanca government 250 million lire. All future shipments were to be paid for with 50 percent in free currencies or lire derived from this loan, and the other 50 percent in merchandise that Italy normally bought from abroad. Fagiuoli's SAFNI was designated by the Italians to act as intermediary in all Italian purchases of Spanish materials. The sale of two warships and of sixty air planes was not covered by the terms of this agreement. The Spaniards promised to pay for them separately, half in free currencies and half in lire.[97]

Over all, the terms Rome obtained were far less favorable than those the Nationalists granted the Germans the month before, when they agreed to pay all their debts in Reichsmarks and promised to sign with Germany their first general economic treaty.[98] The Germans were far more aggres-

[95] Anfuso, unnumbered telegram to Ciano, July 4, 1937, MAE, Ufficio Spagna, b. 3.

[96] Anfuso, unnumbered telegram to Ciano, July 8, 1937, MAE, Ufficio Spagna, b. 3.

[97] Ciano, note for Mussolini, August 11, 1937, MAE, Ufficio Spagna, b. 3; Guarnieri, *Battaglie economiche*, II, 134. The note speaks of 125 million lire, but Guarnieri gives the figure of 250 million, and by December 31 Franco had already used 194 million lire of the credit. Perhaps the original 125 million ceiling was increased later in the year.

[98] GD, D, III, 421 and 612–13.

sive and insistent in pursuing their economic interests and far more determined to win valuable concessions from the Spaniards in return for their aid. Rome occasionally attempted to obtain mining concessions or to guarantee payment in convertible currencies, but Mussolini's lack of real interest in such questions fatally weakened the bargaining position of men like Guarnieri, who knew that a direct appeal from Franco to the Duce would usually be sufficient to override any objections they might offer. Mussolini was more interested in appearing to be the generous and farsighted leader of a great country than in the arid facts of Italy's limited resources and deficient balance of payments.

INTERNATIONAL TENSION

The six months after Guadalajara, during which Franco eliminated the northern front, was the period in which Italian foreign relations were most dramatically affected by the international consequences of the Spanish conflict. In retrospect, it is clear that none of the incidents actually brought Europe close to a general conflict, but tension ran high throughout the period. During the crisis provoked by attacks on Italian and German ships engaged in the nonintervention patrol and by Italian submarine attacks on Mediterranean shipping bound for Republican ports, it seemed to contemporary observers that little more was needed to start a European war. This period of international tension that centered around the Spanish Civil War was closed by the Nyon Conference in September 1937. During the following eighteen months, the Civil War took on an entirely different character, if viewed in terms of its international repercussions. European statesmen were still concerned about it, but it had become relatively clear that the great powers would not fight over Spain; and from the spring of 1938 onwards, Hitler's expansion in central Europe came to occupy the center of the international stage. From an independent driving variable, Spain became a dependent one.

International tension was exacerbated in the spring of 1937 by British and French press coverage of the battle of Guadalajara, which raised the temperature of the international debate over Fascist intervention in Spain, and made it more difficult for leaders in London and Paris to ignore the seriousness and extent of Italian violations of the Non-Intervention Agreement. The Italians, for their part, did nothing to ease the situation. On March 23, Ambassador Grandi allowed himself to be provoked into declaring at a meeting of the Non-Intervention Committee that Italy did not consider the time ripe for discussing the question of the withdrawal of volunteers, although in fact he had been authorized to do so. He added that he hoped no Italian volunteers would leave Spanish soil until Franco's victory was assured.[99] This outburst is surprising in a diplomat of Grandi's ability and self-control, and constitutes an eloquent index of the extent to which Italian leaders felt their country's prestige had been affected by the defeat.

The Italian press soon launched into violent criticism of French aid to the Republic. The almost daily articles in all the major Italian newspapers obviously represented a deliberate government-sponsored campaign, and naturally led to further deterioration of Italo-French relations. It has been suggested that after Guadalajara, Italian intervention in Spain tended toward "overturning the ratio of forces in the western Mediterranean with the final objective of disqualifying France."[100] This hypothesis is a suggestive one, but lacks any documentary basis. As noted previously, there seems to be a strong anti-French strain in Italian policy during this whole period, but there is no real evidence of a fundamental change to a more markedly anti-

[99] *Ibid.*, p. 263. A vivid account of the incident is found in Maisky, *Spanish Notebooks*, pp. 215–26.

[100] D'Amoja, *La politica estera dell'Impero*, p. 175.

French policy at this juncture, despite the heated tone of the Italian press.

The weeks following Guadalajara also witnessed a sharp increase in Italo-British tension. The Italian troop buildup in Spain during January and February had effectively destroyed whatever goodwill had been generated by the Gentlemen's Agreement. London now found new cause for concern in the growth of an assertive and belligerent Italian presence in North Africa. While the battle of Guadalajara was raging in Spain, Mussolini visited Libya. A ceremony on March 18 in which he accepted a symbolic "sword of Islam" seemed to point to a desire to extend Italian influence among the Arabs outside the narrow confines of Libya and Tripoli. Arab-language radio broadcasts from Radio Bari tended to foment discontent in British-ruled countries, and became one of the most frequent subjects of British diplomatic remonstrances in Rome.

Partly as a reaction to British reporting on the battle of Guadalajara, the Italian press became increasingly violent and abusive in its refutation of attacks on Italy in the British press and in its anti-British colonial propaganda. On March 31, 1937, for example, the *Corriere della sera* carried on the front page an article on India entitled "London Governs with the Sword rather than with the Rights of the Majority." A second lengthy article on the same page was titled, "The Usual Liar. The Inexhaustible Falsehoods of *The Times* on the Situation in Addis Ababa." The unsigned article describes the British press as the world's greatest specialist in the invention of false news for "indefinable sectarian political aims."

Early in May, British press commentary on the difficulties encountered by Italian troops at Bermeo incensed Mussolini. The Italian press responded with exaggerated accounts of the "Heroic Defense of Bermeo by Italian Volunteers of the 'Black Arrows',"[101] and with savage attacks on the British press. The *Corriere della sera* reported bitterly that

[101] *Popolo d'Italia*, May 6, 1937.

some English papers claimed Italian soldiers had fled before the women of Bermeo. "It is well that our Italian readers know what is being written about them abroad . . . so that their national sentiment and their Fascist pride grow even larger in the face of the limitless misery of such people."[102] Only two days later, the *Corriere* launched yet another deliberately insulting attack on the British press, castigating "the miserable representatives of a journalism that lies deliberately, speculating on the infinite imbecility of its readers."[103] The following day, the ministry for press and propaganda took the extreme step of recalling all Italian correspondents from England and prohibiting the entrance of most English papers into Italy. Not until July would Italian correspondents resume their work in London or British papers be allowed into Italy.

Against this general background of tense relations, a crisis developed in May and June, when Italian and German ships participating in the international patrol of the sea lanes leading to Spain were attacked by Republican aircraft. On May 24, the Italian ship *Barletta* was lying in the harbor of Palma de Mallorca when it was hit by a bomb. Grandi immediately lodged a vigorous protest with the Non-Intervention Committee, calling upon it to "reassert its authority."[104] On May 29, two Republican aircraft attacked the German battleship *Deutschland* while it lay at anchor off the island of Ibiza. Two days later, a German cruiser and four destroyers shelled the Spanish

---

[102] *Corriere della sera*, May 5, 1937.

[103] *Ibid.*, May 7, 1937.

[104] The committee deplored the incident and reserved the right to examine it again when full reports had been received. Thomas notes that Palma lay outside the Italian patrol zone and infers that the *Barletta's* "presence in Palma could not have been entirely innocent" (Thomas, *The Spanish Civil War*, p. 564). Vessels of all the countries in the patrol had, however, developed the custom of stopping briefly in Spanish ports. On the 24th, for instance, a British ship was also in Palma, although Palma was part of the French zone. The accusation, therefore, seems unfounded.

town of Almería in retaliation. Later the same day, the German government notified the Non-Intervention Committee of its decision to "cease to take part in the control scheme, as well as in the discussions of the Non-Intervention Committee" until it had received guarantees that such events would not recur.

These German decisions were taken without consulting Italy and without informing her beforehand. In response to an Italian inquiry, von Neurath said that it would be better for Italy to continue to attend the Non-Intervention Committee. Mussolini, however, was unwilling to follow a course of action different from that of Germany. To do so, he argued, would give rise to speculation about a divergence in the view of the two countries which could only weaken their influence. He therefore instructed Grandi to inform the committee that Italian ships would be withdrawn from the patrol and that the Italian ambassador would no longer participate in the meetings.[105] According to some observers, Mussolini was concerned at this time that Germany was gradually drifting away from Italy and welcomed these complications, since they brought the two countries back together again.[106]

London was alarmed by the Italo-German reaction. Fears ran high that the two Fascist countries meant to resume complete freedom of action and that this would greatly increase the danger of a European war, which the nonintervention policy, despite its evident failings, seemed to have much reduced. Many in high British diplomatic circles believed that the incident had been deliberately provoked by the Valencia government, possibly at the urging of Moscow, for the purpose of breaking up the Non-Intervention Agreement. Anthony Eden told the American ambassador in London that "it looked as if the Soviet Government wanted the British to pull its chestnuts out of the fire and would not be disturbed if Germany was at war with Eng-

[105] GD, D, III, 298–300.
[106] *Dez Anos,* 4, p. 408

land and France leaving Russia with a completely free hand on the other side."[107] The British ambassador in Berlin, Sir Neville Henderson, urged von Neurath repeatedly "not to do the Reds the compliment of expanding the Spanish situation into a world war."[108]

The main concern of both London and Paris was to prevent the total breakdown of the nonintervention policy and thus avoid the outbreak of a European conflict. They therefore agreed that in the case of future attacks the four patrol powers would take joint action, and that the country whose ship had been attacked would retain its right to act on its own initiative if not satisfied with the results of joint action. On this basis, Italy and Germany agreed to resume the patrol and return to the meetings.

Renewed Italo-German participation in the patrol scheme was nonetheless to prove short-lived. On June 18, the German cruiser *Leipzig* reported that four torpedoes had been fired at it by a submerged submarine. The British and French refused to take any action until further investigation had verified the reported attack, whereas the Germans, backed by the Italians, pressed for an immediate four power naval demonstration. No compromise could be reached on this issue, and on June 22 negotiations broke down. This time Germany did not take any retaliatory action, but withdrew permanently from the patrol scheme, while continuing to participate in the Non-Intervention Committee. Italy immediately followed the German example.

The definitive withdrawal of Italy and Germany from the patrol scheme forced the Non-Intervention Committee to abandon its attempts to establish international control of arms shipments to Spain and turn its attention to two issues which had been raised previously but not resolved: the granting of belligerent rights to the parties in Spain and the withdrawal of volunteers.

[107] FRUS, 1937, I, 318.
[108] GD, D, III, 299.

A proposal for granting belligerent rights to both sides in the conflict was put forward by Italy and Germany in response to British inquiries as to a viable alternative for the now defunct international patrol scheme. From the strictly juridical point of view, the Italo-German proposal was not without merit. The fighting in Spain was certainly of sufficient dimensions to justify recognizing the combatants as belligerents. It was widely believed, however, that in practice, the granting of belligerent rights would give General Franco a considerable advantage over the Republican government, since his superior naval strength guaranteed that he would be able to enforce an effective blockade, whereas the Republicans were unlikely to be able to do so. This feature, which made the proposal attractive to Italy and Germany, made it unacceptable to the governments of Russia and France. Conversely, the British and French were anxious to see foreign combatants withdrawn from Spain under international supervision, whereas the Italians were unwilling to accept any effective plan of supervised withdrawal. The committee soon found itself in a complete deadlock. By the end of July, it was clear to all parties that no progress could be expected until some sharp change in the international diplomatic situation or in Spain modified the conditions enough to move one or more of the powers off its position.

"PIRACY IN THE MEDITERRANEAN" AND THE NYON CONFERENCE

At this juncture, the growing frequency of torpedo attacks and other attacks on shipping in the Mediterranean provoked a new crisis and shifted attention away from the committee's work to the more pressing question of the safety of maritime traffic in the Mediterranean. On August 3, the Nationalist ambassador in Rome received an urgent telegram from Salamanca, announcing reports of massive Soviet shipments to the Republic. He was instructed to inform the Italian government immediately, requesting that Italian destroyers observe the position and routes of ships leaving Odessa and report them to the Nationalist fleet. Salamanca admitted that the reports might be exaggerated, but nonetheless requested that the Italians either provide them with the necessary ships or use their own fleet to stop the transports as they passed through the straits south of Italy and to block the route to Spain.[109]

The proposal found a ready response in Mussolini. A meeting was arranged for August 5 in Palazzo Venezia between the Duce and Nicolás Franco.[110] The personal letter from the Generalissimo, which his brother brought to Rome, repeated the plea for assistance in stopping the flow of Russian arms to the Republic, and stressed the dangers that would arise if the USSR were to gain "a strategic position in the West that would constitute a powerful center of propaganda and a future base for naval or aerial actions."[111] Mussolini refused Franco's request for surface vessels, but agreed to establish an elaborate net of safeguards to prevent Soviet ships from reaching the Republic. The Italians would intensify their vigilance at Constantinople. Submarines would be stationed at Cape Matapan and four destroyers in the Canal of Sicily would spot ships on their way to Spain. A string of submarines would be stationed between Cape Bon and Cape Lilibeo to torpedo vessels carrying arms to Spain. Spanish ships could patrol the sea between Cape Spartivento and the African coast,

[109] *Ibid.*, p. 432. The Italian ambassador in Berlin first received word of the new Spanish proposal from Count von Weizsacker. His reaction, which he reported to Rome on August 4th, was that the idea was too childish to be taken seriously (Attolico, telegram 5426, August 4, 1937, MAE, Gabinetto, b. 2). Two days later, Ciano curtly told the ambassador, "The proposal is so far from being childish that we have already decided on it and adopted it" (Telegram 1379/284, August 6, 1937, MAE, Gabinetto, b. 2).

[110] Summary of the Spanish Question from March 1937 to February 1938, MAE, Politica, b. 33.

[111] Franco to Mussolini, August 3, 1937, MAE, Gabinetto, b. 2.

and six Italian submarines would blockade the Republican ports of Barcelona, Valencia, and Cartagena.[112]

Available Italian records offer no information as to how Mussolini reached this decision, nor is it possible to ascertain the position taken by the ministers and other people who may have influenced him. The only thing that is clear is that the decision was made rapidly, in a period of forty-eight hours or less, and that it was a sign of the Duce's deepening commitment to supporting Franco until final victory. As we have seen, Guadalajara and the subsequent attacks on Fascist Italy in much of the world press had goaded Mussolini into identifying himself ever more closely with Franco's success. The minister for foreign exchange, Guarnieri, who was in close daily contact with him during this period, testifies that the Spanish conflict gradually took on in the Duce's mind the importance of "a symbol of an ideological war that deeply involved the honor and the prestige of the regime."[113] Consequently, he had made up his mind to do whatever was necessary short of European war to insure Franco's victory, irregardless of the cost.

The overall state of Italy's diplomatic situation, and especially of her relations with Great Britain, must have weighed heavily in the decision to interdict traffic in the Mediterranean. Toward the end of July, Mussolini had indicated to Chamberlain that he was still anxious to improve relations, and that he had no political, much less territorial, ambitions in Spain. Chamberlain immediately responded favorably to these overtures with a note assuring him that Great Britain would be ready at any time to begin conversations to clarify the situation and remove causes of suspicion and misunderstanding.[114] The British prime minister be-

[112] Minutes of the meeting between Nicolás Franco and Mussolini, MAE, Gabinetto, b. 2.

[113] Guarnieri, *Battaglie economiche*, II, 132–33. The publication three months after the event of Mussolini's anonymous article on Guadalajara in *Il popolo d'Italia* is another index of the Duce's profound irritation with the humiliation of his troops at Guadalajara.

[114] FO R 6096/1/22.

lieved that the Duce sincerely desired better relations. He was not alone in this belief. The American ambassador in Berlin held that despite her efforts to secure a speedy Franco victory, Italy was "ultimately concerned with her relations with England in the Mediterranean."[115]

The true importance of Mussolini's advances to Chamberlain can only be gauged by considering them against the background of Italy's behavior during the entire spring and summer of 1937. Throughout the Muslim world, Rome was carrying out a violent campaign of anti-British propaganda. In April 1937 a High Command for North Africa was formed, and plans were made for creating a white metropolitan army corps in Libya.[116] The tightly controlled Italian press published more and more articles that betrayed great animosity toward England. Mussolini's violent unsigned article on "Guadalajara," published on June 17 in *Il popolo d'Italia*, closed with the warning that "the dead of Guadalajara will be vindicated." The appearance of this article, with its bitter attacks on England and its thinly veiled threats of vendetta, may well have been motivated by a desire to make the atmosphere less propitious for von Neurath's projected visit to London, which had been announced on June 13. The announcement of this visit had come as an unwelcome surprise to the Italians, who feared that Germany might attempt to improve her relations with England at the expense of the Axis.[117]

Even after von Neurath's visit was indefinitely postponed, the Italian press continued its anti-British campaign. Two more editorial attacks on England were published in the *Popolo d'Italia* in a single week,[118] and in *Regime fascista* Farinacci practically called for preventive war.[119] The British chargé found the atmosphere unpleasantly reminiscent

[115] FRUS 1937, I, 352.
[116] FO R 3831/1/22.
[117] GD, D, III, 339.
[118] *Popolo d'Italia*, June 26 and July 1, 1937.
[119] *Regime fascista*, June 25, 1937.

of the early months of 1935, and believed that if Mussolini wanted to work public opinion up for war, this was how he would do it.[120] The secretary general of the French foreign ministry also feared that Mussolini was trying to provoke a war.[121] These fears were exaggerated. The Duce certainly did not want to become involved in a war at this time, but contemporary observers in London and Paris considered the situation serious.[122]

Toward the end of the summer Mussolini again assumed a very belligerent posture toward the Western powers. In mid-August, in a widely publicized speech given in Palermo, Mussolini declared his unwillingness to allow Franco to be defeated: "Let it be said in the most categorical fashion, that we will not tolerate the presence of Bolshevism or anything similar in the Mediterranean."[123] At the end of the month, he made public a telegram to Franco celebrating the exploits of Italian troops in the battle of Santander:

I am particularly glad that during ten days of hard fighting, the Italian legionary troops have made a valiant contribution to the splendid victory of Santander, and that that contribution finds today in your telegram the recognition to which they aspired. This comradeship of arms, which has become so close, is a guarantee of the final victory which will liberate Spain and the Mediterranean from all threats to the civilization we share.[124]

The French chargé in London, Cambon, interpreted the telegram as an open admission that Italy had violated the Non-Intervention Agreement in letter and in spirit, and described its publication to Eden as a public challenge

---

[120] Eden, *Facing the Dictators,* p. 506.
[121] FRUS, 1937, I, 356–57.
[122] GD, D, III, 391.
[123] Mussolini, *Opera omnia,* XXVIII, 242.
[124] Ciano, *Ciano's Diplomatic Papers,* p. 137.

to the nonintervention powers. Eden pointed out that the statement was mostly intended for domestic consumption, but nonetheless many English leaders were disturbed by the Duce's cavalier disregard for the most elementary forms in his international relations.[125]

Viewed in this context, Mussolini's overtures to Chamberlain seem a merely tactical move, without lasting significance. About this time, Ciano said explicitly to a young Fascist writer that he was maintaining contacts with the English ambassador to keep Great Britain quiet while he carried out his policy in Spain, and to keep anglophile elements in Italy content, but that he had no intention of modifying the basic lines of Italian policy.[126]

If Mussolini had in fact abandoned hope of a lasting Anglo-Italian settlement at the time he decided to interdict traffic in the Mediterranean, he may have seen no real cost to Italy in further alienating the British by attacking shipping on the high seas, so long as he did not go so far as to run any grave risks of provoking a war. In addition, he may have been convinced that British passivity and ineffectiveness were so great that he could fly in the face of their interests without doing any serious or irreparable harm to his relations with them, or at least without their declaring war on Italy.

These considerations probably entered Mussolini's calculations, although it is impossible to exclude the possibility that his decision may have been taken without much reflection and without weighing well the costs and risks involved. He could show on occasion a high degree of caution and circumspection, but at other times he acted impulsively, taking important decisions without consulting his advisors or even thinking through their implications.

In any case, by August 10 Italian submarines were in place and began a series of concerted attacks on shipping to Spain. During the first ten days of the month, one British,

---

[125] FO W 16299/23/41.

[126] Zangrandi, *Il lungo viaggio attraverso il fascismo*, p. 147.

one French, one Greek, and one Italian merchantman had been bombed by aircraft apparently belonging to the Spanish Nationalists. On the 11th, the Spanish tanker *Campeador*, carrying eight thousand tons of gasoline, was torpedoed and sunk in the Canal of Sicily. On the 12th, a Danish cargo ship was sunk by Italian aircraft off Barcelona, and on the following day, the Spanish cargo ship *Conde de Albasola* was torpedoed near Pantellaria. On the 13th, for the first time, a non-Spanish ship was attacked by submarines. The French *Parame* escaped without damage, but the following day the Panamanian tanker *MacKnight* was shelled and set on fire near Tunis. Three Spanish freighters and a Spanish destroyer were sunk between the 14th and the 18th.

Then there was a lull. During the next week, no ships were sunk, although one British vessel was attacked by airplanes between Marseilles and Barcelona. On the 30th, the Russian *Timiryazev* was sunk by a submarine near Algiers, and a second ship, the *Blagoiev*, sank off Cape Matapan. On the night of August 31-September 1, the Italian submarine *Iride*, which was blockading the Spanish coast under direct orders of the navy ministry in Rome, spotted a ship which its commander identified as a destroyer of the Spanish Republican fleet. The *Iride* launched torpedoes against the ship, which was in fact the British destroyer *Havock*. The *Havock* counterattacked with depth charges, but the *Iride* eventually managed to escape without being damaged or identified. Two days later, a British merchantman, the *Woodford*, was sunk by a torpedo near Valencia.[127]

On September 4, Ciano ordered Admiral Cavagnari to suspend the submarine attacks until further notice, despite the fact that Franco's emissary had told him the blockade

[127] Royal Institute of International Affairs, *Survey of International Affairs, 1937*, II, 341; research notes of Professor Willard C. Frank of Old Dominion University; interview with the commander of the *Iride*, Valerio Borghese, Rome, June 18, 1970.

would be decisive if continued through September. Ciano did not deny that it might indeed prove decisive, but ordered the suspension anyway in the face of British protests.[128] The following day, the British and French governments issued invitations to a conference on security in the Mediterranean to be held in the small Swiss town of Nyon, near Geneva, on September 10.

Ciano's first reaction to the invitation was favorable, and Italy would probably have participated in the conference if the USSR had not sent a strongly worded note of protest to Rome, accusing her of being responsible for the sinking of Russian ships and demanding reparations. The Italians indignantly rejected the accusations and said they could not participate in a conference with the Russians unless the charges were withdrawn. For once, the British and French acted with a certain amount of energy. Eden pressed the Italians to attend, arguing that if the Soviet Union were in fact trying to sabotage the conference, as Ciano charged, Italy could thwart the plan by attending anyway. In any case, he said, the need to put a speedy end to the situation in the Mediterranean made it necessary to go ahead with the meeting, even if Italy felt unable to attend.

The conference met in Nyon on September 10 without Italian or German participation. By the next evening an agreement had been worked out, which was signed on September 14.[129] The Nyon Agreement stipulated that the participating powers would destroy any submarine which attacked a merchant vessel not belonging to either party to the Spanish conflict, and any submarine encountered in the vicinity of a position where a merchant vessel had just been attacked if circumstances made it appear that the submarine was responsible. The decisions were to be carried out in the western Mediterranean and the Malta

[128] Ciano, *Diary*, September 4, 1937.
[129] The text of the agreement is found in League of Nations, *Official Journal*, XVIII, 7 (July–December 1937), 671–74.

Channel, with the exception of the Tyrrhenian Sea, by the British and French navies. In the eastern Mediterranean, it would be executed by the participating countries in their own territorial waters and by the British and French on the high seas except in the Adriatic. Neither the British nor the French had any desire to exclude Italy from adhering to the agreement, and the patrol of the Adriatic and Tyrrhenian was deliberately left open so that it could be assigned to her.[130]

The Italians were unpleasantly surprised by the fact that their refusal to attend the conference had not prevented its meeting as scheduled, nor even made it difficult to reach an agreement. Little would be gained, however, by refusing to participate in the arrangements made at Nyon, and Italy's claims to great power status would be hurt if the sea which Mussolini fondly called the *mare nostrum* were to be patrolled exclusively by French and British vessels. There was some satisfaction to be found, furthermore, in the fact that the Soviet Union had not been assigned a patrol zone in the Mediterranean, but was confined to the Black Sea. On the other hand, Italian sensibilities were wounded by the relatively insignificant zone which had been reserved for them if they decided to accept the plan. On September 14, Ciano declared that Rome could not agree to patrol only the Tyrrhenian, but insisted on "absolute parity with any other power in any part of the Mediterranean."[131] The British and French were willing to be

---

[130] The British were more inclined toward taking a soft line than the French. On September 18, the French foreign secretary proposed to Eden that France and Great Britain make a joint démarche in Rome to clarify Italy's intentions with respect to Spain. Italy should be required to stop dispatching men and to withdraw at least some volunteers. If not, the two governments should reserve their freedom of action (FO W 17863/7/41). The British were not receptive to this proposal. The foreign office felt that British interests in the conflict were not sufficient to justify the risks involved in an energetic stance.

[131] *Nuova antologia*, October 1, 1937, p. 337.

flexible on this subject, and by the end of October final arrangements were made for Italian participation in the patrolling of the Mediterranean, to begin on November 11. Italy also accepted the supplementary agreements reached at Nyon in an attempt to prevent attacks by surface vessels and aircraft on shipping in the Mediterranean.[132]

The Nyon arrangements proved successful for several months, and no new submarine attacks were reported until January 1938, when the strength of the patrols had been reduced due to their evident success. Nyon is often presented as a triumph of firmness, and a proof of the assertion that "Mussolini would respect a show of force."[133] Ciano interpreted the whole episode in an entirely different key. On September 21 he noted in his diary: "It is a fine victory. From suspected pirates to policemen of the Mediterranean—and the Russians, whose ships we were sinking, excluded." Neither version fully represents the facts, but Ciano's seems in many ways more satisfactory. True, there were no more submarine attacks in the Mediterranean for some months, but it does not seem that this is to be attributed to Franco-British firmness at Nyon.

[132] League of Nations, *Official Journal*, XVIII, 7 (July–December 1937), 685–86.

[133] Taylor, *Origins of the Second World War*, p. 125. Eden wrote: "There are those who say that at all costs we must avoid being brought into opposition with Germany, Japan and Italy. This is certainly true, but it is not true that the best way to avoid such a state of affairs is continually to retreat before all three of them. To do so is to invite their converging upon us. In any retreat, there must on occasion be counter-attack and the correct method of counter-attack is to do so against the weakest member of the three in overwhelming force. This is the justification of Nyon" (*Facing the Dictators*, p. 471). Churchill described Nyon as "proof of how powerful the combined influence of Britain and France, if expressed with conviction and readiness to use force, would have been upon the mood and policy of the Dictators" (*The Gathering Storm*, p. 248). A recent historian calls it "one of the few occasions during the interwar period when the Western Powers made a resolute stand against totalitarian aggression" (Dreifort, *Yvon Delbos at the Quai d'Orsay*, p. 76).

It must have been evident to the Italians from the beginning that they could not expect to attack shipping on the high seas over an extended period of time without running a serious risk of touching off a major international conflict, which Italy certainly did not desire. Nor was a long campaign likely to be necessary to achieve the limited objective of discouraging the Soviet Union from attempting to ship large amounts of material to Spain throughout the Mediterranean. It seems unlikely, therefore, that Rome ever intended the submarine campaign to last indefinitely. In fact, it was suspended before the Anglo-French invitations to the Nyon conference were ever issued, and well before the British and French had had an opportunity to display their determination of carrying through with the conference whether or not the Italians participated. The suspension of the campaign was due to the fact that it had already at least partially achieved its objectives by late August or early September, and also to the unintentional attack on a British warship, which raised the risks involved to unacceptably high levels. The decision was quite independent of the show of firmness given at Nyon.[134] Nonetheless, the Nyon Conference does mark the end of serious international tension over Spain. After Nyon the leading role on the international stage passed to others, and combatants in the Spanish Civil War became principal supporting actors rather than protagonists.

[134] Broué and Témime, *The Revolution and the Civil War in Spain*, pp. 489–90. Cortada, "Ships, Diplomacy and the Spanish Civil War: Nyon Conference, September, 1937," pp. 688–89.

NINE

TO THE BITTER END:
OCTOBER 1937–APRIL 1939

Reinforcement of Italian Units in Spain

AFTER the fall of Santander and the final elimination of the northern front, a prolonged period of quiet ensued as Franco prepared his forces for yet another assault on Madrid. The calm would be broken only by the beginning of the Republican offensive against Teruel in December 1937 (see map 8). During this period, the commander of the CTV was changed once again, and its forces strengthened and reorganized. General Bastico had had some success in molding the CTV into an efficient fighting force after Guadalajara, but his relations with Franco were badly strained. He was not the sort of man who would adapt easily to the subordinate position Franco expected from his commanders, and he attempted to maintain a degree of independence the Generalissimo was unwilling to concede. For instance, he repeatedly refused to allow the Arrow brigades, whose Spanish troops were commanded by Italian officers, to be used other than as part of the CTV. After the battle of Santander, he requisitioned for his troops large amounts of captured material that Franco wanted to assign to other Nationalist units whose needs were far more pressing. His direct dealings with the Basques and efforts to protect the Basque prisoners who had surrendered to the CTV also contributed to Franco's decision to request his replacement in late September.[1] Mussolini was annoyed by what he

[1] A copy of Franco's letter to Pedro García Conde of September 21, 1938, instructing him to request Bastico's substitution, is found in SHM CGG, L. 387, C. 38.

317

Map 8

Division of Spain: October 1937

Nationalist territory

considered Franco's "nasty letter",[2] but acceeded to the request, naming General Berti as new commander of the CTV. Berti had been Bastico's second in command.

When Berti took over, Italian ground forces in Spain numbered 32,560 troops, 3,768 NCOs, and 1,922 officers. The Santander campaign had taken its toll of the CTV, which had received only 1,200 new men since February. Two infantry battalions, an artillery battalion, and an engineers' battalion from the army were on their way to Spain, with a total of 96 officers and 4,000 troops. In addition, another 100 officers were being shipped there.[3] Berti complained to Ciano that even these forces, which amounted

[2] ACS, segreteria particolare del Duce, carteggio riservato, 463/R Spagna.

[3] Report of the ministry of war to Mussolini, October 1, 1937, ACS,

to more than 10 percent of his current totals, were not sufficient to permit the CTV to carry out "decisive actions," and he requested further reinforcements, adding that the withdrawal of the CTV would put the Nationalists in a dangerous situation.

At this time, the Italian undersecretary for war, General Pariani, was pressing for the dispatch of Italian Alpine units to launch an attack on Valencia. Ciano feared that massive new troop shipments, coming close on the heels of the submarine campaign in the Mediterranean, might set off a European conflict, but the Duce did not share his fears. In fact, in mid-October he immediately acceded to Franco's request for another division to help liquidate the northern front.[4] The troops never actually embarked for Spain, since the fall of Gijón made their dispatch unnecessary,[5] but what is important is that a month after the Nyon Conference Mussolini was willing to provide another full division of Italian troops if the military situation warranted it.

Italian aerial and naval support of Franco also increased significantly in the weeks following Nyon. At the end of September a new group of modern S 79 bombers were sent to the Balearic Islands.[6] Among the pilots who reached Spain at this time was Mussolini's son Bruno, who would fly twenty-seven missions before he was withdrawn in March 1938.[7] Four Italian submarines, with Italian crews

---

segreteria particolare del Duce, carteggio riservato, 463/R Spagna. Ten battalions of Black Shirts, with a total of 200 officers and 6,000 troops, were in training in Italy at this time, awaiting shipment to Spain.

[4] Ciano, *Diary*, October 2, 5, and 19, 1937.

[5] During the months of September and October a total of 4,487 men were shipped to Spain (Final Report of the Ufficio Spagna, appendix 6, MAE, Ufficio Spagna, b. 1).

[6] Note of the Ufficio Spagna on the Spanish Question from March 1937 to February, 1938, MAE, Politica, b. 38.

[7] Rachele Mussolini, *Benito. Il mio uomo,* p. 71.

and officers, were assigned to Port Soller in Majorca. With a Spanish flag and a Spanish communications officer, these submarines operated along the coasts of Spain, under the control of the Spanish navy, for approximately a year.[8]

The Nationalist navy was also strengthened in early October with the transfer of two Italian destroyers, the *Aquila* and the *Falco*, which were renamed *Ceuta* and *Melilla* and manned by Spanish crews.[9] The Nationalists had first requested surface vessels at the end of June. At that time, Mussolini, apparently without consulting either the foreign ministry or the navy ministry, had agreed to sell them the 4,500-ton cruiser *Taranto*, laid down in 1910, and five smaller ships. In return for the ships, he asked 40 million lire, to be paid immediately in convertible currencies or ores.[10]

Mussolini's proposal had caused considerable concern among the officials of the foreign ministry. In an unsigned note of the European and Mediterranean affairs section dated July 15, it was pointed out that the sale of warships was expressly prohibited by the Non-Intervention Agreement. Even if other countries were to recognize Franco as a belligerent, Italy would still have little legal basis for selling him warships. The only way to effect the transfer would be clandestinely and indirectly.[11] Five days later the under-secretary of state for the navy pointed out the immense practical difficulties that stood in the way of a clandestine transfer. The composition of Franco's navy was perfectly well known, and since he had only one destroyer it would be impossible to keep his acquisitions secret. Furthermore, a ship could not simply be handed over with a set of written instructions; Italian officers and crews would have to re-

[8] Interview with Valerio Borghese, Rome, June 18, 1970.
[9] Research note of Professor Willard C. Frank.
[10] Note from the Capo di Gabinetto of the navy to the foreign ministry, Doc. B 9156, July 9, 1937, MAE, Politica, b. 29. See also Cervera Valderrama, *Memorias de guerra*, pp. 184–85.
[11] Memorandum of AEM/1, July 15, 1937, MAE, Politica, b. 29.

main on board during a more or less lengthy training period. And finally, it would be very difficult to explain the disappearance of six ships from the Italian fleet.[12] Despite these objections, by late August the sale of the *Aquila* and the *Falco* had been concluded. The transfer was delayed until November because Ciano insisted that the ships' silhouettes be modified.[13]

To the observer looking back on the events from some distance, it is clear that the Nyon Conference marked the end of the period in which Spanish problems occupied the center of the European diplomatic stage. It was followed, however, by a brief flurry of activity during which tensions once again ran high. On October 2, London and Paris issued a formal invitation to Rome to participate in three-power talks on Spain.[14] The Anglo-French note contained a veiled threat of abandoning the entire policy of nonintervention unless steps were taken to make it really effective. It also held out the hope that if progress could be made on withdrawing volunteers, it might be possible to grant belligerent rights to Franco.[15]

Tension was sharply increased by rumors reported in Paris during the first week of October that Italy was planning to invade the island of Minorca. Twenty to thirty

[12] Undersecretary of state for the navy to ministry of foreign affairs, Doc. B 9677, July 20, 1937, MAE, Politica, b. 29.

[13] Report from Faupel to German ministry of foreign affairs Sa 3-3145/37, August 21, 1937, NA German Naval Reconds T 98 A, PG 3310. A copy of this report was supplied to me by Professor Frank.

[14] The proposals appear to have been related to the declarations made by the Italian representative to the League in a conversation with Delbos on September 22, 1937. Signor Bova Scopa had said that no more Italian troops would be sent to Spain and that Italy had no designs on Spanish territory. Though their substance was not new, the tone of these declarations and the apparent success of the Nyon Conference convinced Delbos that there were grounds for hope that Italy would respond favorably to an invitation to three-power talks (GD, D, III, 444–45; Van der Esch, *Prelude to War*, pp. 99–100).

[15] The text was printed as CP 234 (37).

thousand Italian troops were said to be being concentrated in Majorca, while Italian air forces were being strengthened in preparation for the attack.[16] Minorca lay even closer than Majorca to the major routes connecting French Mediterranean ports with North Africa, and possessed in Mahón the only port in the Balearic group capable of being developed into a major naval base.

Rome was fully aware of the increasing international tension. On October 8, Ciano noted: "There can be no doubt that the Spanish problem is going toward an international crisis. There will be a break or a clarification."[17] On the 10th, nonetheless, the Anglo-French overtures for tripartite talks were rejected with a note that reiterated Italy's position in favor of treating the Spanish problem in the Non-Intervention Committee, and that refused to discuss the problem without the participation of Germany. Simultaneously with the presentation of this reply, the Italian press launched a new attack on French violations of the Non-Intervention Agreement.[18]

The French government wished to respond by officially opening the frontier with Spain, but once again London prevailed upon them to delay any official move, and reopen the frontier unofficially.[19] As a result, the only Anglo-French response to the Italian refusal to discuss the Spanish problem outside the Non-Intervention Committee was verbal protest. Ciano was greatly relieved: "The Franco-British reaction to my note is flabby. Delbos's *passez á l'action*

[16] Royal Institute of International Affairs, *Survey of International Affairs, 1937*, II, 364. As we have seen, another group of bombers was sent to Majorca at this time, but no major troops concentrations took place; there is no evidence that Italy was planning to occupy Minorca, a move which would have been strongly opposed by General Franco, who was trying to improve his relations with Great Britain.

[17] Ciano, *Diary*, October 8, 1937.

[18] A lengthy front-page article by Virginio Gayda, for instance, included a list of 154 ships said to have carried arms from France to the Republic (*Giornale d'Italia*, October 10, 1937).

[19] FRUS, 1937, I, 434.

is already losing its bite. I think they will confine themselves to continuing the exchange of views."[20] Rather than seeing in the moderation of the reply a sign of international sense of responsibility, Ciano considered it a sign of weakness. "After the threats of the last few days, this withdrawal is enough to make one speculate about the decline of the French and British peoples," he mused. "The moment will come, it has perhaps already come, when we shall be able to stake all on the final throw."[21] To avoid unnecessary provocation, however, Rome decided to refrain for the moment from further troop shipments.[22] A semiofficial statement was also made to the effect that the number of Italian volunteers in Spain was about 40,000, not 100,000 to 110,000, as had been stated in the French press.[23]

The significance of Italy's attitude during this brief diplomatic crisis is unequivocal in the light of the new troop shipments, the dispatch of more aircraft, and the transfer of four submarines and two destroyers to the Nationalists. The transfer of the destroyers is particularly important in this regard, since it might easily have been discovered and could have had serious international repercussions. Mussolini was renewing and even sharply increasing his commitment to Franco, despite the recent Nyon accords. This fact confirms that the Duce was far less impressed with Anglo-French firmness at Nyon than has generally been believed.

ITALIAN RELATIONS WITH SPAIN AND GERMANY

After his victory in the North, Franco began to give some clues that he was determined to improve his relations with

[20] Ciano, *Diary*, October 12, 1937.
[21] *Ibid.*, October 14, 1937.
[22] *Ibid.*, October 12, 1937.
[23] "Informazione Diplomatica" n. 3, in Mussolini, *Opera omnia*, XXIX, 486. It was generally believed in Europe that the real figure was considerably higher than 40,000, but in fact that number was approximately correct.

Great Britain rather than remain isolated within the Italo-German orbit. In early November 1937, for example, the Nationalist press was ordered to refrain from attacks on Great Britain and British institutions.[24] Simultaneously, the newly named Nationalist commander of the Balearic Islands was instructed to maintain cordial relations with English authorities.[25] All of this naturally occasioned concern in Rome.

In a conversation with Ribbentrop on November 6, 1937, Mussolini discussed the need to be on guard in order to protect German and Italian financial and political interests in Spain. "We wish to be paid and must be paid," he said. But even more than the financial aspects, Mussolini stressed the political importance of keeping Franco from drifting into the British orbit. "We want Nationalist Spain, which has been saved by virtue of all manner of Italian and German aid, to remain closely associated with our maneuvers. . . . Rome and Berlin must, therefore, keep in close contact so as to act in such a way that Franco will always, and to an increasing degree, follow our policy."[26]

Later in the conversation, Mussolini again underlined the need for pressure to prevent Franco from breaking away from the Axis and laid out a two step plan for assuring his fidelity. "First, he must adhere to the Anti-Communist Pact. Second, we will undertake to bring Spanish policy into line with that of the Rome-Berlin Axis."[27] For the moment, he instructed Ambassador Viola to intensify his contacts with Franco and to collaborate closely with the Germany embassy in an effort to guarantee that "the Generalissimo's policy be always in close harmony with the system of the Rome-Berlin Axis, in conformity with the common ideologies, avoiding any possible devia-

[24] Telegram 725, November 4, 1937, MAE, Politica, b. 31.
[25] Report 3664/1384, November 2, 1937, MAE, Politica, b. 16.
[26] Ciano, *Ciano's Diplomatic Papers*, p. 144.
[27] *Ibid.*, p. 145.

tions."[28] Viola foresaw no difficulties in inducing Franco to adhere to the Anti-Comintern Pact as Mussolini desired. In fact, he reported, Franco had already told him that he would like to join it in the near future. But in his opinion, the ambassador added, it would be preferable to avoid any public adhesion to the pact until the Civil War was over, so as to increase its value and importance in Franco's own eyes.

Repayment of Italian credits would not, in Viola's opinion, be a major problem either. Franco's government would meet its obligations once the war was over. On the Italian side, he said, it would only be necessary to grant a sufficiently long term repayment schedule.[29] The contrast between Fascist and Nazi diplomatic styles is particularly marked here. Rome seems to have been content with Viola's generic assurances that Franco could be counted on to pay his debts in due time if a reasonable repayment schedule was offered. Berlin, on the other hand, was examining the economic situation in great detail and attempting to obtain from Franco written guarantees of its mining claims in Spain—despite Franco's October decree that had annulled all mining concessions granted since the beginning of the Civil War.[30] The Germans were consistently very active in their efforts to obtain economic advantages, particularly minerals and other strategic raw materials, from Spain. The Italians occasionally expressed interest in the economic aspects of the conflict, but never actually proceeded much beyond the stage of negotiating clearing agreements, which the Spaniards promptly circumvented.

A clue that the ambassador's optimism about Franco's political reliability was excessive was given in mid-November, when the Nationalists accredited the Duke of Alba, who had long been acting unofficially in London, as their

[28] Telegram 1952, November 9, 1937, MAE, Politica, b. 14.
[29] Ajeta report to Ciano on a conversation with Viola, Rome, November 18, 1937, MAE, Gabinetto, b. 2.
[30] GD, D, III, 496–619.

agent to the British government, and accepted the appointment of Sir Robert Hodgson as British agent in Nationalist Spain. The event was not a serious one, but it did suggest Franco's determination not to be a mere puppet of the Italians and Germans. From this point on, concern over the future orientation of Franco's foreign policy was to be a constant, if minor, element in Italian foreign policy.[31]

A far more important element was the increasing closeness of Italo-German relations. Less than two weeks after the conclusion of the Nyon Conference, Mussolini travelled to Germany to meet with Hitler. Parades and public demonstrations left little time for serious political conversations, although Ciano did reassure von Neurath that Mussolini was fully determined not to deviate from the Rome-Berlin axis.[32] In the course of Mussolini's brief discussions with Hitler, German assurances were repeated that Berlin considered Spain and the Mediterranean in general as areas of special Italian interest, just as Austria was an area of special German interest. Hitler also agreed with Mussolini that it was vital to bring the Spanish hostilities to an end as soon as possible.[33] This did not mean, however, that Hitler had really decided to make an all-out effort to help Franco. In fact, only a few weeks later he once again told a secret high level meeting of German leaders that a total victory for Franco was not desirable from a German point of view, since a continuing conflict in Spain might lead to a direct Italo-French confrontation from which Germany could benefit.[34] Not until almost a year later would Germany undertake the massive arms shipments that Franco needed to achieve final victory.

[31] As early as July 1937, the Portuguese foreign ministry had become convinced that Franco was determined to make good relations with Great Britain a cardinal element of his foreign policy (*Dez Anos*, 4, p. 400).

[32] *Documents secrets du ministère des affairs étrangères d'Allemagne*, III, 19–20.

[33] GD, D, I, 1.

[34] *Ibid.*, p. 37.

The importance of Mussolini's trip does not lie in these few relatively banal conversations, but rather in the effect the visit as a whole had on the Duce, who fell increasingly under Hitler's influence. He was "intoxicated by the spectacle of so much power, and fascinated by the man who was plainly resolved to wield it."[35] He had become convinced that Nazi power was irresistable and invincible, and this conviction rapidly became a fundamental postulate of his foreign policy.[36] The tightening of the bonds between Rome and Berlin was publically announced on November 6, 1937, when Rome joined the Anti-Comintern Pact. On December 11, 1937, she also withdrew from the League of Nations.

An index of Mussolini's fascination with German militarism and growing subservience to Hitler can be found in the intensification of his efforts to transform Italy on Prussian models, and in the social legislation he introduced in the country for the first time in 1938.

In October 1937, the existing youth group, the *Opera nazionale balilla*, was replaced with the far more militaristic *Gioventù italiana del littorio*. Military exercises, parades, camps, and uniforms became more than ever the order of the day for Italian youth. In January 1938, the army adopted 'the Roman step,' which even the least perceptive observers recognized as the Prussian goose step. Simultaneously, a decree was issued calling for the use of the comradely *voi* instead of the formal second personal pronoun *Lei*, which was condemned as being a foreign invention requiring the use of feminine forms unsuited to the heroic military spirit of Italy in the sixteenth year of the Fascist era.

---

[35] Kirkpatrick, *Mussolini. A Study in Power*, p. 354.

[36] This point is made by practically all his biographers. See, for example, Fermi, *Mussolini*, pp. 352–53; Monelli, *Mussolini piccolo borghese*, pp. 246–47; Gallo, *L'Italia di Mussolini*, pp. 253–54. The most penetrating and extended treatment is found in Giudice, *Benito Mussolini*, pp. 561–66.

In July 1938, a statement of "Italian scholars" on racial questions was published. The statement, which was in fact almost entirely written by Mussolini himself, presaged the regime's anti-semitic legislation. The high point of this legislation was the racial laws of October 7, 1938, prohibiting marriages between Italians and persons of Semitic or other "non-Aryan" races, and the organic laws of November 10, 1938, excluding all Jews from the civil and military administrations of the state, the party, and their affiliated organizations. Mussolini's newly adopted anti-semitism was partially due to a desire to strengthen his position of self-appointed "protector of Islam" and to his competition with the Reich for the favor of the anti-Jewish elements in Hungary, Rumania, and Yugoslavia. But above all, it signalled the growth of Nazi influence in Italy. Among its victims was the chief of staff of one of the Arrow Divisions, Colonel Morpurgo. On December 20, 1938, he was relieved of his duties because of his Jewish ancestry. On the 21st, Morpurgo deliberately crossed the no-man's-land between the lines well ahead of his troops, and was killed by Republican machine gun fire.[37]

Less serious in their effect, but perhaps equally important as signs of the increasingly bellicose and militaristic attitude Mussolini exhibited after his trip to Berlin, were a number of minor measures, such as the decree putting all government employees into uniform, and the institution of gymnastic contests for members of the Fascist hierarchy. The spectacle of middle-aged public officials jumping through firy hoops and over barrels was in itself ludicrous, but the fact that they had been ordered to do so by the undisputed ruler of a major European power bode ill for the future peace and security of the Continent. Ridiculous though the procedures were, Mussolini's intentions were clear: "The [Fascist] revolution," he told Ciano, "must affect the way of life of Italians. They must learn to be

[37] Gambarra, "La ultima parola sulla guerra di Spagna," *Tempo*, August 8, 1957, p. 34.

less *simpatici*, to become hard, implacable, hateful. That is, masters."[38]

NAMING OF THE NATIONAL COUNCIL OF THE FALANGE

Within Nationalist Spain, the development of political institutions continued to move forward at a slow pace. Franco apparently recognized the need for some form of civilian government, but was extremely reluctant to commit himself to anything that might tie his hands in the future or alienate any of the diverse groups on which he depended for support.

On October 19, 1937, he finally issued a decree establishing the national council of the Falange, a body clearly patterned on the grand council of Fascism.[39] It was composed of fifty members, all named by Franco. In choosing them, he was careful to avoid the predominance of any one political group. Fewer than half the appointees were Falangists and several were definitely anti-Falange at the time of their appointment.[40] The post of secretary general was first offered to Franco's brother-in-law, Ramón Serrano Suñer. After he declined, Raimundo Fernández Cuesta, the secretary general of the original prewar Falange, was appointed.[41] Fernández Cuesta was well disposed toward the Italians, who were pleased by his appointment.[42]

The naming of the national council was interpreted by the Italian embassy as a cautious step in the direction of normalizing Spanish internal politics and regularizing the state that had been born of the military uprising, although the ambassador hastened to add that it did not mean a common denominator had been found for the various ideological tendencies of Nationalist Spain. In his opinion, the

---

[38] Ciano, *Diary*, July 10, 1938.
[39] Ansaldo, *¿Para qué?*, p. 78.
[40] Clark, *The Evolution of the Franco Regime*, II, 631–35.
[41] Payne, *Falange*, pp. 179 and 186–87.
[42] Report 4200/1578, December 4, 1937, MAE, Politica, b. 14.

development of government in Franco's Spain had utterly failed to keep pace with the growth of military power. Although Franco's arms already dominated two thirds of the country, "what is now called the government is in fact nothing more than one aspect of his headquarters."[43] The establishment of the Falange council was a first step toward the formation of a government, but a very timid one, he said. Franco was being careful not to take any position publicly. In Falangist meetings he acted like the most ardent Falangist, but among Carlists he seemed a thoroughly convinced Requeté.[44] He had found it necessary to "bring together fifty people in order to leave some room for everyone and balance out the representation of the various organizations and tendencies."[45]

In Viola's opinion, Italy's best hopes in Spain lay with the Falange, which would in all probability provide the "leading exponents of a new Spain, which will be necessarily friendly to Fascist Italy."[46] In view of the situation, however, he advised against taking sides with the Falange

[43] Report 3625/1367, October 31, 1937, MAE, Politica, b. 14.
[44] Ajeta, report to Ciano on a conversation with Viola, Rome, November 18, 1937, MAE, Gabinetto, b. 2.
[45] Report 3625/1367, October 31, 1937, MAE, Politica, b. 14.
[46] Ajeta, report to Ciano on a conversation with Viola, Rome, November 18, 1937, MAE, Gabinetto, b. 2. Similar opinions were expressed about this time by Italo Sullioti, a Fascist party propagandist sent to southern Spain in October, 1937. The tone of Sullioti's reports is generally more pessimistic than that of Viola's. "In every city, in every little town," he wrote shortly after reaching Spain, "the vast majority of the population has remained red." Only the Falangists struck him as well disposed toward Italy and toward Fascism. "What little, what very little there is tendentially Fascist in this country is owed to them." "Only the Falangists have understood Italian Fascism and Mussolini. Only the Falangists try without false pride to understand us with intelligence and faith." Not only were enthusiastic Fascists hard to find in Spain, but even Franco, Sullioti reported, was "far from enjoying the popularity that he is believed in Europe to have" (Sullioti, letters to the ministry of popular culture, October 17, October 27, and November 17, 1937, ACS, ministero della cultura popolare, b. 91).

against the Carlists. Such a move would be premature at best and possibly damaging. All Rome could do, he believed, was to press Franco to form a regular government.[47]

In fact, for some time Italy had been doing just that. In July 1937, for example, Ciano had taken advantage of Anfuso's trip to Spain to instruct him to suggest to Franco that he announce the formation of a government on the first anniversary of the July 17 uprising. To do so, he argued, would "not only consecrate the triumph of the national cause, but would represent the consolidation of the state," and would help to "win recognition for his regime from countries that were still undecided."[48]

Shortly after the naming of the Falange council in October, *Il popolo d'Italia* printed a front page article in which it mistakenly said a government would be named within a few days.[49] In fact, it would still be several months before Franco would get around to naming a government. The article represented a sharp break with the *Popolo's* usual practice of not commenting on Spainish developments, much less anticipating them. The close attention Mussolini paid to the Fascist party's leading organ suggests that the publication of this article was a subtle attempt to move Franco to hurry in the formation of his government. For the moment such low-keyed maneuvers represented the full extent of Italian intervention in the internal politics of the Nationalist zone.

One reason for particular restraint on the Italians' part at this time was that despite Bastico's replacement, their relations with Franco continued to be tense because of friction between the CTV and the Spaniards. Ciano's personal secretary and frequent emissary to Spain, Filippo Anfuso, reported in mid-October that Franco could hardly wait for the Italian ground forces to be withdrawn, although

[47] Report 3625/1367, October 31, 1937, MAE, Politica, b. 14.
[48] Telegram 1178/486, July 6, 1937, MAE, Ufficio Spagna, b. 3.
[49] *Popolo d'Italia*, November 1, 1937.

331

he wanted to retain the air force and the artillery. The German ambassador informed his government that the roots of the problem lay in "the extravagant glorification of Italian deeds of arms, the presumptuousness of Italian military authorities, the conduct of the troops at the front and especially in the rear echelons, the smuggling of Italian goods promoted by the Italian military, which appears now and again, and other encroachments."[50] Authorities in Rome only complicated the question with their own concern for prestige and exaggerated appraisal of the CTV's contributions. Ciano's reaction to Anfuso's report that Franco wished to see Italian troops withdrawn, for instance, was to think that he was "jealous of our successes and afraid of those that are still to come."[51] In this atmosphere it is not surprising that Rome continued to avoid any overt attempts to influence Franco on political matters.

TERUEL

Franco's preparations for the renewed offensive against Madrid proceeded very slowly and were marked by repeated delays, partly because large armed bands continued to resist in the nominally conquered montainous territories of northern Spain. Preparations were finally almost completed when the Republican command, which had learned of the upcoming Nationalist offensive, launched a surprise attack on December 15, 1937, against the city of Teruel. The initial onslaught succeeded in surrounding the town by evening of the first day. Two weeks went by before Franco could even mount a counter offensive to relieve the beleaguered garrison, and in the meantime plans for the offensive on Madrid had to be abandoned as all available aircraft and artillery were moved into the Teruel sector.

In Rome the result of the Teruel offensive was profound

[50] GD, D, III, 521.
[51] Ciano, *Diary*, October 17, 1937.

gloom. "Franco," Ciano complained, "lacks a synthetic concept of war. He carries out his operations like a magnificent battalion commander. His objective is always the ground. Never the enemy. He just doesn't realize that wars are won by destroying the enemy."[52]

The new commander of the CTV, General Berti, had requested reinforcements and described the CTV as essential to the Nationalists' victory only a few months earlier. Now he was, if anything, even more discouraged than Ciano by the new turn of events and travelled to Rome to argue in favor of withdrawing all Italian infantry from Spain. In addition to the usual criticism of the Spaniards' lack of desire to finish the war quickly, and of the disastrous effects of the lack of a really unified Nationalist command, Berti argues that Italy could ill afford to risk her prestige on the performance of an expeditionary corps of twenty infantry battalions. Ciano was much impressed by this consideration, but he was afraid that a withdrawal at a time when Franco was encountering difficulties would give Franco an excuse for liquidating cheaply his debt of gratitude to Italy. "Every decision has its unfavorable aspect. This Spanish business is long and burdensome," he lamented.[53]

If Ciano was undecided, the Duce believed he had no alternative but to continue supporting Franco. He rejected Berti's plea, and on December 29 gave the CTV's commander written instructions that he was to communicate to Franco on his return to Spain. He pledged that the Fascist government would support the Nationalists until they achieved a complete victory, and offered to maintain the CTV in Spain if Franco intended to use it. Italian infantry, however, was to be used "qualitatively," not in battles of attrition. As for overall strategy, he urged Franco to speed up the war, and warned him against considering diplomatic recognition by foreign countries a substitute for

[52] *Ibid.*, December 20, 1937.
[53] *Ibid.*, December 28, 1937.

victory, or hoping for the eventual collapse of the Republican zone. Nothing short of military defeat, he said, would cause the collapse of the Republic, which had survived even the bitter partisan fighting of May 1937 in Barcellona. Similarly, Mussolini cautioned Franco not to be deluded about the attitude of the French and the British. Against all evidence, he asserted they would remain implacably hostile to the Nationalists. Finally, he called for a fully unified command, with the assistance of Italians and Germans, in order to execute mass attacks.[54]

Not content with pressing Franco directly to institute a unified command, Ciano also attempted to enlist German support.[55] In Berlin, the Italian military attaché spoke with General Keitel, who agreed that Franco showed no inclination whatsoever to launch a new offensive that would put an end to the war. The proposals of the Italian and German headquarters were always courteously received by Franco, but never seemed to have any outcome. Franco's personality, Keitel acutely observed, seemed to split between the military man who willingly accepts the suggestions offered, and the politician who draws back from carrying them out.[56]

German military authorities were not, however, enthusiastic about the idea of creating a mixed Italo-German-Spanish command, which would carry with it the danger of isolating the Italian and German commanders from direct personal contact with Franco, and of permitting the Spanish military leaders to unload their responsibility on the new organism.[57] Marshall Blomberg informed the Italian chargé, Magistrati, that the German commander in Spain, General

[54] A copy of the instructions is attached to Ciano's letter to Massimo Magistrati, December 28, 1937, MAE, Gabinetto, b. 2.
[55] Ciano, letter to Magistrati, December 28, 1937, MAE, Gabinetto, b. 2.
[56] Report of military attaché to Magistrati, N. 1926, December 30, 1937, MAE, Gabinetto, b. 2.
[57] Magistrati, letter to Ciano, January 5, 1938, MAE, Gabinetto, b. 2.

Volkmann, would be instructed to urge greater haste and maintain close contact with General Berti, but he did not pursue further the idea of a joint command.[58] In view of the lack of German support for the idea, Mussolini stopped pressing for it.[59]

Intense cold and blinding snow storms hindered the Nationalists in their attempts to relieve Teruel. On January 8, 1938, the remnants of the beleaguered garrison were finally forced to surrender to the Republicans, who now became in turn the besieged. Despite the limited strategic importance of Teruel, more and more forces were thrown into the battle on both sides. As the days and weeks dragged on without any decisive action, and with ever greater forces committed to the reconquest of what was at best a secondary objective, Mussolini became more and more agitated. It was apparent that Hitler would soon make a move in Austria, and the Duce was anxious to see the Spanish situation resolved before Italy's international position was further complicated by German occupation of her northern neighbor.

On February 2, he decided to bring pressure to bear on Franco with a letter that threatened the withdrawal of Italian support unless the pace of the war was increased.

You cannot count on the internal breakup of the Reds behind the lines. . . . Their breakup and the appearance of a fifth column will come about as the result of your victory, not sooner. If you do not wish to make the war chronic—with the enormous dangers that would bring with it on the international plane as well—it is necessary to prepare a battle of masses that will destroy the enemy apparatus. Once the plan is made, there should be no more deleterious postponements. And once the attack

[58] Magistrati, letter to Ciano, January 8, 1938, MAE, Gabinetto, b. 2.

[59] Report 562/185 from Berlin, January 25, 1938, MAE, Politica, b. 32.

begins, it should be carried out to the fullest. If that is your plan, ask me for whatever I can do for you. If not, if you expect the final decision from other factors, it is clear that at a certain point, the Italian Legionaries will have to be withdrawn since it would make no sense for them to stay longer. I await your reply.[60]

The letter was reinforced with an order to suspend all shipments of men and material to Spain until further notice, although the Italian airforces already in Spain were ordered to intensify their bombing of coastal cities in the hope of weakening Republican morale.[61]

Fighting continued in the Teruel sector for several more weeks. Not until February 20, 1938, did Franco's troops manage to retake the town. The battle had lasted two months, and cost the Republic more than 10,000 dead and 14,500 prisoners.[62] The Republicans had gained no lasting strategic advantages from the battle and had suffered heavy losses, but once again they had disrupted Franco's plans and prevented him from carrying out decisive offensive actions. Battles like Teruel could never, in themselves, lead to a Republican victory, but they might conceivably put off defeat for a long time.

From a purely military point of view, Franco could probably have afforded to leave Teruel in Republican hands and press ahead with his plans for another attack on Madrid. For political reasons, however, he was unwilling to allow the Republic to retain control of any territory which he had once occupied. This pattern of behavior, which reappeared repeatedly during the war, was perhaps dictated by his belief that in a civil war the occupation of territory is of primary importance as one of the few reliable

[60] Mussolini, letter to Franco, February 2, 1938, reproduced in Magistrati, *L'Italia a Berlino*, pp. 176–77.

[61] Report of the Ufficio Spagna on the Spanish question from March 1937 to February 1938, MAE, Politica, b. 33.

[62] Thomas, *The Spanish Civil War*, p. 649.

indicators by which the public can judge the course of the war. Mussolini was concerned exclusively with putting an end to the conflict through a series of crushing military victories, but Franco had to balance the military advantages of a single-minded offensive policy against the effects on the morale of the areas he already held of allowing the Republic to claim even a limited success.

During the entire battle, Franco had used the CTV artillery and aviation, but held Italian ground troops in reserve, much to the Duce's disgust. On February 20, therefore, Ciano telegraphed Viola that at some point at least part of the troops would have to be withdrawn. "Since the use of the troops in action has been, at least for the moment, discounted, it seems to us that their evacuation can be used advantageously in the negotiations now in course [with the British]."[63] On February 23, Mussolini himself telegraphed Franco, urging him to fight, and insisting that he chose between employing the CTV and sending it home.[64] By February 26 he was frantic, since Franco not only continued to hold the CTV in reserve but still had not responded to his letter written more than three weeks earlier.[65] Orders were given to the Italian air forces in the Balearic Islands to abstain from all further operations until Franco decided to employ the infantry.[66]

Franco's reply to Mussolini is dated February 16, but evidently was not delivered until very late February or early March. Just as he would do with Hitler at Hendaye in 1940, Franco seems to have deliberately kept Mussolini waiting. His letter is worth examining in some detail, since it illustrates well the tone of his relations with the Fascist

---

[63] Telegram 166, February 20, 1938, MAE, Gabinetto, b. 2.

[64] Ciano, *Diary*, February 23, 1938.

[65] In view of the success of the offensive begun by the Nationalists on February 7, Berti had waited several days before actually delivering the letter, but it had now been in Franco's hands for several weeks (GD, D, III, 582).

[66] Ciano, *Diary*, February 26, 1938.

leader. Even under considerable pressure, Franco seems a fatherly superior, who is attempting to calm unreasonable fears, rather than a nervous disciple anxious to please a demanding master.

I would like to communicate to your spirit my own faith in the victorious outcome of the campaign. That faith is founded on solid realities, the result of a year and a half of victories and of continuous fighting, during which we have not rested a single day nor allowed our troops to waste any time that wasn't made good use of.

Against Mussolini's argument that the Teruel setback was a result of his excessive caution and failure to launch an earlier offensive, Franco argued that Teruel demonstrated precisely the need for extreme caution, since even such a minor setback had caused an enormous impression in Italy and in the rest of the world, leading people to doubt his final victory.

Franco accepted Mussolini's argument that victory would have to be achieved on the battlefield. "I have never counted on the spontaneous breakup of the enemy's rear areas. I have always planned on bringing it about with a crushing victory and the destruction of the enemy army." Italian forces would be an important element in that victory, both militarily—as a forty thousand-man force of maneuver—but even more important, morally, since "their remaining in Spain is considered throughout the world an act of solidarity with our nation and their absence would cause, on the international plane, an impression of abandonment." Franco made no direct pleas for the retention of Italian troops in Spain. Rather, he took for granted that they would remain and went on to request more supplies.[67]

Franco's reply and the victory at Teruel won Mussolini over completely. The argument that withdrawal of the CTV

[67] Franco, letter to Mussolini, February 16, 1938, MAE, Gabinetto, b. 2. Also Viola to Ciano, telegram in arrivo 942/R, February 18, 1938, MAE, Gabinetto, b. 2.

would be interpreted as deserting the cause he had begun to defend was well calculated to guarantee that he would abandon the idea, if indeed he had ever really considered it seriously. His only request was that the legionaries be given the opportunity to fight "one good decisive battle."[68]

FRANCO'S FIRST GOVERNMENT; THE SPAINISH LABOR CHARTER; ITALO-SPANISH ECONOMIC RELATIONS

During the early weeks of 1938, Franco attempted to offset the adverse political effects of Teruel and bolster his domestic and international position by means of internal political activity. On January 31 he finally announced his first regular civilian government, as if in an attempt to show that even in a moment of military stalemate he was thinking of the future and confident of final victory.

Rome was pleased with the composition of the new government. According to Ambassador Viola, it represented "a reinforcement, even if not yet well defined, of the political influence of Italy and of Mussolinian Fascism." Its most important member was the minister of the interior, Serrano Suñer, who had studied in Bologna and had clearly shown his preference for Italian over German models in organizing the new state. The minister of education, Pedro Sainz Rodríguez, was a Catholic monarchist, and as such could be expected to prefer Fascism to pagan Nazism. Even before his appointment, he had contacted the Italian embassy, expressing interest in recent Italian experiences in the field of education. The minister for foreign affairs, General Gómez Jordana, was a monarchist who had a reputation as an anglophile, but Viola thought he could be expected to execute faithfully Franco's desires, whatever his personal preference. The exclusion of the pro-British Sangróniz and

[68] Mussolini, letter to Franco, March 3, 1938, MAE, Gabinetto, b. 2.

of Franco's own brother Nicolás from the cabinet was a final source of satisfaction in Rome.[69]

News of the formation of the government was given considerable attention in Italian papers, but no commentaries were made on the political significance or tendencies of its members. The *Giornale d'Italia,* whose comments may be considered typical, merely pointed out that Franco retained full and exclusive legislative power.[70] During the following days Franco made several declarations about the character of his government. The *Giornale d'Italia* gave special importance to his statement that "the Government will claim the great role that belongs to Spain in the world and will contribute to European peace without forgetting those who have befriended us in our days of trial."[71] The *Corriere della sera* reproduced sections of an interview Franco had granted to *O jornal do Brasil:* "Spain will be organized according to a broad totalitarian concept through national institutions that will guarantee its totality, its unity and its continuity. . . . In agreement with the corporative spirit, the Nation will manifest its will through the Corporations and technical organs. We want to avoid absolutely class struggle, introducing harmony between capital and labor."[72]

The favorable composition of the cabinet was, at least to some degree, a result of Italian efforts. The Italian embassy had lobbied against a cabinet post for Sangróniz, and had vigorously opposed the nomination as undersecretary of State of Domingo Barcenas, who was supported by conservative anglophile elements.[73] These are the only two instances I know of in which Italy clearly influenced Franco in his choice of collaborators, but they give some

[69] Report 751/259, February 5, 1938, MAE, Politica, b. 34.
[70] *Giornale d'Italia,* February 1, 1938.
[71] *Ibid.,* February 4, 1938.
[72] *Corriere della sera,* February 4, 1938.
[73] Telegram 026, March 3, 1939, MAE, Politica, b. 52.

grounds for thinking that similar pressures may have been brought to bear on other occasions of which no record has been found.

Among the first tasks facing the new Nationalist government was the preparation of some form of labor legislation. Italy had been urging the passage of measures that would improve the image of the Franco regime, and thereby help to justify Rome's support in the eyes of both Italian and foreign opinion.[74] Thus far Franco had not progressed much beyond the very rudimentary anti-Communism and calls for internal order that had characterized the early days of the revolt. After over a year and a half of fighting and the loss of hundreds of thousands of lives, the need for a more elaborate ideological justification of the war was painfully obvious, and the stalemate on the battlefields made it urgent to do something to bolster morale.[75]

Even before the official announcement of the naming of the government, a committee of the national council of the Falange had been appointed to begin studying the future corporative bases of Nationalist Spain. As soon as word of this decision reached Rome, the Italian foreign ministry requested the ministry of popular culture to include more items about Fascist corporativism in the Stefani news bulletins distributed in Spain and in the radio news for Spain.[76] The labor attaché of the Italian embassy, a left-wing Fascist labor leader named Marchiandi, had been sent to Spain as a propagandist at the suggestion of the

---

[74] Interview with Dionisio Ridruejo, Madrid, June 30, 1972.

[75] Serrano Suñer himself admits that "the uprising had been in its origin merely negative, an act of defense against the criminal claudication of the Republican government and against the certain danger of a Communist revolution. But once under way, it could no longer be a question merely of overthrowing that government and returning to the situation prior to the triumph of the Popular Front" (Serrano Suñer, *Entre Hendaya y Gibraltár*, p. 27).

[76] ACS, ministero della cultura popolare, b. 92, f. 7, sf. 1; NA T 586, roll 429, frames 013641 and 013673.

ministry of foreign affairs in the summer of 1937.[77] He was in close contact with various members of the national council of the Falange, to whom he expounded Fascist social theories. His interest lay less in gaining the approval of concrete measures than in seeing to it that a declaration of principles be made "to fully justify on ideal grounds Italian intervention in Spain."[78]

The fruits of the special committee's efforts were two drafts of a labor charter, one prepared by the conservative minister of syndical organization, Pedro González Bueno, and the other by a more radical Falangist group composed of Joaquín Garrigues, Francisco Jávier Conde, and Dionisio Ridruejo. The second project was championed by Fernández Cuesta, who held the posts of secretary of the national council of the Falange and minister of agriculture. It called for syndical control of the entire economy, and was based on a mildly anticapitalist concept of property. It did not provide for nationalization of industry, but proposed extensive state intervention and control of business.[79]

The Italian press predicted approval of a labor law at the meeting of the Council of Ministers on February 8, 1938. The ministers, however, rejected the second proposal as overly radical, yet refused to approve González Bueno's more conservative one. The entire question was referred to the full national council of the Falange. This was the Falange council's first opportunity to act on an important legislative matter, and was also to be its last.

A bitter struggle developed within the council on March 1, 1938, between the Falange "left" and conservatives who objected to any hint of social radicalism in the proposed law. Serrano Suñer, who had remained neutral in the earlier discussions, intervened to suggest that both sides were acting hastily in attempting to draft legislation on such an

[77] *Telespresso* 223757 from ministry of foreign affairs to ministry for corporations, July 13, 1937, MAE, Politica, b. 14.
[78] Report 1464/472, March 16, 1938, MAE, Politica, b. 34.
[79] Payne, *Falange*, p. 186.

important issue without long study and specialized knowledge. It would be better, he suggested, to merely enunciate some general principles without attempting to make specific legislative proposals.

The deep divisions between the members of the council would probably have made it difficult to reach a compromise even on general principles had not Franco himself intervened. He stressed that reasons of both internal and foreign policy made it essential to promulgate immediately a programmatic declaration, and demanded that one be approved within forty-eight hours. The urgency of providing some sign of progress in order to offset the impression created by Teruel was increased by the fact that the press had already announced the imminent publication of the legislation. A regime that spoke in the rhetoric of national unity under the leadership of the Caudillo could hardly afford to admit that the newly named government was incapable of reaching an agreement on the first important question set before it.

Serrano Suñer had described the labor law as the most important issue facing the Nationalist government,[80] but the extremely brief time alloted for its preparation is an eloquent index of how little importance Franco attached to its actual content. What was important to him—and to Italy as well—was merely that some declaration of principles be made. During the following two days a commission, whose active members were Ridruejo and Eduardo Aunós, the former minister of labor under Primo de Rivera, prepared an entirely new text. During this final stage a number of members of the commission, including Aunós, Yangüas Messía, and Esteban Bilbao, were in contact with Marchiandi, whose advice was influential in bringing the project into line with Italian corporative theory.[81]

The labor charter approved by Franco on March 9, 1938, contained a sixteen-part declaration of principles, calling

[80] *Popolo d'Italia,* February 6, 1938.
[81] Report 1464/472, March 16, 1938, MAE, Politica, b. 34.

for government protection of the rights of labor, including guaranteed employment, a family wage, vacations, and other fringe benefits. It defended private property and declared that the management of business concerns should be in the hands of their directors. Without specifically mentioning strikes, the charter characterized as seditious all individual or collective acts that in any way disturb normal production. It called for the establishment of vertical syndicates which would include all the workers and businessmen involved in a given productive sector, ordered hierarchically under the direction of the state. None of these measures was implemented by the charter itself, which was merely to serve as a guideline for specific legislation.[82]

The most obvious influence in the text of the charter was that of the Catholic social doctrine set forth by Leo XIII and Pius XI. Not only the underlying ideas but also many verbal formulations are strongly reminiscent of the encyclicals *Rerum Novarum* and *Quadragesimo Anno*. Within this general framework, the influence of Spanish corporative thinkers, such as the traditionalist Juan Vázquez de Mella, is also apparent.[83] Naturally, the document also contains echoes of both National Socialism and Fascism. Throughout the text the general parallels between the Spanish *Fuero del trabajo* and the Italian *Carta del lavoro* are apparent.[84] The only striking dissimilarity between the two documents was that the Italian system provided for separate syndicates for workers and industrialists, which were then united in the corporations, whereas the Spanish system had no such separate organizations.[85]

[82] The text of the Labor Charter is found in Clark, *Evolution of the Franco Regime,* appendix I, pp. 173–79.

[83] For a summary of Mella's theories, see Codón Fernández, *La tradición en José Antonio y el sindicalismo en Mella.*

[84] It is perhaps significant that one of the final drafts of the document bears the title *Carta del Trabajo,* which was only changed to *Fuero del Trabajo* at the last moment. A copy of this draft is in the private archives of Dionisio Ridruejo.

[85] Fernández Cuesta, *Intemperie, victoria y servicio: discursos y*

Overall, the Italians were well pleased with the *fuero*. It mattered little to them how closely it followed their own corporative system. What really counted was its propaganda value. On the international level, and even more importantly at home, it could be used to refute the charge that Italy was supporting in Spain a reactionary regime whose policies were contrary to Fascism's proclaimed goals of social revolution.[86]

This brief flurry in the early months of 1938 marked the high point of political activity in Franco's Spain during the Civil War. We have been at pains to discover and highlight the role Italy played, but what is truly remarkable is how limited and secondary that role was. Overall, her direct intervention in the internal political development of the Nationalist zone was all but negligible, although Franco's dependence on her for arms and for diplomatic support would surely have permitted her to exercise much more influence had she so desired. After Guadalajara, Mussolini returned to the policy he had briefly abandoned during the Farinacci mission of allowing the Nationalists to organize their political life as they saw fit, without Italian tutelage or interference. Had his objective been to establish in Spain a Fascist state patterned on Italian models, he would certainly have wanted to influence its development more actively. His passive "hands-off" policy confirms that his aims were more strategic and political in the classical

---

escritos, pp. 91 and 101–102, quoted in Payne, *Falange*, pp. 187–88. Genco, *Precedenti e contenuto della Carta del Lavoro Spagnola*, pp. 112–16. Genco concludes (p. 116) that "the Fuero conceives of the corporative undertaking in substantially the same terms as our *Carta del Lavoro*, even if the form is different." Also Incisa, *Spagna nazional sindacalista*, pp. 136–38 and 162–64. For a good description of Italian corporative organization in theory and practice, see Neufield, *Italy. School for Awakening Countries*, pp. 419–91.

[86] It will be recalled that even Ambassador Cantalupo was deeply disturbed about Italy's support of what he considered a reactionary regime.

sense, and that ideologically he was interested only in preventing the victory of the anti-Fascist republic.

The same generally passive attitude also continued to characterize Italy's economic relations with Spain. In late March 1938, Franco again sent his brother Nicolás to Rome to negotiate the financing of further aid. The minister for foreign exchange, Guarnieri, was already unhappy about the Spaniards' failure to meet their payments under the clearing agreements negotiated the previous year, and unwilling to see new agreements reached that would jeopardize Italy's precarious exchange position. At the first official meeting between the Italian and Spanish delegations, a complete deadlock arose over questions of payment. The Spaniards, who were desperately short of exchange, wanted to pay their existing debts in kind, whereas the Italians insisted on payment in cash, as had been established in the clearing agreements signed the previous year. For the future, the Spaniards offered to pay 50 percent in goods and requested credit for the other 50 percent, whereas the Italians demanded immediate payment, 50 percent in cash and 50 percent in goods.[87]

Ciano, like Guaranieri, was put off by the size of the requests: "They want a billion lire worth of goods," he complained, "payment to be mostly in kind and very problematical. We must keep our tempers. We are giving our blood for Spain—do they want more?"[88] Franco, however, successfully appealed to Mussolini's vanity and a few days later in a meeting between Nicolás Franco, Ciano, and Guarnieri, an agreement was reached. The Spaniards agreed to pay their existing debts, one third in cash, and two thirds in kind, mostly olive oil. Future supplies, for a maximum of 150 million lire, would be paid for 50 percent in cash and 50 percent in kind.[89] Once again the Nationalists had won exceptionally favorable terms and the Italians

---

[87] Guarnieri, *Battaglie economiche*, II, 276.

[88] Ciano, *Diary*, March 26, 1938.

[89] Guarnieri, *Battaglie economiche*, II, 277–78. The conclusion of the letter requesting the sale of the *Taranto* is a good example of

had failed to exact even a beneficial repayment arrangement, much less any real economic advantages.

THE ARAGON CAMPAIGN AND THE EASTER AGREEMENT

The very day the labor charter was published, the Nationalists initiated an offensive in the Aragon sector. Its aim was to drive through to the sea, cutting off Catalonia from Valencia and the rest of Republican-controlled central and southern Spain. In response to Italian pressure, the CTV was given a prominent position in the offensive formation. It formed the center column, advancing on Alcañiz, between Yague's Army of Morocco, which would attack Caspe, and Aranda's Army of Galicia, whose objective was Alcorisa.[90] By March 14, the first objectives fixed in Franco's plans had been achieved, and the CTV had occupied Alcañiz, taking a large number of prisoners (see map 9).

The anxiety and disappointment of a few weeks earlier gave way in Rome to an atmosphere of equally exaggerated optimism. Ciano believed the Republic was on the point of collapse. To hasten its demise Mussolini ordered the Italian air forces stationed on Majorca to attack Barcelona. The attacks, begun on March 16, were carried out indiscriminately, with no effort to distinguish between civilian and military targets.[91] They continued at three-hour intervals until the afternoon of March 18, killing and injuring large numbers.[92]

---

the sort of approach that regularly disarmed the Duce: "I request your able collaboration and effective support for the solution of these problems . . . so as to overcome the obstacles and the difficulties that such requests always encounter in administrative organisms. In their severity and legitimate defense of the public interests, they become obstinant, and need to be spurred on by the political genius of someone who, like yourself, directs the destiny of an empire" (*ibid*, p. 276). In the face of such an appeal, cautious arguments about the Italian balance of payments and the condition of state finances lost all interest for the Duce.

[90] Belforte, *La guerra civile in Spagna*, IV, 10.
[91] GD, D, III, 624–25.
[92] Bowers, *My Mission to Spain*, p. 376.

Aragon & Levante
Offensives:
March–July 1938

March 9–May 26

May 26–July 20

50 Miles

50 Km.

In Rome, Ciano took a certain sadistic glee in the results. A report on a raid carried out a month earlier had greatly impressed him with the destructive power of aerial bombardment. "I have never read a document so realistically horrifying. . . . Large buildings demolished, traffic interrupted, panic on the verge of madness, and 500 dead, and 1,500 wounded."[93] Mussolini, according to his son-in-law, was "delighted that Italians should be horrifying the world by their aggressiveness for a change, instead of charming it with their guitar. In his opinion, it will increase our standing with the Germans, who love total, pitiless war."[94]

In fact, the attacks served no real military purpose and failed to weaken the morale of the Catalans. Nor did the Germans approve. Ambassador Stohrer condemned them as unlikely to achieve their intended psychological effect but destined to stir up hatred against Germany and Italy after the war.[95] Mussolini's savagery may be partially explicable in terms of his need to achieve psychological compensation for the *Anschluss*. He had been forced to watch passively while Hitler aggrandized himself at his expense, and despite a brave propaganda front, he had been deeply humiliated both at home and abroad. The bombing of Barcelona may have served as a relief from that humiliation.

Indignation was widespread, not only among supporters of the Republic. Before the experience of World War II had blunted their moral sensibility, men of all political convictions regarded with horror and outrage the senseless killing of civilians. On March 20, the Vatican representative in Salamanca, Msgr. Antoniutti, informed the Italian embassy that he had made an appeal to Franco in the Pope's name to stop the bombing.[96] Franco himself was unhappy with the attacks, which he requested Mussolini to suspend.[97]

[93] Ciano, *Diary*, February 8, 1938.
[94] *Ibid*, March 20, 1938.
[95] GD, D, III, 625.
[96] Report 1672/529, March 20, 1938, MAE, Politica, b. 41.
[97] GD, D, III, 626.

Italian troops pushed ahead rapidly from Alcañiz, apparently in an attempt to be the first to reach the Mediterranean,[98] but they were held up both by the difficulties of the rugged terrain and by the stubborn resistance of Lister's division, one of the best Republican units.[99] After the Nationalists reached the sea at Viñaroz on April 15, cutting the Republican zone in two and isolating Catalonia, the CTV marched on the town of Tortosa, occupying the sections that lay on the right rank of the Ebro on April 19. No attempt was made at this time to cross the river and occupy the rest of the town.

The Italian contribution to the Aragon campaign, while not as decisive as some apologists would have it,[100] appears to have been underrated by many authors. The CTV succeeded in advancing rapidly against the best units of the

[98] According to British sources, Ambassador Viola claimed that Italians were to have been the first to reach the sea but were jockeyed out of position at the last moment (FO W 12150/83/41).

[99] Alcofar Nassaes, *CTV*, p. 148.

[100] On March 18, 1938, Luigi Barzini wrote in a letter to his editor, Barella: "The Nationalists are still timid. They are frightened by rapid events and if left to themselves would stop. But there is the Legionary Corps which pulls them along. Our general does nothing but spur Franco to act, to act soon, rapidly and in depth. Franco seems convinced of the plans for maneuvers that are suggested to him, but he always wants to pause to catch his breath and take his bearings. He is a little amazed. 'Yes, we must act quickly and continue the advance without ceasing,' he says.
" 'What will you do?'
" 'I'll give the necessary orders!'
" 'When?'
" 'Tomorrow.'
" 'No, today. Immediately.'
" 'All right.'
" 'What are your orders?'
"This is the tone of their meetings. If it weren't for the Legionaries, the advance would still be beginning. . . . The Legionaries, in the center, have served as a wedge all the time, taking the flanks along with them" [Barzini to Barella, March 13, 1938, ACS, segreteria particolare del Duce, carteggio riservato, 241/R (Barzini)]. Also see Belforte, *La guerra civile in Spagna*, IV, 37.

Republican army at a cost of some five hundred dead and twenty-five hundred wounded, and particularly in the early stages of the offensive helped set the rapid pace of advance.[101]

As the separation of Catalonia from the rest of Republican Spain made the total collapse of the Republic and the end of the war appear imminent, a new attempt was made to liquidate it on the diplomatic plane with yet another Anglo-Italian agreement. A new agreement had been hanging fire for six months, since the apparent success of the Nyon Conference had led London to intensify its efforts to reach a general understanding with Rome.

Whitehall was already beginning to view Spain not as a crucial European problem to be dealth with on its own merits, but as an obstacle to a broadly based settlement between Great Britain and Italy. In negotiating with Rome, Britian was not, as one author has suggested, "acting in good faith, and expecting the same identity between words and deed from Germany and Italy," nor was she "always inclined to put the best possible interpretation on the motives of the totalitarian powers."[102] Foreign office officials were aware that Mussolini was "too deeply implicated to relax his support of Franco, unless the latter's victory is assured," and they generally estimated quite accurately the probable outcome of diplomatic maneuvers with respect to Italian intervention in Spain. They were fully convinced that "while we shall keep our word, it is less certain that the Italians will."[103] The reason for British willingness to negotiate under these circumstances lies in the belief that Britain's interests in a Republican victory were less important than an improvement in her relations with Rome. Personally, Chamberlain was especially anxious for a rapprochement with Rome, which he viewed as a way of weakening the Axis. So great was his determination to achieve

[101] *Almanacco del regio esercito,* p. 485.
[102] Van der Esch, *Prelude to War,* pp. 118–19.
[103] FO R 6746/1/22; minute by Ingram, October 18, 1937.

it, that he willingly accepted Eden's resignation when the foreign minister opposed signing any new agreement before substantial progress had been made toward withdrawing the CTV from Spain.

Mussolini did not at first share Chamberlain's enthusiasm for improved Italo-British relations. He still wanted to obtain British recognition of his conquest of Ethiopia, since it would greatly enhance his prestige and might make available the funds of London's financial markets for projects there. To secure recognition, he was willing to consider signing a new general accord, but he was in no great hurry to do so. The Duce only began to wish a quick agreement in February 1938, when the proximity of a German move in Austria lent new urgency to the question. Italy was rapidly becoming the junior partner in the Axis, and had lost much of her freedom of action. An improvement in her relations with England that would allow her to take a somewhat more independent stance in her dealings with Berlin became more desirable as growing tension in Austria pointed toward the proximity of a German move there.

Formal negotiations were opened in Rome on March 8. Ciano informed Chamberlain that Italy was willing to accept a formula proposed earlier by the British for the withdrawal of volunteers from Spain and the granting of belligerent rights. Among the other topics to be discussed were the position of Italy and Great Britain in the Red Sea, Italian propaganda in Arab countries, and various boundary questions in East Africa.

On March 11, 1938, Nazi troops invaded Austria, and the next day an all-Nazi government was installed in Vienna. Ciano had told London that once the *Anschluss* was consumated, Italy's hands would be tied and she would be unable to sign a pact with Britain,[104] but in fact Rome pressed ahead with the negotiations anyway. The Spanish question was the only one on the original agenda

[104] Ciano, *Ciano's Diplomatic Papers*, pp. 161–62; Eden, *Facing the Dictators*, p. 658.

which offered substantial difficulties. Italy at first maintained that her formal acceptance of the British proposal for troop withdrawals was a sufficient contribution to a solution of the Spanish problem to justify British recognition of the Ethiopian conquest. Chamberlain might personally have been willing to accept this position, but when the *Anschluss* had just increased the pressure of public opinion to avoid "giving in to the dictators," he could hardly recognize the Italian conquest of Ethiopia without getting something more than promises and expressions of goodwill in exchange. To speed the negotiations, Mussolini authorized Ciano to propose that the agreement be signed but not to go into effect until a satisfactory settlement in Spain had been reached.[105] This proposal found favor in London because the British, like the Italians, believed that Franco's Aragon offensive would soon lead to the complete collapse of the Republic, after which Italian troops could easily be withdrawn from Spain.

Accordingly, on April 16, 1938, an Anglo-Italian accord, generally known as the Easter Agreement, was signed in Rome.[106] In an accompanying exchange of notes, the Italian government confirmed its acceptance of the British plan for the withdrawal of foreign volunteers from Spain, pledged that it would apply the conditions established by the Non-Intervention Committee, and guaranteed that at war's end it would withdraw all remaining Italian soldiers and war material. The British government, for its part, welcomed these declarations and stated that the agreement would come into force when the Spanish question had been settled.[107] Both governments still confidently expected that Franco's final victory and the withdrawal of Italian troops would soon open the way for British recognition of the Italian empire.

[105] Ciano, *Diary*, March 17, 1938.
[106] Text printed as Cmd. 5726.
[107] Texts in Royal Institute of International Affairs, *Survey of International Affairs, 1938*, I, 141.

353

VALENCIA AND THE EBRO

After Franco reached the Mediterranean, almost all observers expected him to turn north immediately and occupy the rest of Catalonia, including Barcelona. The Caudillo, however, ordered his armies to turn south toward Valencia rather than north into Catalonia. His decision may have reflected a belief that the Republic could be crushed by destroying its striking force in the South, where the lines were dangerously extended,[108] but it was more probably due to a healthy respect for his opponent, which led him to fear that the Catalans might still be capable of inflicting a major setback on him. He was acutely aware of the effect on morale in the Nationalist zone of any defeat, and had gone to great lengths throughout the war to avoid risking any serious reverse, even when this obliged him to forego promising offensive opportunities. In addition, occupation of the heavily populated Catalan region would have posed serious problems if it did not lead to the immediate collapse of the Republic. Much of the population was strongly affected by regional nationalism, and Barcelona had long been an anarchist stronghold, so that policing the area would be a difficult operation. Furthermore, feeding Barcelona and the other urban centers of Catalonia would place a strain on the rest of the Nationalist zone, which thus far had enjoyed cheap and plentiful food, since Franco controlled the major agricultural regions and had few large cities to feed.

The offensive against Valencia soon proved more difficult than expected, thanks in part to an influx of arms from France and from the Soviet Union. On March 13, 1938, Leon Blum formed his second cabinet, with Paul Boncour as foreign minister. Four days later he issued a secret order in council, opening the frontier. Blum's government fell less than a month later, but for some time his successor,

[108] Broué and Témime, *The Revolution and the Civil War in Spain*, pp. 475–76.

Edouard Daladier, kept the frontier open and allowed the transport of Soviet aircraft and equipment across France. According to one estimate, during the months of April and May three hundred Soviet aircraft and twenty-five thousand tons of war material crossed the French border into Spain.[109] This influx of aid revitalized the Republican armies, which managed to bring the Nationalists to a halt in the difficult terrain north of Valencia. The illusion of a rapid end of the war soon disappeared as the Nationalists found themselves stalled once again.

The CTV took no part in the unsuccessful spring Valencia offensive. For over six months, only a trickle of reinforcements had reached Spain, and it was now becoming urgent to send more men if the CTV was to be maintained with its present formations.[110] Since Franco's inability to advance rapidly against Valencia dashed all hopes for a rapid conclusion of the war, Mussolini ordered Ciano to begin new troop shipments, sending the men in small groups and in civilian clothes. Over three thousand men left Italy for Spain during June 1938, and another twenty-five hundred in July, for a total of 5,697 during the two months.[111] Another two Italian destroyers, the *Poerio* and the *Pepe*, were transferred to the Nationalists at this time.[112] More airplanes were also sent, including twenty-five S 81, twelve S 79, and seven Br 20 bombers, in addition to fighter planes. These shipments make the summer and

[109] Pike, *Conjecture, Propaganda, and Deceit*, p. 165.

[110] Berti wanted his troops to go into the reserve to rest and reorganize after the Aragon offensive, but Franco insisted on using them to man part of the line on the Ebro (GD, D, III, 652).

[111] Final Report of the Ufficio Spagna, appendix 6, MAE, Ufficio Spagna, b. 1. One group of 29 officers, 16 NCOs and 254 militia men were shipped to Spain on the hospital ship *Aquilea*. The men wore Red Cross badges and were supposed to be nurses, but according to an official report they were so poorly dressed and so careless of their appearance that they seemed more like beggars. MAE, Politica, b. 35.

[112] Research note of Professor Willard C. Frank.

early fall of 1938 one of the most active periods of the entire war in terms of Italian aid to Spain.[113]

In mid-July, the Nationalists made another attempt to push their way through to Valencia. This time the CTV, reinforced with new troops, arms, and equipment, played an important role. In addition to the Littorio and the March 23rd Divisions, it was composed of the Blue Arrows Mixed Brigade and the Spanish 5th Navarrese Division.[114] The offensive began on July 13. During the first two days, the CTV captured the railway center of Albantosa, which had been heavily fortified by the Republicans, and during the following days overthrew the defenses of Sarrión. The difficulty of the terrain and the strength of Republican defenses made the advance costly, but by July 25 the CTV had gained more than fifty kilometers and taken almost two thousand prisoners. The advance cost 232 killed and 1,613 wounded, of whom probably about half were Italians, and the rest Spaniards of the 5th Navarrese Division and the Blue Arrows Brigade.[115] During the twelve-day offensive, the Italian air force based on the continent flew 2,808 missions for a total of 5,630 hours, dropping 758,000 kilograms of bombs and claiming 24 Republican aircraft downed, while reporting losses of 11 planes. Italian bombers based in the Balearic Islands flew another 318 missions for a total of 690 hours, dropping 80,000 kilograms of bombs.[116]

The Nationalists' Valencia offensive had to be suspended

[113] ACS, Aeronautica, Gabinetto, 1938, Varie, OMS.

[114] In mid-June, the Arrows Division was dissolved and its separate brigades passed directly under the orders of the commander of the CTV. At the moment of its dissolution, the division had 969 officers and 17,191 men. SHM CTV, L. 10.

[115] Berti's unnumbered telegraphic report of July 27, 1938, ACS, segreteria particolare del Duce, carteggio riservato, 463/R Spagna; Barzini, letter to Barella, August 9, 1938, ACS, Aeronautica, Gabinetto, 1938, N 2/11 Spagna, relazioni sulla situazione militare; *Almanacco del regio esercito*, *XVIII, 1939–40*, p. 486; Canevari, *La guerra italiana*, I, 477.

[116] Belforte, *La guerra civile in Spagna*, IV, 85–86.

before it reached its objective because during the night of July 24–25 the Republicans crossed the Ebro at numerous points, establishing a large bridgehead ten miles east of Gandesa. The attack caught Franco's forces totally unaware, although Italian sources claim that CTV intelligence had provided full information on Republican preparations and troop movements.[117] The Nationalists could not halt the offensive until August 2, when they finally contained it just short of Villalba and Gandesa after giving up some five hundred square kilometers. In the long run, the Ebro offensive would prove to be a terrible mistake for the Republic, which could ill afford to expend its slender supplies in a large-scale diversionary maneuver.[118] For the moment, however, it seemed immensely successful. Franco's plans were completely upset, as all available aviation and artillery were diverted to the Ebro. The optimism which had reigned in Rome when it seemed that Valencia might fall any day disappeared completely.

Throughout the rest of the summer of 1938, the Nationalist armies strove unsuccessfully to throw the Republicans back across the Ebro. The weight of air power and artillery lay with them, but the Republicans had the advantage of holding the high ground, and were determined not to be driven back. The CTV artillery was placed directly under the command of the Army of the North, which used it for concentrated aerial and artillery attacks against relatively restricted areas. Between August 19 and October 9, 1938, Italian artillery fired a quarter of a million shells in support of Franco's troops.[119] Despite their overwhelming superiority in armament, however, the Nationalists were

[117] Barzini, letter to Barella, August 9, 1938, ACS, Aeronautica, Gabinetto, 1938, N 2/11 Spagna, relazioni sulla situazione militare; FO W 12150/83/41.

[118] Thomas, *The Spanish Civil War*, pp. 686–90.

[119] Belforte, *La guerra civile in Spagna*, IV, 100. The Ebro was the only theater of the Spanish Civil War in which concentrated artillery fire was used to drive out the defenders from restricted areas which were then occupied by small infantry units.

357

held by the Republicans until fall. As late as mid-October, they had still recovered less than half the territory lost in July.

ITALO-BRITISH RELATIONS

During the spring and summer of 1938, while Franco's forces battled inconclusively with the Republicans, the Anglo-Italian agreement was held in suspense, since no progress was made toward withdrawing Italian troops from Spain. On several occasions Mussolini publicly professed his interest in proceeding along the road to better relations with London, but both his private conversations[120] and his actions in the Civil War belied any real desire for rapprochement. The resumption of Italian bombing of Barcelona and other towns in late May 1938, and the celebration in Italy of an official day of solidarity with Nationalist Spain[121] gave rise to popular indignation throughout Britain, while new aerial attacks on British-registered shipping stirred irate protests. Between mid-April and mid-June, twenty-two British registered ships were attacked from the

[120] In mid-July Mussolini talked to Ciano about his plans for a "revolution in the way of life" of the Italians, especially through racial legislation. "It will augment foreign hatred for Italy. That's fine. I'm doing everything possible to turn my back more and more on France and England" (Ciano, *Diary*, July 17, 1938).

[121] A Spanish delegation, led by General Millan Astray, the commander of the Spanish Foreign Legion, and composed of various members of the Falange, spoke to meetings throughout Italy. At the explicit orders of the ministry of popular culture, considerable front page space was dedicated to the arrival of the Spanish delegation and to the celebrations arranged in their honor (ACS, agenzia Stefani, carte Morgagni, velline, May 20 and 21, 1938). The Fascist party's newspaper said that Italy supported Nationalist Spain because in Spain "our civilization, our very history" are being defended. The task undertaken by the leaders of Nationalist Spain was described not merely as one of liberating territory from "Bolshevik barbarism" but "the same one proclaimed by Fascism in ordering in martial form an entire people against the enemies of civilization" (*Popolo d'Italia,* May 29, 1938).

air in Spanish ports and eleven were sunk or seriously damaged. Indignation rose so high that observers began to predict Chamberlain's iminent fall.

It was clearly to Italy's advantage to see to it that the Chamberlain government remained in power, since the prime minister had shown he would acquiese in almost any Italian undertaking in Spain and was anxious to bring the Easter Agreement into effect. To facilitate Chamberlain's position, therefore, Grandi was instructed to take a cooperative line in the meetings of the Non-Intervention Committee, where endless discussions of the meaning of "substantial progress" and of the date on which international control of the Spanish borders should be reinstated were threatening to postpone indefinitely the actual execution of the British plan for withdrawing volunteers.[122]

Italian interest in helping Chamberlain and bringing the Easter Agreement into effect was not sufficient, however, to lead to any substantial concessions. In late June, renewed attacks on British registered ships by Italian and German airplanes acting under orders from Franco caused a fresh storm of protest in Britain.[123] Seventeen parliamentary questions on the subject in a single day, coming not only from the opposition but from some of Chamberlain's own supporters, provide an index of the degree of indignation aroused. Perth informed Ciano that Chamberlain might well fall on this issue, but Mussolini at first refused to intervene with Franco. Assuming one of his favorite postures, that of the strong man who is unshaken by the tempest, the Duce told Ciano: "If Chamberlain falls, we shall see who takes his place. I shall base my decision on the positive and concrete factors of the situation which then arises. For the moment, I am waiting."[124]

---

[122] Ciano, *Diary*, May 24, 1938. A good summary of the state of the negotiations in the Non-Intervention Committee in May 1938, is found in FRUS, 1938, II, 188–92.

[123] *Dez Anos*, 5, p. 331.

[124] Ciano, *Diary*, June 28, 1938.

Mussolini did eventually ask Franco to call off the attacks,[125] but throughout the rest of the summer Italo-British relations continued basically unchanged. On July 5, the Non-Intervention Committee finally approved a plan for the withdrawal of foreign volunteers. In view of the favorable military situation in Spain, where Nationalist troops were again advancing rapidly on Valencia, the Italians at first encouraged Franco to cooperate in its implementation, so as to ease international tensions and facilitate their rapprochement with Britain.[126] The Republican Ebro offensive, however, once again made gaining time the most important consideration, even if that involved further antagonizing London and Paris. Rome soon advised Burgos to put forward alternate proposals that amounted to a flat rejection of the withdrawal plan.[127]

In addition to encouraging Franco to reject the withdrawal plan, the Italians, as we have seen, resumed their own shipments of troops to Spain. In the face of British protests, Ciano denied that Italy was sending more troops, but confessed that she had indeed made further shipments of material, and brashly asserted she would continue to do so as long as Italian volunteers were engaged in Spain.

No effort was being made at this time to conceal Italy's continuing support for the Nationalists. In a preface to the *Acts* of the grand council of Fascism, dated July 1, 1938, Mussolini himself exalted the Black Shirts' contribution to the fight against Bolshevism and liberalism.[128] On the second anniversary of Franco's uprising, the Fascist party newspaper described "the solidarity between Fascist Italy and Nationalist Spain" as the "best guarantee of the definitive triumph of Mediterranean civilization against Muscovite barbarism."[129]

[125] GD, D, III, 713.
[126] *Ibid.*, pp. 726, 728.
[127] Telegram 10875, July 29, 1938, MAE, Politica, b. 40.
[128] Mussolini, *Opera omnia*, XXIX, 116.
[129] *Popolo d'Italia*, July 17, 1938.

In dealing with Paris, Mussolini was even more belligerent and unyielding than in dealing with London. When Daladier formed his new government in mid-April 1938, the incoming foreign minister, George Bonnet, immediately notified Rome that he wished to negotiate on Mediterranean questions and was willing to recognize the Italian empire. There were only two points upon which the French intended to stand firm, the withdrawal of Italian forces from Spain and Italian acceptance of the status of Italian immigrants in Tunisia.[130]

It soon became clear that the Italians would be flexible about Tunisia, but adamant about Spain. Mussolini was incensed by France's insistence that he offer her the same assurances he had just given Great Britain about the withdrawal of Italian forces from Spain. London, he said, could reasonably ask for such assurances since, on the whole, she had fulfilled her obligations under the Non-Intervention Agreement. France, however, had openly and repeatedly supported the Republic in violation of the agreement and had no right to ask Italy for assurances of any kind, especially since precisely at this time the French frontier was open and arms and material were pouring across the border into Spain every day.[131]

In an important foreign policy speech given at Genoa on May 14, Mussolini surprised all the diplomatic observers by saying he was uncertain whether the conversations in course with France would lead to any result. In the Spanish war, he declared, "we are on opposite sides of the barri-

[130] Bonnet, *De Washington au Quai d'Orsay*, pp. 144–45. It had now been eighteen months since France has been represented in Rome by an ambassador, and six months since the Italian ambassador had been recalled from Paris.

[131] In addition to Spain, difficulties also arose over the Red Sea. Mussolini had no intention of associating the French with the Anglo-Italian declaration on the Red Sea contained in the Easter Agreement. That declaration had virtually converted the Red Sea into an Anglo-Italian lake, and the Duce had no desire to invite the French to participate.

cades. They desire the victory of Barcelona; we, on the contrary, desire and will the victory of Franco."[132] After such a rebuff, the conversations could hardly be expected to lead to any positive results and were suspended indefinitely. Spain had once more proved the most important obstacle to better Franco-Italian relations, as it would do again in the fall after the Munich Conference, when the French would renew their efforts.

Despite the lack of positive response from Rome, Chamberlain continued his efforts to keep the door open for better relations with Italy, especially in view of the impending Czech crisis. Thus, when Franco in effect rejected the Non-Intervention Committee's plan for troop withdrawals, its British chairman, Lord Plymouth, simply refused to convoke a meeting to consider Franco's response. As he specifically told the Italian ambassador, the prime minister wanted "to defuse the Spanish question, and meantime to gain time in which it can be resolved in the way that is most favorable to the interests of Europe and of the Italo-British understanding."[133]

PLANS FOR TROOP WITHDRAWAL AND THE MUNICH CRISIS

Toward the end of summer it began to appear that Rome might soon withdraw enough troops from Spain to permit bringing the Easter Agreement into effect. Italian commanders in Spain had become increasingly annoyed by constant Spanish criticism of their performance in the field and by the Nationalists' tendency to minimize the contribution of Italian aviation and artillery.[134] They were not

[132] Mussolini, *Opera omnia*, XXIX, 101.

[133] Telegram 614 from London, September 2, 1938, MAE, Politica, b. 40.

[134] The British agent in Spain reported in August: "The two allies are heartily tired of one another and look forward to the day when their partnership in arms will be dissolved" (FO W 11582/29/41). The Portuguese ambassador described the moment as "particularly

optimistic about the general situation after the Republican Ebro offensive, and were extremely concerned about the future of their own forces. Since the beginning of the war, the CTV had suffered some 11,500 casualties including 2,352 killed.[135] The constant illusion that the war was about to end had led Rome to replace only the troops killed or wounded, without rotating the rest. This had given rise to a serious morale crisis among the soldiers, who felt condemned to continue fighting until they were killed.[136] Early in August, General Berti informed Mussolini that either large-scale reinforcements would have to be sent or the infantry would have to be evacuated, unilaterally if necessary.

In response to Berti's petitions, Mussolini decided to offer Franco three alternatives: 1) sending the Italian infantry home with all honors; 2) receiving another ten thousand troops to make the CTV an effective fighting force; or 3) receiving several more Italian divisions.[137] The dispatch of more divisions might well provoke a crisis in the Non-Intervention Committee and a reopening of the French frontier, which had been closed since June, but if it did, Mussolini asserted, he would send even more men to finish off the war.[138] The Duce's reckless offers to assist Franco regardless of the international consequences was probably a bluff, since the experience of the previous months gave him every reason to believe that Franco would not accept his offer of more troops. But it may also reflect his growing conviction that European war was all but inevitable. Despite Italian insistence, Berlin obstinately refused to pro-

---

delicate," and found that "each day the impossibility of understanding each other becomes more evident" (*Dez Anos*, 5, p. 426).

[135] Ciano to embassy in Berlin, telegram by courier 16063/PR, October 5, 1938, MAE, Politica, b. 40.

[136] Donosti, *Mussolini e l'Europa*, p. 56.

[137] Ciano to embassy in Berlin, telegram by courier 16063/PR, October 5, 1938, MAE, Politica, b. 40.

[138] Ciano, *Diary*, August 12 and 21, 1938.

vide any concrete information about future plans in central Europe, but by late summer it was clear to all observers that a major crisis was developing over Czechoslovakia.

Franco rejected Mussolini's offer of new divisions. He had no desire to see the outbreak of a major European war, which would probably turn Spain into an international battlefield and bring with it Franco-British assistance to the Republic. He did accept the possibility of Italy's sending ten thousand replacements, but pointed out that their dispatch could not be kept secret.[139] In view of Franco's opinions, the Duce decided on August 22 to concentrate the Littorio and March 23rd Divisions into a single division, repatriating the ten to fifteen thousand men who would be released by this move.[140]

Immediately after this decision was taken, Mussolini received copies of two letters written by the experienced Italian war correspondent, Luigi Barzini. The reports painted a very dark panorama of present and future events in Spain. According to Barzini, Franco lacked broad strategic vision and was incapable of conceiving and executing the daring operations needed to end the war. Each time he began an offensive, the Republic responded with a counteroffensive that forced him to abandon his plans and rush all available artillery and aviation to the threatened sector. When he had successfully contained the attack and even passed over to the offensive again, he regularly failed to take advantage of the opportunities for a crushing blow. Thus, the projected offensive against Madrid had been abandoned because of the Republican threat at Teruel, but when the Nationalist counterattack in Aragon had met with success and reached the sea, Franco turned toward

---

[139] GD, D, III, 766.

[140] Mussolini, telegram to Berti 2118/2, August 22, 1938, MAE, Gabinetto, b. 2. There is a summary of these events in the German diplomatic correspondence, where the general outline is correct, although the dates are slightly wrong (GD, D, III, 765–66).

Valencia, instead of attempting to march north into Catalonia. And in July, when it seemed that the Nationalists were about to take Valencia, the Ebro offensive had forced Franco to go on the defensive again. The Italian general staff officers in command of the CTV had repeatedly suggested possibilities for successful offensive operations, but their ideas had been systematically rejected, Barzini reported. "The relations of the Legionary Corps with the Nationalist Command are still those of a subordinate, whose ideas are of no interest and whose advice need not be taken into account."

After Teruel, the Aragon campaign, the costly attempt to march to Valencia through the mountains, and now the Ebro, Franco's forces were depleted and his reserves all but nonexistent. The Generalissimo refused, however, to call up more soldiers, principally out of fear of the social and political repercussions of doing so, particularly in a moment when it was clear to the entire country that his forces were in difficulty. The Nationalists' problems, though grave, were less so than those of the Republic, in Barzini's opinion. The situation could still be turned in their favor, but that would require energetic action that he believed was unlikely to be forthcoming. The most likely prospect, he thought, was that once the Ebro campaign was over, Franco would turn his attention once again toward the indecisive Valencia offensive.[141]

Barzini's reports deeply disturbed the Duce, who told Ciano to record in his diary "that today, August 29, I prophecy the defeat of Franco. Either the man doesn't know how to make war or he doesn't want to. The Reds are fighters—Franco is not." Military leaders were also un-

[141] Copies of Barzini's letters to Barella dated August 9 and August 19, 1938, in ACS, Aeronautica, Gabinetto 1938, N 2/11, Spagna, relazioni sulla situazione militare. At this time, the Portuguese ambassador was also sending pessimistic reports to his government (*Dez anos*, V, 427.), and the German ambassador believed the two sides had reached a stalemate (GD, D, III, 743).

happy about the idea of leaving a single division in Spain. To do so, they argued, would not appreciably reduce Italy's international commitments and would add to the danger of a major setback on the battlefield with loss of prestige. Mussolini, therefore, dashed off another telegram to Berti, instructing him to press Franco to allow all the troops to be withdrawn. Franco accepted the proposal, but only grudgingly, since he feared the withdrawal would be interpreted as a slackening of Italian support for his regime.[142] Mussolini again changed his mind and offered to maintain one division in Spain, lest his withdrawal be interpreted as a lack of loyalty. Franco accepted this offer, and on September 13, Berti was ordered to begin forming a single division and preparing the remaining men for repatriation.[143] Some delay was occasioned by the fact that the Italian troops were being used to stem a minor Republican offensive, but by September 22 final arangements had been made between the Italian command and General Franco.[144]

Before any steps could be taken, the situation was modified again by the Czech crisis. For months the Negrin government had seen in international war its last real hope of salvation. It had decided in the event of the outbreak of hostilities to declare war immediately on Italy and Germany, thereby forcing France and England to accept Republican Spain as an ally.[145] Franco was deeply con-

[142] In a conversation with Viola, Spanish Foreign Minister Jordana requested especially that he be informed about the exact timing and form of the public announcement, so that the withdrawal would not appear to be something foreign to Franco's will, and so that no opportunity would be given for speculation about the weakening of Italian support for Franco (Viola, telegrams 150 and 151, September 23, 1938, MAE, Politica, b. 40).

[143] Ciano to embassy in Berlin, telegram by courier 16063/PR, October 5, 1938, MAE, Politica, b. 40; Mussolini, telegram to Berti, 2278, September 7, 1938, MAE, Gabinetto, b. 2.

[144] Viola, telegram 150, September 23, 1938, MAE, Politica, b. 40.

[145] Broué and Témime, The Revolution and the Civil War in Spain, p. 497.

cerned that this would lead to an immediate French occupation of Catalonia, Spanish Morocco, Minorca, and perhaps the territories around San Sebastián and Irun at the western end of the Pyrenees.[146] From September 18 on he worked feverishly to convince London and Paris to dissociate Spain from any possible conflict over Czechoslovakia. His representatives informed the British and French governments that should war break out Nationalist Spain intended to observe strict neutrality.[147]

These assurances were sympathetically received in both capitals, but the problem remained of convincing Italy and Germany to respect his neutrality. The Germans were no more forthcoming with Franco than they were with Mussolini about what they planned to do, and the arrival of the *Deutschland* in the port of Vigo aroused his fears that Berlin might be planning to use Spain as a base of operations.[148]

On September 26 Franco informed Berlin that in the event of war he would be forced to remain neutral, and that he wished to negotiate with London and Paris to insure that they would respect his neutrality.[149] The Italians first learned of his proposed neutrality from the Germans. Ciano was indignant at the news and accused Franco of "direct betrayal of the common cause."[150] "How disgusting," he wrote, "our dead must be turning over in their graves."[151] His first reaction was to begin thinking of concentrating all Italian ground forces in Majorca and withdrawing the air force altogether. After a few hours, however, Mussolini decided that it would be better to leave the CTV in Spain to continue fighting against the Republic. There is no evi-

---

[146] GD, D, II, 950–51.
[147] Broué and Témime, *The Revolution and the Civil War in Spain*, p. 499.
[148] GD, D, III, 741 and 747–48.
[149] GD, D, II, 951.
[150] *Ibid.*, p. 972.
[151] Ciano, *Diary*, September 26, 1938.

dence as to the Duce's motives in taking this decision
It may have been due simply to the practical logistical
problems of moving the troops if war were to break out
in the next few days. In any case, the order to repatriate
the ten thousand troops was once again suspended.[152]

The Munich Conference definitely defused the Spanish
Civil War as a potential source of European conflict. The
fact that the Czech crisis could be solved peacefully seemed
to demonstrate that Europe could settle without recourse
to arms problems far more critical than those arising from
the Spanish conflict. In the words of a British foreign office
official, "the Powers who did not fight over Czechoslovakia
will surely not fight over Spain."[153] After Munich no one
any longer seriously feared that complications in Spain
might lead to a general European war.

For a moment there was even a flicker of hope that
the powers who had settled the Czech crisis might be able
to negotiate a settlement in Spain. Chamberlain discussed
this possibility with Mussolini on September 29, and with
Hitler on September 30. Neither was very encouraging,
although neither rejected the idea out of hand.[154] A compromise peace would only have been possible if Italy and
Germany had been interested simply in frustrating the success of the revolution in Spain and securing, in the German
case, certain economic advantages. Their aims, however,
went well beyond that. They wanted "a strong Spain that
leans toward the Rome-Berlin Axis" and would not be satisfied with anything less than "total victory for Franco."[155]
Consequently all mediation proposals were doomed to
failure.

On October 3, Ciano officially informed the British ambassador that ten thousand men would soon be returning

---

[152] *Ibid.* and GD, D, II, 972.
[153] Foreign office memorandum, October 21, 1938, partially reproduced as annex XVII of CP 231(38).
[154] BD, III, 2, pp. 636–37.
[155] GD, D, III, 759.

to Italy from Spain and proposed that the Easter Agreement be put into effect immediately.[156] In reply to the ambassador's queries, he gave formal assurances that no further troops would be sent to Spain, but refused to promise that there would be no future increases in the number of aircraft and pilots.[157]

The Italian proposal came at a propitious time. At Munich Mussolini had played the role of the honest broker. The Western powers were grateful for his assistance in avoiding war and anxious to be able to count on his collaboration in the future. The four-power pact which Chamberlain had so doggedly pursued seemed finally to have come into existence. The foreign office felt the cause of general European peace would be served by helping Mussolini to regain his freedom of action with respect to Germany, and believed that the improvement of Anglo-Italian relations that would follow on British recognition of the Italian empire could be an important step in that direction.[158]

The French, who were generally more deeply concerned than the British about Spain, and who had consistently favored a harder line in dealing with Italy, now took the initiative in an effort to improve their relations with Rome. On October 5, they announced their dicision to recognize without further delay the Italian conquest of Ethiopia. This made British recognition almost a foregone conclusion, and in mid-November the Easter Agreement was finally brought into effect.

By this time, however, Mussolini was explicit in his declarations to Ciano that improved relations with Great Britain left untouched the basic outlines of Italian policy. "All this is very important," he said after the signing of the Anglo-Italian accord, "but does not alter our policy. In Europe the Axis remains fundamental. In the Mediter-

[156] FO R 7949/23/22.
[157] BD, III, 3, p. 325.
[158] FO R 7966/23/22.

ranean we will collaborate with the English as long as we can. France remains outside."[159]

Despite the implementation of the Anglo-Italian agreement and France's recognition of the Italian empire, neither Mussolini nor Ciano showed any inclination to improve relations with Paris. In response to a question from the newly appointed ambassador to Paris, Rafaele Guariglia, as to what he ought to accomplish, Ciano had responded, "Nothing."[160]

The deterioration of Italo-French relations during the winter of 1938–39 cannot be explained only in terms of economic, political, or ideological factors. Some account must also be taken of Mussolini's almost pathelogical antipathy toward France, and more concretely toward the new French ambassador, François-Poncet, who arrived in Rome on November 7.[161] "I shall do everything," Mussolini told Ciano, "to help him to break his head. I don't like the man."[162] Among the objective obstacles to improved relations, however, Spain ranked among the most important. As French Foreign Minister Bonnet observed, it was "the real bone of contention" between the two countries."[163]

During his first conversation with the new French ambassador on November 9, Ciano met his offers of better relations with protests of Italian goodwill, but stated categorically that Spain continued to be a barrier between the two countries, as Mussolini had declared at Genoa in the spring. He rejected any possibility of mediating a settlement in Spain, and pressed for an immediate grant of belligerent rights to Franco. "It would be difficult to start exhaustive conversations on the subject of our relations with France," he said, "until the Spanish affair has been disposed of."[164] After this inauspicious opening only a

[159] Ciano, Diary, November 16, 1938.
[160] Guariglia, Ricordi, p. 357.
[161] Toscano, Origins of the Pact of Steel, p. 89.
[162] Ciano, Diary, November 5, 1938.
[163] BD, III, 3, p. 465.
[164] Ciano, Ciano's Diplomatic Papers, pp. 248–49.

purblind optimist could have expected much improvement in Italo-French relations, and in fact they deteriorated throughout the rest of 1938.[165]

THE OCCUPATION OF CATALONIA AND THE END OF THE WAR

On October 15, 1938, ten thousand Italians sailed from Cadiz. They arrived in Naples on October 20, where they paraded through the streets of the city and were reviewed by the king and crown prince. This partial withdrawal made it necessary to reorganize the CTV once again. The Italian troops left in Spain were formed into the twelve thousand-man Littorio Assault Division. Three additional divisions under the orders of the CTV command were constituted with Spanish troops and about a hundred Italian officers and 575 Italian NCOs.[166] In addition, the CTV had a tank group with a hundred light tanks and about a thousand men; six hundred artillery pieces served by seven thousand officers and men; two thousand engineers; and roughly eight thousand men in services.[167] Simultaneously

[165] On November 30, during a speech on foreign policy delivered at the Chamber of Deputies, Ciano spoke of the "natural aspirations of the Italian people." Cries were immediately heard throughout the chamber calling for Tunisia, Corsica, Nice, and Savoy. These claims on France, which seem to have been motivated by tactical considerations rather than by any deep-seated interest in the territories in question, may be viewed as a reply to and a counterrhythm of German expansion. Plans were already well advanced for the occupation of Albania, but in the meantime Italy needed to lay some claims if she were to preserve her dignity as an equal member of the Axis, which had already netted Austria and the Sudetenland for Germany. The claims were probably also designed to make more difficult any eventual German-French rapprochement at a moment when Mussolini feared an improvement in their relations.

[166] SHM CTV, 9, 19.

[167] The figures on material are taken from ACS, segreteria particolare del Duce, carteggio riservato, 463/R Gambarra. Those on the number of men are from FO R 7966/23/22. These estimates by Brit-

371

with these organizational changes, General Berti was recalled to Rome and replaced as commander of the CTV
by Gastone Gambarra, who had been his chief of staff.
Gambarra was still a colonel at the time of his appointment,
but was immediately promoted to brigadier general. Both
Mussolini and Ciano were enthusiastic about Gambarra,
whose undoubted courage and considerable bragadoccio
made him the prototype of the ideal Fascist officer. Roatta
was assigned to act as Franco's military advisor and as
his chief of staff for the remaining units of the CTV.[168]
The withdrawal of ten thousand troops, many of whom
had been in Spain for more than eighteen months and
were heartily weary of the war, may well have made the
CTV a more efficient and effective fighting unit. It is a
mistake to believe it meant that Italy was slackening its
support of Franco.[169] Mussolini was determined to continue
providing arms and other material, as he clearly signified
by his refusal to guarantee to the English ambassador that

ish military intelligence merit a high degree of confidence. In cases
in which it is possible to compare British estimates with official Italian
secret information—for instance, on the number of aircraft—they are
shown to be extremely accurate. The British estimate of the total
number of Italian ground soldiers in Spain—30,000—is confirmed
by Belforte, who states that there were 2,077 Italian officers and
25,935 men in Spain in December 1938, in addition to some 2,200
Italian aviators and supporting personnel, with a total of 250 aircraft,
of which about 180 were on the mainland and 70 in Majorca (Belforte, La guerra civile in Spagna, IV, 117–18). Maisky's allegation that
after the withdrawal Franco still had about 150,000 German and
Italian troops is so exaggerated as to suggest that the former Soviet
ambassador to London deliberately lied in his memoirs (Maisky,
Spanish Notebooks, p. 202).

[168] Note Q56125 from ministry of war to Nulli, October 12, 1938,
MAE, Gabinetto, b. 2. The appointment of Roatta to this delicate
post confirms that Mussolini failed to realize what a bad impression
the Guadalajara affair had made on Franco. A note on the organization of the CTV with the names of all its commanding officers is
found in SHM CGG, L. 387, C. 44.

[169] This interpretation is widely accepted, even by authors as reliable
as Deakin, The Brutal Friendship, p. 8.

no more airplanes would be sent to Spain. If, for the moment, he excluded the possibility of sending more men because Italy was closely watched and dispatching them would harm her relations with England, time would show that even this condition would be abandoned again as soon as it seemed that more troops were needed.

Not until October 30, 1938, did the Nationalists launch their final offensive in the Ebro sector. Supported by Italian artillery and aviation, Franco's troops advanced irresistibly across the ground the Republicans had won in July. On November 18, 1938, the last Republican units abandoned the right bank of the Ebro (see map 10). Total Republican casualties in the five-month battle may have reached seventy thousand. In addition, the Ebro had cost the Republic some two hundred aircraft, eighteen hundred machine

Map 10

Division of Spain: Fall 1938

Nationalist territory

373

guns, and twenty-four thousand rifles. With only limited supplies now arriving from Europe, these were losses that it could ill afford. The French border had been officially closed since June, and Stalin was far too concerned with events in Manchuria and Eastern Europe to continue supporting the Republic. In fact, many Soviet advisors had been withdrawn during July and August, and no significant quantities of arms were shipped to Spain from Russsia after early summer.[170] The Popular Front, which Stalin had tried for two years to build on the basis of collaboration in Spain, had evidently failed, and he now turned his attention to other strategies for guaranteeing Russia's interests, abandoning the Republic to its fate.

In contrast, after Munich the Germans began to want to liquidate the war as quickly as possible. During the closing months of 1938 it was Berlin, not Rome, that was most anxious to bring the Spanish conflict to a victorious end. The outcome of the Munich conference had convinced Mussolini that Franco's efforts would soon be crowned with success, and he was no longer troubled by the pace of events in Spain.[171] Italian shipments of aircraft, arms, and other war materials declined sharply during the last quarter of 1938.[172] Not until January 1939 would Mussolini again become concerned about ending the Spanish conflict quickly. The Germans, on the other hand, dramatically increased their aid once Franco had agreed to grant them extensive mining rights and to pay the full expenses of the Condor Legion.[173] It was this massive German aid that gave Franco the margin of victory and enabled him to break the stalemate that had arisen after the battle of the Ebro.

[170] Thomas, *The Spanish Civil War*, pp. 703–704; Whealey, "Foreign Intervention in the Spanish Civil War," p. 227.

[171] See Ciano's *Diary* for the last quarter of 1938, especially October 25, 1938.

[172] ACS, Aeronautica, Gabinetto, 1938, Varie, OMS.

[173] GD, D, III, 785–96.

The conclusion of the battle of the Ebro reopened for the Nationalists the question of whether to attempt a new attack in central Spain, directed against Madrid or Valencia, or turn north toward Barcelona. As late as mid-November, Franco was apparently leaning toward another attack on Madrid.[174] Italian military leaders in Spain resolutely opposed this plan and strongly favored an offensive in Catalonia. The CTV's intelligence indicated that over the past few months the Republicans had considerably improved their military situation in central Spain. In Catalonia, the situation was far less favorable to the Republic. Due to the losses suffered on the Ebro, its forces there were numerically insufficient and critically short of supplies.[175]

Franco, under pressure from many of his own generals as well as from the Italians, eventually decided to attack Catalonia.[176] The offensive was originally scheduled to start on December 10, but was postponed several times. After a number of fruitless encounters with the Nationalist commander in the Catalan sector, General Davila, Gambarra went directly to Franco to demand that the offensive begin immediately.[177] The date was finally set for December 23. The Holy See's request that an armistice be observed for Christmas was rejected by an irritated Franco with the curt observation that it would be militarily harmful.[178]

For the offensive, which was destined to be decisive, Franco assembled a powerful striking force along a line

[174] Report of General Porro to General Valle, November 21, 1938; ACS, Aeronautica, Gabinetto, 1938, 7, 19.

[175] CTV, Ufficio I, Report on the Political and Military Situation in Red Spain, November 6, 1938, SHM CGG, L. 388, C. 64.

[176] Report of General Porro to General Valle, November 21, 1938, ACS, Aeronautica, Gabinetto, 1938, 7, 19.

[177] Gambarra, "L'ultima parola sulla guerra di Spagna," *Tempo*, August 1, 1957, pp. 31–32.

[178] Viola, telegram by courier, 117, December 21, 1938, MAE, Politica, b. 53.

from the Pyrenees to the Ebro and the sea. In the north was a new army corps of Urgel, under General Muñoz Grandes, and the Army of the Maestrazgo, commanded by García Valiño. In the center, the Army of Aragon under Moscardó, together with Gambarra's four divisions, and the Army of Navarre under Solchaga, was to cross the Segre river at Lerida and various points to the southwest. The Army of Morocco, commanded by Yagüe, was to advance along the coast toward Barcelona. Franco's original plans had called for the CTV to be held in reserve, but Gambarra convinced Davila to give his troops a front-line position (see map 11).[179]

An overwhelming barrage from five hundred artillery pieces emplaced along a four-kilometer front supported the first wave of the offensive in the Italian sector.[180] Exploiting initial surprise, his superiority in artillery and air support, and the mobility of his units, Gambarra leaped ahead some thirty kilometers to the line of the Sed River. The Spaniards on Gambarra's right flank under Solchaga's command advanced more cautiously and slowly. On December 27, the Italian command in Spain cabled Ciano, requesting Rome to bring pressure to bear on Franco to have his troops advance.[181] In answer to this request, Mussolini instructed Gambarra to "go immediately to Franco and tell him that I do not understand why the two lateral army corps have remained stopped when the CTV has broken through on a front that permits a strategic maneuver that may be definitive. If they do not advance, the CTV cannot push further ahead without grave danger, and once again he will miss the opportunity for a decisive victory."[182] Not content with taking the initiative himself,

[179] Gambarra, "L'ultima parola sulla guerra di Spagna," *Tempo*, August 1, 1957, pp. 31 and 34.
[180] *Ibid.*, August 15, 1957, p. 29.
[181] ACS, segreteria particolare del Duce, carteggio riservato, 463/R Spagna.
[182] Gambarra, "L'ultima parola sulla guerra di Spagna," *Tempo*, August 29, 1957, p. 36.

Map 11

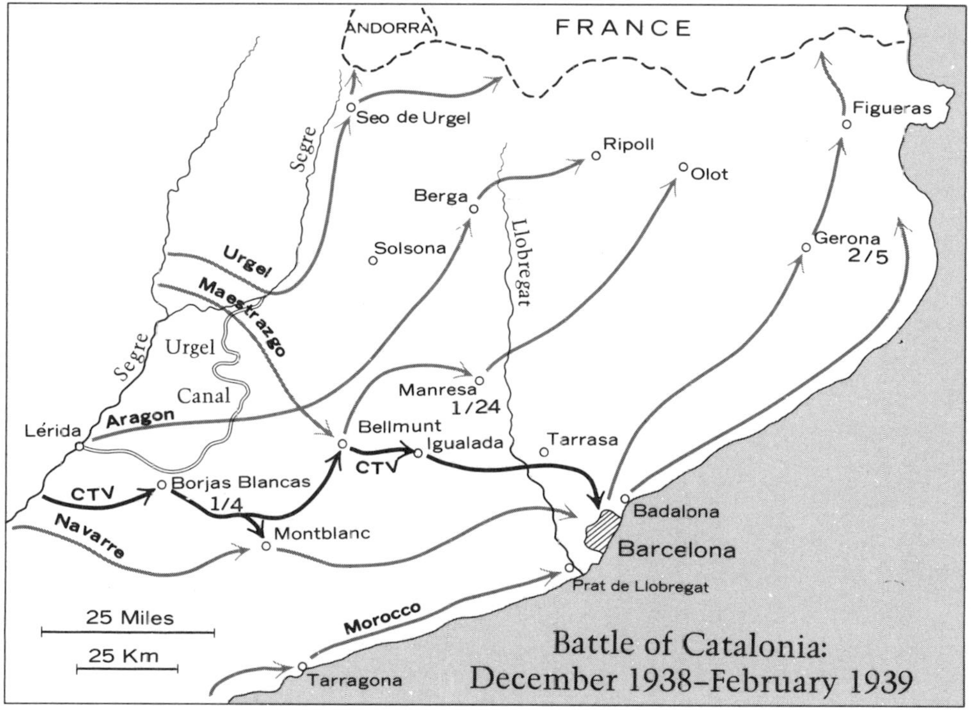

Battle of Catalonia:
December 1938–February 1939

Mussolini also requested the Germans to press for a rapid advance, and sent Ambassador Viola together with Colonel Bodini to urge Franco on.[183]

A powerful Nationalist attack forced Lister to retreat all along the line where he faced the CTV on January 3, 1939. The next day, Borjas Blancas fell to the Navarrese and Italian offensive,[184] and the CTV advanced virtually unopposed along the Lerida-Taragona road. The battle of Catalonia had become a rout as the Republicans proved incapable of coping with the rapid movements of the CTV.

The successful beginning of Franco's Catalan offensive further strained Italo-French relations. The French government again opened the frontier to allow war material to flow into Spain, and rumors began to circulate about the possibility of massive French intervention to save Catalonia *in extremis*. On January 3, a note from Viola was received in Rome describing Franco's anxiety about French intervention.[185] To counter this danger, Ciano repeatedly threatened London and Paris that Italy would send regular army units to wage war against France on Spanish soil should the French intervene.[186] In view of the French and British record on Spain, this threat involved very little risk for Italy, but its sharp tone reflects the increasing firmness of Mussolini's commitment to a policy of alliance with Germany and his growing belief in the inevitability of war with France and England.[187]

[183] *Ibid.*, September 5, 1957, p. 32.
[184] Chiodini, *Roma o Mosca*, pp. 610–11.
[185] Telegram 0121, n.d., MAE, Politica, b. 52.
[186] Ciano, *Diary*, January 5 and 16, 1939.
[187] On New Year's day, 1939, Mussolini told Ciano that he was ready to sign a tripartite pact with Germany and Japan during the last ten days of January, since a clash with the western democracies seemed more and more inevitable, and it was well to provide for a military alignment in advance (Ciano, *Diary*, January 1, 1939). This decision would eventually bear fruit in the Pact of Steel signed between Germany and Italy on May 28, 1939, two months after the conclusion of the Spanish Civil War. The details of the negotiations,

This bold Italian threat undoubtedly weighed heavily in Daladier and Bonnet's decision to oppose the French Left's pressure for massive aid to the Republic. Without such aid, the Catalans were unable to resist. In Barcelona, the heavy losses incurred during the battle of the Ebro and the long feud between the Catalan *Generalitat* and the central government, as well as the Communist campaign against the P.O.U.M. and the anarchists, made it impossible to rally the population for a defense of the city like that of Madrid two years earlier. On January 24, Italian troops helped overcome Republican resistance at Manresa and Martorell. The following day, as they crossed the Llobregat river, Mussolini telegraphed Gambarra that he wanted a sizeable contingent of the CTV to be among the first troops to enter the city.[188]

The Catalan capital fell to the Nationalists on January 26, 1939. The entire front page of most Italian newspapers was filled with the story. The ministry of popular culture ordered that prominent place be given to Franco's telegram to Gambarra praising "the brilliant effort of the Italian legionary troops who will receive in Barcelona with their Spanish comrades the laurels of triumph."[189] From the balcony of Palazzo Venezia, Mussolini harangued an enormous crowd that filled the square. "The splendid victory of Bar-

which were protracted by Japanese hesitation and resistance, are of less interest here than Mussolini's perception of the inevitability of conflict and his willingness to bind Italy irrevocably to the Nazi cart. This disposition would be shaken by the German takeover of Bohemia in March, but only momentarily. Mussolini's pride and self-respect had become involved in keeping faith with his commitments to Hitler. This concern, together with his unwillingness to face up to the realities of the extremely unpleasant situation into which he had gotten Italy, was sufficient to maintain him within the German orbit even though he recognized that all the benefits of the Axis were going to his northern partner.

[188] Gambarra, "L'ultima parola sulla guerra di Spagna," *Tempo*, September 12, 1957, p. 27.

[189] ACS, agenzia Stefani, carte Morgagni, velline, January 25, 1939.

TO THE BITTER END

celona is another chapter in the history of the new Europe we are creating," he exulted. "Franco's magnificent troops and our intrepid legionaries have not only defeated the government of Negrin. Many other enemies of ours bite the dust in this moment. The motto of the Reds was this: 'No pasarán!' We have passed, and I assure you we will pass."[190] At Ciano's suggestion, Gambarra, who had been made a brigadier general only two months earlier, was given a promotion for war merit to major general, and the news of his promotion was prominently displayed in Italian papers.[191] No effort to dissimulate the extent of Italian involvement in Spain was now being made in Rome. Quite the contrary, the newspapers were specifically ordered to give prominence to incidents such as the wounding of General Bitozzi.[192]

The troops that had failed to defend Barcelona could not be expected to hold the rest of Catalonia, and their retreat soon turned into flight. The city of Gerona fell on February 5, and within five days the entire Hispano-French border was occupied by Nationalist troops. During the Catalan offensive, the CTV suffered more than twenty-eight hundred casualties, with 385 killed and 2,430 wounded.[193]

After the collapse of Catalonia, fighting broke out on the Republican side between partisans of surrender and advocates of resisting to the bitter end. This complex series of events elicited no interest in Rome, where Ciano and Mussolini were concerned only with the rapid conclusion of the hostilities so that they could get on with their plans for the invasion of Albania. There was no longer any real doubt about Franco's eventual victory, but it was not altogether clear that the major fighting was over.

In Rome, the conviction was widespread that the speed

[190] Mussolini, *Opera omnia*, XXIX, 228–29.
[191] *Il messagero*, January 28, 1939.
[192] ACS, agenzia Stefani, carte Morgagni, velline, February 4, 1939.
[193] *Almanacco del regio esercito XVIII* (*1939–1940*), p. 498; Canevari, *La guerra italiana*, I, 481.

and success of the Catalan offensive was due to the contribution of the CTV. Although somewhat exaggerated, there was a good deal of truth in this position, as General von Stohrer confessed.[194] Ciano and Mussolini believed that the rapid occupation of Valencia, Madrid, and the other Republican-held areas of central Spain would also depend on the CTV.[195] It was this conviction, rather than any long-range plans to remain in Spain, that explains why during the final months of the war Italian troops again began to be dispatched to Spain in large numbers. In January, 2,035 army officers and troops were shipped to Spain, and another 1,857 in February. During the first two months of the year, an additional 926 members of the Fascist militia also left for Spain. In March close to five thousand men, were sent. 3,776 were from the army and 1,090 were from the militia.[196]

For the first time in almost three years, Rome proved overly pessimistic about the duration of the war. Before the new Italian contingents had time to reach the front, the fall of Catalonia and the infighting among its own supporters led to the complete collapse of the Republic. Madrid was occupied on March 28, and on April 1, 1939, Franco officially announced the end of the war.

The final weeks of the war witnessed a series of maneuvers on the international level as the various powers attempted to guarantee their positions for the future. The British and French on their side decided the time had come to improve their relations with Franco, whereas Italy shifted its attention primarily to the problem of keeping him from becoming overly friendly with them. Rome could

[194] GD, D, III, 844.

[195] "There remains only the final blow at the center. To that end we shall immediately begin to reorganize the CTV, which must again take on itself the task of carrying the Spanish along" (Ciano, *Diary,* February 4, 1939).

[196] Final Report of the Ufficio Spagna, appendix 6, MAE, Ufficio Spagna, b. 1.

not, of course, object to Franco's establishing normal diplomatic relations with other countries, but as a delaying measure she advised him to insist on full recognition, without accepting any half-way measures.[197]

The circumstances which surrounded the Nationalist occupation of the island of Minorca soon showed that the Italians had reason to be concerned about Franco's political reliability. French military planners had long been concerned about the island and anxious to avoid any Italian presence there. Early in 1939, rumors began to circulate that to forestall an Italian invasion French leaders were considering invading Minorca themselves.[198] At the end of January, the Nationalist air force commander in Majorca approached the British consul in Palma to inquire whether it would be possible for a British destroyer to take him to Minorca to arrange a surrender.[199] After obtaining assurances that the operations had Franco's approval, the British agreed to cooperate, with the condition that no foreign troops would take part in the occupation of the island.

On February 9, 1939 the British ship *Devonshire* carried Nationalist negotiators to the island and took off Republican leaders, who were transported to France. Subsequently, the island was occupied by Spanish troops. While it was being occupied, Italian bombers carried out several raids against it. They were described by the Italian embassy as part of the CTV's cooperation in the occupation, but seem rather to have been a sign of Italian pique.[200] Rome instructed Viola to lodge a protest in Burgos about the fact that a Nationalist agent had used a British warship to reach Minorca.[201]

[197] Telegram 79/26 R, February 2, 1939, MAE, Politica, b. 56.
[198] *Tribuna,* January 22, 1939; *Lavoro Fascista,* January 22, 1939.
[199] FO W 1404/314/41.
[200] Telegram 020, February 12, 1939, MAE, Politica, b. 50. FO W 2630/314/41; Hassell, *The Von Hassell Diaries. 1938–1943,* p. 36.
[201] Telegram 97/R, February 10, 1939, MAE, Politica, b. 50.

During the closing weeks of the war Fascist leaders continued to do what they could to prevent the rapprochement between Burgos and Paris and London from becoming too cordial. They urged the Germans to reach a quick agreement with the Nationalists on a treaty of friendship that had been under negotiation for some time,[202] and they began to press Franco to adhere to the Anti-Comintern Pact. At the end of February, Franco told the Italian ambassador that he had decided to adhere immediately, even though the decision was to be kept secret until the end of the war. Mussolini was elated, since he mistakenly thought this meant Nationalist Spain was prepared to play an anti-French role in European politics, to the benefit of his plans for increasing Italy's influence in the Mediterranean. "Those silly people who tried so hard to criticize our intervention in Spain will one day perhaps understand," Ciano noted with an air of triumph, "that on the Ebro, at Barcelona, and at Málaga, the foundations were laid for the Roman Mediterranean Empire."[203]

[202] Ciano, *Diary,* February 8, 1939.
[203] *Ibid.,* February 22, 1939.

TEN

EPILOGUE AND CONCLUSIONS

EPILOGUE

LESS than one week after the end of the Civil War, the first Italian troops landed in Albania. The presence of sizeable Italian units in Spain during the Albanian crisis was a useful restraint on France lest she should feel inclined to take any serious measures in response to the new Italian aggression. For this reason Mussolini was in no hurry to withdraw the CTV,[1] but he did not seriously consider maintaining a military presence in Spain much beyond the end of the Civil War.[2] Some discussion took place at the foreign ministry of plans for demobilizing in Spain soldiers who expressed a desire to remain there and work,[3] and for establishing Italian labor battalions to help reconstruct the country,[4] but there was no thought of keeping military units there.

The public announcement of Franco's adherence to the Anti-Comintern Pact made London and Paris all the more nervous about the continued presence of German and Italian troops in the Iberian peninsula. In response to anxious queries, Rome replied that her troops would be withdrawn as soon as the final victory parade had taken place. After repeated delays, the parade was held in Madrid on May 19, 1939. For diplomatic reasons, General Gambarra and the CTV were given the place of honor at the head of

[1] GD, D, III, 887.
[2] Ciano, *Diary*, March 5, 1939.
[3] ACS, pubblica sicurezza, direzione generale degli affari generali e riservati, 1920–1945, 1939, b. 15.
[4] Correspondence in MAE, Politica, b. 52.

the more than a hundred thousand troops who marched past Franco's reviewing stand. Soon afterwards, preparations for the departure were put in train; and on May 31 some twenty thousand Italians sailed from Cádiz for Naples, accompanied by Ramón Serrano Suñer and three thousand Spaniards, who would participate in the parade planned to welcome the CTV back to Italy. Over the course of the next month and a half the remaining Italians sailed for home, leaving behind them nearly four thousand dead and large amounts of equipment, including artillery, tanks, and aircraft.

During his two-week stay in Rome, Serrano Suñer found the Duce enthusiastic about the possibilities of future Italo-Spanish collaboration. Mussolini suggested that Spain ought particularly to strengthen her navy, and urged the construction of four 35,000-ton battleships. To his son-in-law he confided his plans for North Africa: Morocco should go to Spain and Tunisia and Algeria to Italy, while an agreement with Spain would guarantee Italy's permanent access to the Atlantic through Morocco.[5] In an article published in the party magazine, *Gerarchia,* Ciano extolled the comradeship-in-arms between the Spanish and Italian people, "born of this war which we have fought in common." General Kindelán, the commander of the Spanish air force, was more explicit: "The union of the Italian and Spanish air forces has made the Mediterranean a lake which cannot be traversed by the enemy. I do not know what tomorrow will bring, but no arm of the Spanish services, particularly not the air force, will be able to remain idle if the Italian forces are engaged."[6]

In July Ciano returned Serrano Suñer's visit and engaged in conversations with General Franco. The Spanish leader confirmed his intention "to follow more and more definitely the line of the Rome-Berlin Axis while awaiting the day when Spain's general condition and military preparations

[5] Ciano, *Diary,* June 14, 1939.
[6] Both quoted in Ciano, *Ciano's Diplomatic Papers,* pp. 289–90.

will allow him to identify himself with the political system of the totalitarian countries." More significantly for the future, the Caudillo insisted that Spain was exhausted and that if war were to come in the near future she would be forced to remain neutral.[7]

On the economic plane also, negotiations were being carried on between Rome and Madrid. Some Italian representatives hoped to establish close links between the two countries, and to win for Italy a prominent place in the Spanish program of reconstruction. As on previous occasions, expressions of good will were not lacking on the Spanish side, but few concrete results were forthcoming. According to Guarnieri, the Italian economic ministries had to make strenuous efforts to keep Mussolini from simply canceling the entire Spanish debt. An agreement was finally reached in May 1940, that stipulated that Spain would pay 5 billion lire toward the 6 to 8.5 billion lire which the war had cost Italy.[8] Five billion lire represented 3 percent of Italy's estimated gross internal product, and about 12 percent of her governmental expenditures in 1939.

During the early stages of World War II, not only Spain but Italy as well remained neutral. Even after Italian entrance into the war in June 1940, Franco continued to remain neutral, although for a time after the collapse of France he gave some signs of willingness to join the Axis in its successful war against England. In August he declared he would enter the war once a landing in Great Britain took place, if Germany would provide him with military and economic assistance and guarantee that Spain would receive Gibraltar, French Morocco, and Oran, along with territories

[7] *Ibid.*, p. 291.

[8] 6 billion lire is the replacement cost of the material sent as calculated by the Ufficio Spagna (Final Report of the Ufficio Spagna, p. 24, MAE, Ufficio Spagna, b. 1). 8.5 billion, the figure given by Guarnieri, seems a reasonable estimate of the cost including salaries (Guarnieri, *Battaglie economiche fra le due grandi guerre, II*, 353–54). Ciano's claim that the war had cost Italy 14 billion was almost certainly an exaggeration.

adjoining the Spanish colonies in the Rio d'Oro and the Gulf of Guinea. In a letter to Mussolini he asked the Duce's assistance in having his requests met by Hitler. Mussolini in reply urged him to join the Axis but made no effort to force him to do so.

It is far from clear whether Franco ever really intended to enter the war, but certainly by September whatever enthusiasm he may have felt had faded, together with the likelihood of a successful German invasion of England. He continued to proclaim his willingness to fight, but was exceedingly careful to avoid any firm commitments. By October Hitler's desire to see Spain join him in the war was great enough to bring him to the Spanish frontier, where he met Franco in the town of Hendaye. The Caudillo used to best advantage all the guile for which his native Galicia is known, and succeeded in avoiding any specific engagements.[9]

During the following months the military position of the Axis became more difficult, largely because of Italian failures in Libya and Albania. In the new strategic situation, control of Gibraltar became an increasingly vital Axis objective. In December Hitler decided to attack it from Spanish territory, but had to withdraw this proposal in the face of strong opposition from Franco, who insisted that Gibraltar must be taken by Spanish forces.

By mid-January 1941, Hitler had begun to despair of bringing Spain into the war himself, but still hoped that Mussolini, who had always boasted of his special relationship with the Caudillo, might be able to do so. At Hitler's request, the Duce reluctantly agreed to meet with Franco. Although he had forced Hitler to come to the Spanish

[9] Accounts of the meeting are found in GD, D XI, pp. 371–80 and 383; Serrano Suñer, *Entre Hendaya y Gibraltár*, pp. 261–65; Trythall, *Franco. A Biography*, pp. 171–74; and Crozier, *Franco*, pp. 329–31. For a full discussion of German attempts to bring Spain into World War II, see Detwiler, *Hitler, Franco, und Gibraltar: Die Frage des spanischen Eintritts in den zweiten Weltkrieg*.

border to see him, the Spanish leader did Mussolini the courtesy of traveling to the town of Bordighera on Italy's Ligurian coast, near the French border.

The Duce was not deceived by this courtesy, and confided to Anfuso before the meeting that he was convinced Spain would not enter the war. He had never been one for unpleasant conversations, and could not bring himself to make any real effort to convince Franco. To judge from the minutes of their curious meeting, one would not know that Spanish entrance into the war would have benefited Italy at least as much as Germany.[10] Perhaps Mussolini's own feeling of servitude to Hitler and his memories of his own neutrality and subsequent ill-timed entrance into the war made him more understanding with the Spanish leader.[11] In any case, he limited himself to outlining the situation and inquiring about Franco's conditions for joining the war, stressing that "the date and form of her participation in the war are matters for Spain herself."[12]

In the face of such a half-hearted attempt, Franco had no difficulty in avoiding any further commitments. A few days later he wrote Hitler to tell him that in view of the changed situation even the vague promises made at Hendaye were now outdated.[13] From this point on, Fascist Italy and Nationalist Spain were to follow increasingly divergent paths. The bonds between Rome and Berlin were to prove solid enough to drag Mussolini and his regime down to final destruction, but the much vaunted solidarity between Spain and Italy could not bring Franco into the conflict.

ITALIAN FOREIGN POLICY AND THE SPANISH CIVIL WAR

It has been the contention of this book that Italian intervention in Spain was motivated largely by traditional foreign

---

[10] Ciano, *Ciano's Diplomatic Papers*, pp. 421–30; and Serrano Suñer, *Entre Hendaya y Gibraltár*, pp. 261–65.

[11] For an excellent discussion of Mussolini's state of mind at this time, see Guidice, *Benito Mussolini*, pp. 606–608.

[12] Ciano, *Ciano's Diplomatic Papers*, p. 423.

[13] Kirkpatrick, *Mussolini*, p. 492.

policy considerations relating to Italy's political and military position in Europe and the Mediterranean, particularly her relations with France.[13a] From 1922 until the outbreak of the Civil War, Mussolini thought of Spain primarily in terms of strengthening Italy's position vis à vis France by denying Paris the possibility of transporting troops across Spain from North Africa. To a lesser extent he may also have considered the desirability of obtaining bases in the Balearic islands athwart the routes between North Africa and France's Mediterranean ports, but his interest in Spain was a function more of the negative goal of preventing France from improving her position than of a positive desire to obtain new bases for Italy.

The coming to power of Blum's Popular Front government intensified Mussolini's animosity toward France, adding an ideological note to Italo-French rivalry. This coincided with a growing polarization and a sharp swing to the left in Spanish political life. Mussolini viewed with distaste, if not alarm, the prospect of a revolution or even of the consolidation of a left wing government in Spain. Either would probably bring Madrid closer to Paris and the success of a revolution in a nearby Latin country threatened to reawaken protest and discontent in Italy and generally weaken the cause of counterrevolution in Europe. Mussolini's initial decision to support the Spanish rebels was, therefore, motivated both by anti-French sentiments and by a desire to crush any possible revolution in Spain.

These initial motives persisted throughout the civil war, but were soon reinforced by other considerations. Support of Franco provided a common ground on which to collaborate with Hitler's Germany. Despite Rome's concern over German influence in the Mediterranean, Spain repre-

[13a] The most recent and most thorough student of German intervention in Spain highlights the importance of "considerations typical of a policy of traditional interests" in Hitler's initial decision to intervene in Spain. (Viñas, *La Alemania nazi y el 18 de julio,* p. 442).

sented one of the few areas in which Rome and Berlin could work together in furtherance of a common goal. Hitler deferred to Mussolini on questions of Spanish policy and allowed him to take the lead, in gratifying contrast to his general tendency not even to inform Rome before taking major steps such as the occupation of Austria.

Success in Spain soon became a question which involved the prestige of the Fascist regime and of Mussolini himself. Mussolini's reaction to the Italian defeat at Guadalajara and the Italian press's glorification of Santander as a great Fascist victory underline the importance of prestige factors in Italian policy in Spain. What was at stake was not only the Duce's personal pride, but his reputation as an infallible leader whose followers were asked to believe that "the Duce is always right." The party's own propaganda about Fascist volunteers in Spain and the success of the European anti-Fascist press in presenting the Spanish civil war as an anti-Fascist crusade made it essential to see Franco through to victory. A mobilizational regime which trades heavily on the personal prestige of its carismatic leader cannot accept failure in a foreign venture to which he has committed himself without danger of serious damage to itself.

Fascist ideological aims in Spain were more negative than positive. Mussolini was more concerned about preventing a successful revolution in Spain than he was about promoting Fascism there. Except for the incidents surrounding the Farinacci mission during the first quarter of 1937, Rome made no serious attempt to induce the Spanish Nationalists to follow Fascist models nor did she try to strengthen and support pro-Fascist groups within the Nationalist coalition. This passive and defensive attitude did not spring from a lack of desire to see Fascist regimes established abroad. Mussolini's public statements from the early thirties onwards and the propaganda activities carried out in other countries, particularly Brazil, demonstrate that he wanted to spread Fascism. Rather it shows

390

that in Spain traditional foreign policy considerations of power and prestige and the negative ideological aim of avoiding defeat for forces to which he had committed himself outweighed the desire to promote Fascism whenever they came into conflict.

There is no sign in Italy of the kind of tension between foreign ministry and party which characterized German foreign policy under Hitler. The Spanish question was handled largely by Ciano's personal entourage, who had replaced the career diplomats as chief advisers of the foreign minister, but the professionals made only feeble attempts to exert any influence and there was no equivalent in Italy to the *Bureau Ribbentrop*. In so far as there was a distinctive fascist influence, it was exercised by men who had been placed within the state apparatus, rather than by party organs.

Italian policy in Spain was Mussolini's personal preserve. The day to day decisions were left to Ciano and his subordinates, but all major decisions were the Duce's. Many were taken on the spur of the moment, without consulting anyone and without any rational analysis of costs and benefits. The erratic character of the resulting policy was particularly apparent in the late summer and early fall of 1938 when the Duce seemed unable to decide whether to keep some Italian troops in Spain or withdraw them all. As he once confessed to Ciano, he tended to be swayed by the last argument he had heard, and so he alternated back and forth, making a decision one day only to reverse it the next. The record of his vacilating policy in Spain confirms that after 1936 the Duce began to lose his grip and to become a less and less effective decision maker.

Italy's Contribution to Franco's Military Victory

Italian support was an essential element in the Nationalist victory. A critical factor that is frequently forgotten was diplomatic support. Paris, as we have seen, had strong political and ideological motives for assisting the Republic.

Had the rebels not received the backing of at least one major power, in all probability France would have taken whatever steps were necessary to insure a Republican victory. The diplomatic support of a great power was, therefore, an essential condition of Franco's success.

German support alone would have been sufficient, even without Italian backing, but it seems unlikely that Germany would have committed herself fully had Italy remained on the sidelines. It is true that the first German commitment was made without consulting Rome and prior to Mussolini's decision to aid Franco, but initial German aid was small and involved few risks. Once it became clear that much greater aid would be needed, Germany would probably have withdrawn had not Italy also been backing the Nationalists. German interests in the Mediterranean were not sufficient to justify the risks involved in single-handedly defying France in a distant theater, where all the geographic factors were in France's favor. Italian support of the rebels reduced the political and economic costs to Germany of aiding them, while the benefits for overall German policy of acting in collaboration with Rome gave the Nazis added incentive for continuing their aid. In this sense, Italian diplomatic—and military—backing was a crucial element in Franco's victory.

Italy and Germany were Franco's only significant sources of modern arms and equipment. The most important supplies sent from Italy are summarized in table 7. The total cost of the material supplied by the ministry of war amounted to 4.2 billion lire, while the air ministry spent another 1.8 billion. The total value of the material supplied by Germany was somewhere between a half and three fourths of this amount.[14] Aircraft are the item which

[14] Figures on Italian aid are from the Final Report of the Ufficio Spagna, p. 24, MAE, Ufficio Spagna, b. 1. The sterling equivalent of 6 billion lire at the official 1939 exchange rates was 64 million pounds. The best available estimates put total German aid at between 412 and 540 million RM, equivalent to between 35 and 46 million

TABLE 7
Italian War Material Sent to Spain
July 1936–March 1939

Army and Militia

Cannon	1,801	Small arms ammunition	320
Mortars	1,426	(millions of rounds)	
Machine guns	3,436	Artillery shells (millions)	7.7
Tanks	157		
Motor vehicles	6,791		

Air Force

Bombers		Fighters	
S 81	84	Cr 32	376
S 79	100	Ro 41	28
Br 20	13	Other	10
Ca 310	16		
Total	213	Total	414
Assault planes	44	Reconaissance	68
Sea planes	20		

SOURCE: Ufficio Spagna, final report, pp. 20–22, MAE, Ufficio Spagna, b. 1.

it is easiest to compare with some assurance. Italy sent 414 fighters to Germany's 282.[15] No exact statistics have been found on the total number of bombers provided by Germany, but at the end of 1938 Italian bombers in service in Spain outnumbered German ones by a ratio of 9 to 7.[16]

Italian army material was inferior in quality to that provided by Germany. Most of the cannon sent from Italy were of World War I vintage, and most of the rifles were the 1891 model. Germany had no stockpiles of antiquated equipment, since she had been forced to disarm by the

pounds. The lower estimate is found in GD, D, III, 783, the higher in Whealey, "Foreign Intervention in the Spanish Civil War," p. 219.

[15] Salas Larrazábal, La guerra de España desde el aire, p. 431.

[16] Ibid., p. 433.

treaty of Versailles, and so provided superior modern supplies.

Overall, Italian aircraft were probably not inferior to the German ones. The Me 109 and the He 112 fighters were certainly far superior to the Italian CR 32s, but they constituted only a little over half the fighters sent from Germany. The He 51, which made up the other 50 percent, were so antiquated that in the later phases of the war they could not be used as fighters at all, whereas the CR 32s continued in active service through the end of the war with considerable success. The Italian S 81 bomber did not compare unfavorably with the JU 52, and the S 79 was an excellent medium bomber whose toughness, maneuverability and top speed of 430 kilometers per hour—considerably faster than the He 111 or the Do 17— enabled it to serve as the workhorse of the Italian airforce during World War II. On balance, considering both the quantity of aid provided and the quality of the material, Italian arms probably contributed as much as German ones to Franco's victory. If they were inferior, it can only have been by a small margin.

We have seen in chapter 4 the importance of Italian and German aircraft in enabling Franco to offset initial Republican control of the sea, and so transport the Army of Africa to the peninsula. Italian naval support was also an important element in the Nationalists' final victory. The submarines put at Franco's disposal in the fall of 1936 and the arming of the *Canarias* considerably strengthened his fleet. This, together with the timidity of the Republican navy, especially after the Italian submarine attack on the *Cervantes* in December 1936, enabled the Nationalist navy to gain control of the sea during the first six months of the war, despite its initial inferiority. Nationalist naval superiority made it more difficult and expensive for the Republic to receive supplies from the Soviet Union, and hindered communications and transportation between Republican controlled territories in the north and the rest of

Republican Spain, as well as denying the Republicans the benefits of coastal shipping.

During the summer of 1937, attacks by Italian submarines in the Mediterranean took a heavy enough toll of Soviet shipping to hinder badly Soviet supply efforts and force the Soviet Union to divert most future shipping away from the Mediterranean. Even after the Nyon Conference put an end to the "piratical" attacks, the Russians generally preferred not to run the risks of the Mediterranean. Their reliance on French Atlantic ports and overland transshipment through France made supporting the Republic slower and more costly. Italian naval support thus helped to reduce sharply the flow of aid to the Republic.

The distinctive thing about Italy's intervention in the Civil War was the large number of men she sent. Summary figures for the entire war are presented in table 8. One Spanish historian has gone so far as to call manpower "obviously the greatest contribution of Fascist Italy to the Nationalist side."[17] Italian pilots and other air force personnel certainly played a vital role in Franco's triumph, both in direct combat and in training Spanish pilots. Most of the Spanish air force had remained loyal to the Republic, so the vast majority of Franco's pilots were either Italians and Germans, or men trained by them during the course of the war. Italian artillery crews were also a valuable element in the Nationalist war effort. Throughout the conflict, the majority of the artillery pieces sent from Italy were served by Italian artillerymen. In March 1937, Italian officers established a number of training schools for officer candidates, tank and artillery crews, engineers, and chemical warfare specialists. By the end of the conflict, twenty five thousand men and officers had passed through the courses.[18]

[17] La Cierva, "The Nationalist Army in the Spanish Civil War," p. 204.

[18] Final report of the Ufficio Spagna, p. 31, MAE, Ufficio Spagna, b. 1.

TABLE 8

Italian Forces Sent to Spain
July 1936–March 1939

	Ground Forces		
	Army*	Militia	Total
Officers	3,301	1,736	5,037
NCOs	2,895	27,910	67,738
Troops	36,933		
Total	43,129	29,646	72,775

	Air Force		
	Pilots	Other	Total
Officers	862	203	1,065
NCOs	573	1,196	1,769
Enlisted	—	2,865	2,865
	1,435	4,264	5,699

SOURCE: Final report of Ufficio Spagna, p. 81,
and appendices 5 and 6, MAE, Ufficio
Spagna, b. 1.
* Numbers for the Army should be increased by
1,500 men sent prior to December 1936 who
cannot be divided among officers, NCOs and
troops.

At no time during the war did Italian—or German—
officers play a central role as Franco's advisors in the
planning of operations. In this field Italo-German influence
on the Nationalists was less direct and less significant than
Soviet influence on the Republicans. The Republic had
fewer politically reliable generals and field grade officers,
and so was forced to rely more heavily on foreigners. On a
number of occasions, Russian advisors were extremely influential in planning and conducting operations, whereas the

Italians and Germans rarely if ever succeeded in swaying Franco's decisions.

Most Italian attempts to influence Franco involved the pace of the war. Mussolini, as we have seen repeatedly, was anxious to end his commitment in Spain and was convinced that Franco could win the war more quickly if he really tried. From a purely military point of view he was probably correct. During the early months of the conflict, Franco had attempted to put an end to the fighting by capturing Madrid. The stubborn defence of the capital and a growing awareness of the degree of popular resistance to his rule appear to have convinced him that excessive haste in conquering the country would make it more difficult to govern at the war's end.

This and other similar political considerations frequently weighed heavily in Franco's decisions and led him to reject proposals that might have materially shortened the war. We have mentioned that in talking with the Italian military attaché in Berlin, General Keitel observed that Franco's personality seemed to be split between the military man who willingly accepted Italian and German suggestions for decisive new offensives, and the politician who drew back from carrying them out. The commander of the Nationalist Air Force also refers in his memoirs to the preponderance in Franco's decisions of "psychological considerations which perhaps ought in principle to take second place to the rules of warfare, but which are especially important in a civil war."[19]

The effects of these considerations on the battles of Guadalajara, Brunete, Teruel, and Catalonia have already been noted. That Franco was able to carry out the war in his own way and at his own pace, despite Rome's vigorous protests and threats of discontinuing its aid, is a clear indication that he managed to retain almost total

[19] Report of the military attaché to Magistrati, N. 1926, Berlin, December 30, 1937, MAE, Gabinetto, b. 2; Kindelán, *Mis cuadernos de guerra, 1936–1939*, p. 67.

operational independence despite heavy reliance on foreign support.

Italian infantry troops, despite their number, were not a significant factor in Franco's victory. This is not to deny that they made valid contributions at Málaga, Santander, etc., but simply to say that with over a million men under arms by the end of the war, Franco did not vitally need seventy thousand foreign infantry soldiers. They never fulfilled the function of an elite shock force, as did the International Brigades, whose mortality rate seems to have been close to 33%. The CTV's casualty rates appear to have been roughly similar to those of the Navarrese and Falangist units for which figures are available—5 percent killed for the Italians and 6 percent for the Carlists and Falangists.[20] The Italian infantry did not greatly alter the overall balance of forces.

It is often supposed that Italian and German aid to the Nationalists far exceeded aid to the Republic. The absence of reliable figures on the supplies that reached the Republic and on the size of the International Brigades makes it difficult to discuss the question intelligently. The scraps of evidence I have been able to assemble, which are presented in the preceeding chapters, seem to indicate that while the Nationalists received more aid, the difference was nowhere near as great as propagandists claimed and as some historians have believed.[21]

[20] Thomas, *The Spanish Civil War*, p. 637; Payne, *Politics and the Military in Modern Spain*, p. 461.

[21] Van der Esch asserts that Franco-Russian aid "cannot be compared to that of the Axis." She describes it as "small and spasmodic" (*Prelude to War*, p. 35). Puzzo writes: "While Italo-German support of the rebels amounted to a veritable invasion of Spain by the fascist powers, Russian support of the Loyalists, albeit of importance militarily and significant in the political life of the Republic, did not alter the essentially Spanish character of the Republic's military effort. Thus, while the Republicans fought Germans, Italians, Moors, and the Tercio, with formations of the small, conscripted Spanish Army and other Spanish contingents, principally the Navarrese *requetés* inter-

Effects on the Political Configuration of Nationalist Spain
The outcome of the Civil War was the installation in Spain of a conservative authoritarian regime with certain similarities to Fascism, in which effective power was highly concentrated in the hands of General Franco. Beyond permitting the establishment of such a regime by contributing to the military victory of the rebels, what role did Italy play in its configuration?

As we have seen, the three phases of the Civil War witnessed quite different Italian policies with respect to intervention in the internal politics of the Nationalist zone. During the first phase, when Italy's military commitment was limited to supplying material and instructors, Rome was extremely cautious not to attempt to favor one political group over another. During the second phase, as Italy's military presence in Spain grew, so did her political presence. The Farinacci mission clearly signaled Rome's determination not to remain an idle spectator as Franco began to form a new political regime. During the third phase, Rome returned to the policy of intervening in Nationalist politics only on a very limited scale, perhaps because the defeat at Guadalajara had undermined the moral basis for Italian attempts to influence Nationalist politics.

At no time was direct Italian influence sufficient to alter

spersed among them, the rebels fought Spaniards who, for a time, enjoyed the support of the numerically weak but hard fighting International Brigades" (*Spain and the Great Powers 1936–1941*, p. 169).

One Spanish author with privileged access to military records maintains that the Republic received more aircraft than the Nationalists during the course of the war. Salas Larrazábal, "La intervención extranjera y las ayudas exteriores," in Palacio Atard, La Cierva, and Salas, *Aproximación histórica a la guerra española (1936–1939)*, pp. 200–201. His sources are not open to examination by independent scholars, but the figures he gives for the number of Italian planes are accurate. Thomas's calculations for all kinds of aid show a proportion of about 4:3 in favor of the Nationalists (*The Spanish Civil War*, pp. 793–97).

fundamentally the character of the regime that was being formed. The political decisions which were taken were primarily the result of the balance of political forces within Nationalist Spain. Italian—and German—intervention in the war had fewer repercussions on the internal politics of the Nationalist zone than did Russian intervention on the politics of the Republic. Control of Soviet arms allowed Spanish Communists to win for themselves an influence that was disproportionate to the strength of their position at the outbreak of the war and which they probably could not have achieved solely on the basis of their superior organization and spirit.[22] No similar development took place in Nationalist Spain. The Falange, which was ideologically closest to Fascism and the logical candidate for Italian and German support, was firmly under Franco's personal control—a useful instrument but one with no independent power of its own. Italy made no real effort to change this situation and seemed quite content to allow Franco to exercise his authority as he saw fit.[23]

In terms of the future political configuration of Spain, one of the most important effects of Italian intervention was the contribution it made to General Franco as he consolidated his preeminent position. The process was largely completed during the first phase of the war, when Italy was being most cautious about not meddling in the internal politics of the Nationalist zone, and there is no evidence that Mussolini deliberately sought to help Franco establish himself as the sole leader of Nationalist Spain. Nonetheless, the fact that the bulk of Italian aid was directed—in large part for geographic reasons—to Franco's Army of Africa certainly enhanced the future Caudillo's position with respect to the other leaders of the rising. His name has become so closely linked with the Nationalist cause that it

[22] Cattell, *Communism and the Spanish Civil War*, passim.

[23] Horton notes that Faupel's efforts to support the Falange were personal ones which received little encouragement from Berlin. *Germany and the Spanish Civil War*, pp. xiv–xv.

is hard to realize that others, particularly Mola, might well have aspired to share power with him. Control of Italian arms contributed in no small measure to the consolidation of Franco's position during the early months of the war. During its later phases, Italy's continued backing helped Franco to maintain his position, and Rome's failure to provide vigorous support to the Falange helped Franco retain a high degree of personal power.

As we have seen, the leaders of Fascist Italy occasionally refered to the Civil War as a defense of Fascism, but they never spoke of it as an opportunity to spread it, nor did they quote Franco's Spain as an example of a Fascist state. The Italian press carried occasional articles about the development of Fascist regimes in other countries, particularly Brazil,[24] but only rarely was much attention paid to the political development of Franco's Spain. When information was given, the word *Fascist* was carefully avoided. There were, it is true, a few references to Italian casualties in Spain as martyrs of the "Fascist Idea," and other similar phrases, but nothing more concrete than this was said. Franco himself was equally careful to avoid publicly equating his regime with Fascism. Typical of his attitude is a telegram to Mussolini which describes the Italians killed in Spain as having died "for the defense of Christian civilization."[25]

Nonetheless, the political system Franco gradually developed did bear at first glance considerable resemblance to that of Fascist Italy. A one-party system was established, and an effort was made to invest the Caudillo with a charismatic halo like that of the Duce. Propaganda based on an authoritarian and nationalistic rhetoric was initiated, and Spain blossomed with uniforms and "Roman" salutes. An attempt was even made to promote interest in a new "imperial" era of Spanish history. A system of state-con-

---

[24] For example, a front page article by Federzoni was published in *Popolo d'Italia*, September 12, 1937.

[25] *Corriere della Sera*, October 30, 1937.

trolled labor unions was established, and the new Spanish labor legislation was in large measure copied from the Italian *Carta del lavoro.* The similarities were, however, more formal than substantive, more cosmetic than real. Spain's state party, the *Falange Española Tradicionalista y de las JONS,* for instance, was little more than a forced coalition of heterogeneous elements wedded by Franco to prevent infighting among supporters of the National movement and to facilitate his own control of political life. It had no independent political power and was not the basis of his power, as the *Partito Nazionale Fascista* was the basis of Mussolini's.

The Franco regime can be described in Linz's terminology as a bureaucratic-military authoritarian regime, but not a fully Fascist one. Even when it came closest to Fascism, prior to 1945, it allowed a greater—although quite limited—degree of pluralism, and was significantly less mobilizational and participatory than the Italian Fascist regime. Spain's experience with mass democratic politics was short enough and the country's social and economic development was slight enough that it was not essential to give the majority of the citizens a sense of participation. Despite some effort at political mobilization in the years immediately following the war, Franco was usually content to accept apathy without demanding active support.[26]

Mussolini's regime, as we have seen, soon reached a working agreement with Italy's traditional political, social, and economic elites, but the Fascist party had originally been built on a bourgeois base. Franco's dependence for political power on the traditional elites was more direct and more crucial. Furthermore, his support came less from a modern bourgeoise than from Spain's traditional *clases medias* of lawyers, bureaucrats, etc. Until the outbreak of the civil war, these groups had proven relatively impervious

[26] Juan Linz, "Totalitarian and Authoritarian Regimes," draft of an article to appear in Greenstein and Polsby (eds.), *Handbook of Political Science;* cited by permission of the author.

to the appeals of the Falange and other pro-Fascist groups. Their support of Franco was less the result of successful ideological mobilization than of the exigencies of the situation once the war began.[27]

What significant imitation of Fascist models did take place was due more to force of circumstance than to the direct results of Italian intervention. At the outset of the war, the Nationalist leaders intended only to restore order and establish a strong conservative government. Their plan, which had no particular theoretical underpinnings, was practicable only on the premise of a successful coup or, at most, a brief, decisive civil war. As the months dragged on with no end of fighting in sight, the necessity of a more elaborate political program capable of justifying a long and bloody conflict began to be felt. Of the available models, Italian Fascism would have been the most obvious candidate for imitation even had Italy not been providing active military support. Fascism was at the height of its internal success and had recently scored an international victory with its conquest of Ethiopia in defiance of the League of Nations. Its ideology, which suited the authoritarian tastes of the military and their backers, was more congenial to many Spaniards than the rigid anti-Christian theories of German National Socialism. Even before the war began, the Falange had introduced a generically Fascist program into Spanish political life, and its rapid growth after the outbreak of the war was a guarantee that it would receive a favorable hearing.

The Fascist elements in Franco's new state are to be attributed less to direct Italian intervention in the Civil War than to the historical moment in which the regime was born and the tastes and interests of the Caudillo and his supporters. Throughout the war, Franco managed to retain a degree of political as well as military autonomy that can only be described as remarkable in view of his

[27] *Ibid;* Broué and Témime, *The Revolution and the Civil War in Spain*, p. 459.

dependence on Italy and Germany for diplomatic support and arms. He fought the war at his own pace and in his own way, and adopted only those political institutions he found useful. Even in the economic sphere, he compromised himself surprisingly little until he was finally forced to sign mining agreements in order to obtain the German arms he required for the Catalan offensive at the end of 1938.[28]

The Spanish Civil War and Italy's Participation in World War II

Shortly after the outbreak of the Spanish Civil War, Mussolini referred for the first time to the "Rome-Berlin Axis," and one year after its end Italy joined Germany in the Second World War. We have examined in some detail the effects of Italian participation in the Civil War on her international relations, but it may be useful to summarize them briefly here.

Despite their much vaunted ideological solidarity, in 1936 Italy and Germany still had little in common and few common objectives. Their initial decisions to aid Franco were taken independently and without consulting each other; but the Spanish venture soon became a joint enterprise, and for almost three years provided an area in which they could collaborate on a common project. During the first four or five months of the war, Germany took the initiative. It was Hitler who sent envoys to Rome in August 1936 to propose coordinating efforts, and he provided most of the aid sent to Franco up to January 1937. From the beginning, however, he allowed Italy to play the leading role in the Non-Intervention Committee, where the German representative was instructed to follow Grandi's line.

In December 1936, after the signing of the secret political

[28] "Despite his ever-increasing debt to the Reich and constant heavy pressure from Berlin, Generalissimo Franco largely succeeded in preserving his own freedom of action" (Harper, *German Economic Policy in Spain during the Spanish Civil War, 1936–1939*, p. 135).

treaty between Rome and Burgos, Mussolini decided to increase radically his commitment in Spain by beginning to provide not only material and instructors but infantry. Hitler's refusal to follow the Duce in this step implied a reversal of roles. During the next two years, it was Italy who sent more aid, although German assistance continued to be sizeable. Germany did not cut back her aid to Franco; she simply did not multiply it as Italy did in early 1937. As we have pointed out, Italo-German collaboration in Spain was frequently tainted with rivalry, and Rome was never altogether pleased with the prospect of an increased German presence in the Mediterranean. Consequently, although he would have liked the Germans to provide more aid in the hope of helping Franco to a quick victory, Mussolini was not angered by their failure to do so and seems to have considered the level of Berlin's aid satisfactory. During the final months of the war, German support again became preponderant.

In addition to providing a basis for Italo-German collaboration, the Civil War also focused Rome's attention on the western Mediterranean, preventing her from devoting too much thought to Central Europe. Germany's highly successful efforts to increase her influence in the Danube basin and her occupation of Austria and Czechoslavakia might have provoked greater concern in Rome had not Italy been preoccupied with Spanish affairs. It is easy, however, to overstress the role of the Spanish conflict in this regard. The fact that Mussolini abandoned his efforts to preserve Austrian independence no later than June 1936, before the Civil War began, indicates that even when not engaged in Spain he was aware there was relatively little Italy could do about German expansion other than register ineffectual protests.

Together with the Ethiopian War, Italian participation in the Spanish Civil War helped to polarize the international climate by creating a sizeable body of anti-Fascist opinion in England and the United States. Prior to 1936, anti-Fascism had been mostly limited to Communists and Socialists and to small groups of non-Marxist democrats in France. Many British and American democrats and liberals had shown a great deal of toleration toward Fascism, which they judged an acceptable solution for Italy's problems. The Spanish Civil War, ably exploited by the powerful propaganda machine of the Comintern, contributed to a shift of opinion. Increasingly, large numbers of people came to see Fascism as the natural enemy of democracy. Italy's flagrant violations of her obligations under the Non-Intervention Agreement made her seem an unreliable ally and a dangerous and deceitful enemy.[29]

If Italy's support of Franco converted many former well-wishers into enemies of Fascism, the failure of Great Britain and France to react energetically to his Spanish adventure helped convince Mussolini that the Western democracies had neither the will nor the ability to resist him. Together with their feeble efforts to prevent his invasion of Ethiopia and their passive acquiescence in Hitler's remilitarization of the Rhineland and occupation of Austria and Czechoslovakia, their reaction to his aid for Franco contributed to his scorn for countries that seemed unable to defend their own interests.

Soviet leaders also drew their own lessons from the impunity with which Italy and Germany were allowed to support Franco. Like Mussolini, they concluded that France and England were in an advanced state of decline. More importantly, they found confirmation for their belief that Fascism was really a tool of Western capitalism in its struggle against Socialism, and that the capitalist countries

[29] Valiani, "L'intervento in Spagna," p. 12. Also see Watkins, *Britain Divided. The Effects of the Spanish Civil War on British Political Opinion;* and Guttmann, *The Wound in the Heart. America and the Spanish Civil War.* Diggins, however, does not believe that the Spanish Civil War had much effect on American views of Italian Fascism (Diggins, *Mussolini and Fascism: The View from America,* pp. 322–25).

would be only too glad to see the Soviet Union invaded by Nazi Germany. The failure of their efforts to enlist the aid of France and Great Britain in a "popular front against Fascism" in Spain must have weighed heavily in the Soviet decision to abandon collective security with the West and sign the Nazi-Soviet Non-Aggression Pact.

The Spanish Civil War exacerbated the tensions between Italy and France. As the months went by, Mussolini showed an ever increasing hostility toward France that contrasted sharply with his relatively open attitude toward Great Britain. Had London and Paris not been so closely related, Chamberlain's efforts to win Mussolini away from the Axis might conceivably have met with some success. The Duce was not unaware of the costs and risks involved in his alignment with Hitler, but Italo-French emnity, fed by the incidents of the Civil War, was a major obstacle in the path of Italian rapprochement with England. In many ways this factor is more important in explaining Italy's adhesion to the Pact of Steel and eventual entrance into the world war on Germany's side than the fact of Italo-German collaboration in Spain or Mussolini's disdain for the impotence of the democracies.

The importance of these factors taken together could easily be exaggerated. It should be remembered that the Second World War was nine months old before Italy finally entered, and that she did so only when it seemed that Germany was on the verge of winning a crushing victory. Had the allies been more successful in resisting the Nazi onslaught, Mussolini might very well have remained neutral or even eventually joined them if it seemed that in so doing he could better achieve his goals.

The Second World War soon revealed Italy's woeful lack of preparation for a major conflict. One obvious explanation lay in her prolonged participation in the Spanish Civil War shortly after the Ethiopian conflict. Italy, it has frequently been said, was exhausted before the world war ever began by her efforts in Spain. Her supposed exhaustion has even been described by one eminent historian as "perhaps the only significant effect of the Spanish Civil War."[30] The facts do not support these allegations.

The 6 billion lire in war material that Italy sent to Spain represented only slightly more than one year's ordinary budget for the armed services and amounted to about 3.5 percent of her estimated gross internal product for 1939. It is important to note, furthermore, that a high percentage of the material was sent to Spain quite early in the conflict. Of the 4.2 billion lire total for the ministry of war, 2.9 billion had already been sent by mid-September 1937.[31] Similarly, by the end of September 1937 the air force had already spent at least 700 million of the 1.8 billion lire it was to spend during the war.[32] This means that over half the material was sent to Spain almost three years before Italy's entrance into World War II, allowing plenty of time for its replacement. The expenditures made for Spain were sizeable, but not so large that the arsenals and arms depots could not have been restocked over a three-year period.

Most of the arms sent to Spain were antiquated and needed to be replaced anyway. The artillery pieces were all World War I models. Their loss in Spain should have served as a stimulus to increase production, but did not materially reduce the Italian army's capacity to wage war against a well-equipped enemy. Similar observations may be made about many other categories of equipment. Italian commanders in Spain repeatedly noted in their reports, for instance, that the 45-mm mortars they had been sent

[30] Taylor, *The Origins of the Second World War*, 2nd ed., p. 245; Spigo, *Premesse techniche della disfatta*, p. 45; Italy, Ufficio storico stato maggiore esercito, *L'esercito italiano tra la prima e la seconda guerra mondiale*, p. 134.

[31] Report prepared by Ufficio Spagna, MAE, Ufficio Spagna, b. 2.

[32] The figure for September 1937 is taken from ACS, Aeronautica, Gabinetto, 1937, 7, 1, 3. The somewhat confused figures found in this category of the air ministry's files give a total of 1.1 to 1.5 billion lire for the entire war, rather than the 1.8 billion mentioned in the text and taken from the final report of the *Ufficio Spagna*.

were too light to be effective. The rifles employed were the 1891 model, better suited to trench warfare than to the conditions under which Italian troops would fight in World War II. The tanks were all 3.5-ton L-3 models, armed only with machine guns, whose inadequacy was clearly demonstrated in Spain.[33] Of the more than 750 aircraft sent to Spain, only the one hundred S 79 bombers could have made a significant contribution in World War II.[34]

Far from weakening Italy militarily, the experience of combat and the loss of antiquated equipment should have served as a stimulus and contributed to improving efficiency. It did not in fact do so. Despite Mussolini's bellicose statements and conviction that war was inevitable, few serious efforts were made actually to prepare for war. The problem was only partly one of lack of industrial capacity and raw materials. As late as 1939, the army was purchasing only 17 percent of Italian industrial production.[35] According to the director of war production, in that crucial year the country was producing only seventy artillery pieces per month of the same types of which she had turned out eight hundred per month in 1917–18.[36] Although events in Spain had clearly demonstrated the inadequacies of light tanks

[33] "The thesis that the enormous inferiority in armament of our army in 1939 and during the war was a consequence of the Ethiopian war and of our participation in the Spanish Civil War [is] completely unfounded. . . . Our units cannot have lost or used up in Ethiopa and in Spain the *modern* arms and equipment which we never possessed" [Roatta, *Otto milioni di baionette*, p. 13 (emphasis in original)].

[34] The S 81 was an antiquated bomber which played no significant role in World War II and could not have done so. The same observation may be made about almost all the fighters employed in Spain. The workhorse of the Spanish Civil War, the CR 32, was a biplane designed in the early thirties. With a top speed of 375 kilometers per hour and armed with two 12.7-mm machine guns, by 1940 it was "out of date from every point of view" (Barbieri, *I caccia della seconda guerra mondiale*, p. 209).

[35] Romeo, *Breve storia della grande industria in Italia*, p. 180.

[36] Favagrossa, *Perchè perdemmo la guerra*, p. 14.

armed with machine guns, in 1939 Italy manufactured only 194 tanks armed with cannon.[37]

Italian political and military leaders not only failed to respond to the stimulus the Spanish Civil War offered them to improve the country's armament, they also failed to learn from the experience of the war. The air force did make a conscious effort to rotate its men regularly in order to give them combat experience, but its relative success in Spain seems to have confirmed its commitment to individual heroism and bravado rather than to mass employment of planes in standardized patterns, as could be seen in training programs which laid more stress on aerial acrobatics than on group tactics.[38] The army did not attempt to use Spain as a proving ground, and Italian officers were usually changed only for reasons of service, with no regular pattern of rotation.[39] No major effort was made to substitute obviously deficient equipment, such as the 45-mm mortar or the L–3 tank. Combat experience in Spain had tended to show that the new two-regiment divisions then being adopted as the basic organizational unit of the army were too light to do their job effectively, but the reform was pushed through nevertheless.[40]

Italy was unprepared for World War II not because she had exhausted herself in Spain, but because her political and military leaders failed to respond adequately to the changing situation, and to make use of the opportunities offered by the Spanish Civil War to improve both equipment and organization.

[37] Italy, Ufficio storico stato maggiore esercito, *Il esercito italiano tra la prima e la seconda guerra mondiale*, p. 270.

[38] Favagrossa, *Perchè perdemmo la guerra*, p. 43; and Bocca, *Storia d'Italia nella guerra fascista*, p. 135. The former subsecretary of the air force, when asked during an interview in Rome what the air force had learned in Spain, immediately replied, "Nothing." He then added that its equipment had been perfected and its crews trained, but his first instinctive answer came closer to expressing the truth that no important lessons were learned. (Interview with General Valle, Rome, June 17, 1970).

[39] Interview with General Giuseppe Bodini, Rome, July 5, 1970.

[40] Canevari, *La guerra italiana*, I, 560–63.

APPENDICES

TEXT OF THE SECRET ITALO-SPANISH AGREEMENT OF NOVEMBER 28, 1936

The Fascist Government and the Spanish Nationalist Government, united in solidarity in the common struggle against Communism, which at the present moment more than at any other menaces the peace and security of Europe, animated by the desire to develop and reinforce their own relations and to further with all their strength the social and political stabilisation of the European nations, have examined in detail the questions affecting the two states through the agency of their respective representatives in Rome and Burgos, and have agreed on the following points:

1. The Fascist Government will in future pledge to the Spanish Government its support and aid for the conservation of the independence and integrity of Spain, including both metropolitan territory and colonies, as well as for the re-establishment of social and political order within the country itself. Technical agencies of both parties will in future maintain contact to this end.

2. Convinced that close collaboration between them will be useful for both countries and for the political and social order in Europe, the Fascist Government and the Spanish Nationalist Government will maintain close contacts with each other, and will concert their actions on all questions of common interest, particularly on those concerning the western part of the Mediterranean on which it may prove necessary to co-ordinate their respective actions, and will lend each other mutual support in the effective defence of their common interests.

3. Each of the two Governments undertakes not to participate in any other grouping of Powers, or agreement between Powers, which might be directed against the other party, and will not contribute directly or indirectly to measures of a military, economic or financial nature, directed against one of the contracting parties. In particular, they undertake not to permit the exploitation of their territories, ports and inland seas, for

413

any kind of operation directed against one of the contracting parties, or for the preparations for such operations or for the free passage of the materials or troops of a third Power. With this end in view, the two Governments undertake to consider all agreements previously concluded and incompatible with the present text to be invalid, and to suspend the implementation of all undertakings arising from the above mentioned agreements.

4. The Fascist Government and the Spanish Nationalist Government have agreed on the subject of Article 16 of the League of Nations Covenant, concurring in the opinion that the manner in which it has recently been interpreted and applied is full of grave dangers to peace, and that it must therefore be abolished or radically modified. In the event of one of the contracting parties finding itself involved in a conflict with one or more Powers, or if collective measures of a military, economic or financial character are applied against one of the parties, the other Government undertakes to adopt towards the first-mentioned Government an attitude of benevolent neutrality, to guarantee it the necessary supplies, to put at its disposition all facilities, the use of ports, of air-lines, of railways and roads, as well as the maintenance of indirect commercial relations.

5. With this object in view, the two Governments believe it is of value to lay down, with effect from the conclusion of peace, the method to be adopted for the exploitation of their own economic resources, particularly raw materials, and of the means of communication. The technical agencies of both Governments will shortly conclude the agreements necessary to this end.

6. The Fascist Government and the Spanish Nationalist Government consider it possible and in accordance with the interests of both parties to develop as much as possible all forms of economic relations and sea and air communications. With this object in view, and having regard to their particularly friendly relations, they concede each other all possible facilities for exchange of goods, for the mercantile marine and for the civil aviation.

Source: Ciano, *Ciano's Diplomatic Papers*, pp. 75–77.

OFFICERS OF THE CTV AT THE BEGINNING OF THE BATTLE OF GUADALAJARA

Commander: General Mario Roatta
Chief of Staff: Colonel Emilio Faldella
Assistant Chief of Staff: Lt. Colonel Giacomo Zanussi
Chief of Operations Office: Lt. Colonel Emilio Molteni
Chief of Services Office: Lt. Colonel Giorgio Morpurgo
Chief of Information Office: Major Umberto Beer
Liaison Officer with Spanish Headquarters: Colonel Fernando Gelich
Commissar: Colonel Michele Scaroina

1st Division: "God Wills It"
Commander: General Edmondo Rossi
Assistant Commander: General Giovanni Bocchio
Chief of Staff: Colonel Roberto Nasi
1st Regiment: Colonel Aristide Nasi
2nd Regiment: Colonel Costantino Salvi
3rd Regiment: Colonel Mario Mazza

Autonomous group "March 23"
4th Regiment: Consul General Francesco Gidoni
5th Regiment: Consul General Enrico Francisci

2nd Division: "Black Flames"
Commander: General Amerigo Coppi
Chief of Staff: Major Giuseppe Bodini
6th Regiment: Consul Mario Pittau
7th Regiment: Consul Mario Marino
8th Regiment: Consul Fausto Vandelli

3rd Division: "Black Feathers"
Commander: General Luigi Nuvoloni
Chief of Staff: Major Bruno Lucini
9th Regiment: Consul General Azeglio Bulgarelli
10th Regiment: Consul General Giovanni Martini
11th Regiment: Consul General Alberto Liuzzi

415

"Littorio Division"
Commander: General Annibale Bergonzoli
Assistant Commander: General Gualtiero Gabutti
Chief of Staff: Lt. Colonel Tullio Giannotti
1st Infantry Regiment: Colonel Daniele Pescarolo
2nd Infantry Regiment: Colonel Ugo Sprega
Artillery Regiment: Colonel Giuseppe Amico

Services: Colonel Francesco Rippa

Armored cars: Colonel Carlo Rivolta

Artillery: General Ugo Zanotti

Engineers: General Michele Molinari

Aviation: General Vincenzo Velardi

The 1st and 2nd Mixed Brigades, "Blue Arrows" and "Black Arrows" commanded by Colonel Guassardo and Colonel Piazzoni, were not in the Guadalajara sector, although nominally part of the CTV.

Source: Conforti, *Guadalajara*, pp. 418–19.

APPENDIX C

ITALIAN TROOP SHIPMENTS TO SPAIN
FROM NOVEMBER 25, 1936 TO MARCH 15, 1939

Month	Army	Army to Date	Militia	Militia to Date	Total Month	Total to Date
11/36	149	149	3543[1]	3543	3692	3692
12/36	553	702	4158	7701	4711	8403
1/37	16026	16728	15900	23601	31926	40329
2/37	3606	20334	3241	26842	6847	47176
3/37	—	20334	—	26842	—	47176
4/37	—	20334	—	26842	—	47176
5/37	363	20697	—	26842	363	47539
6/37	657	21354	—	26842	657	48196
7/37	—	21354	—	26842	—	48196
8/37	173	21527	—	26842	173	48369
9/37	2320	23847	25	26867	2345	50714
10/37	2142	25989	—	26867	2142	52856
11/37	367	26356	—	26867	367	53223
12/37	168	26524	—	26867	168	53391
1/38	—	26524	—	26867	—	53391
2/38	—	26524	—	26867	—	53391
3/38	126	26650	—	26867	126	53517
4/38	242	26892	—	26867	242	53759
5/38	711	27603	—	26867	711	54470
6/38	3238	30841	—	26867	3238	57708
7/38	1696	32537	763	27630	2459	60167
8/38	384	32921	—	27630	384	60551
9/38	546	33467	—	27630	546	61097
10/38	211	33678	—	27630	211	61308
11/38	728	34406	—	27630	728	62036
12/38	1107	35513	—	27630	1107	63143
1/39	2035	37548	—	27630	2035	65178
2/39	1857	39405	926	28556	2783	67961
3/39	3776	43181	1090	29646	4866	72827
Total	43181	43181	29646	29646	72827	72827

SOURCE: Final report of the Ufficio Spagna, Appendices 5 and 6, MAE, Ufficio Spagna B. 1.
[1] The statistical appendices of the Final Report of the Ufficio Spagna are the only official Italian sources that mention this group of 3,500 militia men leaving Italy between November 25 and November 30, 1936. Since they are not mentioned in the body of the report, it seems quite likely that a mistake was made in compiling the statistics. The men probably actually left during December. From other sources we know that some 8,700 men left Italy during the month of December. (See *supra*, p. 170.) It should be noted that this table does not include some 1,500 men sent by the Italian army prior to Italian recognition of the Franco regime.

417

ITALIAN CASUALTIES IN THE SPANISH CIVIL WAR

According to official Italian figures, the Spanish Civil War cost 3819 Italian lives. Of these 1824 belonged to the Army, 1777 to the Fascist Militia, 180 to the Air Force, and 38 to the Navy.[1] In addition another 11,000—12,000 men were wounded,[2] of whom about half the Army and half from the Militia.[3]

The mortality rate was 4.5% for the Army and 6% for the Militia. The total combined casualty rate including men killed and wounded for the Army and Militia was between 20 and 22%. The only Spanish units for which data are available—the Falangist and Carlist militia—show comparable mortality rates (6%), but a significantly higher number of men wounded. In fact the Italians suffered roughly 3 nonfatal wounds for every man killed whereas the Spanish units show a 5 to 1 ratio of wounded to killed.[4]

The distribution of Italian casualties over the course of the war is shown in Table A. Table B classifies Italian mortalities by region and province of origin.

[1] Final Report of the Ufficio Spagna, p. 81 and Appendices 5 and 6. MAE, Ufficio Spagna, b.1.

[2] Rispoli (*La Spagna dei Legionari*, p. 245) lists 11,186 wounded from the Army and Militia. The figures he gives for men killed are slightly lower than those of the Ufficio Spagna.

[3] No breakdown of men wounded by services is available, but the war ministry's publication on the army's participation in the war lists 5,282 wounded. (Italy, Ministero della guerra, *Volontari dell'esercito nella guerra di Spagna*, p. 61).

[4] Payne, *Politics and the Military in Modern Spain*, p. 461.

TABLE A

Italian Army and Militia Casualties by Campaign

Campaign	Killed[1]	Wounded	Missing
Madrid	2	11	—
Málaga	74	221	2
Guadalajara	415	1969	163
Estremadura	13	26	1
Bilbao	105	427	3
Santander	486	1546	1
Brunete	—	1	—
Zuera	39	71	1
Teruel	9	40	—
Aragon	731	2481	13
Levante	321	1456	3
Ebro	39	206	—
Viver	3	33	—
Catalonia	527	2141	38
Sickness and Accidents	277	557	—

SOURCE: Rispoli, *La Spagna dei Legionari*, p. 245
[1] The total number of men killed–3071–is 15% lower than the official totals given above.

TABLE B

Italians Killed in Spain by Region and Province of Origin

Region/Province	% of Population	% of Army Dead	% of Militia Dead	Index of Percent of Army Dead to Percent of Population	Index of Percent of Militia Dead to Percent of Population
North	*46.5*	*23.9(429)*	*36.7(638)*	*.51*	*.79*
Piedmont	8.0	2.8(51)	4.5(78)	.35	.56
Liguria	3.4	1.2(22)	2.4(42)	.35	.71
Lombardy	13.6	5.9(106)	13.5(235)	.43	.99
Venezia-Tridentina	1.6	1.0(18)	1.0(18)	.63	.63
Veneto	9.9	8.6(154)	6.0(104)	.87	.61
Venezia Giulia and Zara	2.3	1.1(20)	1.1(20)	.48	.48
Emilia	7.7	3.2(58)	8.1(141)	.42	1.05
Center	*17.8*	*11.9(213)*	*21.4(373)*	*.67*	*1.20*
Tuscany	6.9	3.6(64)	10.3(179)	.52	1.49
Marche	2.9	2.3(42)	2.8(50)	.79	.97
Umbria	1.7	0.5(9)	2.0(35)	.31	1.25
Lazio	6.3	5.4(98)	6.2(109)	.86	.98
South	*23.9*	*36.7(657)*	*30.0(522)*	*1.54*	*1.26*
Abruzzi and Molise	3.7	5.0(90)	10.9(189)	1.35	2.95
Campania	8.7	10.3(185)	6.0(104)	1.18	.69
Puglie	6.2	8.7(156)	8.4(145)	1.43	1.36
Lucania	1.2	3.4(62)	1.2(20)	2.83	.92
Calabrie	4.1	9.1(164)	3.6(64)	2.22	.88
Islands	*11.7*	*27.4(493)*	*11.3(198)*	*2.34*	*.97*
Sicily	9.3	19.1(344)	7.3(128)	2.05	.78
Sardinia	2.4	8.3(149)	4.0(70)	3.46	1.66

Source: Calculated from data in Giardina, "La guerra per la civiltà fascista in terra di Spagna" (typescript) in ACS, Mostra della rivoluzione fascista, Iª parte, b. 49.

A NOTE ON SOURCES

This study is based on archival materials, printed collections of documents, newspapers and magazines of the period, and interviews, in addition to books and articles published during or after the war. The following note provides a synoptic view of the sources quoted. It does not in general cover material I have consulted but not quoted.

I. ARCHIVAL MATERIALS CONSULTED

Archivio centrale dello stato (Rome)
Agenzia Stefani. Carte Morgagni
Carte Mussolini
  autografi
  telegrammi autografi
Ministero dell'interno.
  pubblica sicurezza, direzione generale
  degli affari generali e riservati
  ufficio cifra
Ministero dell'aeronautica militare
  gabinetto del ministro
  rapporti al capo del governo
Ministero della cultura popolare*
Ministero della marina: gabinetto
Mostra della rivoluzione fascista

* A large part of these papers was captured by the Allies during the War and is available as National Archives Microfilm Publication T 586, *Personal Papers of Benito Mussolini together with Some Official Records of the Italian Foreign Office and Ministry of Culture 1922–1944*. Whenever possible reference has been made to the microfilm rather than to original files in the Archivio Centrale dello Stato.

Partito nazionale fascista
  direttorio
  situazione politica delle provincie
Presidenza del consiglio dei ministri
  gabinetto
  provvedimenti legislativi
Segreteria particolare del Duce. Carteggio riservato*
  Verbali consiglio dei ministri
Archivio storico del ministero degli affari esteri (Rome)
  direzione generale degli affari politici
  gabinetto del ministro
  "ufficio Spagna"
Public Records Office (London)
  Papers of the British Foreign Office
Servicio histórico militar. Archivo de la Guerra de Liberación (Madrid)
  Documentación nacional. Cuartel general del generalísimo
  Documentación nacional. Tercera sección de estado mayor. CTV.
  Documentación nacional. Quinta sección de estado mayor. CTV.

II. Printed Collections of Documents

Documenti diplomatici italiani. Rome, 1952–
Documents diplomatiques Français, 1932–1939. Paris, 1963–
Documents on German Foreign Policy, 1918–1945. Washington, 1949–
Documents secrets du ministère des affaires étrangères d'Allemagne. Paris 1946–
Foreign Relations of the United States. Washington, 1861–
Dez anos de politica externa (1936–47). Lisbon, 1961–
Trattati e convenzioni fra il Regno d'Italia e gli altri stati. Turin, 1865–1931.

III. Newspapers and Magazines

In addition to selected articles from the major European and American newspapers in the clipping file of the Royal

Institute of International Affairs (London), the collections of the following publications have been consulted in the Emeroteca Nazionale (Rome).

L'avvenire d'Italia (Bologna)
Il corriere della sera (Milan)
Critica fascista
La civiltà cattolica
Il giornale d'Italia (Rome)
Gerarchia
Nuova antologia
L'osservatore romano (Vatican City)
Il popolo d'Italia (Milan)

IV. OTHER PRINTED SOURCES

The following list is restricted to books and articles cited in the notes and is intended primarily to give the reader their full title and publication date.

Albrecht-Carrie, René, *Italy from Napoleon to Mussolini.* New York, 1950.

Alcofar Nassaes, José L., *CTV. Los legionarios italianos en la guerra civil española 1936–39.* Barcelona, 1972.

Allison, Graham T. "Conceptual Models and the Cuban Missile Crisis," *American Political Science Review* 63 (September 1969), 689–718.

Almanacco del regio esercito, XVIII (1939–1940). Milan, 1939.

Alvarez del Vayo, Julio. *Freedom's Battle.* New York, 1940.

Ansaldo, Juan Antonio. ¿*Para qué?* *De Alfonso XIII a Juan III.* Buenos Aires, 1952.

Aquarone, Alberto, "La guerra di Spagna e l'opinione pubblica italiana," *Il cannocchiale* 4/6 (1966), 3–36.

———. *L'organizzazione dello Stato totalitario.* Turin, 1965.

Araquistain, Luis. "Las grandes potencias y la guerra de España (1936–1939)," *Cuadernos* 23 (March/April 1957), 65–73.

Arrarás, Joaquín. (ed.). *Historia de la cruzada de España.* 44 volumes. Madrid, 1940–1943.

Artieri, Giovanni. *Quattro momenti di storia fascista.* Naples, 1968.

Askew, William. "Italian Intervention in Spain: The Agreements of March 31, 1934, with the Spanish Monarchist Parties," *Journal of Modern History* 24 (June 1952), 181–83.

Azaña, Manuel. *La velada en Benicarló.* Buenos Aires, 1939.

Aznar, Manuel. *Historia militar de la guerra de España.* 3 volumes. Madrid, 1958–1963.

Baer, George W. *The Coming of the Italian Ethiopian War.* Cambridge, Mass., 1967.

Bahamonde, Antonio. *Memoirs of a Spanish Nationalist.* London, 1939.

Bajo la bandera de la España republicana. Moscow, 1967.

Barbieri, Corrado. *I caccia della seconda guerra mondiale.* Parma, 1970.

Barros, James. *Betrayal from Within. Joseph Avernol, Secretary General of the League of Nations, 1933–1940.* New Haven, 1969.

Baumont, Maurice. *La faillite de la paix: 1919–1938.* Volume I, 4th ed., Paris, 1960. Volume II, 3rd ed., Paris, 1950.

Bayo, Alberto. *Mi desembarco en Mallorca.* Guadalajara, Mexico, 1944.

Beck, Clarence Dempsey. *A Study of German Involvement in Spain, 1936–1939.* Ph.D. diss., University of New Mexico, 1972.

Belforte, Generale Francesco. *La guerra civile in Spagna.* 4 volumes, n.p., 1938–1939.

Bernanos, Georges. *Les grands cimetières sous la lune.* Paris, 1938.

Beumelburg, Werner. *Kampf um Spanien.* Berlin, 1940.

Blythe, Henry. *Spain over Britain. A Study of the Strategical Effects of Italian Intervention on the Defense of the British Empire.* London, 1937.

Bocca, Giorgio. *Storia d'Italia nella guerra fascista, 1940–1943*. Bari, 1969.

Bolín, Luis A. *Spain: The Vital Years*. London, 1967.

Bolloten, Burnett. *The Grand Camouflage. The Spanish Civil War and Revolution 1936–1939*. New York, 1961.

Bonnet, Georges. *De Washington au Quai d'Orsay*. Geneva, 1946.

Bonomi, Ruggero. *Viva la muerte*. Rome, 1941.

Bottai, Giuseppe. *Vent'anni e un giorno. 24 luglio 1943*. 2nd ed., Rome, 1949.

Bowers, Claude G. *My Mission to Spain*. New York, 1954.

Brenan, Gerald. *The Spanish Labyrinth*. 2nd ed., Cambridge, 1960.

Broué, Pierre and Témime, Emile. *The Revolution and the Civil War in Spain*, Cambridge, Mass., 1973.

Burgo, Jaime del. *Conspiración y guerra civil*. Madrid, 1970.

Canevari, Emilio. *La guerra italiana. Retroscena della disfatta*. 2 volumes. Rome, 1948.

Cantalupo, Roberto. *Fu la Spagna. Ambasciata presso Franco (febbraio-aprile 1937)*. Milan, 1948.

Carlton, David. "Eden, Blum, and the Origins of Non-Intervention," *Journal of Contemporary History* 6:3 (1971), 40–55.

Carocci, Giampiero. *La politica estera dell'Italia fascista 1925–1928*. Bari, 1969.

———. "Salvemini e la politica estera del fascismo," *Studi Storici* 9 (1969), 218–24.

———. *Storia del fascismo*. 3rd ed., Milan, 1963.

Carr, Raymond (ed.), *The Republic and the Civil War in Spain*. London, 1971.

———. *Spain, 1808–1939*. Oxford, 1966.

Cassels, Alan. *Mussolini's Early Diplomacy*. Princeton, 1970.

Castronovo, Valerio. *Giovanni Angelli*. Turin, 1971.

Catalano, Franco. *L'economia italiana di guerra, 1935–1943*. Milan, 1969.

———. *L'Italia dalla dittatura alla democrazia 1919–1948*. Milan, 1962.

Cattell, David. *Communism and the Spanish Civil War*. Berkeley, 1957.

———. *Soviet Diplomacy and the Spanish Civil War*. Berkley, 1957.

Cervera Valderrama, Admiral Juan. *Memorias de guerra. Mi labor en el estado mayor de la armada afecto al cuartel general del generalísimo durante la Guerra de Liberación Nacional 1936–1939*. Madrid, 1968.

Chabod, Federico. *A History of Italian Fascism*. London, 1963.

———. *L'Italia contemporanea*. Turin, 1961.

Chiodini, Luigi. *Roma o Mosca. Storia della guerra civile spagnola*. Rome, 1966.

Churchill, Sir Winston. *The Gathering Storm*. London, 1948.

Ciano, Conte Galeazzo. *Ciano's Hidden Diary 1937–1938*. Translated by Andreas Mayor. New York, 1953.

———. *The Ciano Diaries. 1939–1945*. New York, 1946.

———. *Ciano's Diplomatic Papers*. London, 1948.

Clark, Clyde. *The Evolution of the Franco Regime*. 2 volumes and 3 appendices. Washington, D.C., 1954.

Codón Fernández, José María. *La tradición en José Antonio y el sindicalismo en Mella*. Madrid, 1962.

Colodny, Robert. *The Struggle for Madrid*. New York, 1958.

Conforti, Olao. *Guadalajara. La prima sconfitta del fascismo*. Milan, 1967.

Conti, Clara (ed.). *Il processo Roatta. I documenti*. Rome, 1945.

Cortada, James W. "Ships, Diplomacy and the Spanish Civil War: Nyon Conference, September, 1937," *Il Politico* 37 (1973), 673–89.

Cot, Pierre. *Triumph of Treason*. Chicago, 1944.

Coverdale, John F. "I primi volontari italiani nell'esercito di Franco," *Storia contemporanea* 2 (1971), 545–54.

Crozier, Brian. *Franco*. Boston, 1967.

D'Amoja, Fulvio. *La politica estera dell'Impero. Storia della politica estera fascista dalla conquista dell'Etiopia all'Anschluss.* 2nd ed. Padova, 1967.

D'Aroma, Nino. *Vent'anni insieme: Vittorio Emanuele e Mussolini.* Rome, 1957.

Deakin, Frederick W. *The Brutal Friendship. Mussolini, Hitler and the Fall of Italian Fascism.* London, 1962.

De Angelis, Giovanni Battista. *Aspetti navali della guerra civile di Spagna sino agli accordi di Nyon (30 settembre 1937).* Ph.D. diss., University of Rome, 1966.

De Begnac, Yvon. *Palazzo Venezia: Storia di un regime.* Rome, 1950.

De Felice, Renzo. *Il fascismo. Le interpretazioni dei contemporanei e degli storici.* Bari, 1970.

Delperrie de Bayac, Jacques. *Les Brigades Internationales.* Paris, 1968.

Deschamps, Bernard. *La verité sur Guadalajara.* Paris, 1938.

Detwiler, Donald S. *Hitler, Franco und Gibraltar: Die Frage des spanischen Eintritts in den zweiten Weltkrieg.* Wiesbaden, 1962.

Díaz-Retg, Enrique. *Les italiens dans la guerre d'Espagne.* Paris, 1939.

Diggins, John. *Mussolini and Fascism: The View from America.* Princeton, 1972.

Di Nolfo, Ennio. *Mussolini e la politica estera italiana (1919–1933).* Padova, 1960.

Donosti, Mario. *Mussolini e l'Europa. La politica estera fascista.* Rome, 1945.

Driefort, John E. *Yvon Delbos at the Quai d'Orsay.* Lawrence, Kan., 1973.

Duroselle, Jean Baptiste. *Histoire diplomatique de 1919 à nos jours.* 4th ed., Paris, 1966.

Eden, Sir Anthony. *The Eden Memoirs.* Volume 1, *Facing the Dictators.* London, 1962.

Faldella, Emilio. *Venti mesi di guerra in Spagna.* Florence, 1939.

Favagrossa, C. *Perchè perdemmo la guerra. Mussolini e la produzione bellica.* Rome, 1946.

427

Fermi, Laura. *Mussolini*. Chicago, 1961.

Fernández Cuesta, Ramón. *Intemperie, victoria y servicio: discursos y escritos*. Madrid, 1951.

Fischer, Louis. *Men and Politics. Europe between the Two World Wars*. New York, 1966.

Fornari, Harry. *Mussolini's Gadfly: Roberto Farinacci*. Nashville, 1971.

François-Poncet, André. *The Fateful Years: Memoirs of a French Ambassador in Berlin, 1931–1938*. New York, 1949.

Frank, Willard C. *Sea Power, Politics, and the Onset of the Spanish War, 1936*. Ph.D. diss., University of Pittsburg, 1969.

Freidlander, Robert A. *The July 1936 Military Rebellion in Spain. Background and Beginnings*. Ph.D. diss., Northwestern University, 1963.

Fuà, Giorgio. *Notes on Italian Economic Growth*. Milan, 1965.

Gabrieli, Manlio. *Una guerra civile per la libertà*. Rome, 1966.

Galindo Herrero, Santiago. *Los partidos monárquicos bajo la Segunda República*. Madrid, 1956.

Gallagher, M. D. "Leon Blum and the Spanish Civil War," *Journal of Contemporary History* 6:3 (1971), 56–64.

Gallo, Max. *L'Italia de Mussolini. Vignt ans d'ère fasciste*. Paris, n.d.

Gambetti, Fidia, *Gli anni che scottano*, Milan, 1967.

Garriga, Ramón. *Guadalajara y sus consecuencias*. Madrid, 1974.

Garosci, Aldo. *La vita di Carlo Rosselli*. 2 volumes. Rome, 1946.

Genco, Raoul. *Precedenti e contenuto della Carta del Lavoro Spagnola*. Milan, 1942.

Giannini, Amadeo. "I rapporti italo-spagnoli (1860–1955)," *Rivista di studi politici internazionali* 24 (1957), 8–63.

Gigli, Guido. *La seconda guerra mondiale*. Bari, 1964.

Gil Robles, José María. *No fue posible la paz.* Barcelona, 1968.

Gilbert, Felix. "Ciano and His Diplomats," in Gordon Craig and Felix Gilbert (eds.), *The Diplomats.* Princeton, 1953, pp. 512–36.

Giménez Caballero, Ernesto. "Lettera dalla Spagna: una situazione drammatica," *Critica fascista* (March 1, 1936), pp. 141–42.

Giudice, Gaspare. *Benito Mussolini.* Turin, 1969.

Gomá, Colonel José. *La guerra en el aire. Vista, suerte y al toro.* Barcelona, 1958.

Granados, Anastasio. *El cardenal Gomá.* Madrid, 1969.

Gray, Ezio Maria. *L'Italia ha sempre ragione.* Milan, 1938.

Guariglia, Raffaele. *Ricordi, 1922–1946.* Naples, 1950.

Guarnieri, Felice. *Battaglie ecomomiche fra le due grandi guerre.* 2 volumes. Milan, 1953.

Gutiérrez-Ravé Montero, José. *Antonio Goicoechea.* n.p., 1965.

Guttmann, Allen. *The Wound in the Heart. America and the Spanish Civil War.* New York, 1962.

Harper, Glenn T. *German Economic Policy in Spain during the Spanish Civil War, 1936–1939.* The Hague, 1967.

Hassell, Ulrich von. *The Von Hassell Diaries. 1938–1943.* New York, 1947.

Herriot, Edouard. *Jadis.* Volume II. *D'une guerre à l'autre 1914–1936.* Paris, 1952.

Horton, Albert G. *Germany and the Spanish Civil War.* Ph.D. diss., Columbia University, 1966.

How Mussolini Provoked the Spanish Civil War. Documentary Evidence. London, 1938.

Ibarruri, Dolores, *et al. Guerra y revolución en España.* 2 volumes. Moscow, 1967.

Incisa, Luigi. *Spagna nazional sindacalista,* Bologna, 1941.

Invrea, Massimo. "La verità su Guadalajara, *Secolo XX* 1 (May 7, 1963), 20–30.

Italy. Istituto Centrale di Statistica. *Sommario di statistiche storiche dell' Italia 1861–1965.* Rome, 1968.

Italy. Ministero della guerra. *Volontari dell' esercito nella guerra di Spagna.* Rome, 1942.

Italy. Ufficio storico stato maggiore esercito. *L'esercito italiano tra la prima e la seconda guerra mondiale.* Rome, 1954.

Jackson, Gabriel. *The Spanish Republic and the Civil War 1931–1939.* Princeton, 1965.

Kennan, George F. *Russia and the West.* Boston, 1960.

Kindelán, Alfredo. "La aviación en nuestra guerra," *Guerra de liberación.* Zaragoza, 1961.

———. *Mis cuadernos de guerra, 1936–1939.* Madrid, n.d.

Kirkpatrick, Sir Ivone. *Mussolini. A Study in Power.* New York, 1964.

Kleine-Ahlbrandt, William L. *The Policy of Simmering.* The Hague, 1962.

Kogan, Norman. *The Politics of Italian Foreign Policy.* New York, 1963.

Krivitsky, Walter G. *I Was Stalin's Agent.* London, 1939.

La Bruyère, René. "La Espagne et les routes navales de la France en Afrique," *Politique étrangère* 2 (1937), 523–30.

La Cierva, Ricardo de. *Historia de la guerra civil española.* Volume 1, *Antecedentes: monarquía y república 1898–1936.* Madrid, 1969.

———. "The Nationalist Army in the Spanish Civil War" in Raymond Carr (ed.), *The Republic and the Civil War in Spain,* London, 1971, pp. 188–212.

La Francesca, Salvatore. *La politica economica del fascismo.* Bari, 1972.

Lajolo, Davide. *Il "Voltagabbana".* Milan, 1963.

Largo García, Ramiro. "La batalla de Guadalajara," *Ejército* 60 (January 1945), 23–30.

Laurens, Franklin D. *France and the Italo-Ethiopian Crisis 1935–1936.* The Hague, 1967.

Ledeen, Michael A. *Universal Fascism. The Theory and Practice of the Fascist International, 1929–1936.* New York, 1972.

Lister, Enrique. *Neustra guerra. Aportaciones para una historia de la guerra nacional revolucionaria del pueblo español, 1936–1939.* Paris, 1966.

Lizarza Iribarren, Antonio. *Memorias de la conspiración.* 4th ed., Pamplona, 1957.

Longo, Luigi. *Le brigate internazionali in Spagna.* Rome, 1956.

Macartney, M. H. H. and Cremona, P. *Italy's Foreign and Colonial Policy, 1914–1937.* London, 1938.

Mack Smith, Dennis. *Italy. A Modern History.* Ann Arbor, 1959.

Madariaga, Salvador de. *Spain. A Modern History.* New York, 1958.

Maddison, Angus. *Economic Growth in the West. Comparative Experience in Europe and North America.* New York, 1964.

Magistrati, Massimo. *L'Italia a Berlino (1937–1939).* Milan, 1956.

Maisky, Ivan. *Spanish Notebooks.* London, 1966.

Malaparte, Curzio. *Viva la muerte.* Special issue of *Prospettive,* 1939.

Malefakis, Edward. *Agrarian Reform and Peasant Revolution in Spain. Origins of the Civil War.* New Haven, 1970.

Martínez Bande, Colonel José Manuel. *La campaña de Andalucía,* Madrid, 1969.

———. *El final del frente norte,* Madrid, 1972.

———. *La invasión de Aragón y el desembarco en Mallorca.* Madrid, 1970.

———. *La lucha en torno a Madrid.* Madrid, 1968.

Mayer, Arno J. *The Dynamics of Counterrevolution.* New York, 1971.

Melograni, Piero. *Gli industriali e Mussolini. Rapporti tra Confindustria e fascismo del 1919 al 1929.* Milan, 1972.

Merkes, Manfred. *Die Deutsche Politik gegenüber den Spanischen Bürgerkrieg, 1936–39.* Bonn, 1961.

Monelli, Paolo. *Mussolini piccolo borghese.* n.p., 1950.

Montú, Carlo. *Storia dell'artiglieria italiana.* Volume 16, Rome, 1955.

Mussolini, Benito. *Opera omnia,* edited by Edoardo and Duilio Susmel. 36 volumes. Florence, 1954–1963.

Mussolini, Rachele. *Benito. Il mio uomo.* Milan, 1958.

————. *La mia vita con Benito.* Milan, 1948.

Nellessen, Bernd. *Die verbotene Revolution.* Hamburg, 1963.

Nenni, Pietro. *La guerre d'Espagne.* Paris, 1960.

Neufeld, Maurice. *Italy. School for Awakening Countries.* Ithaca, 1961.

Nicolson, Sir Harold. *Diaries—Letters.* New York, 1966.

Nolte, Ernst. *The Three Faces of Fascism.* New York, 1969.

Packard, Reynolds and Packard, Eleanor. *Balcony Empire. Fascist Italy at War.* New York, 1942.

Padelford, Norman J. *International Law and Diplomacy in the Spanish Civil Strife.* New York, 1939.

Palacio Atard, Vicente; La Cierva, Ricardo de; and Salas Larrazábal, Ramón. *Aproximación histórica a la guerra española (1936–1939),* Madrid, 1970.

Payne, Stanley G. "Catalan and Basque Nationalism," *Journal of Contemporary History* 6 (1971), 15–41.

————. *Falange. A History of Spanish Fascism.* Stanford, 1961.

————. *A History of Spain and Portugal.* 2 volumes. Madison, 1973.

————. *Politics and the Military in Modern Spain.* Stanford, 1967.

————. *The Spanish Revolution.* New York, 1970.

Pemán, José María. *Un soldado en la historia. Vida del capitán general Varela.* Cádiz, 1957.

Petersen, Jens. "La politica estera del fascismo come problema storiografico," *Storia contemporanea* 3 (December 1972), 661–706.

Phillips, William. *Ventures in Diplomacy.* North Beverley, Mass. 1953.

Piazzoni, Sandro. *Le "Frecce Nere" nella guerra di Spagna* (*1937–1939*). Rome, 1939.

Pike, David W. *Conjecture, Propaganda, and Deceit and the Spanish Civil War.* Stanford, 1968.

Pini, Giorgio and Susmel, Duilio. *Mussolini: L'uomo e l'opera.* 4 volumes. 2nd ed., Florence, 1957–1958.

Pollina, Paolo M. *I sommergibili italiani.* Rome, 1962.

Puzzo, Dante. *Spain and the Great Powers 1936–1941.* New York, 1962.

———. *The Spanish Civil War.* New York, 1969.

Quaroni, Pietro. "Le diplomate italien," in K. Braunias and G. Stourzh (eds.), *Diplomatie unserer Zeit.* Graz, 1959.

Ratcliff, Dillwyn F. *Prelude to Franco: Political Aspects of the Dictatorship of Migual Primo de Rivera.* New York, 1957.

Reyes Heroles, Jesús. *Tendencias actuales del estado.* Buenos Aires, 1946.

Rispoli, Tullio. *La Spagna dei legionari.* Rome, 1942.

Roatta, Mario. *Otto milioni di baionette. L'esercito italiano in guerra dal 1940 al 1944.* Milan, 1946.

Robinson, Richard. *The Origins of Franco's Spain. The Right, the Republic and the Revolution, 1931–1936.* n.p., 1970.

Rochat, Giorgio. *Militari e politici nella preparazione della campagna d'Etiopia.* Milan, 1971.

———. "Mussolini e le forze armate," *Il movimento di liberazione in Italia* 95 (April/June 1969), 3–22.

Rodimtsev, A. "En la dirección de Guadalajara" in *Bajo la bandera de la España republicana.* Moscow, n.d., pp. 257–318.

Rojo, Vicente. *Así fue la defensa de Madrid.* Mexico City, 1967.

Romeo, Rosario. *Breve storia della grande industria in Italia.* Bologna, 1961.

Rosachi, Andrew J. *Italian Intervention in Spain. 1934–1939.* Master's thesis, Stanford University, 1947.

Rossi, Cesare. *Trentatré vicende mussoliniane*. Milan, 1958.

Royal Institute of International Affairs. *Survey of International Affairs 1937*, Volume II, *The International Repercussions of the War in Spain*. London, 1938.

———. *Survey of International Affairs 1938*, Volume I. London, 1941.

Rumi, Giorgio, *Alle origini della politica estera fascista (1918–23)*. Bari, 1968.

———. "Tendenze e caratteri degli studi sulla politica estera fascista (1945–1966)," *Nuova rivista storica* 51 (1967), 146–68.

Salas Larrazábal, Jesús. *La guerra de España desde el aire. Dos ejércitos y sus cazas frente a frente*. Barcelona, 1969.

Salas Larrazábal, Ramón. "The Growth and Role of the Republican Popular Army," in Raymond Carr (ed.), *The Republic and the Civil War in Spain*, London, 1971, pp. 159–87.

———. *Historia del ejército popular de la República*, 4 vols., Madrid, 1973.

———. "La intervención extranjera y las ayudas exteriores" in Palacio Atard, La Cierva and Salas, *Aproximación histórica a la guera española (1936–1939)*, pp. 167–204.

Salvatorelli, Luigi. *Il Fascismo nella politica internazionale*. Modena, 1946.

Salvatorelli, Luigi and Mira, Giovanni. *Storia d'Italia nel periodo fascista*. Revised ed., Turin, 1964.

Salvemini, Gaetano. *Mussolini diplomatico 1922–1932*. Bari, 1952.

———. *Prelude to World War II*. London, 1953.

———. *Preludio alla seconda guerra mondiale*. Edited by Augusto Torre. Milan, 1967.

Sánchez, José M. *Reform and Reaction: The Politico-Religious Background of the Spanish Civil War*. Chapel Hill, 1964.

Santamaria, Aldo. *Operazione Spagna (1936–1939)*. Rome, 1965.

Santarelli, Enzo. *Storia del movimento e del regime fascista.* 2 volumes. Rome, 1967.

Sarti, Roland. *Fascism and the Industrial Leadership in Italy, 1919–1940.* Berkeley, 1971.

Schwartz, Fernando. *La internacionalización de le guerra civil española. Julio de 1936—marzo de 1937.* Barcelona, 1971.

Seco Serrano, Carlos. *Edad contemporánea.* Volume VI of the *Historia general de los pueblos hispánicos.* Barcelona, 1962.

Serrano Suñer, Ramón. *Entre Hendaya y Gibraltár.* Madrid, 1947.

Siebert, Fernand. *Italiens Weg in den Zweiten Weltkrieg.* Frankfurt, 1962.

Slaughter, Margaret J. *Italian Antifascism: The Italian Volunteers in the Spanish Civil War.* Ph.D. dissertation, University of New Mexico, 1972.

Soleri, Marcello. *Memorie.* Turin, 1949.

Spain. Ministerio de Ultramar. *Spanish White Book. The Italian Invasion of Spain: Official Documents and Papers Seized from Italian Units in Action at Guadalajara.* Washington, D.C., 1937.

Spigo, Umberto. *Premesse tecniche della disfatta.* Rome, n.d.

Steer, G. L. *The Tree of Guernika.* London, 1938.

Tamaro, Attilio. *Vent'anni di storia, 1922–1943.* 3 volumes. Rome, 1953–1954.

Tannenbaum, Edward R. *The Fascist Experience. Italian Society and Culture 1922–1945.* New York, 1972.

Taylor, A. J. P. *The Origins of the Second World War.* 2nd ed., New York, 1968.

Taylor, F. Jay. *The United States and the Spanish Civil War (1936–1939).* New York, 1956.

Thomas, Hugh. *The Spanish Civil War.* Revised ed., Harmondsworth, 1965.

Toscano, Mario. "L'Asse Roma-Berlino—Il patto Anti-Comintern—La guerra civile in Spagna—L'Anschluss—

435

Monaco" in *La politica estera italiana dal 1914 al 1943*. Rome, 1963.

——. *The History of Treaties and International Politics*. Volume I. Baltimore, 1966.

——. *The Origins of the Pact of Steel*. Baltimore, 1967.

——. *Pagine di storia diplomatica contemporanea*. Volume II, *Origini e vicende della seconda guerra mondiale*. Milan, 1963.

Traina, Richard P. *American Diplomacy and the Spanish Civil War*. Bloomington, 1968.

Trythall, John W. *Franco: a Biography*, London, 1972.

Ubieto, Antonio; Reglá, Juan; Jover, José María; Seco, Carlos. *Introducción a la historia de España*. 3rd ed., Barcelona, 1967.

Ulam, Adam B. *Expansion and Coexistence. The History of Soviet Foreign Policy, 1917–1967*. New York, 1968.

Valiani, Leo. "L'intervento in Spagna," *Il Mondo*, Nov. 15, Nov. 22, Nov. 29, Dec. 6, and Dec. 13, 1960.

——. "L'intervento in Spagna," in Franco Antonicelli (ed.), *Trent'anni di storia italiana (1915–1945)*. Turin, 1961.

Van der Esch, P. A. M. *Prelude to War. The International Repercussions of the Spanish Civil War (1936–1939)*. The Hague, 1951.

Vansittart, Robert. *The Mist Procession*. London, 1958.

Vanutelli, Cesare. "Occupazione e salari dal 1861 al 1961," in *L'Economia italiana dal 1861 al 1961*. Milan, 1961, pp. 560–96.

Vedovato, Giuseppe. *Il non intervento in Spagna*. Volume I. Florence, 1938.

Villella, Giovanni. *Rivoluzione e guerra di Spagna (1931–39)*. Rome, 1971.

Viñas, Angel. *La Alemania nazi y el 18 de julio. Antecedentes de la intervención alemana en la guerra civil española*. Madrid, 1974.

Warner, Geoffrey. "France and Non-Intervention in Spain,

July-August 1936," *International Affairs* (London) 38 (April 1962), 203–220.

Watkins, K. W. *Britain Divided. The Effects of the Spanish Civil War on British Political Opinion.* London, 1963.

Watt, D. C. "Soviet Military Aid to the Spanish Republic in the Civil War 1936–1938," *Slavonic and Eastern European Review* 38 (June 1960), 536–41.

Weinberg, Gerhard. *The Foreign Policy of Hitler's Germany. Diplomatic Revolution in Europe 1933–1936.* Chicago, 1970.

Weintraub, Stanley. *The Last Great Cause. The Intellectuals and the Spanish Civil War.* New York, 1968.

Whealey, Robert H. "Foreign Intervention in the Spanish Civil War," in Raymond Carr (ed.), *The Republic and the Civil War in Spain.* London, 1971, pp. 213–38.

———. *German-Spanish Relations January-August 1939.* Ph.D. diss., University of Michigan, 1963.

Wiskeman, Elizabeth. *The Rome-Berlin Axis: A History of the Relations between Hitler and Mussolini.* Revised ed., London, 1966.

Zangrandi, Ruggero. *Il lungo viaggio attraverso il fascismo.* 4th ed., Milan, 1963.

INDEX

Advisors: role of Italian and German compared with Russian, 396–98

Africa, Army of: blocked in Morocco, 69–85

Africa, North: visited by Mussolini, 302; Italian High Command for instituted, 309.

Agreements: between Italy and Spanish monarchists, 50–54, 74, 154; Italo-Spanish economic and clearing, 118, 298––99, 346–47; Anti-Comintern Pact, 324–25, 327, 383; Italo-British Easter agreement: 351–53, 368–70. See also Treaties.

Aguirre, José Antonio, 286, 287, 289, 290

Aircraft: Italian sent to Nationalists, 3–4, 74, 106, 108, 113, 114, 133, 136, 174, 177, 355, 392–94; initial distribution of, 68; German sent to Nationalists, 86, 108–09, 114–15, 174, 392–94; French sent to Republic, 92, 109; Soviet sent to Republic, 99, 109, 176, 276, 355

Airforce: contribution of Italian to Nationalist victory, 395

Airlift: of troops from Africa to Spain, 85–87

Airplanes. See Aircraft

Ajuriaguerra, Juan, 287, 288

Alaminos, 225

Albania, 10, 384

Alcalá de Henares: Italian and Spanish troops to meet in, 221

Alcalá Zamora, Niceto, 59

Alcañiz, 347

Alcorisa, 347

Alfonso XIII, King of Spain, 34, 36, 72

Almadrones, 225, 227

Almería, 303–04

Alto del Leon, 72

Anarchists: propaganda of Italian on SCW, 266–67

André Marty battalion, 231

Anfuso, Filippo: refuses aid to Franco, 72; reports of on conditions in Spain, 101, 122–23; negotiates treaty with Nationalists, 153–56; discusses further aid with Franco, 298–99

Anti-Comintern Pact: Italian efforts to bring Spain into, 324–25; joined by Italy, 327; Franco's decision to join, 383

Anti-Fascism: of Spanish Republic, 38–39; of Republic's supporters, 88; stimulated in Europe by SCW, 405–06

Ansaldo, Juan, 41–42, 49, 50

Anschluss, 27, 352–53

Antoniutti, Msgr. Hildebrando, 349

Aquila, 320

Aragon offensive, 347–51

Argecilla, 225

Arms shipments. See Italy—Aid to Nationalists; Germany, aid to Nationalists; France, aid to Republic; Union of Soviet Socialist Republics, aid to Republic

Aunós, Eduardo, 343

439

INDEX

Austria, 26, 27, 55
Autarky, 22
Avernol, Joseph, 198
Avanti!, 266
Axis: Formation of, 110–13; and anti-communism, 111; weakness of in early stages, 112–13; strengthened by SCW, 162. *See also* Italy—Relations with Germany.
Azaña, Manuel, 39, 42, 59

Badajoz, 88
Badoglio, General, 270
Balbo, Italo, 41–42, 50, 51–52
Balearic islands: and 1926 Italo-Spanish treaty, 34; Italian interest in, 41, 53, 76–77, 127–28; strategic importance of, 90, 127–28; French concern over Italian presence on, 90, 155, 198; Nationalist concern over Italian designs on, 154; British concern over, 198; and Italian foreign policy, 389. *See also* Majorca; Minorca; Ibiza; Formentera
Balkan wars, 9, 25–26
Barcelona: bombing of, 347–49; capture of, 379–80
Barcenas, Domingo, 340
Barletta, 303
Barrera, General Emilio, 50
Barroso, Col., 214, 218
Barthou, Jean Louis, 54
Barzini, Luigi, 157, 364–65
Bases: Italian right to establish in Spain, 155
Basque surrender, 285–94
Bastico, General Ettore: named commander of CTV, 275; demands major role for CTV, 279–80; and Basque prisoners, 293; replaced as commander

of CTV, 317–18
Bayo, Capt. Alberto, 133–34, 137–38
Beer, Major Umberto, 290
Belligerent rights, 305–06
Benavente, Jacinto, 47
Berchtesgaden, 110
Bergamo, Mario, 19
Bergonzoli, Gen. Annibale, 176, 245
Bermeo, 280, 302–03
Bernanos, George, 139
Berti, General Mario: sent to reorganize CTV, 275; named commander of CTV, 318; requests withdrawal of CTV, 333; urges withdrawing or strengthening CTV, 363; recalled to Italy, 372
Berzin, Ian, 98
Bilbao, Esteban, 343
Bilbao, 277–80, 287–88
Blagoiev, 312
Blitzkrieg. See Guerra celere
Blomberg, Marshall, 334
Blum, Leon, 29, 89, 354
Bolín, Luis, 70–72
Bonaccorsi, Arconovaldo: sent to Majorca, 134–35; rallies defence of Majorca, 135–36; forces change of commander, 136; urges Italian attack on Republican ships, 137; ordered to restrict his activities, 137; organizes victory parade, 138–39; organizes Falange, 139; and repression in Majorca, 139–40; his friction with Juan March, Jr., 141–42; proposes invading Minorca, 142; and proposed coup in Majorca, 143–45; withdrawn from Majorca, 199–200
Boncour, Paul, 354

440

Bonnet, Georges, 361
Bordighera, 338
Borjas Blancas, 378
Brihuega, 229, 231, 242–46
Brunete, 281
Bucard, Marcel, 57
Business interests in Italy, 7, 15

Calvo Sotelo, José, 49–50, 60, 63
Campeador, 312
Canaris, Admiral: meets with Roatta, 87; mission to Rome, 103–06; proposes naval support of Nationalists, 114–15; proposes funneling all aid through Franco, 119–20; attends December 1936 meeting in Rome, 160
Cantalupo, Roberto: named ambassador, 188; protests against Nationalist repression, 191–92; his opinion of Franco, 192; requests withdrawal of CTV from Guadalajara sector, 248; suggests reconsidering Italian commitment, 263; recalled to Rome, 272; criticizes Italian policy, 274; his critics, 272–74
Cape Espartel, battle of, 108
Carlists: trained in Italy, 52; united by Franco to Falange, 295–97
Carocci, Giampiero, 15
Carta del lavoro, 344
Casares Quiroga, S., 59–60
Caspe, 347
Casualties, 210, 248, 351, 356, 363, 373, 380, 398
Catalonia, 100–01, 375–80
Catholic Church: role of in Italy, 7, 265–66. See also Vatican
Cavaletti, Marchese di, 285–86, 287–88, 290

C.E.D.A., 44, 122
Ceuta, 320
Chamberlain, Neville: desires rapprochement with Italy, 308; and Easter agreement, 351–53; Italian efforts to keep him in power, 359–60; tries to avoid conflict with Italy, 362
Ciano, Costanzo, 70–71
Ciano, Galeazzo: named foreign minister, 27; orders subsidies to José Antonio Primo de Rivera, 57–58; early career of, 70–71; first reaction to request for aid, 71–72; meets with Goicoechea, 73–74; convinced the fall of Madrid is imminent, 87; visits Germany, 110–12; vetoes proposals to influence Nationalist domestic politics, 121–22; orders Bonaccorsi to restrict his activities, 137, 141–42; vetoes proposed invasion of Minorca, 142; authorizes occupation of Minorca, 150; and German presence in Mediterranean, 173; explains Italy's Spanish policy to Cantalupo, 188–89; his plans for war, 206; orders suspension of attacks on shipping, 312; his opinion of Nyon Conference, 315; considers Great Britain and France decadent, 323; criticizes Franco's conduct of war, 333; and bombing of Barcelona, 349; his reaction to Franco's proposed neutrality, 367; visits Spain, 385–86
Ciaurriz, Doroteo, 286–87
Civil War. See Spain—Civil War
Civilian government: Italy presses for formation of in Spain, 331; composition of, 339–41

Clearing agreements. *See* Agreements

Cogollor, 225, 227

Comitato d'azione per la università di Roma, 47

Communism and Italian foreign policy, 12–13, 40, 78–83, 98–102, 111

Communist party: propaganda of Italian on SCW, 267

Conde, Francisco Javier, 342

Conde de Albasola, 312

Condor Legion, 11, 113–14, 160. *See also* Germany, aid to Nationalists

Confederación española de derechas autónomas, 44, 122

Conte Rossi. *See* Bonaccorsi, Arconovaldo

Coppi, General Amerigo, 176, 225, 236

Corfu incident, 10, 33

Corporativism, 343–44

Corpo Truppe Volontarie: formation of, 166–71; relations with Germans in Spain, 166; decision to form separate Italian divisions, 169; organization of, 176, 212, 222–23, 275–76, 318–19, 371–72; motives of volunteers, 181–86; recruitment of, 181–86; pay of, 182; geographic origin of volunteers, 182, 184; Malaga offensive, 206–10; casualties, 210, 249, 351, 356, 363, 380, 398; quality of troops of, 256–58; plans for offensive against Valencia, 212–13; Franco opposed to using it as single unit, 215–17; refuses to carry out diversionary offensive, 218; armament of, 222–24; motorization of,

223–24; in battle of Guadalajara, 225–48; morale of, 257–58; reorganization of after Guadalajara, 275–76; refuses to participate in Bilbao offensive, 279–80; in Santander offensive, 281–84; Berti named commander of, 318; friction with Franco, 331–32; Berti requests its withdrawal, 333; in Aragon offensive, 347–51; reinforcements for sent, 355; in Valencia offensive, 356; artillery of in battle of Ebro, 358; plans for withdrawing troops, 362–69; Mussolini's decision to leave it in Spain in case of European war, 367–68; ten thousand troops return to Italy, 371–72; Gambarra named commander of, 372; in battle of Catalonia, 377–81; withdrawn from Spain, 384–85

Corriere della Sera, 302, 303, 340

Costa, Joaquín, 35

Cot, Pierre, 90–91

Counterrevolution, 12–13, 82–83, 389. *See also* Anti-Comintern Pact; Italy—Foreign policy, ideological factors in

CTV. *See Corpo Truppe Volontarie*

Czechoslovakia, 25, 266–68

Daladier, Edouard, 355

Danube basin, 25–26, 29

Darland, Admiral, 147

De Carlo, Col., 288, 290

Decoux, Admiral, 147

Delbos, Yvon, 147

Deutschland, 303–05, 367

Devonshire, 382

Díaz de Freijo, Col., 135–36, 140–41

Diplomatic recognition of Franco government, 24–26
Diplomatic support: importance of Italian to Franco's victory, 391–92
Diplomats: and foreign policy formulation in Italy, 7–8
Di Nolfo, Ennio, 14
Dollfuss, Engelbert, 27, 55
Domestic politics: of Nationalist Spain and Italian intervention, 117–23, 128–30, 138–46, 330–32, 340–45, 399–404; effects of on Italian foreign policy, 14–15, 82–83
Durini di Monzo, Ercole, 38–42 *passim*
Dragoons of Death, 136

Easter Agreement, 351–53, 368–70
Ebro, battle of, 356–58, 373–74
Economic conditions and Italian foreign policy, 15, 20–24, 75
Economic relations between Spain and Italy, 31, 118, 145–46, 298–99, 325, 346–47, 386
Eden, Sir Anthony: and Italian presence on Majorca, 147–49, 198–99; and Italo-British relations, 195–96; proposes tripartite talks on Spain, 197; and *Deutschland* incident, 304–05; resigns over Easter agreement, 352
XI International Brigade, 227–28
Ente nazionale fascista per la cooperazione, 146
Escudo pass, 282
Espartel, Battle of Cape, 108
Estrada, Capt. Rafael, 132
Ethiopia, 12, 14, 19, 28–29, 54
Expansionism, 8–13

Facchi, Abraham, 132
Fagiuoli, Vincenzo, 298–99
Falange: formation of, 46; subsidized by Italy, 57–58; and outbreak of Civil War, 83; praised by Pedrazzi, 122; Anfuso's opinion of, 123; in Majorca, 145; and mixed brigades, 177–79; contacts with Farinacci, 193; united by Franco to Carlists, 295–97; statutes of, 296–97; National Council of named, 329; and Labor Charter, 342–43; Italian relations to, 400; compared to Fascist Party, 402–03
Falco, 320, 321
Faldella, Col. Emilio: informs Franco about Italian troop shipments, 168; meets with Franco, 215–16; meets with Col. Barroso, 213–14; refuses to carry out diversionary offensive, 218
Farinacci, Roberto: candidate for ambassador, 187–88; hostility toward Great Britain, 188; urges Franco to create national party, 190–91; mission to Spain, 190–91, 193–94; protests against repression, 191; his contacts with *Falange*, 193; his opinion of Franco, 193; criticizes Cantalupo, 272–73; calls for preventive war with Great Britain, 309
Fascism: and Italian foreign policy, 8–13, 24–25, 166, 390–91; and militarism, 10–11; popularity of, 19–20; Italian support of in Spain, 46–49; Italy's lack of interest in implanting in Spain, 83–84, 345–46; its failure to motivate

troops at Guadalajara, 257–58; and Italian intervention in Spain, 401–04
Fascist International, 45
Fascist Party: original composition of, 6; depolitization of, 6; and monarchy, 6; and Catholic Church, 7; and army, 7; and business interests, 7; and political mobilization, 11; and expansionism, 11–12; disappointment of its left wing with Italy's role in SCW, 269–70; and Italian foreign policy, 391
Ferretti, Captain Giovanni, 114, 117
Fernández Cuesta, Raimundo, 329
Fiume, 33, 134
Foreign policy. See Italy—Foreign policy
Foreign trade, Italian, 22–23
Formentera island, 133
France: conflict of interests with Italy in Central Europe, 25; relations with Italy (June-July 1936), 29–30; Italian hostility toward, 33, 40–41, 43, 51, 53, 54–55, 65, 75–76, 127–28, 154–55, 370–71, 389; relations with Spain and supposed secret treaty, 40–41; initial decision to aid Republic, 7, 90; motives for aiding Republic, 89–90; right-wing opposition to aid, 90; renounces overt aid, 90; strategic posture of and SCW, 90; announces closing of frontier, 91; arms shipments to Republic, 91–92, 109, 354–55; concern over Balearic islands, 147, 198; proposes mediation of SCW, 196–97; invites Italy to tripartite talks, 321–22; dis-

suaded by Great Britain from officially opening border, 322; her overtures rebuffed by Italy, 361–62; recognizes Italian empire, 369; opens frontier, 378
Francisci, Consul General Enrico, 228, 229
Francisme, 57
Franco, Gen. Francisco: request Italian aid, 69–70; aided by Italy to achieve preeminence, 118–20, 400–01; named commander-in-chief, 119; avoids concrete commitments to Italy, 156; annoyed by Italian troop shipments, 168; and monarchy, 191; meets with Faldella, 215–16; his concern over political implications of CTV, 215–17; prefers slow advance, 216; rejects proposed Valencia offensive, 216; accepts plan for Guadalajara offensive, 217, 219–21; insists that CTV continue Guadalajara offensive, 238–42; fails to support Italians at Guadalajara, 253–56; attitude toward Italians, 255–56; accepts Italian suggestions for Basque surrender, 289–90; unites Falange and Carlists, 295–97; names National Council of Falange, 329; annoyance with CTV, 331–32; his concern for political aspects of war, 336–37; his reply to Mussolini's threat to withdraw support, 337–39; demands immediate passage of Labor Charter, 343; and bombing of Barcelona, 349; attacks Valencia rather than Catalonia, 354; rejects offer of new divisions, 364; de-

clares neutrality in case of European war, 367; and World War II, 386–88; visited by Hitler, 387; interview with Mussolini at Bordighera, 388; and pace of war, 397

Franco, Nicolás: signs economic agreement with Italy, 299; meets with Mussolini, 307–08; excluded from first civilian government, 340; negotiates clearing agreement with Italy, 346–47

Franco, Ramón, 39

François-Poncet, André, 82, 370

Frezza, Col., 243, 246

Fuero del trabajo, 340–45

Gambarra, Gastone: named chief-of-staff of CTV, 275; named commander of CTV, 372; directs CTV during battle of Catalonia, 377–78; promoted, 380

Gandesa, 357

García Ruiz, Col., 136, 143

Garibaldi battalion, 229, 231–32, 243

Garrigues, Joaquín, 342

Gayda, Vigilio, 250

General staff: joint Italo-German accepted by Franco, 172

Genoa, 361–62

Gentlemen's agreement, 199–202

Germany: interest of in Central Europe, 25; aid to Nationalists, 86, 103, 108–09, 111, 113–15, 163–64, 174, 374, 392–94; coordinates with Italy aid to Nationalists, 102, 110, 116, 160–64, 171–75; gives assurances to Italy on Mediterranean, 104–05; visited by Ciano, 110–12; and domestic politics of Na-

tionalist Spain, 120–21; recognition of Franco government, 124–26; agrees to strengthen airforce in Spain, 160; renounces naval operations in Mediterranean, 160; opinion of on Italian policy in Spain, 161–64; decides Italy should provide most aid, 161–64; refuses combat troops, 161, 172; fear of Anglo-Italian understanding, 162; limits aid to Nationalists, 163–65; and duration of SCW, 163–64; accepts proposed prohibition of volunteers, 202; Mussolini's visit to, 326–27. *See also* Axis; Italy—Relations with Germany

Gibraltar, straits of, 69, 85, 93, 108

Gil Robles, José María, 44, 122

Giménez Caballero, Ernesto, 47, 61

Giolitti, Giovanni, 9

Giornale d'Italia, 340

Gioventù italiana del littorio, 327

Giral, José, 80, 99

Giustizia e libertà column, 89

Goded, General, 135

Goicoechea, Antonio, 50, 52, 73–74

Gomá, Cardinal, 286

Gómez Jordana, General, 339

González Bueno, Pedro, 342

Gorev, Vladimir, 98

Göring, Hermann, 171–74

Great Britain: relations with France, 28; relations with Germany, 28; relations with Italy (summer 1936), 28–29; foreign policy of, 92–93; neutrality of, 92–94; strategic interests of in Spain, 93; investments of in Spain, 93; supports noninter-

445

vention, 93–94; its strategic position in Mediterranean, 147–48; and Italian presence on Majorca, 147–50, 198–99; proposes mediation of SCW, 196–97; Gentlemen's agreement with Italy, 195–96, 199–200; and Italian troop shipments, 201–02; and Italian withdrawal from control scheme, 304; invites Italy to tripartite talks, 321–22; names representative to Nationalists, 325–26; Easter agreement with Italy, 351–53, 370; her shipping attacked, 358–59; relations with Italy (summer 1938), 358–60; and occupation of Minorca, 382

Guadalajara, battle of: planning of, 215–22; Republican forces at beginning of, 224; initial Italian advance, 225–30; coordination with Jarama sector, 227, 233, 252–54; tanks in, 229; aerial aspects of, 230; morale of CTV, 233; alternate plan vetoed by Franco, 233–34; Republican propaganda during, 236–38; Roatta proposes suspending offensive, 238–42; Republican counterattack, 242–47; Republicans break off contact, 247; final Republican attacks repulsed, 247–48; Cantalupo requests withdrawal of CTV, 248; strategic significance of, 248; casualties in, 248–49; Italian arms lost in, 249; psychological significance of, 250; propaganda on, 250–51; causes of Italian defeat, 251–60; effects of on public opinion in Italy, 270–71

Guariglia, Raffaele: named ambassador in Spain, 43; instructed to cultivate Spanish Right, 45; encourages Spanish fascists, 46–49; named ambassador to France, 370

Guarnieri, Felice, 297, 346

Guerra celere, 210, 212, 222, 259–60

Grand Council of Fascism, 204

Grandi, Dino: told to obstruct activity of Non-intervention Committee, 96–97; discusses Balearic islands with Eden, 149; informed CTV will remain in Spain, 271–72; expresses hope Italians will stay in Spain, 301

Greece, 10, 28

Hassel, Ulrich von, 155

Havock, 312

Hedilla, Manuel, 178, 193

Hendaya, 387

Hitler: and duration of SCW, 163–64; visits Franco at Hendaya, 387

Hontanares, 225

Hossbach memorandum, 326

Hughes, H. Stuart, 14

Ibarra Palace, 230–33, 232, 236

Ibiza, 130, 133

Ideology: effects of on Italian foreign policy, 8–13, 29, 33, 37, 38, 40, 53, 65, 78–84, 345–46, 389–91

Imperialism in Italian foreign policy, 8–13

Infantes, Col., 224

International brigades: organization of, 99; in defense of Madrid, 124; in battle of Guadalajara, 227–29, 231–32, 243–45

Iride, 312

Italy: army in, 6–7; monarchy in, 6–7; business interests in, 7; Catholic Church in, 7; and Mediterranean, 8–9, 40–41, 53, 65, 127–28, 173, 389; and imperialism, 8–13; motives for intervention in Spain, 11–15; relations with USSR, 12; domestic politics of (1936), 19; economic situation of, 20–24; foreign trade, 22–23, 25; foreign relations of (July, 1936), 26–30; treaty with Spain (1926), 34; aid to monarchist conspirators, 41–42; encourages Spanish fascists, 46–49; propaganda in Spain, 47, 56, 186–87; agreement with monarchists, 50–54; subsidies to José Antonio Primo de Rivera, 57–58; and preparation of military rising against Republic, 60–64; responsibility for outbreak of SCW, 65; receives first reports on SCW, 68–69; accepts nonintervention, 95–96; state of foreign relations (fall 1936), 112–13; policy of in Spain executed by military, 117–18; and domestic politics of Nationalists Spain, 117–23, 128–30, 138–46, 186–94, 285–97, 330–32, 340–46, 399–404; economic relations with Spain, 118, 145–47, 155–56, 297, 300, 325, 346–47, 386; Ministry for press and propaganda, 121; recognition of Franco government, 124–26; treaty with Nationalists, 153–56; decides to send combat troops, 157–61; army ministry subordinated to *Ufficio Spagna,* 165–66; foreign ministry of and Fascism, 166; protests against Nationalist repression, 191–92; rejects proposed tripartite talks, 197, 322; accepts prohibition of volunteers, 202; bans departure of volunteers, 203; expresses solidarity with Spain, 204; negotiates Basque surrender, 285–92; withdraws from nonintervention control scheme, 304; withdraws from nonintervention patrol after *Leipzig* incident, 305; and Nyon conference, 313–16; aims of in supporting Franco, 324; tries to maintain Spain in her orbit, 324, 381–83; joins Anti-Comintern Pact and withdraws from League, 327; militarism in, 327–29; racial legislation in, 328; presses for formation of civilian government in Spain, 331; commitment to Franco renewed, 333; and naming of civilian government, 340–41; airforce bombs Barcelona, 347–49; threatens massive intervention, 378–79; invades Albania, 384; withdrawal of CTV, 384–85; effects of SCW on foreign relations of, 404–407; effects of SCW on preparedness for WWII, 407–410

—aid to Nationalists: aircraft, 3–4, 74, 106, 108, 113, 114, 133, 136, 174, 177, 355, 392–94; reported in international press, 4, 170; date of first decision, 4 n.; initial hesitation, 69–72; decision to grant, 74; motives for, 74–84; not specifically pro-Fascist, 83–84; arms shipments, 87, 103, 106–07, 108, 113–117, 133, 136, 176–77, 277, 319, 355, 392–94; military mission to Spain, 102; coordination of with Germany, 102, 110, 116, 160–64, 171–75; troops, 102–03, 157–61, 167–71, 173–75, 276, 318–19, 355, 363, 381, 395–98; instructors, 107; naval support, 114–17, 179–80, 319–21, 355, 394–95; decision to send to Majorca, 132; meeting to discuss, 160–61; formation of mixed brigades, 170–71, 177–79; Mussolini threatens to withdraw, 173–74, 335–37; submarines attack shipping, 306–08, 311–12; withdrawal of some troops, 362–69; low level of in late 1938, 374; importance of to final victory, 391–98; advisors, 396–98; effects of on domestic politics of Spain, 399–404; effects of on Italian preparedness for WWII, 407–10

—foreign policy: formulation of, 7, 16–19, 166, 190, 391; prior to Fascism, 8–9; Mediterranean in, 8–9, 127–28, 173, 389; ideological factors in, 8–13, 29, 33, 37–38, 40, 53, 65, 78–84, 345–46, 389–91; prestige factors in, 12, 169, 390; effects of domestic politics on, 13–16, 82–83, 271; and economic conditions, 15, 24; and Fascism, 24–25, 390–91; effects of Ethiopian war on, 28–29; general character of, 32; and counterrevolution, 78–83, 389; strategic and political factors in, 345–46;

motives for intervention in Spain, 388–91

—press; attacks France, 301; attacks Great Britain, 302, 309–10; reports on naming of government in Spain, 340; proclaims solidarity with Spain, 360; and Fascism in Spain, 401

—public opinion and propaganda: state of in 1936, 19–20; and SCW, 183, 264–71; and battle of Guadalajara, 250; and Catholic Church, 265–66; and unification of *Falange* with Carlists, 295–97; and capture of Barcelona, 379–80

—relations with France: ideological factors in, 29; state of in summer 1936, 29–30; hostility toward, 40, 43, 51, 56, 65, 75, 76, 127–28, 154–55, 301–02, 370–71, 389, 407; rejects overtures for rapprochement, 361–62; trreatens massive intervention if France aids Republic, 378–79

—relations with Germany: ideological factors in, 26; and Austria, 26–27; coordination of aid to Spain, 102, 110, 116, 160–64, 171–75; concern over German presence in Mediterranean, 104–05, 173; effects of SCW on, 104–06, 389–90, 404–05; Ciano visits Hitler, 110–12; formation of Axis, 110–13; Mussolini visits Germany, 326–27

—relations with Great Britain: state of in summer 1936, 28–29; Mussolini calls for rapprochement, 112–13; and Majorca, 148–50; Gentlemen's agreement, 195–96, 199–200; tension after Guadalajara, 302–03; state of during summer 1937, 308–11; Easter agreement, 351–53, 368–70; state of in summer 1938, 358–60; threat of massive Italian intervention if France aids Republic, 378–79

—relations with Spain prior to Civil War: refusal to meddle in domestic politics during Dictatorship, 36; reasons for 37–41; attempted rapprochement, 43–45; loss of interest in, 54–58
Izvestiia, 94

Jaime Primero, 68, 133, 137, 179
James, Sir William, 147
Jarama, battle of, 213–14, 217–19
Juntas de ofensiva nacional sindicalista, 46

Keitel, General, 334
Kerensky, Aleksandr, 79
Kindelán, Gen. Alfredo, 385
Krivitsky, General Walter, 98

Labor Charter, 340–45
Ladesma Ramos, Ramiro, 46
Landini, Amadeo, 57–58
Largo Caballero, Ernesto, 75, 99
Laval, Pierre, 54–55
League of Nations: and Corfu incident, 10; and Ethiopian war, 19; appeal to by Spanish Republic, 197–98; Italy withdraws from, 327
Leipzig incident, 305
Leo XIII, Pope, 344
Libertad, 133, 137
Libya, 302
Lister, Enrique, 245, 378
Littorio division, 183, 245; in battle of Guadalajara, 212–60, *passim*
Liuzzi, Consul General Alberto, 235
Lizarza Iribarren, Antonio, 50
Llobregat river, 379
Lombardia, 169, 170
London Naval Pact, 28
Long, Luigi, 237

MacKnight, 312
Madrid, first battle of, 123–24
Magaz, Admiral, 132
Majorca: military revolt in, 130; Nationalists request Italian aid, 130–32; Italian decision to send aid to, 132; Republican forces evacuated, 137–38; Italian interference in domestic politics, 138–46; repression in, 139–40; friction between Bonaccorsi and Nationalists, 140–41; plans for Falangist coup in, 143–44; Italian economic interests in, 145–47; Italian presence on in October 1936, 147; Bonaccorsi withdrawn from, 199. *See also* Balearic islands
Málaga: repression in, 192; battle of, 206–12
Manresa, 379
March, Juan, Sr., 132
March, Juan, Jr., 141
Margottini, Capt.: requests sending of military advisor to Majorca, 134; supports Bonaccorsi, 140–41; his political ac-

tivity, 142; and proposed coup in Majorca, 143–45; and Italy's economic position in Majorca, 145–47

Marín, Major, 143

Martorell, 379

Marzo, Col., 224

Masegoso, 225

Maura, Miguel, 61

Mazza, Col., 245, 246

Mediation, 196–97

Mediterranean Sea: in Italian foreign policy, 8–9, 25, 33, 40–41, 53, 65, 127–28, 173, 389; and Italian conquest of Ethiopia, 54; Italian position in and intervention in Spain, 75–77; Italian fear of German presence in, 104–05; British interests in the SCW, 148; Germany renounces naval operations in, 160; German presence in, 173; and Gentlemen's agreement, 196, 200; submarines attack shipping, 306–08, 311–12; and Nyon Conference, 313–16

Melilla, 66, 320

Miguel de Cervantes, 179

Militarism, 10–11, 327–29

Milizia volontaria per la sicurezza nazionale, 7, 167, 183–86

Millán Astray, Gen., 218

Minorca: military revolt in, 130; Ciano vetoes proposed invasion of, 142; Ciano authorizes occupation of, 150; rumors of planned Italian invasion of, 321–22; Nationalist occupation of, 382. See also Balearic islands

Miralrío, 234

Mixed brigades: formation of discussed with Franco, 159; Mus-solini discusses with Canaris, 161; formation of, 167, 170–71, 177–79

Mola, General Emilio, 70, 72, 85

Monarchist agreement with Italy, 50–54

Monarchy: role of in Italy, 6–7

Montreux Conference, 49

Morocco, 4, 31, 66, 90–91

Moscardó, Gen. 221, 224

Motorization of CTV, 223–24

Mousney, Sir George, 147

Munich Conference, 368

Mussolini, Benito: and labor, 6; and business interests, 6; and foreign policy formulation, 7–8, 8–13, 16–198, 33, 128, 311, 391; ideological factors in his foreign policy, 8–13, 29, 33, 37–38, 40, 53, 65, 78–84, 345–46, 389–91; attitude of toward war, 10–11; antipathy toward Spanish Republic, 13; relation of his foreign policy to domestic politics, 14–15; his scorn for parliamentary government, 38; praises crushing of Sanjurjo coup, 42; and "Century of Fascism," 45; meets with Spanish monarchists, 50–55; hostility toward Spanish Republic, 53; refuses to aid Franco, 70–72; not anxious to implant Fascism in Spain, 83–84; coins term "Axis," 112; calls for rapprochement with Great Britain, 112–13; and armed services, 166; decides to form separate Italian divisions, 169; his personal commitment to Franco's victory, 171–72, 263–64, 308; discusses aid to Nationalists with Göring, 171–74; his opinion of Franco's war

effort, 172; hopes CTV will end war quickly, 212; publishes article on Guadalajara, 251; reaffirms commitment to Franco, 271–75, 333; urges moderation with Basque prisoners, 289; his disinterest in economics, 300; visits Libya, 302; orders submarine attacks on shipping, 307–08; his public declarations of support for Franco, 310–11; meets with Ribbentrop, 324; wants to maintain Spain in Italian orbit, 324; visits Germany, 326–27; convinced that Nazis are invincible, 327; threatens to withdraw Italian support, 335–37; orders bombing of Barcelona, 347–49; his praise of Black Shirts' role in Spain, 360; Genoa speech on foreign policy, 361–62; proposes strengthening or withdrawing CTV, 363; discouraged by Franco's lack of progress, 365–66; urges more rapid advance in Catalonia, 377–78; growing commitment to Germany, 378; his speech on fall of Barcelona, 379–80; his plans for dividing up North Africa, 385; interview with Franco at Bordighera, 388; his scorn for England and France increased by SCW, 406
Mussolini, Bruno, 319
M.V.S.N., 7, 167, 183–86

Nanetti, Nino, 89
Naval support: effects of on outcome of war, 394–95
Nenni, Pietro, 80, 89
Neride, 140
Nolte, Ernst, 12

Nonintervention: motives for France, 91; British support of, 93; Soviet acceptance of, 94–95; Italian acceptance of, 95; formation of committee and early activities, 96–97; and Italian activities in Majorca, 149; and foreign troops in Spain, 196; and control of arms shipments, 202–03; Italy and Germany withdraw from control scheme, 304; and belligerent rights, 305; Italy and Germany return to committee meetings, 305; Italy and Germany withdraw from patrol, 305; and plan for withdrawal of volunteers, 360
North Africa: visited by Mussolini, 302; Italian High Command for instituted, 309
Nuvoloni, Gen. Luigi, 176, 228
Nyon Conference, 313–16, 323

Officer training schools, 395
Olazabal, Rafael de, 50
Onaindía, Fr. Alberto, 286, 287, 288–290
Opera nazionale balilla, 327
Orgaz, General Luis, 221
Orlov, Alexander, 98
Ortega y Gasset, Eduardo, 39
Ossorio, Col., 143

Palazzo Vidoni, Pact of, 6
Parame, 312
Parliamentary government: Mussolini's scorn for, 38
Partito Nazionale Fascista. See Fascist Party
Pavlov, General P.G., 98, 243
Pedrazzi, Orazio: named ambassador to Spain, 55; and Spanish Fascism 57; his opinion of

Spanish situation, 61–62; his first reports on Civil War, 68–69, 81; report on danger of Communism in Spain, 81; urges more active Italian political presence, 120–22; praises Falange, 122

Piazzoni, Col. Sandro, 177–78

Pietromarchi, Conte Luca, 165, 167–68

Pita Romero, Leandro, 45

Pittau, Consul Mario, 243, 245, 246

Pius XI, Pope, 344

Planes. See Aircraft

Poland, 25

Policy making. See Italy—Foreign policy, formulation of

Political mobilization: and Fascist party, 11; degree of in Italy and Spain compared, 402–03

Popolo d'Italia, 157, 309, 331

Popular Front: and Italo-French relations, 29; in Spain, 58–60; abandoned by USSR, 374

Pou Rodelló, Martín, 130

Pravda, 94

Press: reports on Italian aid to Nationalists, 4, 170; and Italian defeat at Bermeo, 280, 302–03. See also Italy—Press

Prestige: importance of in Italian foreign policy, 12–14, 169, 263–64, 390

Prieto, Indalecio, 39

Primo de Rivera, José Antonio, 46, 48, 49, 57–58

Primo de Rivera, Miguel: comes to power, 33; accepts Italian overtures, 33; domestic politics of, 35–36; Italian assessments of, 35–36; dismissed by Alfonso XIII, 36

Propaganda: Italian in Spain, 47, 55–56, 186–87, 250–51, 257–58; and battle of Guadalajara, 236–38, 250–51, 257–58; Italian on SCW, 264–66; of anti-Fascists on SCW, 266–67; Italian on taking of Santander, 282–84

Public opinion: effects of on Italian foreign policy, 13–16; European support of Republic, 89; in Italy and SCW, 183, 264–71; and Mussolini's decision to continue supporting SCW on image of Fascism, 405–06

Quadragesimo anno, 344

Quota novanta, 15

Racial legislation, 328

Radical party, 44

Raw materials, 75

Redondo, Onésimo, 46

Regime fascista, 309

Reinosa, 282

Renovación española, 50

Repression, in Nationalist Spain, 139–40, 191–92, 216

Rerum novarum, 344

Revisionism, 8

Rhineland, 90

Ribbentrop, Joachim von, 324

Ridruejo, Dionisio, 342–43

Riff ores, 299

Roatta, General Mario: meets with Canaris, 87, 103–106; and politics, 117–18; his opinion of Franco's strength, 156–57; named Italian commander in Spain, 166; and Málaga offensive, 206–09; expects little sup-

port from Jarama sector, 219; and battle of Guadalajara, 219–60 *passim;* relieved of command, 275; and Basque surrender, 290, 293; named advisor to Franco, 372
Rodríguez, Commander, 143
Rojo, General Vicente, 228
Rosselli, Carlo, 29, 88
Rossi, General Edmondo, 176, 245–46
Rubí, Lt. Col, 144–45
Ruiz García, Col., 144
Rumania, 25
Russo, General, 167–68

S.A.F.N.I., 298–99
Saniz Rodríguez, Pedro, 73, 131, 339
Salvatorelli, Luigi, 14
Salvemini, Gaetano, 14
Salvi, Col. Costantino, 243, 245, 246
Sanctions, 28, 71
Sanjurjo, General José, 41–42, 70
Santander, 280–84
Santoña, 291–92
Sardegna, 170
Schuschnigg, Kurt von, 27
Second World War: Spain refuses to enter, 386–88; Italian preparation for and SCW, 407–10
Serrano Suñer, Ramón, 339, 342–43, 385
Socialists: propaganda of Italian on SCW, 266
Societa anonima fertilizanti italia, 298–99
Solidarity with Spain: expressed by Grand Council of Fascism, 204; day of, 358
Somosierra, 72
Soria division, 224
Spain

—Dictatorship: Primo de Rivera comes to power, 33; commercial agreement with Italy, 34; and Italian interests in Tangiers, 34–35; domestic politics of, 35; Italy refuses to meddle in internal politics of, 36

—Republic: Italian hostility toward, 13, 37–41; proclaimed, 37; anti-Fascism of, 38–39; supposed secret treaty with France, 40–41; refuses to renew 1926 treaty with Italy, 41; monarchist conspiracies, 41–42; Sanjurjo coup, 42; Italy attempts rapprochement with, 43–44; center-right electoral success, 44–45; rapprochement with Italy, 45; Italian propaganda in, 47; monarchist agreement with Italy, 50–54; public opinion in and Italy, 55–56; government of, 56; Popular Front election, 58; President Alcalá Zamora deposed, 59; social and political conditions in, 59–60; Italy and plan for military coup against, 60–64; political situation in, 80–81; receives aid from France, 91–92, 109, 354–55; receives aid from USSR, 94, 98–100, 109, 176, 276–77, 354–55; Largo Caballero government, 99; international brigades organized, 99; role of Soviet advisors, 99, 101–02 n., 396–97; capital transferred to Valencia, 123–24; appeals to League of Nations, 197–98; decides to declare war on Italy in case of European war, 366; lack of supplies, 374

—Civil War: outbreak of, 66–68; first reports reaching Italy, 68–69; situation on July 30, 1936, 85; Nationalists force straits, 86; Nationalists take Badajoz and Talavera, 88; relief of Toledo, 108; capture of Ronda, 108; Nationalists transport troops from Africa and win control of straits, 108; first battle of Madrid, 123–24; in Balearic islands, 130–38; failure of first Madrid offensive, 156; Coruña road offensive, 171; situation in January, 1937, 205; battle of Málaga, 206–12; battle of Guadalajara, 212–60; battle of Jarama, 213–14, 217–19; northern offensive, 277–84; Santander offensive, 380–84; battle of Brunete, 281; battle of Teruel, 332, 335–37; Aragon offensive, 347–51; Valencia offensive, 354–57, battle of Ebro, 356–58, 373–74; situation in summer 1938, 365; Catalonian offensive, 375–80; Franco declares end of, 381; occupation of Minorca, 382; effects of Italian intervention on outcome of, 391–98; aid to Nationalists and Republicans compared, 398

—Nationalists: aid for Germany, 86, 103, 108–09, 111, 113–15, 163–64, 174, 374, 392–94; Italy and domestic politics of, 117–23, 128–30, 138–46, 186–94, 285–97, 330–32, 340–46, 394–404; political divisions within, 121–22; repression in, 139–40; 191–92, 216; treaty with Italy, 153–56; concern over Italian designs on Balearic islands, 154; mobilization of troops, 157; opens recruiting office in Rome, 158–59; and Italian offer of mixed brigades, 167; attitudes toward Italians, 255–56; unification of Falange and Carlists, 295–97; economic relations with Italy, 297–300, 325, 346–47; attempts to improve relations with Great Britain, 323–24; and Anti-Comintern Pact, 324–25; names representative in London, 325; naming of National Council of Falange, 329; civilian government in, 331, 339–41; Labor Charter, 341–45; declares neutrality in case of European war, 367; joins Anti-Comintern Pact, 383; role of Italian and effects of Italian aid on political configuration of, 399–404. *See also* Italy—Aid to Nationalists

Spanish Civil War. *See* Spain— Civil War
Stohrer, Gen., 349
Strategic and political factors: in Italian foreign policy, 388–89
Submarines: hinder supplying of Málaga, 211; Italian in service of Nationalists, 116–17, 179–80, 319–20; Italian attack Mediterranean shipping, 306–08, 311–12
Sumshkevich, Y. V., 98
Suvich, Fulvio, 27

Tajuña river, 231
Talavera de la Reina, 88
Tangiers, 34
Tanks: German, 119, 114–15; Russian, 110, 228, 243, 259;

Italian, 110, 259, 409–10; in battle of Guadalajara, 229, 231
Taranto, 320
Tardieu, André, 40
Tellini, General, 10
Teruel, 332, 335–37
Tetuán, 66
Thomas, Capt. Juan, 130–31
Timiryazev, 312
Toricelli, 179
Torija, 225, 228
Tortosa, 350
Trade, Italian foreign, 22–23
Traditionalists. *See* Carlists
Training schools, 395
Treaties: Italo-Spanish (1926), 34, 41; supposed secret Franco-Spanish, 40–41, 53, 154; Italo-Spanish (1936), 153–56. *See also* agreements
Tripcovich steamship lines, 140
Tripoli, 9
Troops: contribution of Italian to Nationalist victory, 395–98
Troop shipments, 161–71, 173–75, 276, 318–19, 355, 381
Turkey, 28

Ufficio Spagna, 165–66
Unemployment in Italy, 20–21
Union of Soviet Socialist Republics: relations with Italy, 12; collection in favor of Spanish workers, 94; and nonintervention, 94–95; aid to Republic, 98–100, 109, 176, 276–77, 355; reported sending massive aid to Nationalists, 306–07; abandons Popular Front, 374, effects of SCW on its foreign policy, 406–07

Unión patriótica, 35

Valdeiglesias, Conde de, 73
Valencia, 214–16, 354–57
Valle, General Giuseppe, 3–4, 137
Vansittart, Sir Robert, 149
Vatican, 349, 375. *See also* Catholic Church
Vázquez de Mella, Juan, 344
Vélez Málaga, 209
Viana, Marqués de, 70
Victor Emanuel III, King of Italy, 69
Villalba, 357
Viñaroz, 350
Viola, Guido: appointed ambassador to Spain, 296; instructed to keep Spain close to Axis, 324–25; his opinion of National Council of Falange, 329–31; his report on Franco's first civilian government, 339
Voronov, N. N., 98

Wages, in Italy, 20–21
Walwal incident, 54
Warlimont, Col., 118
Weapons. *See* Italy—Aid to Nationalists; Germany, aid to Nationalists; France, aid to Republic; Union of Soviet Socialist Republics, aid to Republic; Aircraft; Tanks
Woodford, 312
World War II. *See* Second World War

Yugoslavia, 25, 28

Zayas, Marqués de, 131–34, 143
Zunzunegui, Luis, 73

Library of Congress Cataloging in Publication Data

Coverdale, John F   1940–
  Italian intervention in the Spanish Civil War.

  Bibliography: p.
  Includes index.
  1. Spain—History—Civil War, 1936–1939—
Foreign participation—Italian.   I. Title.
DP269.47.I8C65   946.081   74-25604